IN SEARCH OF SYNERGY
IN SMALL GROUP PERFORMANCE

IN SEARCH OF SYNERGY

IN SMALL GROUP PERFORMANCE

JAMES R. LARSON, JR.

Ψ Psychology Press
Taylor & Francis Group

New York   London

Psychology Press
Taylor & Francis Group
270 Madison Avenue
New York, NY 10016

Psychology Press
Taylor & Francis Group
27 Church Road
Hove, East Sussex BN3 2FA

© 2010 by Taylor and Francis Group, LLC
Psychology Press is an imprint of Taylor & Francis Group, an Informa business

Printed in the United States of America on acid-free paper
10 9 8 7 6 5 4 3 2 1

International Standard Book Number: 978-0-8058-5943-0 (Hardback) 978-0-8058-5944-7 (Paperback)

Library of Congress Cataloging-in-Publication Data

Larson, James R.
    In search of synergy in small group performance / James R. Larson, Jr.
        p. cm.
    Includes bibliographical references and index.
    ISBN 978-0-8058-5943-0 (hardcover : alk. paper) -- ISBN 978-0-8058-5944-7
    (pbk. : alk. paper)
    1. Small groups. 2. Small groups--Psychological aspects. 3. Group decision
making. 4. Social groups. I. Title.

HM736.L37 2010
302.3'4--dc22   2009034605

Visit the Taylor & Francis Web site at
http://www.taylorandfrancis.com

and the Psychology Press Web site at
http://www.psypress.com

*To JRL and JMG, whose footsteps
I followed into the academy, and to IRG,
who once again has given up much so that I could write.*

CONTENTS

PREFACE

The relationship between the group and the individual is at the heart of many long-standing scholarly debates in psychology, sociology, and philosophy. One such debate concerns the task-performing capabilities of groups relative to individuals and is typified by the question, Are two heads better than one? We might ask, for example, whether people are any more or less creative, productive, or wise when working collaboratively than when working alone. Given a task that can be performed either by several people working together as a group or by those same people working individually, does it matter which work arrangement is employed? What are the costs and benefits of working interactively versus working independently, and is one approach more likely than the other to yield superior performance outcomes? These are the sorts of questions to which this book is addressed.

There exists a significant body of published empirical research bearing on the performance implications of working in groups relative to working individually. However, it is scattered across numerous scientific journals, academic disciplines, and time. The fields of social psychology (my home discipline), organizational psychology, and organizational behavior lay claim to much of this literature, but substantial contributions also have been made by researchers in cognitive psychology, human communications, education, and sociology. Further, although some of this work is fairly recent, having been published in the last dozen years or so, a good bit of it is older. In a few cases, relevant lines of research can be traced back a century or more. As a result of all this, it is hard to gain perspective on the literature in its entirety. One purpose I had in writing this book was to bring together in one place the most important empirical research concerning group versus individual task performance. By doing so, my hope was not only to foster a better appreciation of the breadth and depth of this literature, but also to encourage additional research on the many questions about group versus individual performance that remain unanswered.

A second purpose I had in writing this book was to contrapose—and hopefully change—what I perceive to be an unjustified "shared mental model of group ineptitude" that pervades much of the field. There is a subtle but persistent tendency among scholars to couch group performance in negative rather than positive terms. Although there is much evidence of both strength and weakness in group task performance, we seem more keenly attuned to the latter than the former. This is particularly true for colleagues who are only causally acquainted with the group performance literature, but it exists as well even among those who contribute directly to that literature. We find it easier to recall evidence of group failings than group accomplishments. It is the shortcomings of groups, not their successes, that more readily surface in our classroom lectures. We are more curious about the etiology of problematic rather than proficient group performance. And our research is more often geared to investigate how things that can go wrong in groups might be avoided rather than to learn how things that can go right might be exploited.

While no doubt there are many reasons for this unfavorable stance toward group performance, the one that is of greatest concern to me is the meta-theoretic interpretational framework that dominates this literature. We think poorly of group performance in part because that framework is itself quite negative. It is structured in a way that can do little else but call attention to the shortcomings of group performance. It identifies weaknesses but is blind to strengths. This, in turn, shapes how we think about and communicate our research results to others in the field (e.g., in journal articles and conference presentations) and, ultimately, to the broader audience beyond. Simply put, we tend to view group performance negatively because the meta-theoretic framework implicitly adopted by most of the field does not allow us to think of it in any other way.

This book is an attempt to reorient the study of small group performance by introducing a more balanced interpretational framework—one that gives just as much heed to what can go right in groups as to what can go wrong, and so acknowledges the benefits as well as the costs of working collectively. In proposing this alternative framework, my intention is to be critical, not Pollyannaish. But being critical means attending to the good as well as the bad in small group performance and giving proper credit for each.

This book is intended as a high-level, integrative treatment of the small group performance literature. I have tried to be integrative in the sense of bringing together in one place a discussion of the multiple subareas within the literature, including those concerned with idea generation, problem solving, judgment, decision making, learning and memory, motivation, and the dynamics of group composition. Further, I have tried to tie these various topics together via the interpretational framework that is introduced in Chapter 1. One benefit of that framework is that it provides a common metric for comparing group performance across otherwise incommensurate task domains. It allows us to see, for example, how group performance on problem-solving tasks compares to group performance on idea-generation tasks. Thus, it enables us to think about the various segments of the group performance literature in relation to one another and so in a more sophisticated, holistic way.

I have also tried to convey in this book a sense of the developmental progress that has been made in this literature, particularly in those subareas that have a longer history of empirical research. To fully appreciate the literature, I think it is helpful to understand how that research has evolved over time. Thus, I have also sought to make the book integrative in a temporal sense, by calling attention to some of the older research and highlighting its relationship to what has been done more recently.

Finally, I have endeavored to write a book that will appeal to graduate students, advanced undergraduates, academics, and researchers alike. My aim was to present the material in a way that is both accessible and engaging for those who do not have an extensive background in the study of groups. The small group performance literature is rife with complexity and subtlety. I have sought to convey both without getting bogged down in either. Thus, I hope that students will find it a useful point of entry into the small group performance literature. At the same time, I have tried to introduce content and analysis that will be of interest to the seasoned scholar already conversant with that literature. Chief among these is the interpretational framework that I employ throughout the book.

Surprisingly, I found the book more difficult to end than to start. As I was trying to wrap it up, new issues of journals kept appearing in my mailbox, conference notices kept popping up in my email, and well-meaning colleagues kept passing along references that I may have missed. All of this played incessantly on my hope of finding the next breakthrough study before finally bringing the book to a close. But eventually a line had to be drawn, the last words written, and a reality admitted: This book is necessarily incomplete, as it tells a story that is still unfolding.

ACKNOWLEDGMENTS

I am indebted to Debra Riegert, who acquired this project for Lawrence Erlbaum Associates, and to Paul Dukes, who saw it through to completion after Erlbaum and Psychology Press were merged. The project was tossed into Paul's lap at a turbulent time, both for Psychology Press and for the book. He managed that turbulence with just the right mix of support and flexibility. I am grateful to Gary Stasser for his substantial input on a very early draft of Chapter 4. I would also like to thank Guido Hertel and Franziska Tschan, who reviewed a prepublication draft of the book. All were very helpful, and the book is better for their efforts.

I thank the American Psychological Association for permission to adapt and reprint the material presented in Tables 2.1, 3.2, 8.1, and 8.2, and in Figures 6.3 and 6.4. I gratefully acknowledged the permission of Behavioral Measurement Database Services (BMDS; Pittsburgh, PA) to adapt and reprint the material presented in Figure 2.1. Figure 2.3 is reprinted by permission of Pearson Education, Inc., Upper Saddle River, NJ. I thank Sage Publications for permission to adapt and reprint the material presented in Table 7.1 and Figure 9.2. Figure 7.1 is reprinted with permission of the authors and publisher, copyright 2001, The Institute for Operations Research and the Management Sciences (INFORMS), 7240 Parkway Drive, Suite 300, Hanover, Maryland 21076. Finally, Table 7.2 is adapted with permission of the *British Journal of Psychology* © The British Psychological Society.

CHAPTER 1

Introduction

Mapping the Territory

Groups are sometimes maligned for their incompetence. Most of us have heard the joke about the camel being a horse designed by committee, and at one time or another we've all derided a particularly inept group as certain evidence of the core truth in such jokes. But wholesale ineptness is not what most people usually expect from groups. On the contrary, judging by the frequency with which groups are used in the pursuit of important organizational and societal goals, there would seem to be a rather widespread faith in the performance capabilities of groups. Task-performing groups abound in every kind of organization and in all corners of society: architectural firms are rife with design teams, the core work of an airline is done by flight crews, accounting firms field auditing teams, fire departments maintain emergency rescue squads, hospitals play host to surgical teams, television networks depend on film crews, police departments rely on crime investigation details, and atop most organizations are innumerable management committees, taskforces, and policy groups. Indeed, the pervasiveness with which groups are used in every conceivable functional area within modern organizations has prompted one set of critics to declare this the "age of groupism" (Locke, Tirnauer, Roberson, Goldman, Latham, & Weldon, 2001).

To be sure, certain kinds of tasks seem to demand the use of interacting groups. The technology employed to accomplish a task, for example, may necessitate the closely coordinated interaction of several people. No large ship can be sailed safely by a crew of one, and it's hard to imagine a hip replacement operation being performed by any surgeon working alone, no matter how skilled he or she might be.

But for many tasks, the use of a group to perform the work is a matter of managerial discretion, not technical necessity. In some cases, the

1

task done by a group might reasonably be performed instead by a single individual. Many problem-solving and decision-making tasks are of this sort. Or the group's task might be divided among the same number of persons who work independently. Several authors who write a textbook together by working collaboratively on each chapter could instead work independently on separate chapters, much in the way an edited collection of essays or short stories is produced.

That such tasks are increasingly assigned to interacting groups rather than to individuals suggests a fundamental belief in the superiority of group work arrangements. Groups are often entrusted with important matters of policy, for example, because they are presumed capable of greater creativity, more effective problem solving, and higher quality judgment and decision making than individuals. This is not to say that performance considerations are the only reason for assigning tasks to groups. Matters of representation and decision acceptance are also important. Still, there remains an abiding interest in using groups simply because groups are presumed to have at least the potential for achieving a higher level of performance than would be possible using an individual-oriented approach.

☐ Synergy in Task-Performing Groups

The term often invoked in connection with this lay belief in the performance potential of groups is *synergy*, a word derived from the Greek *sunergos*, which means "working together." Most dictionaries define synergy as the working together of two or more agents (things, people, organizations), especially when the result is greater than the sum of their individual efforts or capabilities. Consistent with this definition, synergy has gained currency in popular discourse as a way of referring either to the hoped-for performance benefits of a future group interaction, or to the group interaction presumed to have generated an exceptional or unexpected past performance. Those who have recently participated in a very successful group effort might, for example, use the term synergy as a way of expressing the excitement, motivation, or high level of cohesiveness they felt while working together. Outside observers, on the other hand, tend to use the term synergy more directly in connection with the group's performance. Sportswriters, for instance, who are veteran observers of groups, often have some aspect of group performance in mind when applying the term (e.g., "The team's starting line-up showed early signs of synergy in last night's victory over ... "). Likewise, business writers frequently cite "anticipated synergies" at various levels of analysis as the rationale for all sorts of management decisions, not the least of which are those surrounding mergers and acquisitions (e.g., Shaver, 2006). Indeed, synergy has gained such cachet as a synonym for high performance in business that the term has even found its way into many corporate names, including such variants as Cynergy, SynerChange, and Synerdyne.

But synergy is hardly ubiquitous. While commonly understood as something positive, popular conceptions of synergy also imply that it has an ethereal, fleeting, even mystical quality. Though often sought after, synergy is not so often attained. And when it is attained, it seems easily lost. Few who use the term can say specifically how synergy might be conjured when it does not exist, or, when it does exist, how it might be preserved. It seems easier to use synergy to explain a past performance than to predict a performance that is yet to come. So, just what is this fleeting object of faith called synergy? What is the evidence, beyond anecdote and hindsight, that group interaction actually yields synergy? And what are the conditions that foster and maintain synergy? These are questions that a more disciplined, scientific approach to synergy in groups ought to be able to address.

Synergy as a Scientific Concept

The concept of synergy has a long history of use in science, most notably in several disciplines connected with medicine. In physiology, for example, it describes the coordinated action of two or more muscles working together to produce the same effect at the same joint (Marieb, 2004). Here, synergy is used in an additive sense; the forces produced by several muscles are summed to create movement, with each muscle working in the same way at the same time. In endocrinology, on the other hand, synergy is used in either an additive or a complementary sense to describe the combined effect of hormones. Two hormones that each stimulate a different stage of a complex process, and that are both needed in order for the process as a whole to occur, are said to be synergistic; they complement, rather than duplicate, one another's actions (Fox, 1996). And in pharmacology, synergy is used primarily in a multiplicative sense; it refers to a combined effect of two or more drugs that is greater than the sum of the effects of each drug acting alone (Katzung, 1998). For instance, imagine that in a study investigating the palliative effect of two cancer-fighting drugs, each drug by itself is found to provide two units of benefit to patients relative to a placebo control condition. But suppose that when administered together they provide five units of benefit. That is, the study reveals two main effects and an ordinal interaction. The interaction would be taken as evidence of synergy between the drugs (but see Caudle & Williams, 1993). It is just this sort of idea that gives rise to one popular metaphor for synergy: $2 + 2 = 5$.

In sharp contrast to its use in medicine, the term synergy can scarcely be found in the contemporary scientific literature on small-group performance—a surprising state of affairs given the frequency with which synergy is employed colloquially in reference to groups. Further, the few synergy-like concepts that do exist in the group performance literature seem to refer to rather different things. Cattell (1948, 1957), for example, defined synergy in a way that emphasizes members' experiential and motivational states. He applied the term somewhat vaguely to express the "energy going into the group life as a result of satisfaction with fellow members" (1957, p. 791). According to Cattell, synergy can be measured by summing the "interest strengths" of members in their group's life. He was thus concerned with what today might be called group cohesion or morale, especially as these relate to members' underlying motivation to work hard in the pursuit of group goals.

Taking a different tack, both Overstreet (1925) and Collins and Guetzkow (1964) introduced synergy-like concepts that focus more directly on group performance. Overstreet postulated that there would be a gain in understanding or creative insight whenever two or more people work together earnestly to solve a problem (p. 225). He dubbed this gain a "creative plus," and suggested that it is beyond what any one person can attain working a problem alone. Collins and Guetzkow (1964) offered a more elaborate definition of essentially the same construct, but labeled it an "assembly effect bonus." This term, too, refers to group performance that is beyond what could have been achieved by any member of the group working alone, or by a simple combination of individual member efforts. An assembly effect bonus, they suggest, is performance that "exceeds the potential of the most capable member and also exceeds the sum of the efforts of the group members working separately" (p. 58; see also Rosenberg, Erlick, and Berkowitz, 1955). These two terms, *creative plus* and *assembly effect bonus*, are each roughly commensurate with the meaning synergy is given in other scientific disciplines as described above, and they provide a useful stepping stone to the definition of synergy I offer below.

Synergy Defined

I define synergy as a gain in performance that is attributable in some way to group interaction. More specifically, a group is said to exhibit synergy when it is able to accomplish collectively something that could not reasonably have been achieved by any simple combination of individual member efforts. Synergy is thus an emergent phenomenon rooted in group interaction.

Several aspects of this definition warrant comment. First, synergy is synonymous with a group performance gain. It does not refer to the members' feelings, emotional reactions, sense of heightened "energy" in the group, or other experiential states. Synergy is simply a performance gain that is due to group interaction. Although group performance gains may often produce positive affective reactions in members, such reactions are not a defining characteristic of those gains, and indeed may not even be a reliable indicator of them. It has been shown, for example, that members sometimes react very positively to their group's performance even when objectively they have demonstrated an overall performance loss (e.g., Nijstad, Stroebe, & Lodewijkx, 2006; Paulus, Dzindolet, Poletes, & Camacho, 1993).

Second, if synergy denotes a performance gain, then there must exist a standard or baseline for assessing that gain. Because the gain must be one that is attributable to group interaction, the clearest baseline is the performance achieved by the same individuals working independently (i.e., with no interaction). For example, consider a decision that the night manager in a local supermarket might face this evening: deciding whether the three stock clerks on duty are to work as a team to replenish the shelves in each of three grocery aisles (i.e., working together first in one aisle, then in the next aisle, then in the third), or whether they are instead to work independently in different aisles. If they work together as a team, each aisle will be restocked more quickly, but because the aisles are worked sequentially, some will be completed sooner than others. On the other hand, if the clerks work independently in different aisles, progress will be slower on each one, but the three aisles will all be completed at about the same time. If there is any performance gain to be had by working as a team in this situation, it should be manifest in the total hours of labor needed to complete the job when the clerks work together compared to when they work independently.

At an abstract level, the nature of the comparison required to establish a performance gain is straightforward, and tidy examples are easily devised. In actual research situations, however, matters become more complicated. In part, this is because the nature of the task being performed by the group does not always provide an obvious baseline for comparison. Or it may provide several possible baselines. In the latter case, what appears to be a performance gain when compared to one baseline looks instead like a performance loss when compared to another. Such issues have sometimes been inadequately dealt with in past research, and, as a result, investigators have overlooked instances of what would seem to be legitimate examples of synergy in small groups. I will address this "baseline issue" in more detail at several points in later chapters of the book.

Third, I use the term "interaction" to refer broadly to any observable behavior exhibited by a group member that is directed toward, performed in concert with, and/or enacted in the presence of others in the group. Typically, this will consist of the verbal and nonverbal behaviors that members enact when working face-to-face. However, I also wish to include certain behaviors that may be enacted remotely and asynchronously, such as when a geographically dispersed group communicates via email. Further, it is also useful to include the mere presence of other group members.[1] Members who are merely present exhibit the barest possible form of interaction. Still, it is conceivable that their mere presence is enough to spark a response in others that may affect the performance of the group as a whole.

Finally, "interaction" also implies a process of mutual behavioral adjustment among members. Indeed, it is precisely from such adjustments that performance gains take shape. These adjustments might involve enacting certain behaviors more quickly, with greater intensity, or for a longer period of time than when working alone. Alternatively, they might entail performing new behaviors, performing a new mix or sequence of previously enacted behaviors, or abandoning certain behaviors. I do not wish to suggest that members necessarily understand how their interactions impact group performance. In some cases it is likely that they do understand this; in others, it likely that they do not. Either way, such understanding is neither a defining characteristic of, nor a necessary precondition for, synergy. Whether understood by the group or not, successful interactions are those mutual behavioral adjustments that help members perform their task more effectively and so produce a measurable performance gain. A major objective of this book is to examine the conditions promoting interactions that lead to performance gains.

Weak Versus Strong Synergy

Related to the point made above regarding baselines, it is useful at the outset to make a distinction between two generic levels, or degrees, of synergy: weak synergy and strong synergy.

I define *weak synergy* as group performance that exceeds the performance of the *typical* group member when working alone. In the supermarket example, for instance, we might ask whether the total labor hours required to restock the grocery aisles by the three clerks working as a team is any less (i.e., better) than the average labor hours that would be required for any one of those clerks to do the whole job alone. This average provides a reasonable index of the solo performance of the "typical" group member. If the clerks exceed this baseline when working as a team, weak synergy (at least) would be demonstrated. (Note that the variable of interest here is labor hours, not elapsed clock time. Labor hours takes into account the larger quantity of human resources the group is able to apply to the task at any one moment—three persons versus one—whereas clock time does not. The group will almost certainly complete the job in less clock time than any one person working alone would be able to do. Less clear is whether they can complete it in fewer labor hours.)

In contrast, I define *strong synergy* as group performance that exceeds the solo performance of even the *best* group member. If the supermarket clerks working as a team require fewer labor hours to restock the aisles than would normally be required by even the most proficient of them working alone, strong synergy would be demonstrated. Thus, whereas weak synergy refers to performance gains within a range that at least some members of the group could reasonably achieve working alone, strong synergy refers to performance gains that go beyond that range. In some cases, strong synergy may arise from the same underlying interaction processes that generate weak synergy. In other cases, strong synergy is likely to arise from wholly different interaction processes.

There is substantial empirical evidence for the existence of weak synergy, although even weak synergy can sometimes be difficult to attain. One way to achieve weak synergy on divisible tasks is for members to specialize on those subtasks for which they have the greatest skill (i.e., optimize the person–subtask fit). For tasks that cannot be meaningfully divided (e.g., many types of judgment tasks), weak synergy can be achieve by giving greater weight to the ideas, opinions, and preferences of those members who have the most relevant expertise. The theoretical significance of weak synergy has often been overlooked in the small group performance literature, despite the fact that it can be of considerable practical consequence in real-world settings. This is especially true when it is not possible to specify in advance who among the members has the greatest skill or expertise and so who, on his or her own, might be the best individual performer.

In contrast to weak synergy, there is relatively sparse evidence for the existence of strong synergy, especially on tasks that require mental rather than physical effort. There are several reasons for this state of affairs. First, strong synergy is undoubtedly a much rarer phenomenon than weak synergy, as might be expected, given the definitions of the two constructs. Second, strong synergy is likely to be more difficult to predict in advance, based on an analysis of the task to be performed and the persons who will perform it. This is because, compared to weak synergy, strong synergy is apt to depend on more complex forms of interaction. Finally, the research designs used to study group performance have not always provided adequate tests of strong synergy. A major goal of this book is to examine in detail what little evidence of strong synergy currently does exist, to consider how research designs might be improved in order to better detect strong synergy, and to suggest where the search for synergy might best be directed in the future.

An Example of Synergy: Bicycle Racing

To better understand what I mean by synergy, it is helpful to consider an example that can easily be appreciated by anyone who has ridden a bicycle on a blustery day.

Imagine yourself riding a bicycle home from work on a warm but windy September afternoon. Most of your route is along a wide asphalt path that runs uninterrupted for miles in a nearly-straight line over flat, open terrain. Just such a path can be found in Chicago, running north and south along its Lake Michigan shoreline. It is a scenic route, and for the serious cyclist it is a route that invites speed. But speed is not easily attained on this breezy afternoon. As you make your way homeward, you find yourself fighting a steady 15-mph headwind. So, progress is slow and difficult. You struggle to maintain just 10 mph. The energy you expend to keep up this modest pace is substantial, nearly what it would be if you were traveling 25 mph on an otherwise calm day.

After pedaling vigorously for some distance, another cyclist in a bright yellow jersey gradually overtakes you. As she does, you decide to fall in behind her. You muster a burst of energy, pedal faster to catch up, and then maneuver your bicycle in close, allowing your front wheel to dance just inches from her back wheel. You concentrate on maintaining this position— as close as possible, and directly behind—by mimicking her every move. When she drifts to the left, you drift left. When she edges right, you edge right. Your purpose in doing this is simple: It will enable you to maintain a faster pace while spending noticeably less energy. These are the rewards of drafting. You can ride faster and farther with much less effort if you can manage to tuck in behind someone else. With the lead cyclist breaking the wind, the following cyclist enjoys a substantially easier ride.[2]

If you continue to draft in this way, two things will happen. First, you will begin to sense your strength returning. The relative ease of riding in the pocket of low pressure immediately behind your newly found cycling partner will allow you to rest and so recover from the draining experience of fighting the wind. Second, you will also begin to notice a gradual slowing of the pace as your partner is herself progressively drained of energy. Eventually, the pace will become so slow, and you will have recovered enough of your own strength, that you will be able to break out of the pocket and assume the lead yourself. Your riding partner can now slip back and tuck in behind you, where she can rest until it is once again her turn to lead. And so it goes, riding together mile after mile, alternately leading and resting, until finally one of you, nearing home, signals good-bye and turns sharply off to leave the path.

What has been accomplished in this unexpected encounter is an every-day occurrence, yet still quite remarkable. By taking turns leading and drafting, you will have traveled together at a significantly faster pace than either of you could have managed riding by yourselves. Suppose that each of you, riding alone, could have covered the distance home in 30 minutes. It is not unrealistic to expect that you might cover that same distance in just 25 minutes by riding as a team—a 20% increase in speed.

This improvement in performance is a clear example of synergy. Recall that synergy refers to group performance that exceeds what reasonably could be accomplished simply by combining the separate efforts of the members when working independently. The cycling scenario fits this definition perfectly. First, it seems legitimate to consider these two homeward-bound cyclists as a group, albeit an informal, temporary one of minimum size. They are a group by virtue of their working together in pursuit of a common goal—to propel themselves forward as fast as they can.[3] Second, it should be obvious that the separate transit times these two cyclists would make over a given distance riding alone cannot be added, averaged, or combined in any other straightforward way to produce a result equal to their transit time over the same ground riding as a team. By riding together (and assuming that they are not wildly dissimilar in ability) they can exceed the speed that even the faster of the two would be able to sustain riding alone. Finally, I have also said that synergy is an emergent phenomenon rooted in the interaction among group members. In the case of the two cyclists, one critical element of their interaction is their systematically taking turns as leader and follower. This coordinated action gives each rider an opportunity to rest and so to recover enough strength to retake the lead and restore the pace whenever it begins to sag.

But suppose the two riders in our cycling scenario did not employ the turn-taking strategy. Rather, let us imagine that they instead rode the entire distance home in the same configuration, with one leading the whole way and the other steadfastly drafting behind. In this case, their joint speed would be no greater than could be achieved by the lead rider traveling alone.[4] If the leader happens to be the stronger of the two, then the team will still travel faster than the average of their solo speeds, and this would still qualify as a performance gain. However, it is a gain that does not exceed the performance that the best member could have achieved alone and so would be an example of only weak synergy. In contrast, the original scenario is an example of strong synergy, because they were able to ride faster together than *either* would have been able to do riding alone—including the stronger of the two.

Scholarly Interest in Bicycle Racing: A Historical Note

To this point I have focused only on the physical aspects of the cycling scenario. Of course, a full understanding of the performance gain produced in this situation also requires an analysis of its psychological dimensions.

It seems reasonable to suppose, for example, that an informal competition might arise between riders traveling in close proximity, which should spark greater effort in each. Greater effort, in turn, should translate into greater speed. Thus, we might wonder what portion of the performance gain observed in this situation is due to the competitive motives of the riders, as opposed to their turn-taking strategy.

Motivation as a source of performance gain in groups is a theme that will be examined in detail in Chapter 8. Here, I simply call attention to the fact that interest in this topic, especially as it relates to cycling, dates to the earliest days of both social psychology and bicycle racing. Norman Triplett (1898) is widely credited with having published one of the very first empirical studies in social psychology. In that paper, he provides an analysis of bicycle racing records obtained from the Racing Board of the League of American Wheelmen, the main governing body of professional bicycle racing in the United States at the time. Among other aspects, Triplett examined the record times achieved by individual cyclists racing alone against the clock for distances of up to 25 miles. He compared these to the record times set by individual cyclists who raced against the clock while being paced by a faster vehicle, typically a swift tandem or quadricycle. Triplett noted that substantially faster record speeds were attained by cyclists in paced races (M = 31.17 mph) than by those in unpaced races (M = 24.02 mph). Further, the speeds attained in paced races remained nearly constant through 25 miles, whereas the speeds reached in unpaced races steadily declined with increasing distance.

Triplett (1898) wanted to know the extent to which these performance differences reflected an underlying motivational advantage of the paced racing format. He hypothesized that the presence of the riders on the pace vehicle might have aroused the racer's "competitive instinct ... releasing or freeing nervous energy for him that he cannot of himself release; and, further, that the sight of movement [of the pace vehicle] suggesting a higher rate of speed, is also an inspiration to greater effort" (p. 516).

Unfortunately, Triplett (1898) was not able to draw any firm conclusions about this hypothesis from the bicycle racing data themselves. This is because there was another clear advantage that paced racers enjoyed: they always rode their bicycles very closely behind the pace vehicle for the entire length of the race, and so gained significant shelter from the wind. As one champion rider of the day put it, "No matter which way it blows there is always a place where the man following pace can be out of the wind" (p. 514). This benefit at the very least confounds, if not completely overshadows, any gain that might be due to a boost in competitive motivation aroused by the paced racing format.

Interestingly, and as if intentionally to prove this point, just a year after Triplett published his seminal work, Charles Murphy, a cyclist from Brooklyn, NY, dramatically demonstrated the overwhelming benefit of being sheltered from the wind by becoming the first person ever to ride a bicycle one mile in under one minute. As described in a front-page article in *The New York Times* (Beat a Mile a Minute, 1899), he accomplished this by riding at an average rate of over 62 mph immediately behind a Long Island Railroad train on a smooth wooden bicycle track laid down in the space between the rails of the train track. Importantly, the last car of the train had been fitted with a specially designed hood that extended aft from the roof and sides of its rear end. Murphy rode under this hood, which gave him near-perfect protection from the wind, much better than is normally provided by riding behind either another cyclist or a standard pace vehicle. This eliminated nearly all of the aerodynamic drag that otherwise would have been at play, making it possible for Murphy to ride a full mile in just 57.8 seconds. It would be another four years before an automobile would travel a mile at Murphy's speed.

Triplett (1898) was clearly aware of the interpretational ambiguities created by the wind-sheltering properties of the paced racing format. The same concern also plagued his ability to draw conclusions about competitions involving more than one racer, whether or not a pace vehicle was involved. Here, the racers could gain significant shelter from the wind by following one another. Ultimately, Triplett escaped these interpretational problems by moving his research into the laboratory, where he could employ tasks for which the aerodynamics of drafting was not a factor. I will return to these experiments on pacemaking and competition in Chapter 8. It is sufficient here simply to note that the ingredients for synergy, in bicycle racing at least, have in one way or another been of concern to researchers for a very long time.

Synergy as Challenge to the Status Quo

Although bicycle racing is a useful way to introduce the concept of synergy in task-oriented groups, the relevant scientific literature has concerned itself more with group performance on mental tasks than on physical tasks. I review much of this literature in Chapters 3 through 6. Before doing so, however, it is important to call attention to the rather incongruous theoretical position that the concept of synergy holds within the field of small-group performance. As will be seen, the very idea of synergy represents a significant challenge to the zeitgeist that has grown to dominate this field during the past half-century.

Developments Prior to About 1970

The earliest empirical literature on small-group performance dates from the 1920s and 1930s and is marked by a number of findings that initially seemed to support the idea that synergy occurs not just when groups perform certain physical tasks like bicycle racing, but also when they perform such intellective tasks as idea generation, problem solving, and decision making (e.g., Barton, 1926; Husband, 1940; Osborn, 1953; Shaw, 1932; Timmons, 1942; Watson, 1928). Among the best known of these is Marjorie Shaw's (1932) study of group problem solving.

Shaw (1932) had 41 students from a graduate course in social psychology attempt six different problems: Two of these were variants of Alcuin's river-crossing problem (husbands-and-wives and missionaries-and-cannibals), one was Lucas's Tower of Hanoi problem, one was a bus routing problem, and two required the completion of a sonnet and a short piece of prose, respectively.[5] The husbands-and-wives problem, for example, asks how three wives and their three jealous husbands might be transported across a river by means of a rowboat that can accommodate no more than three passengers at a time, under the restrictions that all of the men and none of the women can row, and that no man will allow his wife to be in the presence of another man unless he, too, is present.[6] Approximately half of the students worked as members of interacting four-person groups and were asked to produce a single group solution for each problem. The remaining students worked alone to produce their own individual solutions for each problem. Shaw reported that on four of the six problems the students performed better when they worked in groups than when they worked as individuals.[7] On the husbands-and-wives problem, for example, 60% of the groups, but only 14% of the individuals, solved the problem correctly. Shaw argued that one reason for the superior performance of groups on these problems was their ability to correct one another's errors as they worked.

To be sure, not every study from that era yielded such positive results (e.g., Burtt, 1920; Jenness, 1932; Marston, 1924). Nevertheless, the body of evidence was sufficiently consistent to suggest that the performance of groups often is superior to that of individuals. And while the term synergy was never employed, the early literature nevertheless seemed to suggest its existence.

By the 1950s, however, claims of group superiority gradually gave way to skepticism about the performance capacity of group. This was due in large part to two methodological weaknesses identified in the early studies. First, many of those studies relied on what Campbell and Stanley (1966) called preexperimental research designs, in which groups and treatment conditions were formed on the basis of convenience rather than random assignment. Second, and more important for the present discussion, the opportunity for group interaction in those studies was often confounded with the number of people performing the task, and so with the quantity of intellectual resources that could be brought to bear. For example, in Shaw's (1932) study, not only could members of the four-person groups interact to correct one another's errors, they also brought to the task four times the mental resources possessed by those who worked the problems individually. This is an important point, because synergy is defined as a product of group interaction, not greater resources. A grand piano that is too heavy for any one person to lift can nevertheless be lifted success-fully by six people working together, not so much because of the synergy emerging from their interaction, but because of the substantially greater strength they collectively possess. Similarly, it is possible that the superior performance of groups relative to individuals initially reported by Shaw and others was due less to group member interaction than to the greater pool of intellectual resources available to groups than to individuals.

In 1955 two related strategies for addressing this latter difficulty were proposed. One was offered by Lorge and Solomon (1955), who suggested that the performance of problem-solving groups should be evaluated not against the raw percentage of persons who are able to solve the problem individually, but against the mathematical probability that *at least one* member of the group could have solved the problem alone. They sug-gested that even without the benefits of group interaction (e.g., error cor-rection), a group should be able to solve a problem correctly if it contains at least one member who can solve that problem correctly when working alone. By this logic, it would not be particularly remarkable to find that more groups than individuals can solve a given problem, if the proportion of groups solving the problem is commensurate with the proportion that would be likely to contain at least one member who could have solved that problem alone.[8]

Essentially the same idea underlies an alternative strategy proposed independently by Marquart (1955) and by Taylor (1955). They suggested that the performance of interacting groups should be evaluated not against the performance of individuals, but against the performance of nonin-teracting "nominal groups" (the term itself is Taylor's, not Marquart's). Nominal groups are groups that comprise the same number of members as the interacting groups with which they are compared, but those mem-bers perform the task independently without any interaction. Indeed, the members of a nominal group are not even aware of their member-ship and so do not constitute a group in any truly psychological sense. Rather, they are a group in name only, existing merely as a statistical entity.[9] Nominal groups provide a useful standard for evaluating the per-formance of interacting groups because they bring the same quantity of intellectual resources to the task but offer no opportunity for interaction among members.

Paralleling Lorge and Solomon (1955), Marquart (1955) and Taylor (1955) both suggested that a nominal group be considered to have solved a prob-lem correctly if at least one of its members can solve it correctly. This might be called a "best member" criterion, because if there is only one person in the group who is able to solve a particular problem, that person is clearly the best performer in the group vis-à-vis that problem. It is important to note, however, that this is not the only performance criterion that can be derived from nominal groups. Another is the "average member" criterion. Here, the nominal group is considered to have solved a problem correctly if at least half of its members can solve it correctly. Clearly, many fewer nominal groups will be considered to have solved a problem when an average-member criterion is used that when a best-member criterion is used—because the former requires that more individual members solve the problem correctly than does the latter. This means that the performance standard set by nominal groups (i.e., the percentage of nominal groups considered to have solved the problem) will be lower, and so more easily surpassed by interacting groups, when an average-member criterion is applied than when a best-member criterion is applied. Even so, it was the standard set by the best-member criterion that captured the attention of most small group researchers.

In response to the methodological problems identified in earlier studies, during the 1950s empirical research on small group performance began to use more robust experimental designs and to assess the performance of interacting groups against standards inspired by the work of Lorge and Solomon (1955), Marquart (1955), and Taylor (1955). This new wave of research yielded a more sobering picture than the one previously painted. Although a great many studies found that interacting groups often did perform better than the standard set by an average-member criterion, they also found that those same groups typically did not perform as well as the standard set by a best-member criterion (Davis, 1969; Hill, 1982; Lorge, Fox, Davitz, & Brenner, 1958).

To illustrate, Marquart (1955) performed a near-exact replication of Shaw's (1932) original study. When following Shaw's data-analytic procedure, Marquart was able to replicate Shaw's original findings: A larger percentage of groups than individuals correctly solved the problems. But Shaw's procedure is equivalent to evaluating interacting groups against the performance of nominal groups using an average-member criterion. On the other hand, when Marquart evaluated her interacting groups against nominal groups using a best-member criterion, her results were reversed: A *smaller* percentage of interacting groups than nominal groups correctly solved the problems. On the husbands-and-wives problem, for example, Marquart found that only 50% of the interacting groups, but 75% of the nominal groups, solved the problem correctly.

These new findings were often presented as evidence that groups frequently fall short of what they should be capable of doing (i.e., they should be capable of perform as well as their best member). Furthermore, this shortfall was generally blamed (though often vaguely) on faulty group interaction (cf. Hill, 1982). The interaction among members was seen as suboptimal, either in the benign sense of being insufficient to the task, or more malevolently as actively interfering with the group's performance. How else can one explain the inability of a group to solve a problem that one or more of its members could reasonably have solved alone? After all, in order to produce a correct answer, such groups have only to adopt the solution proposed by their correct member(s). That groups too often failed to do this seemed clearly to implicate one or more problematic elements of group interaction.

Despite the mounting evidence that groups often do not perform as well as their best members, some researchers nevertheless continued to hold out hope for group superiority, at least under some circumstances. Most notable among these were Collins and Guetzkow (1964), who, it will be recalled, introduced the idea of an assembly effect bonus—roughly comparable to the notion of strong synergy as I define it here. But even they seemed ambivalent on the matter. They cited no convincing empirical evidence of an assembly effect bonus, they did not suggest the circumstances under which such a bonus might occur, and their review of the literature in fact emphasized the obstacles to such a bonus that can arise from group interaction.

Steiner's Model of Group Performance

The pessimism about group interaction and group performance that began to emerge in the 1950s became so entrenched by the 1970s that it was codified in formal theory. Nowhere is this codification clearer than in the model of group performance proposed by Ivan Steiner. Steiner presented his model first in a short journal article (1966), then in a highly influential book-length monograph (1972). In these two works, Steiner sketched a deceptively simple framework that set the direction and tone for a generation of subsequent small-group researchers. According to this model, the actual productivity of a group is a direct function of its potential productivity minus any losses that result due to faulty group process, or:

Actual Productivity = Potential Productivity − Process Loss.

According to Steiner (1966, 1972), potential productivity is a joint function of task demands and member resources. Task demands include all the requirements imposed by the task itself and by the rules under which that task must be performed. Task demands specify not only the resources that members must bring to bear in order to complete their assignment (i.e., the knowledge, skills, abilities, and tools they must possess), but also how those resources must be applied in order to achieve the best outcome possible (cf. Roby & Lanzetta, 1958). Thus, the members of a bicycle racing team must all possess balance and stamina. Further, if they expect to draft effectively, they also must be able to judge accurately the waxing and waning of each others' strength and energy levels so they can rotate the lead at precisely the moment it will do the most good. In like fashion, the task of safely landing a large commercial airliner in adverse weather conditions demands that the crew be able to interpret their flight instruments correctly, follow hard-to-hear verbal instructions over a crackling radio, and execute a sequence of coordinated actions in just the right order and at just the right time. Task demands, in other words, specify the behaviors (including their timing, intensity, and duration) that must be enacted in order for the group to perform optimally, as well as the personal characteristics of the group members (physical, mental, and otherwise) that are needed to enact them. When fully documented, task demands provide a complete recipe for success.

The other determinant of potential productivity in Steiner's (1966, 1972) model is member resources. Whereas task demands specify the knowledge, skills, abilities, and tools that any group must possess in order to be maximally effective at that task, member resources are the knowledge, skills, abilities, and tools that a particular group actually does possess. Included here is knowledge of the appropriate timing, intensity, and duration of task-relevant actions. Such information might be stored as explicit procedural knowledge about the task—knowledge that can be articulated verbally—or as implicit knowledge that is part and parcel of the members' repertoire of skills and abilities. Also captured in the member resources variable is the way in which task-relevant knowledge, skills, abilities, and tools are distributed across members. In group decision-making situations, for example, it is apt to make a difference whether every member possesses a critical piece of decision-relevant information prior to discussing the issue and making a decision, as opposed to that information being possessed by one (or just a few) group members beforehand. At the very least, the latter scenario requires that the member holding the information mention it during discussion. If it is not mentioned, the rest of the group will be unable to take this information into account as they consider the decision. The same is not true for information that is held by every member prior to discussion. Here, it is possible for the information to be taken into account by all members even if it is not openly discussed (e.g., Gigone & Hastie, 1993, 1997a).

A group's potential performance—the highest level of productivity it can hope to achieve—depends on the degree to which its members' resources match the resources demanded by the task. If the members possess all the resources demanded by the task, and those resources are appropriately distributed among them, then they have the potential to perform maximally well. However, if they are deficient in one or more resources, or if those resources are distributed inappropriately, then their potential will be less than maximal. Just how much less will depend on both the degree and criticality of the resource deficiency. Minor deficiencies imply a potential that is only slightly below the maximum, whereas more serious deficiencies imply a potential that is far worse. Thus, according to this model, one reason why performance varies across groups is that groups differ in the resources they bring to the task. Other things being equal, two groups attempting the same task will perform differently to the extent they command different amounts of the required resources.

The final variable in Steiner's (1966, 1972) model is process loss, which is defined as a reduction in performance that is attributable to faulty or deficient group interaction. Group interaction refers to the actual behaviors enacted by the group members while engaging in the task. For example, it refers to the cyclists peddling at breakneck speed, following pace, shouting for a new leader, and trading positions. It also refers to the flight crew working methodically through its pre-landing checklist, reconfirming flight system settings after a sudden burst of turbulence, and discussing the likely content of a garbled air traffic control radio transmission. Thus, just as Steiner's model distinguishes between member resources demanded by the task and those actually possessed by the group, it also distinguishes between behaviors demanded by the task and those actually enacted by the group. If there is an exact one-to-one correspondence between the two, the group will perform to its capacity. Oftentimes, however, their behavior will deviate from what is required for optimum performance. This may be due in part to a lack of skill or ability (resources), which, as described above, constrains their potential performance. But a group's behavior will frequently depart from what is demanded simply because the members do not effectively apply the task-relevant resources that they do possess. This is the root of process loss, and it will drive their actual performance downward, below their resource-adjusted potential. This may come about, for example, as the result of poor coordination or low task motivation. The members of a group might enact the right behaviors but at the wrong time or in the wrong sequence. Alternatively, they might choose behaviors that are easier to enact but less effective. Or they may fail to take any action at all for a period of time, perhaps missing important opportunities for a better outcome simply because they are temporarily paralyzed by conflicting opinions about what to do next. And there are innumerable patently counter-productive behaviors that, if enacted, might interfere with the group's performance. These range from otherwise benign distractions, both private (e.g., worries and daydreams) and public (horseplay), to manifestly hostile actions born of frustration and intragroup tension that are meant specifically to harm the group's performance. However it arises, process loss detracts from the group's performance, and, according to Steiner's model, constitutes the second reason why task accomplishment varies across groups. Just as groups differ in the resources they bring to a task, they also differ in the extent to which they effectively utilize those resources.

Sizing Up Steiner's Model

Taken as a whole, Steiner's (1966, 1972) model is seductive in its simplicity and breathtaking in its sweep. It contains relatively few terms and is intended to apply to all task-oriented groups. At the same time, the model is also unquestionably negative in its view of group process. It does not admit even to the possibility that group interaction might result in process gain, or what I refer to equivalently as synergy. It entertains only the possibility—indeed, likelihood—of process loss. Not only is there no term in the model to represent process gain, the model's use of potential productivity as its central point of reference eliminates, by definition, all hope of process gain; it simply is not possible for a group to perform beyond its potential! Although I am not the first to take note of this pessimistic outlook (cf. Hackman, 1987; Hackman and Morris, 1975), few have suggested alternative ways of conceptualizing group process and performance that take account of both the losses and gains that might occur.

Beyond its unwelcoming stance toward process gain, there is another serious limitation of Steiner's (1966, 1972) model: it fails as a useful theory because (a) its central point of reference (potential productivity) is impossible to unambiguously assess, and, as a consequence, (b) the formulation as a whole is not falsifiable. As noted, a group's potential productivity is a function of the match between task demands and member resources. To determine potential productivity, it is therefore necessary to assess both the task to be performed and the people who will perform it. Both chores pose substantial measurement challenges. Tasks must be assessed at a level of detail that is sufficiently fine-grained to capture every important behavioral nuance that can impact performance. The assessment of member resources must be equally detailed. Further, and as Steiner (1966) himself cautioned, the latter must be done under optimal conditions in order to ensure that each member demonstrates accurately his or her full capacity. Optimal conditions are those that, among other things, elicit high levels of motivation. But how do we know when such conditions have actually been attained?

Consider, for example, a study by Messé, Hertel, Kerr, Lount, and Park (2002), who asked female research participants to perform a simple physical endurance task—holding a 1.75 lb. weight in one hand at arm's length for as long as they felt comfortable doing so. Participants performed this task both individually and in dyads. When working as a dyad, the two members each performed the task but did so simultaneously and in the presence of one another. Messé et al. found that on dyadic performance trials the amount of physical effort exerted by the weaker of the two members was often greater (i.e., the weight was held up longer) than the amount she exerted when working alone under conditions that, to many observers, would seem optimal for eliciting high motivation, and so for assessing maximum strength and endurance (i.e., there were no distractions of any kind, the experimenter urged the participant to do her best, and a financial incentive was offered for holding the weight up longer). In other words, the participants' performance when working alone often did not accurately index the full extent of their resources, at least as far as strength and endurance are concerned. This raises the more general question of how we might ever know when maximum task-relevant effort, ability, knowledge, etc., has been demonstrated, and so when the full extent of the group members' resources has been revealed.

But if there is doubt about whether or not we have accurately assessed the group members' task-relevant resources, then there will also be doubt about whether or not we have accurately determined their potential productivity. This, in turn, makes a decisive falsification of Steiner's (1966, 1972) overall model impossible. How should we interpret a result that shows a group to have performed better than our initial estimate of its potential productivity? Should we conclude that Steiner's model is wrong and deserves to be modified by adding a process gain parameter? Or should we conclude instead that we did a poor job of measuring the group's true potential? Any such challenge to Steiner's model is almost certain to become mired in alternative explanations involving the underestimation of group potential. Consequently, as a practical matter, Steiner's model seems quite untestable.

These limitations have generally been ignored by small group researchers. Instead, Steiner's (1966, 1972) model has been accepted at face value and has strongly influenced thinking about group process and performance for 40 years. This has had two unfortunate consequences. First, it has promoted a research literature that has become decidedly unbalanced. The literature on small-group performance gives rather strong emphasis to the weaknesses of groups while largely ignoring their strengths (cf. Wang & Thompson, 2006). As a result, we know more about what can go wrong in groups, and how to avoid process losses, than about what can go right and how to harness process gains. Second, during this model's tenure there has been a marked decrease in interest in group performance as a topic of study, at least within social psychology (Moreland, Hogg, & Hains, 1994). Undoubtedly, there are numerous factors that have contributed to this state of affairs (cf. Levine & Moreland, 1990, 1998; McGrath, 1997). I am suggesting here simply that one such factor is the pessimistic view of group process that Steiner's (1966, 1972) model has encouraged. If groups are so troublesome, and there is no hope of achieving genuine process gain, then why bother with groups at all? If this assessment is correct, and Steiner's model has in fact contributed to the declining interest in group research within social psychology, it would be ironic indeed, for Steiner himself was among the loudest voices lamenting the onset of this decline (Steiner 1974; 1986).

Perhaps, then, a reframing of the central questions of process loss and process gain is in order. Such a reframing would establish a more suitable conceptual platform for examining synergy within groups. It might also yield a more balanced research agenda, one that is oriented as much toward what is good in groups as toward what is bad. Finally, it may even restore some of the enthusiasm that social psychology once had for group performance as a topic of study.

☐ Scope and Content of This Book

My goal in this first chapter has been to define what I mean by synergy, and to suggest how this concept—especially the distinction between weak and strong forms of synergy—might be usefully employed as a framework for thinking about group performance. However, I have not yet precisely defined what I mean by a "group." In this final section of the chapter, I provide that definition, and do so in a way that both puts the book in larger perspective and demarcates its scope. After that, I briefly preview the content of the remaining chapters.

Scope

The focus of this book is small, task-performing groups. By *group* I mean a collection of individuals who are mutually aware of, and at least minimally dependent upon, one another. Their mutual awareness includes being cognizant of their interdependence. This, more than anything else, is what makes a group a psychological entity, not merely a physical or statistical one. Their interdependence is rooted in a shared purpose, objective, or goal that together they are trying to achieve. It arises from the behavioral requirements of the task(s) they must perform in pursuit of that goal—how they must interact if they are to reach it—and from the fact that the consequences of achieving (or not achieving) their goal will be felt in some way by all of them. A group of rock-and-roll musicians will find it difficult to gain employment as a band (their goal) if during auditions they cannot manage to play in time with one another (one of the behavioral requirements of their task).

A *small* group is one in which each member can reasonably interact one-on-one with every other member. This implies that it is possible for each member both to influence directly, and to be influenced directly by, every other member of the group. Numerically, small groups range in size from two to about 20 members, although the upper boundary is a fuzzy one. Beyond about 20 members, however, regular one-on-one interaction with everyone else in the group becomes prohibitively time consuming. Thus, a nine-piece jazz ensemble qualifies as a small group, whereas a 90-piece symphony orchestra does not. It is worth noting that the bulk of the small group research literature concentrates on groups with a half-dozen or fewer members. Thus, the upper range of what might justifiably qualify as a small group is relatively understudied.

The phrase *task-performing* group is a convenient one that I employ throughout the book. I do not use it, however, to refer to a particular subtype of group (e.g., task-performing versus non-task-performing). All groups perform tasks, some profound (e.g., deciding the guilt or innocence of an accused murderer) and some profoundly mundane (e.g., deciding where to eat lunch). Certain of these tasks will be central to the group's existence (as deciding guilt or innocence is to a jury), whereas others will be less so (as deciding where to eat lunch is to that same jury).[10] Further, whereas some of the tasks performed by a group may be assigned by an external authority (the courts, a work supervisor, an experimenter), others may be taken up at the group's own initiative. The latter implies that deciding what its tasks will be is itself a task that groups sometimes perform. Regardless, the primary interest in this book is understanding those aspects of small group behavior that are in service of, or somehow relevant to, performing whatever task the group is trying to accomplish at the moment (e.g., reaching a consensus about the choice alternative they will select). Thus, rather than denoting a particular type of group, my use of the phrase "task-performing group" is intended simply to emphasize the aspect of small group behavior with which the book is centrally concerned.

More specifically, the book is concerned with the *performance effectiveness* of small groups, by which I mean the quality or quantity of their productive output vis-à-vis the task they are currently working on. Thus, it is concerned with how well or poorly groups perform particular kinds of tasks, and with whether or not their collective performance reflects any evidence of synergy. Performance effectiveness is best evaluated by reference to one or more externally defined standards of excellence. In some cases, relatively objective standards can be applied, such as the speed or distance achieved by an engineering team's experimental solar-powered car. In other cases, nothing beyond subjective criteria may be available. When evaluating the creativity of an advertising team's proposed media campaign, for instance, the only useful benchmark might be the subjective judgment of a client or marketing manager. The empirical research I review is limited to that concerned with groups whose task output is subject to some form of external evaluation, whether objective or subjective. Research that does not deal in a fairly direct way with task performance defined in this manner is generally not considered here.

To avoid confusion, it is useful to distinguish performance effectiveness from the broader concept of group (or team) effectiveness. Group effectiveness can be defined as the extent to which the group is able to accomplish its task objectives, fulfill member needs, and maintain its integrity as an ongoing system (cf. Hackman, 1987; Kozlowski & Ilgen, 2006; McGrath & Argote, 2003). By this definition, performance effectiveness is only one element of group effectiveness—an effective group is *in part* one that can accomplish its tasks and achieve its goals. But groups also must be concerned with their future viability. Naturally occurring groups often endure for substantial periods of time. They exist long enough to develop a meaningful history and typically are expected to continue functioning as a group into the foreseeable future. If they are to do so, however, it will be necessary for members to interact in ways that maintain, if not enhance, their capacity to work effectively together. A group that "burns itself out" in the process of accomplishing today's task (perhaps because of persistent antagonistic interactions) is unlikely to be around to perform tomorrow. Therefore, an effective group is also, *in part*, one that can maintain itself over time as a viable task-performing unit. Finally, this long-term viability is itself partly dependent on the extent to which membership in the group is satisfying. A satisfying group is one that fulfills its members' personal needs. Members who have important needs met by the group will see membership as rewarding, will strive to maintain their membership, and so will be available to contribute to the group's future endeavors. In contrast, those whose needs are not met by the group will be at risk of terminating their membership. Member attrition, especially if it occurs among those who possess unique technical skills, threatens the future task-performing capability of the group. Thus, an effective group is also, *in part*, one that meets members' needs.

In this book I do not tackle the larger problem of group effectiveness. Instead, I focus only on that part of group effectiveness that relates to task performance in the present—how well or poorly the group does at the task it is currently trying to accomplish, and whether there is evidence of synergy in that performance. To be sure, a complete understanding of small group behavior requires that issues of system maintenance and member need fulfillment be addressed. However, these topics are beyond the scope of the present volume.

Content

The remaining chapters in this book address different segments of the empirical literature on small group performance. The goal in each is to call attention to what its segment of the literature has to say about synergy and to identify important problems that need to be addressed if we are to fully understand synergistic performance gains in groups.

Chapter 2 is a foundational chapter that focuses on the tasks that groups perform. This is the logical place to begin, because group performance, and the possibility of synergy, can be meaningfully understood only in terms of what the group has been asked to do. Different tasks make different demands on groups, and even relatively subtle differences in those demands can sometimes have dramatic effects on group process and performance. A primary research objective in studying group tasks is to identify those task differences that actually make a difference—that account for a meaningful proportion of variance in group process and performance. Chapter 2 defines what a group task is, differentiates tasks and subtasks from performance aggregates, and reviews the most important taxonomic systems that have been proposed for describing and classifying group tasks.

Chapters 3 through 6 then examine group performance in each of four different task domains. In each chapter, I consider both the historical origins and recent developments in the relevant empirical literature. Chapter 3 is devoted to idea-generation tasks. It addresses the question of whether groups are any better than individuals at producing novel and creative ideas (e.g., for stimulating tourism in your city). Chapter 4 deals with group problem-solving tasks. These are tasks for which there is an objectively correct answer (e.g., the shortest driving route among six different points of interest in and around your city). Chapter 5 is dedicated to judgment tasks. These also have an objectively correct answer, but the correctness of that answer is usually more difficult—if not impossible—for members to demonstrate conclusively to one another (e.g., the number of hotel rooms in your city that will be vacant next March). Finally, Chapter 6 is concerned with group decision-making tasks. As with judgment tasks, the best answer to a decision-making task is usually very difficult to demonstrate conclusively. Unlike judgment tasks, however, decision-making tasks typically call for a choice among a small set of discrete alternatives that cannot be arrayed on a single underlying dimension (e.g., three candidates being considered for the job of Director of Tourism in your city). Between them, Chapters 3–6 cover the four types of tasks that have dominated the empirical literature on group versus individual performance. Historically, groups have most often demonstrated only weak synergy when performing these tasks. However, within each task domain there is a small amount of scattered evidence suggesting that, under the right conditions, strong synergy is possible. In each chapter, I examine this evidence in some detail.

Chapters 7 through 9 then deal with a set of topics that cut across task types. Chapter 7 is concerned with learning and memory in groups. It focuses on the performance gains that result from experience working together as a group. It addresses, among other things, whether group learning can be distinguished empirically from the individual learning of group members, and whether there is a benefit to collective recall over individual recall. Chapter 8 is concerned with motivation in groups. Performance gains can sometimes arise from the enhanced effort that members exert when working together as a group. This is likely to occur, however, only under certain conditions. I examine research that identifies some of those conditions. Chapter 9 is concerned with diversity in groups, and with how the distribution of member characteristics impacts group performance. The central question taken up there is whether a group's performance is helped or hindered by diversity among its members.

Finally, Chapter 10 is a capstone chapter that summaries and integrates the main themes and conclusions presented in the rest of the book. An important goal of this chapter is to suggest directions for the future in the search for synergy.

☐ Chapter Summary

My purpose in this book is to evaluate objectively the empirical literature on the task performance capabilities of small groups. I attempt to do so with an eye toward better understanding the performance benefits that can be achieved by working collectively in groups to accomplish tasks. I have suggested in this first chapter that the academic research literature has tended to emphasize the performance shortcomings of small groups, even as the world at large has embraced the use of groups as an effective means of accomplishing many kinds of tasks. I argued that this apparent disconnect—between scientific understanding and lay belief—is not wholly the fault of a misguided laity. Rather, it is due, in part at least, to the rather restrictive way in which questions about group performance gains and losses have come to be framed in the academic literature. As an alternative framework, I introduced the concept of synergy—and, in particular, the distinction between weak and strong forms of synergy. This alternative framework provides a more balanced way to evaluate the research literature. Its use will, I hope, shift the academic conversation away from one that thrives inordinately on exposing the weaknesses of groups to one that also sees value in uncovering their strengths. It is certainly important to know what can go wrong in task performing groups, and how to avoid those difficulties. But it is equally important to know what can go right, and how those benefits might be harnessed. What sorts of performance gains are possible with groups, and what are the prospects for actually realizing them? These are the questions at the heart of the rest of this book.

☐ Endnotes

1. The phrase "mere presence" is used here in its general sense, not in the narrow sense employed by Zajonc (1965, 1980) in his theory of social facilitation.
2. Drafting is inherently dangerous and is increasingly so as the speed of travel increases. It is for this reason that drafting is prohibited in many cycling races open to the general public. Thus, despite its benefits, including the visceral insight it can provide into the nature of synergy, I do not recommend that you try this unless you are a very accomplished rider.
3. I provide a more formal definition of what constitutes a group later in this chapter.
4. Two points are worth noting. First, I confine myself here to a purely physical analysis of this situation, ignoring for the moment any psychological processes (e.g., motivation) that might be at play (but see next paragraph). Second, a full account of the aerodynamics of drafting reveals a benefit not just to the following rider, but to the lead rider, too (Wilson, 2004). In most cases, however, the benefit to the lead rider will be very slight and experientially unnoticeable. Thus, for the sake of simplicity, I ignore this as well.
5 For an easy-to-follow analysis of the mathematics underlying the river-crossing and Tower of Hanoi problems, see Danesi (2004).
6. A fuller statement of this problem, along with two possible solutions, is given in Chapter 4.
7. The two problems on which groups and individuals performed equivalently were the bus routing and sonnet completion problems.
8. See Chapter 4 for a fuller discussion of Lorge and Solomon's (1955) argument and mathematical model.
9. For this reason, nominal groups are sometimes called "statisticized groups."
10. The broader social significance of a task does not, by itself, reveal its centrality to a group's existence. Thus, deciding where to eat lunch may or may not be a central task for a given group. Although it might not be central to, for example, a recently empaneled jury, it might well be central to a group whose purpose is to do no more than get together occasionally in order to enjoy one another's company; some lunch spots are more conducive to relaxation and conversation than others.

2

CHAPTER

Tasks

What Groups Do

It seems impossible to talk about task-performing groups without considering in some detail the properties of the tasks that those groups are asked to carry out. For many real-world groups, the tasks they perform are their raison d'être; if there were no task to accomplish, no goal to achieve, there would be no group. This is typically the case in organizational settings, for example, where tasks are quite predictably the center of attention. Concerns about the nature of those tasks, and about what is required to carry them out, are frequently at the heart of managerial decisions regarding which groups will be assigned to perform which tasks and what kinds of resources will be provided in order to support the work of those groups.

Tasks are quite plainly not all alike. They can make very different demands on groups and command very different sorts of behaviors from them. Performing brain surgery is clearly a different sort of activity from performing a Bach sonata. Running a printing press is obviously not the same as running a relay race. Landing a large commercial jetliner can hardly be compared to landing a large contract to build jetliners. And deciding a defendant's guilt or innocence would seem to have little in common with deciding the best location for a new school, wind turbine, or military base. As a practical matter, the success of an organization hinges—in part, at least—on understanding the differences among the tasks to be performed and using that knowledge to inform the deployment of group resources.

How should we deal with task differences in our theories of group process and performance? On the one hand, it seems impractical to consider developing a different theory for every different kind of task that groups might perform. The number of task-specific theories would quickly become unmanageably large and, ultimately, would undercut one of the main advantages of theory: generalizability. On the other hand, few would take seriously the proposition that we ignore task differences altogether. Even a casual observer is apt to protest that the nature of the task matters greatly, if for no other reason than that different tasks require different skills.

But the issue runs deeper than just differences in requisite skills and ability. Even when ability is held constant, remarkably different outcomes can emerge, depending on the nature of the task being performed. Consider, for example, a group of three students who work together on a hypothetical multiple-choice test that contains just two items: a geography question (e.g., "Addis Ababa is the capital of which country?"), and a statistics question (e.g., "What is the sample variance for the set of scores 1, 2, 3, 4, 5?"). The group must decide on a single agreed-upon answer to each question and has at its disposal only a pencil and the piece of paper on which the questions are written. Suppose that only one student in the group knows the correct answer to each question (though it is not necessarily the same student for both questions), and that the other two students both prefer the same wrong answer in each case. As will be argued later in this chapter, and again in Chapter 4, under these conditions there is good reason to expect that the group is more likely to answer the statistics question correctly than the geography question. This is true even though the group members individually possess exactly the same ability vis-à-vis these two questions: just one member knows the correct answer in each case. There is, in other words, something about the statistics question that makes it easier for the group as a whole to answer correctly, even though it is no easier for the members as individuals (cf. Laughlin & Ellis, 1986).

Nor are task effects limited to activities requiring the expenditure of just mental effort. They can be observed as well when mainly physical effort is called for. For example, tasks that require even very simple physical actions by members (e.g., hand clapping, lifting a small weight, or shouting loudly) can sometimes elicit markedly different patterns of effort among members, depending on the particular way in which those tasks are arranged. Some arrangements encourage members to expend the least amount of effort possible, whereas others encourage them to expend the greatest amount possible. Further, among the latter, certain tasks encourage more effort from the most capable members of the group, whereas others encourage more effort from the least capable members. Indeed, there is evidence that the mere perception of task differences can affect both group process and performance, even though no real differences of any kind actually exist (Karau & Williams, 1993; Messé, Hertel, Kerr, Lount, & Park; 2002; Stasser & Stewart, 1992).

And task effects can be surprisingly powerful. This is illustrated, for example, in a laboratory study jointly conducted by Hackman (1968) and

Morris (1966). They had 108 groups perform a total of 108 different tasks, all of which required a written group product. The tasks fell into three broad categories. Some directed the group to generate ideas or images (e.g., "Write a story about ..."). Others instructed them to evaluate an issue (e.g., "Take a stand on ..."). Still others enjoined them to develop a plan to achieve a goal (e.g., "Devise a way to ..."). Each group performed four tasks within one of these three categories, resulting in 432 different group products. Morris (1966) examined group process by coding the verbal interaction among members as they developed these products. He found that 9 (56%) of the 16 behavior categories he coded were significantly affected by the type of task on which groups worked. Similarly, Hackman (1968) had judges rate the group products on eight descriptive performance dimensions (e.g., degree of action orientation, originality, issue involvement), most of which could be evaluated reliably without knowing the specific task that gave rise to the product. He found that task type significantly affected all but one of these dimensions, accounting for up to 48% of the variance in several cases. Comparable findings have been reported by others (e.g., Hackman & Vidmar, 1970; Kabanoff & O'Brien, 1979; Kent & McGrath, 1969).

It seems clear from results like these that even relatively subtle task differences can sometimes dramatically affect group process and performance. At the same time, intuition suggests that not all task differences are apt to have this kind of impact. Tasks can differ one from another in a great many ways, only some of which are likely to be important for understanding group behavior. Therefore, a primary research objective is to identify those task differences that actually make a difference—that account for a meaningful proportion of variance in group process and performance.

A first step toward this goal is to better understand the nature of group tasks themselves—their underlying properties, and their structural relationships with one another. Task-focused research is an important foundational activity that can yield, among other things, useful taxonomic systems for describing and classifying group tasks. Such systems are potentially of immense methodological and theoretical value because they can

1. Inform judgments about generalizability by suggesting the range of tasks over which a given set of empirical results is and is not likely to apply,
2. Facilitate theory development by suggesting what knowledge, acquired in connection with group performance on one task, might reasonably be used to explain group performance on other tasks,
3. Promote the conceptualization of research results in terms of the deep structure of tasks rather than their surface characteristics, thus

encouraging insights into the underlying mechanisms by which tasks impact group process and performance, and

4. Make it easier to see where research has and has not already been done, thus fostering the systematic accumulation of empirical evidence.

In this chapter, I review several systems for describing and classifying group tasks. My review is restricted to those schemes that focus in a fairly direct way on the tasks themselves, apart from the groups that perform them. Particularly in the organizational behavior literature, there exist numerous examples of classification schemes that categorize groups according to their primary task or function (e.g., Devine, 2002; Klimoski & Jones, 1995; Sundstrom, 1999). Although useful for some purposes, such schemes are generally too coarse to be helpful for understanding performance at the task level of analysis. The reason is that groups in organizations almost always perform many different kinds of tasks, even when one of these might reasonably be considered their primary task. For example, the sound crew on a movie set (a production team, according to many taxonomies) is apt to be involved not only in the direct technical activity of recording the film's soundtrack, but also in planning production schedules, problem-solving around personnel issues, choosing equipment vendors, generating creative ideas for enhancing the artistic quality of the film, and so forth. It would be naïve to treat these activities as if they were all the same sort of thing. Rather, it seems more appropriate to conceptualize the group's primary objective (e.g., producing film soundtracks) as requiring the performance of a number of different tasks, and to consider the various ways in which each of those separate tasks might be described or classified.

But before examining the several available descriptive and classificatory schemes that can be put to this purpose, it is important first to understand clearly what a group task is.

☐ The Nature of Group Tasks

An obvious first step for anyone setting out to study group task performance is to define what is meant by the term "group task." Unfortunately, this first step is routinely overlooked in practice, perhaps because it seems self-evident. As I will illustrate, however, confusion about what is and what is not a group task can lead to incorrect interpretations of empirical results and to false conclusions about the presence of synergy in group performance. Thus, it seems wise to attend carefully to this matter, regardless of how easy or obvious it may at first appear.

Group Task Defined

Instead of offering a new definition of the term "group task," I revive a definition originally proposed by Hackman (1969). Thus, I define a group task as a set of instructions for acting on a particular stimulus complex. A "stimulus complex" is the sum total of all the physical, social, and/or conceptual inputs that the group must work with or act upon. "Instructions," are directives that specify either the goal(s) to be pursued or the procedure(s) to be employed vis-à-vis that stimulus complex. Below I consider each of these elements in turn.

First, every task involves some sort of *stimulus complex*. Groups always work with, or act upon, some preexisting set of materials, ideas, or information. Persons, groups, and organizations in the focal group's environment may also be an important part of the stimulus complex. This would be true, for example, in the case of a sales team whose task is to persuade a prospective client to buy their product or service. Here, the prospective client (whether a single person, a group, or an entire organization) is clearly a central element of the stimulus complex.

A stimulus complex need not be complicated in an absolute sense. Consider, for example, a task employed by Taylor, Berry, and Block (1958) to study group creativity. They asked four-person groups to work together to generate ideas for promoting greater European tourism in America. The statement of the problem was presented verbally to each group, and the groups' ideas were recorded on audiotape as they discussed the problem. Thus, what the group was given to work with was exclusively conceptual, and extremely simple: the mental image of European tourists traveling in America. Compare this to the task employed by Liang, Moreland, and Argote (1995) to study transactive memory in groups. They asked three-person groups that had previously been trained in the assembly of AM transistor radios to construct a radio from the several dozen electronic components provided in a commercially available radio assembly hobby kit. Here, the stimulus complex was clearly more elaborate, comprising all the components in the kit (e.g., a prepunched and labeled circuit board, numerous resistors, capacitors, transistors, etc.), the particular way in which those components were presented to the group, the tools they had at their disposal, and the space in which they had to work.

Second, every group task involves one or more *goal directives*. Goal directives are instructions that indicate what the group is expected to produce or achieve. All group tasks have goals,[1] although a goal by itself does not constitute a task (e.g., to be healthy, wealthy, and wise are goals, not tasks). Thus, the goal of the tourism task is to generate as many creative ideas as possible about stimulating European tourism in America, and the goal of the radio assembly task is to construct a functional AM radio.

It is usually fairly easy to identify the goals associated with tasks employed in laboratory settings, as in the two examples given above. In contrast, it can sometimes be quite challenging to identify *the* goal associated with a particular task performed by real-world groups working in their natural settings. Consider, for example, a study by Hutchins (1990), who observed six-person teams working cooperatively to manually fix (establish) the position of their large naval warship as it navigated through restricted coastal waters. Sailors are trained to perform this task using a technology that has changed very little in the past several hundred years: taking visual bearings and from them plotting intersecting lines of position on a nautical chart. Remarkably, sailors may be required to perform this task as often as once per minute while the ship is underway near shore.

The stimulus complex for this task seems clear enough. It consists of the ship's navigation equipment (e.g., binoculars, bearing compasses, charts, plotting table, communication system, etc.), plus the position and visibility of landmarks on shore. But what is the goal? Most immediately, it would seem to be placing a mark on the nautical chart to indicate the ship's current position. Yet, as is often the case in real-world settings, this task is performed with additional, broader organizational objectives in mind. Fixing their current position on the chart helps to produce a plot of the ship's course made good (the course it has actually traveled), which contributes to the goal of safely navigating the ship (e.g., it helps ensure that the ship will not wander onto a shoal and run aground), which must be done in order to bring the ship to port, which will complete the crew's training mission, which contributes to general naval readiness, which is important for defending the country's territorial waters, etc. In other words, even very small tasks are usually part of a hierarchy of ever-broadening organizational goals. Accomplishing any one of these goals contributes to the attainment of all the goals above it (cf. Simon, 1997).

So, which of these is *the* goal associated with the task? For the purpose of understanding group process and performance, it is most useful to focus on the goal whose achievement is *most immediately, directly, and completely determined by the behavior of the group performing the task*. This is the goal against which the group's performance should be assessed. Thus, in order to understand the group performing the shipboard position-fixing task, it is most helpful to focus on the goal of correctly marking the ship's current position on the chart. One member of the group actually makes this mark, but its placement is the product of numerous inputs (observations, calculations) and interactions (primarily communications about observations and calculations) by the rest of the group. It is considerably less helpful in this example to focus on the goal of safely navigating the ship, because safe navigation also depends in part on the successful completion of additional tasks performed by other individuals and groups beyond the position-fixing team (e.g., the ship must be steered in an appropriate direction, her engines must be maintained so as to provide reliable propulsion, etc.). To be sure, the achievement of certain higher-level goals (e.g., safely navigating the ship) often gives meaning to the goals below them (e.g., correctly fixing the ship's current position) and may therefore have strong incentive value for the focal group. But if so, that incentive value is transferred to the lower-level goal, which in principle can be examined directly.

Finally, in addition to goal directives, task instructions may also contain *procedural directives*. Procedural directives specify how the group is to go about performing its task. It is not necessary that tasks have procedural directives, but, when they exist, they either prescribe or proscribe what is to be done vis-à-vis the stimulus complex. Procedural directives may be formalized as rules and standard operating procedures, or they may exist only as informal instructions communicated at the time the task is assigned. Procedural directives often indicate what does and what does not "count" toward achievement of the group's goal. In the game of baseball, for instance, a ball hit over the outfield fence may or may not be counted as a home run, depending on exactly where it crossed the fence line (i.e., did it cross in fair territory?). Similarly, the shipboard position-fixing team might be instructed not to use the ship's electronic navigation equipment as an aide in determining their location (e.g., because doing so would undermine the training objectives of their cruise). And in the laboratory, groups asked to generate as many creative ideas as possible for stimulating European tourism in America might be cautioned that only "distinctly different ideas will be counted." Thus, a given idea (e.g., "provide German-speaking tour guides for organized tours originating in Germany") may or may not be counted, depending on what other ideas have already been suggested (e.g., "provide French-speaking tour guides for organized tours originating in France"). Note that procedural directives are instructions that come from a source of authority with both the ability and the will to enforce those directives. Often, this is a source outside the group, but it could also be the group itself, as when a group of children decides in advance the rules of a game they will play. If there is little or no likelihood that a given procedural directive will be enforced, then it should not be considered an element of the task.

Group Tasks, Performance Aggregates, and the Search for Synergy

I argued above that, except for the incentive value they may confer, higher-level goals that require the completion of additional tasks by other actors beyond the focal group are not particularly helpful for understanding the focal group's performance. But what about higher-level goals that require the completion of additional tasks *by the focal group itself*? Here the situation is more complex. Under some circumstances, performance measured against such higher-level goals may provide useful insights into group process and performance. There are many situations, however, where group performance measured against such goals is apt to be misleading, perhaps suggesting the presence of strong synergy when none actually exists. Here, I examine this problem in some detail, using as a case in point the familiar activity of taking a multiple-choice exam in a classroom setting.

In most educational settings, classroom exams are taken by students working individually. There is no reason, however, why groups of students could not work collaboratively on such exams to produce a single consensus answer for each question. Indeed, this is exactly what happens in courses that use a team-learning approach to instruction (e.g., Michaelsen, Knight, & Fink, 2004). Team learning makes extensive use of small student work groups (teams) to help accomplish important learning objectives. In a typical team-learning classroom, the instructor assigns students to permanent work teams of 4 to 8 members each. These teams are created early in the academic term, remain intact for the duration of the course, and complete a variety of projects both inside and outside the classroom. They also take the course exams together. These exams are usually administered in two phases during the same class period. In the first phase, team members take the exam individually, just as they would any regular classroom test. Then, after turning in their individual answer sheets, they get together as a group to take the exam again, this time working cooperatively to produce a single set of answers that will determine their team exam score. The students' course grades depend on both their individual and their team's performance.

Michaelsen, Watson, and Black (1989) studied the multiple-choice exam performance of 222 team-learning groups enrolled in a college-level organizational behavior course over a 5-year period. They observed that when the members of these teams took the course exams individually in the first phase of testing, they answered an average of 74.2% of the questions correctly. Further, the best member of each group (i.e., the member with the highest exam score) answered an average of 82.6% of the questions correctly. In contrast, the team scores obtained during the second phase of testing averaged 89.9% correct. In other words, the team scores typically exceeded not only the average of their members' scores, but also the scores of their best members. Indeed, when they looked at the data for each team separately, Michaelsen et al. found that the team score exceeded the score of their best member 97% of the time. On the face of it, these results would seem to be evidence of what I defined in Chapter 1 as strong synergy—performance that exceeds what even the best member of the group is able to accomplish individually. And this is essentially how Michaelsen et al. interpreted them.

However, these results are misleading. Although they seem to indicate the presence of strong synergy, a closer analysis suggests otherwise.

The total score on a classroom exam is typically created by aggregating the scores (i.e., correct vs. incorrect responses) obtained on each of the separate exam items. This is true regardless of whether the exam is taken by an individual or a group. This aggregation occurs in much the same way that a soccer team's final score is determined at the end of a game: by counting the total number of times the team successfully placed the ball inside their opponent's goal. And just as there is nothing in the soccer team's final game score that is not derived directly and completely from the separate goals they scored, there is also nothing in the students' total exam scores that does not derive directly and completely from their separate item scores. Importantly, in neither case is the aggregation process itself affected by the performers' behavior. Note carefully the distinction between the aggregation process, on the one hand, and what is being aggregated, on the other. The students, whether working individually or as a group, affect only *what* is aggregated—exam item answers—not *how* those answers are aggregated. They do not, for example, decide which items will be counted or how many points they will be worth. These are the prerogative of the course instructor. Thus, it is really the instructor, not the students, who creates the total exam scores.[2] Although both individuals and groups may strive for the highest possible total score on a classroom exam, they do not directly produce those scores. Rather, what they directly produce are answers to the individual exam questions. It is these direct products of individual and group behavior that should be the focus of attention when inspecting the data for evidence of synergy. Focusing instead on the aggregate exam scores invites confusion and misunderstanding. Because they are a step removed from what is actually produced by students' test-taking behavior, total exam scores provide an imperfect, and potentially distorted, view of group process and performance (cf. Rousseau, 1985; Sackett & Larson, 1990).

Tindale and Larson (1992) demonstrated precisely this point in a replication of Michaelsen et al.'s (1989) study. Like Michaelsen et al., they observed the multiple-choice exam performance of team-learning groups, this time enrolled in an industrial/organizational psychology course. As in Michaelsen et al., team members first took the exams individually, then as a group, with their overall course grade depending on both. When the total exam scores were analyzed, the results obtained were very similar to those reported by Michaelsen et al. Specifically, when the students took the exams individually, they answered an average of 72.2% of the questions correctly, with the best member of each group answering an average of 85.1% of the questions correctly. In contrast, the team scores averaged 90.1% correct. Thus, once again, at the level of the total exam score, the teams appeared to outperform even their best members.

A different picture emerged, however, when Tindale and Larson (1992) analyzed the students' performance on the individual exam items—an analysis conducted at a level that corresponds to what the cooperative learning teams actually produced. Although there continued to be clear evidence that teams routinely performed better than their average members did when working alone, there was no evidence at all that teams ever performed better than their best member. Specifically, and consistent with the idea that teams typically performed better than their average member, teams were highly likely to answer a given item correctly even when a majority of their members had individually gotten that item wrong during the first phase of testing, as long as either one or two members (depending on group size) had, in fact, gotten it right. For example, and as can be seen in the bottom panel of Table 2.1, five-person teams answered items correctly 79% of the time, even when just two of their members had answered those same items correctly as individuals. A different way to express this results is that five-person teams were able to answer a given item correctly

TABLE 2.1 Multiple-Choice Test Item Performance for Four-Person and Five-Person Teams

N Exam Items[a]	N Correct Members in Team	Proportion of Items Answered Correctly
Four-Person Teams		
43	4	1.00
59	3	1.00
28	2	0.86
19	1	0.32
6	0	0.00
Five-Person Teams		
70	5	1.00
91	4	1.00
50	3	0.92
19	2	0.79
16	1	0.38
5	0	0.00

[a] Number of exam items answered by teams of the indicated size with the indicated number of correct members.

Adapted from "Assembly bonus effect or typical group performance? A comment on Michaelsen, Watson, and Black (1989)," by Tindale & Larson, 1992, *Journal of Applied Psychology, 77*, 102–105. With permission of the American Psychological Association.

with a probability of .79, even though their members individually were able to answer that same item correctly with a probability of just 2/5 = .40 (an objectively difficult item). This is clear evidence that the teams outperformed their average members. On the other hand, these same data indicate that the five-person teams failed to give the correct answer 21% of the time, despite the fact that two of their members had answered correctly as individuals. In other words, more than one fifth of the time the teams did not perform as well as their best members (i.e., those who answered correctly as individuals).[3] Further, if just one member in a five-person team was able to answer correctly as an individual, the teams failed to match this one best member's performance more than three fifths (62%) of the time. And when *none* of the team members were individually able to answer a particular item correctly, the team as a whole *never* answered correctly. This latter result is particularly important, because it deals with the one circumstance in which it was even *possible* for the teams to surpass—not just match—the performance of their best members (because no member was actually good enough to answer correctly as an individual). Yet, teams never did this—they never answered correctly when none of their members could answer correctly as individuals. Thus, while these data clearly indicate that the team-learning groups surpassed the performance of their average members, they also indicate that these teams never surpassed the performance of their best members. This pattern fits the definition of weak synergy, not strong synergy.

In summary, different approaches to analyzing these data yield different conclusions. When analyzed at the level of the total exam score, they suggest the presence of strong synergy in team-learning groups. But when analyzed at the level of the individual exam items, they suggest the presence of only weak synergy. Why?

The root of the problem lies in the total exam scores and, in particular, in what it means to be the "best" member in the team based on those scores. When total exam scores are the focus of the analysis, the "best" member is defined as the person in the group with the highest individual total score. However, this person is not necessarily best on every single item. Although this person will be the one who most often can answer an item correctly when others cannot, there are apt to be at least a few occasions when one or more other members can answer an item correctly that this "best" member cannot (cf. Stasson & Bradshaw, 1995). So, on these items, someone else is actually best. Therefore, the "best" member, as defined by the total exam score, is really only "best on average" when the separate exam item scores are considered. Consequently, an analysis of total exam scores that compares a team's performance with that of its "best" member is in reality comparing the team's performance with that of its "average best" member. Because total exam scores are one step removed from what is actually produced by students (i.e., exam item answers), they hide the fact that the "best" member is usually not the best on every single item. If the best person in the group, as defined by the total test scores, were in fact also best on every item, then the conclusions based on the two different levels of analysis—total scores and item scores—would agree.

It is important at this point to emphasize that taking a multi-item exam is not itself a single task. Rather, it comprises many different tasks. These are the exam items. Although the goal (choose the correct answer) and procedural directives (e.g., do not look for answers in the textbook; mark only one answer per question) may be the same for all items in an exam, the stimulus complex (the substance of the question and of the choice alternatives presented) varies from one item to the next. It is this variation in stimulus complex that makes each item a different task.

The search for synergy is a search for group performance gains *at the task level of analysis*. Conclusions about both weak and strong synergy must therefore be based on standards of comparison that faithfully represent what actually happens at the level of the task. With regard to the team-learning groups we have been considering here, it is not appropriate to draw conclusions about strong synergy based on comparisons of total test scores for teams and best members, because these do not faithfully represent what actually happened at the level of the task—that is, on each of the separate exam items. In particular, the person with the highest overall exam score is often not best on every item. On some items, one or more other members may actually be best. Strong synergy is demonstrated when the group's performance *on a given task* exceeds the performance of even its best member *on that task*. It is not demonstrated simply by showing that the group's performance across tasks exceeds the performance of the person who on average is best across tasks. Simply put, the group member with the highest aggregate performance score is usually not a sufficiently high standard for judging the presence of strong synergy.

Tasks and Performance Aggregates: Further Considerations

I intentionally focused above on a very particular type of task, and on a very specific kind of interpretational problem, in order to make the point that group performance should be measured at the level of the task if the objective is to understand the connection between group process and performance. In the present section I address a few loose ends related to the definition of tasks and to the use of performance aggregates, beginning with the latter.

Two Exceptions Regarding Performance Aggregates

The key elements in the argument presented above are that (a) exam scores are measures that aggregate performance over multiple tasks (items), and (b) the group member with the highest total exam score is not necessarily the best performer on every task. These caveats make many aggregate performance measures inappropriate as a basis for conclusions about synergy in group performance. At the same time, they suggest two special conditions under which aggregate scores might legitimately be used in the search for synergy. The first, suggested above, is when the best member as defined by the aggregate score is also best on every separate task. This is apt to be an uncommon condition, and in any case should not be assumed. Rather, it should be verified, which means that a task-level analysis still should be done.

The other special condition under which aggregate scores might legitimately be employed is when the aggregation is over multiple repetitions of exactly the same task. The shipboard position-fixing task studied by Hutchins (1990) is an example. Repeated execution of this task yields a string of fixes on the ship's nautical chart that, when connected by straight line segments, defines the ship's course made good. We might assess performance at this task by aggregating the differences between the ship's true position (perhaps as indicated by its electronic navigation equipment) and the position determined manually by the navigation team for all of the fixes established during a specified period of time. If the position-fixing task is truly the same from one repetition to the next (and assuming no change in the group members' relative ability over time), then variations in performance across repetitions can be attributed to random error, and the aggregate score should be a reasonable estimate of performance at the underlying task level. But the task must really be the same from one repetition to another. Even small variations in stimulus complex or procedural directives can potentially call for different member skills and so make the use of aggregate scores inappropriate, at least when the goal is to understand the processes that contribute to group performance. Thus, for the navigation task, it would likely be a mistake to combine accuracy scores for positions fixed during both daylight and nighttime hours. The same holds for accuracy scores regarding positions fixed manually via both terrestrial and celestial methods. These situations all involve stimulus complexes and procedural directives that are sufficiently distinct from one another as to make them genuinely different tasks. Consequently, combining them for the purpose of studying group process would likely be problematic. The use of aggregate scores in the search for synergy calls for great caution and forethought.

Beyond Aggregates: Tasks with Subtasks

Groups often perform tasks that involve two or more subtasks. Each subtask has its own identifiable stimulus complex, its own goal and procedural directives, and each results in some measurable product. However, unlike the products of a classroom exam (i.e., the individual item responses), which are aggregated by methods quite apart from the activities of the group, subtask products are themselves subsequently used or acted upon by the group in order to achieve a larger, superordinate goal. That is, subtask products become part of the stimulus complex of a higher-level task. In general, one task can be said to be a subtask of another if the product of the first is an important element of the stimulus complex of the second. A budget committee, for example, must accurately forecast both revenues and expenditures in order to develop a realistic fiscal plan for the future. A plan cannot be devised until these two sets of forecasts have been made, as they directly impact what goes into the plan (e.g., they may suggest financial opportunities and constraints that the committee should pay attention to). Developing the two sets of forecasts are thus subtasks of the larger budget planning process.

Tasks and subtasks can be related to one another in a variety of ways. Perhaps the simplest is a one-step hierarchy involving n independent subtasks and one higher-level task. Here, the subtasks can be performed separately, in any order, with their various products all serving as input to the higher-level task. The only limitation is that all of the subtasks must be completed before the higher-level task is performed. Numerous variations on this theme are possible. For example, the hierarchy might involve multiple intermediate-level tasks. Thus, in order to perform a given task, a group might first have to complete several subtasks, each of which in turn has its own set of subtasks, etc. Or, rather than being independent of one another, the various subtasks might be sequentially interdependent, such that the order in which they are performed makes a difference. For instance, it may be impossible to perform certain subtasks unless one or more other subtasks have been performed first. Or, performing a particular subtask might facilitate the performance of one or more other subtasks. Yet another possibility is that the subtasks may be reciprocally interdependent, such that each impacts the other, though perhaps in different ways, depending on which is performed first. Here, it might be advantageous to perform the subtasks simultaneously, or, if that is not possible, to cycle back and forth between them several times in order to refine each subtask product in light of the others. Thus, in the budget planning example, revenues and expenditures might be reestimated several times in light of one another before the committee is able to put forth an acceptable spending plan. Finally, the relationship among subtasks may change over time as the task environment changes. This is akin to what Wood (1986) called "dynamic complexity" (see also Campbell, 1988). If so, different subtask sequences will be optimal under different environmental conditions.

Group performance scores derived from tasks with subtasks thus reflect two things that simple performance aggregates do not. First and foremost, they reflect group action vis-à-vis the subtask products. It is through the group's interaction process that the separate subtask products are acted upon in order to form the overall task product. Different groups might act on exactly the same subtask products in very different ways, and so end up performing very differently on the task as a whole. Simple aggregate scores, by contrast, are constructed by an unvarying, mechanical process that is completely independent of the group's interaction.

Second, when there are multiple subtasks to perform, a decision must be made about the order in which they will be done. In many cases this decision is left to the group.[4] When subtask order does in fact matter, this sequencing decision itself becomes an important subtask that can significantly impact the group's performance on the task as a whole. Simple aggregate scores, on the other hand, typically involve tasks that are independent of one another. Thus, sequencing decisions presumably have no impact on those scores.

Clearly then, overall performance scores on tasks with subtasks reflect the impact of group process in ways that simple performance aggregates do not. If we were to focus only at the subtask level (i.e., excluding subtask sequencing decisions and all activities related to the further use of the subtask products), we would almost certainly miss important aspects of a group's interaction that significantly impact how well they do at the task as a whole. At the same time, it is unlikely that overall performance on such tasks can be fully understood without considering their subtask structure. Thus, it still seems essential to break down such tasks into their elemental parts, recognizing that sequencing decisions and activities that draw on subtask products are themselves important components of group process that must be taken into account. This idea is consistent with action regulation theory, which seeks to understand group performance in terms of cycles of regulatory behavior (orienting, planning, executing, and evaluating) that occur simultaneously at multiple levels of a task/subtask hierarchy (e.g., Tschan, 2002; Tschan & von Cranach, 1996; von Cranach, 1996; see also McGrath & Tschan, 2004).

☐ Group Task Dimensions

I turn now to several systems for describing and classifying group tasks. Each of these focuses on the deep structure of tasks and takes one of two general approaches. One represents the key differences among group tasks in terms of underlying task dimensions, while the other represents those differences in terms of discrete task categories. This section of the chapter focuses on the dimensional approach. The categorical approach is taken up in the next section.

A task dimension is a variable that captures some quantitative way in which tasks differ, such that certain tasks possess more of that quantity than others. Important task dimensions are those that significantly impact group process and performance, either independently or in combination with other factors. Usually it is assumed that most of the variance in group process and performance that is explained by task differences can be accounted for by a relatively small number of such dimensions. It would seem useful not only to catalog those dimensions, but also to specify how they are related to one another. The objective of such an effort would be to define a multidimensional space that captures in a reasonably concise manner all the major similarities and differences among tasks that are relevant for understanding why groups perform as they do. This is not unlike the approach that has been taken by personality psychologists to understand the multitude of differences among persons (e.g., Fiske, 1949; Goldberg, 1993; McCrae & Costa, 1985, 2003; Wiggins & Trapnell, 1997).

Shaw's Multidimensional Analysis of Task Structure

Very few systematic attempts have been made to understand the multidimensional structure of group tasks. By far the most comprehensive effort of this sort is a study conducted by Marvin Shaw (1963). Shaw analyzed the multidimensional structure of 104 group tasks. These tasks were gathered mostly from the extant experimental literature, although a few were developed by Shaw himself specifically for this study. Each task was fairly brief (i.e., could be accomplished in an hour or less), suitable for use in experimental research with college students, and could be described on a single sheet of paper. The full set of 104 tasks covered a diverse array of activities, including mathematical puzzles, arithmetic problems, sorting and transfer problems, word and sentence construction tasks, idea generation tasks, tasks that require the coordinated operation of some piece of apparatus, ranking tasks, and target search tasks. An example of a transfer problem analyzed by Shaw is the Milkman's Quandary, shown in Figure 2.1.[5]

Shaw (1963) analyzed the structural relationship among these 104 tasks by having 49 judges, mostly graduate students in psychology, rate the tasks on each of 10 attributes using the method of "equal appearing intervals" developed by Thurstone and Chave (1929). The 10 attributes used for this purpose were derived informally, based on (a) Shaw's own experience

---

The Milkman's Quandary

This is a group task. Work on the problem cooperatively, and try to arrive at a solution that is acceptable to the whole group.

Problem: A milkman has a 14-quart can full of milk. He wishes to divide the milk into two equal portions. In addition to the 14-quart measure, he has a 5-quart measure and a 9-quart measure. How does he make the division without any waste, using the three measures only, and not guessing at the amounts?

Solution:

Milk Transferred		Amount Left After Transfer		
From Container Size	To Container Size	Container Size = 5	Container Size = 9	Container Size = 14
14	9	0	9	5
9	5	5	4	5
5	14	0	4	10
9	5	4	0	10
14	9	4	9	1
9	5	5	8	1
5	14	0	8	6
9	5	5	3	6
5	14	0	3	11
9	5	3	0	11
14	9	3	9	2
9	5	5	7	2
5	14	0	7	7

Performance Criteria: Number of transfers; time to solution.
Original Source: Marquart (1955).

FIGURE 2.1 An example of a transfer problem analyzed by Shaw (1963). (Adapted with permission of Behavioral Measurement Database Services (BMDS), Pittsburgh, PA.)

with problem-solving groups and (b) an independent review by a panel of social psychologists experienced in small group research. These attributes are listed in Figure 2.2. Judges were required to evaluate all of the tasks on one attribute before moving to the next. They did this by first sorting the 104 task descriptions into four piles representing four levels of a given attribute: highest, second highest, third highest, and lowest. These, in turn, were each subdivided into two piles, resulting in a total of eight piles that were more-or-less evenly distributed across the full range of that attribute. A judge's evaluation of a given task on a particular attribute was defined as the number (1 to 8) of the pile into which he or she had sorted that task for that attribute. A task's attribute score, in turn, was defined as the median

Task Difficulty

1. The amount of effort required to complete the task
2. The number of specialized operations, skills, and/or types of knowledge required.
3. The degree to which the requirements of the task are clearly stated and known to group members (negatively loaded).

Solution Multiplicity

4. The degree to which there is more than one correct solution.
5. The degree to which there is more than one way to reach a correct solution.
6. The degree to which the correctness of a solution can be demonstrated, either by appealing to authority, logical procedures, or by feedback (negatively loaded).

Cooperation Requirements

7. The degree to which integrated action of group members is required to complete the task; the number of persons who are dependent on one another in order to perform functions required for task solution, and the amount of such dependence.

Intellectual-Manipulative Requirements

8. The ratio of mental (thinking, reasoning) to motor (physical) requirements of the task.

Population Familiarity

9. The degree to which the task is commonly encountered by members of the larger society.

Intrinsic Interest

10. The degree to which the task, in and of itself, is interesting, motivating, and attractive to group members.

FIGURE 2.2 Shaw's (1963) empirically derived task dimensions (boldface) and the rated attributes (numbered) loading on those dimensions.

of the 49 judges' evaluations of that attribute. The resulting $104 \times 10 = 1040$ attribute scores were then factor analyzed in order to determine the number of independent dimensions needed to represent them.

Based largely on the results of the factor analysis, Shaw (1963) concluded that the differences among the 104 tasks he studied could best be explained in terms of six underlying dimensions, which he labeled task difficulty, solution multiplicity, cooperation requirements, intellectual-manipulative requirements, population familiarity, and intrinsic interest. As can be seen in Figure 2.2, the first two dimensions were each defined by three attributes. Scores on the three attributes defining the first dimension (task difficulty) were very highly intercorrelated, as were scores on the three attributes defining the second dimension (solution multiplicity). Thus, on empirical grounds, it can be argued that these scores tap just two underlying features, not six. The remaining four dimensions were defined by just one attribute each. According to Shaw, however, the last two of these (population familiarity and intrinsic interest) are relatively weak, and he recommended that they be interpreted with caution. This was partly because the attributes defining these dimensions also had moderately strong loadings on one or more of the other dimensions. Further, a question can be raised about whether these two dimensions really tell us about the tasks per se, or whether they tell us, instead, about the experience and interests of those most likely to perform such tasks (college students in research settings). Still, all six dimensions identified by Shaw appear to be psychologically meaningful, in the sense of having a plausible impact on group process and performance. Population familiarity, for example, is likely to affect the extent to which different group members perceive a task in the same way, and so share a common conceptualization of how it should be performed.

In the abstract, Shaw's (1963) approach to determining the multidimensional structure of tasks would appear to have great potential. Because it is empirically grounded, this methodology can reveal the actual structure that exists among tasks (at least as perceived by judges), as opposed to a structure that is merely postulated. Further, this approach yields useful information about specific tasks, not just about broad task dimensions; it tells us where on a given dimension each of the analyzed tasks falls. Such information is beneficial for both theory and research because it facilitates the systematic comparison of results across tasks known to differ in specific ways. For example, it can help to define the range of tasks over which a particular set of results is apt to generalize.

At the same time, however, Shaw's (1963) study serves to highlight some of the difficulties associated with this approach. The value of any empirical attempt to determine the multidimensional structure of group tasks is necessarily constrained by two factors. One is the sample of tasks analyzed. No study of task structure can reveal dimensions that do not actually exist within the sample of tasks employed in the study. Consequently, it is important that the sample be representative of the population of tasks about which one wishes to draw inferences. Unrepresentative samples, almost by definition, either do not contain all relevant task dimensions or distort the relationship among those dimensions. As a consequence, results that are based on such samples do not fairly represent what exists in the larger population of tasks. In the case of Shaw's study, given the sources from which his tasks were drawn, it is highly unlikely that they are fully representative of the general population of group tasks encountered in everyday life. Indeed, there is reason to wonder whether they are representative of even the population of tasks used in experimental research conducted prior to 1963.[6] But if there is uncertainty about the representativeness of the tasks used in Shaw's study, then there also must be uncertainty about the generalizability of his results.

The other factor that can constrain the usefulness of any empirical attempt to uncover task dimensions is the comprehensiveness of the set of attributes on which the tasks are evaluated. No investigation can hope to reveal task dimensions that are not somehow measured. For example, if the 104 tasks studied by Shaw (1963) differ from one another in some important way that was not captured by any of the 10 attributes on which those tasks were assessed, the dimension underlying that difference could not have emerged in his results. None of the 10 attributes shown in Figure 2.2, for instance, assess the extent to which a given task requires equal participation, contribution, or effort by group members (as opposed to allowing some members to contribute more than others). This attribute—call it the degree to which the task is compensatory[7]—seems very likely to impact group process and performance, so it would be interesting to know how it relates to the six dimensions already identified by Shaw. But because Shaw did not measure this attribute, his study is silent on the matter.

Ensuring the comprehensiveness of the attributes on which tasks are evaluated is not a simple matter. How are we to know if we have assessed all relevant task dimensions when the very purpose of the research is to determine what those dimensions are? Shaw's (1963) approach to solving this conundrum was to have a panel of subject-matter experts (i.e., researchers working in the field of small group performance) independently review his task attributes prior to his using them. Among other things, this panel was encouraged to suggest additional attributes that seemed missing from his original list. One might expand on this idea by making more systematic use of expert panels at every stage in the development of the task attribute list, perhaps employing one of the available structured procedures for working with such panels (e.g., Delbecq, Van de Ven, & Gustafson, 1975; Fine & Cronshaw, 1999; Thorndike & Hagen, 1977). The main point is that one should cast as wide a net as possible when searching for potentially important task attributes.

Laughlin's Intellective–Judgmental Continuum

Shaw's (1963) work stands out as one of the only examples of an empirically based, multidimensional study of group task dimensions. Despite the potential benefits of developing a multidimensional perspective on tasks, few others have taken up the challenges associated with this kind of work. More commonly, researchers have focused on just one task dimension at a time, trying to understand how that one dimension, by itself, impacts group process and performance. One of the best examples of this is the work by Laughlin and his colleagues on the intellective-judgmental task dimension.

Laughlin (1980; 1999; Laughlin & Ellis, 1986) has proposed that cooperative problem-solving tasks can be meaningfully arrayed on a continuum anchored at one end by purely intellective tasks and at the other by purely judgmental tasks. Purely intellective tasks are those for which the correctness of a proposed solution can be readily demonstrated. A simple algebra problem is a good example. Anyone who knows the rules of algebra should be able to assess whether or not a proposed solution is, in fact, correct. Purely judgmental tasks, on the other hand, are tasks for which there is no demonstrably correct answer. Such tasks require an evaluative, behavioral, or aesthetic judgment that establishes—as opposed to matches—what is correct. A good example is the task faced by the awards committee in a juried art show. What criteria should this committee use when deciding which painting or sculpture is best? Should they consider the technical difficulty of the work? Its originality? The degree to which the work is emotionally expressive? Or how about its social relevance? A case might be made for any of these. It is up to the committee to decide which criteria will be used, how they will be weighted, and so which piece of art will be judged best.[8]

There are, of course, many tasks that are intermediate between these two extremes, being neither purely intellective nor purely judgmental. For such tasks, demonstrating the correctness of a proposed solution is more difficult, but not impossible. It seems more difficult, for example, to demonstrate the correctness of the answer to the transfer task given in Figure 2.1 (i.e., to show that that answer involves the fewest possible transfers needed to divide the milk into two equal portions) than to demonstrate the correctness of an answer to a simple algebra problem. Still, a demonstration is possible.

Finally, there are some tasks that seem simultaneously to possess both intellective and judgmental elements. An example is inductive hypothesis testing (Laughlin, 1999, Laughlin & Hollingshead, 1995). Inductive hypothesis testing is arguably the core activity in any empirical science. Given some body of evidence, every pertinent hypothesis (e.g., about a causal relationship between two variables) is either consistent or inconsistent with that evidence. All consistent hypotheses are plausibly correct, whereas inconsistent hypotheses are not. Implausible hypotheses are demonstrably incorrect by virtue of their inconsistency with available evidence. Thus, evaluating implausible hypotheses is an intellective subtask.

Evaluating plausible hypotheses, on the other hand, is a judgmental sub-task. This is because all possible plausible hypotheses are (by definition) consistent with the available evidence, and none can be shown to fit that evidence any better than others. Consequently, without additional data, there is no clear way to differentiate (demonstrate) the one plausible and correct hypothesis from other plausible but ultimately incorrect hypotheses. Thus, inductive hypothesis testing is intellective to the extent permitted by current evidence, but judgmental beyond that. Inductive hypothesis testing will be discussed in more detail in Chapter 4.

The crucial dimension underlying the intellective-judgmental continuum is thus the demonstrability of proposed solutions. On its surface, this dimension appears to be similar to one of the 10 attributes that judges rated in Shaw's (1963) study (i.e., Attribute 6 in Figure 2.2). But what makes the solution to a problem-solving task more or less demonstrable? Laughlin and Ellis (1986) argued that demonstrability depends on four conditions:

1. There must be group consensus on a conceptual system within which the problem can be solved.
2. There must be sufficient information available to solve the problem within that conceptual system.
3. Members who cannot solve the problem themselves must nevertheless have sufficient knowledge of the conceptual system and relevant task information to recognize a correct solution if one is proposed by another member.[9]
4. Members who can solve the problem must have sufficient ability, motivation, and time to demonstrate the solution to the rest of the group.

Laughlin and Ellis (1986) suggest that mathematics is the preeminent domain of demonstrability. To illustrate, suppose a group is given the following problem: $A = \pi r^2$; If r is 5, what is A? If the group members agree that algebra is the relevant conceptual system for solving this problem (Condition 1), if those who cannot themselves solve the problem nevertheless understand enough algebra to follow an explanation offered by someone else (Condition 3), and if those who can solve the problem are willing and able to explain their solution (Condition 4), then given that there is sufficient information to solve this problem (i.e., it involves a single equation in one unknown, which is solvable, as opposed to, for example, being a single equation in two unknowns, which is not solvable; Condition 2), the solution should be fully demonstrable. Under such conditions, if a correct solution is proposed and demonstrated by anyone in the group ($A = 78.5$), the rest of the group should recognized its correctness and so adopt it as their collective answer.

Demonstrability, Faction Size, and Group Problem-Solving Effectiveness

The intellective-judgmental continuum is of value in part because it brings a degree of order to the research literature concerned with faction size and group problem-solving effectiveness. I describe this literature in greater detail in Chapter 4. Here, I give only a brief summary of that material in order to emphasize the importance of considering the nature of the tasks that groups are asked to perform.

Faction size refers to the number of members favoring a particular problem solution prior to group discussion. Of particular interest is the size of the faction favoring the correct solution. I will call this the *solving faction*. Suppose, for example, that a six-person group is attempting to solve a problem presented to them in multiple-choice format. The members of this group can be classified as either solvers or nonsolvers. Solvers are defined simply as those who, if they were to attempt the problem by themselves, would choose the correct answer. Nonsolvers are those who would choose an incorrect answer. The number of solvers within the group defines the size of the solving faction. The number of nonsolvers favoring each of the incorrect answers defines the size of the factions favoring each of those incorrect solutions. These various factions are, in essence, in competition with one another to get their favored solution adopted by the group as a whole. The question is, how large must the solving faction be in order to get the group as a whole to choose its favored solution —the correct solution?

Laughlin and Ellis (1986) proposed that the size of the solving faction that is necessary and sufficient to get the group as a whole to adopt the correct solution is inversely proportional to the solution's demonstrability; the more demonstrable the solution, the smaller the required size of the solving faction. For tasks with highly demonstrable solutions (i.e., intellective tasks), they suggest that a solving faction of size = 1 is all that is required. That is, if a group attempts a problem with a highly demonstrable solution, they should be able to solve it correctly if at least one of their members could have solved it correctly working alone. Research generally bears this out. It appears to be true not only for mathematical problems, but also for "Eureka!" problems. The latter are problems for which the correct solution is obvious once it has been proposed. An anagram task is a common example. Another type of problem that has this quality is the Remote Associates Test (Mednick & Mednick, 1967). Here, the task is to determine the remote verbal association that is shared by a set of stimulus words. For example, given the words "birthday," "line," and "search," the correct response is "party." This task was specifically designed so that the correct answers would be intuitively obvious once proposed (Mednick, 1962). Here, too, a solving faction of size = 1 is usually all that is needed in order for the group as a whole to endorse the correct answer (e.g., Laughlin, Kerr, Munch, & Haggarty, 1976).

For tasks with only moderately demonstrable solutions—those intermediate between intellective and judgmental tasks—the required size of the solving faction is slightly larger. Here, Laughlin and Ellis (1986) suggest that a solving faction of size = 2 is necessary and sufficient for the group as a whole to endorse that solution. Typical of such tasks are world knowledge problems (e.g., Addis Ababa is the capital of which country?). Such problems clearly have correct answers, and their correctness can be demonstrated by reference to books, maps, and other authoritative sources. But without these resources, the correct answers are not necessarily obvious to nonsolvers, even after they have been proposed. In such situations, it is apparently insufficient for one solver alone to propose the correct solution. Rather, support is needed from at least one additional solver who can independently attest to that solution's correctness. When two solvers propose the correct solution, they should together be able to persuade the rest of the group to endorse it. Here, again, the empirical evidence is generally supportive. Besides world knowledge problems, solving factions of size = 2 have been shown to be necessary and sufficient for adoption of the correct answer on vocabulary problems, psychology course exam questions, and analogy problems, all of which appear to be only moderately demonstrable (e.g., Laughlin & Adamopoulos, 1980; Laughlin, Kerr, Davis, Halff, & Marciniak, 1975; Laughlin et al. 1976; Tindale & Larson, 1992). The previously discussed data presented in Table 2.1, which summarize group performance on multiple-choice exam questions about material covered in a college-level industrial/organizational psychology course, are generally consistent with this pattern.

Finally, for tasks with correct solutions that cannot be demonstrated, as well as for tasks that do not have correct solutions, Laughlin and Ellis (1986) argue that only majority or plurality factions will succeed in having their preferred solution alternative adopted by the group as a whole. Tasks with correct solutions that cannot be demonstrated include certain forecasting problems (e.g., predicting which nation's soccer team will win the next World Cup). Such forecasts are highly judgmental, and their correctness cannot be confirmed in the present. Rather, this becomes apparent only with the passage of time. For such tasks, the group is apt to choose the correct solution only when that solution is initially favored by either a majority (in a two-alternative choice situation) or plurality (when there are three or more choice alternatives) of its members. The same holds for tasks that have no correct solution. An example, as already suggested, is jury decision-making. The task of a jury is not to find an a priori correct solution, but rather to establish what solution is correct. Jury decisions have been shown to be strongly determined by predeliberation majority factions (Devine, Clayton, Dunford, Seying, & Pryce, 2001).[10]

In sum, there is relatively consistent evidence across tasks for the proposed inverse relationship between solution demonstrability, on the one hand, and the minimum size of the solving faction that is necessary to get the group as a whole to adopt the correct solution, on the other. From one perspective, differences in solution demonstrability can be thought of as affecting the degree to which numerically small factions within groups are able to prevail. Solution demonstrability gives small factions power that is disproportionate to their size, provided they favor the correct solution. Indeed, even if the solving faction has just one member, that person should still be able to get the entire group to adopt the correct solution if its correctness is highly demonstrable. From a slightly different perspective, groups should be more effective in choosing correct problem solutions when those solutions are highly demonstrable, compared to when they are not. The reason is simply that high demonstrability means fewer members are needed who can solve the problem on their own. Thus, when problem solutions are either moderately or highly demonstrable, the majority does not necessarily rule; minorities can rule if they are right.

Toward Synergy

Although the intellective–judgmental continuum helps to organize the group problem-solving literature, the nature of its underlying dimension—demonstrability—remains incompletely explored. It should be evident that, as Laughlin and Ellis (1986) conceived it, demonstrability is not solely a property of the task. Of their four conditions for demonstrability, only Condition 2 (sufficient information) refers exclusively to the task. The other three conditions refer, in whole or in part, to the members of the group performing that task. The clearest case is Condition 3 (member knowledge), which refers exclusively to members. Conditions 1 and 4 are more complex. Condition 1 (agreement on a conceptual system) might at first seem to be another exclusively member-oriented condition. But consider the two ways in which this condition can be violated. The first is if the group fails to agree on a relevant conceptual system even though one exists (e.g., they cannot decide whether the rules of algebra or chemistry provide the relevant system for solving the problem). The second is if a relevant conceptual system does not exist at all.[11] Here, agreement is not even possible. Thus, whereas the former case implies that some groups might reach agreement and some might not, the latter implies that no group can reach agreement. At least with respect to Criterion 1, therefore, the difference in demonstrability between two tasks performed by two different groups may lie in the tasks themselves (i.e., a relevant conceptual system may exist for one but not the other), in the groups performing those tasks (i.e., a relevant conceptual system exists for both tasks, but only one group is able to agree on what that system is), or in a combination of the two. Finally, regarding Condition 4 (having the ability, motivation, and time to demonstrate the solution), ability is clearly a property of group members, whereas time is a property of the task. Time limits are a type of procedural directive that can make problems more difficult to solve, in part because they restrict a critical resource needed to demonstrate the correctness of proposed solutions. Motivation, on the other hand, speaks to both the members and the task. Tasks that are more consequential, in the sense of having stronger positive and negative outcomes for the group or for others, should elicit greater motivation to demonstrate—and to see demonstrated—the correctness of any solution that is proposed. At the same time, what makes a task consequential depends on the values, preferences, and goals of the group members. Thus, the motivational component of Criterion 4 seems to refer to a combination of member and task factors.

Despite not being exclusively about the task, the four conditions for demonstrability proposed by Laughlin and Ellis (1986) point in the direction of an important set of task demands. The concept of task demands was introduced in Chapter 1 (see pp. 15–17). Task demands refer to the resources (e.g., knowledge, skills, abilities, and tools) that members must possess, as well as the behaviors they must enact, in order to complete an assigned task successfully (cf. Roby & Lanzetta, 1958; Steiner, 1966, 1972). With regard to demonstrability, if a relevant conceptual system exists for solving a given problem, then successful task performance would seem to demand that members agree on what that system is, that nonsolvers understand enough about it to recognize when a correct solution has been proposed by someone else, and that solvers be willing and able to demonstrate the correctness of their solution. To the extent these demands are met, the task becomes more demonstrable, and the group is more likely to perform the task successfully.

As straightforward as these demonstrability-based task demands might seem, more work is needed to specify precisely *how* they are to be met. As currently understood, these demands seem more like a shopping list than a recipe. Recipes do more than enumerate required ingredients; they specify precisely how much of each ingredient is needed, exactly how the ingredients are to be combined, and what specific substitutions might be made and still achieve the same result. For example, little attention has been paid to *how much* agreement is needed among members about the relevant conceptual system, or *how many* nonsolvers must be able to recognize the correctness of solutions proposed by others. Is it necessary that all nonsolvers agree on the conceptual system, and that they all be able to recognize a correct solution when one is presented? Perhaps it is sufficient that a simple majority meet these demands. When majority factions are correct, they almost always succeed in getting the group as a whole to

any deeper meaning to those nominal types. In some cases there may be, but in other cases there may not be.

The advantage of an empirical typology, of course, is that it can reveal the true lines of separation among tasks and so provide an immediate corrective influence on theory development. Conceptual typologies are less efficient in this regard, because they are derived from the very theories that may be in need of correction. It is only when the conceptual typologies prove unhelpful in accounting for systematic differences in group process and performance that they may signal the need for corrective action. However, this is at best a very slow and indirect feedback process.

Surprisingly, despite the likely advantage of an empirical typology, almost no work of any sort has been done to develop such a typology for group tasks (though see Davis & Restle, 1963). This is true despite the fact that there have been numerous attempts to develop empirical typologies of tasks performed by individuals, especially in employment settings (e.g., Buffardi, Fleishman, Morath, & McCarthy, 2000; Fleishman & Quaintance, 1984; Peterson, Mumford, Borman, Jenneret, & Fleishman, 1999; Vincente, 1999). Thus, the focus in this final section of the chapter is necessarily limited to conceptual typologies. I consider in detail two such typologies, one by McGrath (1984) and one by Steiner (1966, 1972).

McGrath's Group Task Circumplex Model

McGrath (1984) proposed a circumplex model that has both typological and dimensional properties. According to McGrath, group tasks can be divided into eight distinct categories: Planning tasks, creativity tasks, intellective tasks, decision-making tasks, cognitive conflict tasks, mixed motive tasks, contests, and performances. These eight categories are intended to be mutually exclusive and exhaustive. Thus, it should be possible to fit any given group task into one and only one of these categories and, when taken together, these eight categories should accommodate all possible group tasks. These categorical features of the model are typological properties. However, McGrath also proposed that these eight categories are logically related to one another according to an underlying two-dimensional structure. One dimension is the degree to which the tasks in each category involve activity that is primarily mental or conceptual, as opposed to being primarily physical or behavioral. The other dimension concerns the degree to which the tasks in each category involve conflict as opposed to cooperation among group members. Organizing the categories according to these two underlying dimensions yields the circumplex structure shown in Figure 2.3.

As can be seen, the conceptual-behavioral dimension is represented along the horizontal axis of the figure, whereas the cooperation-conflict

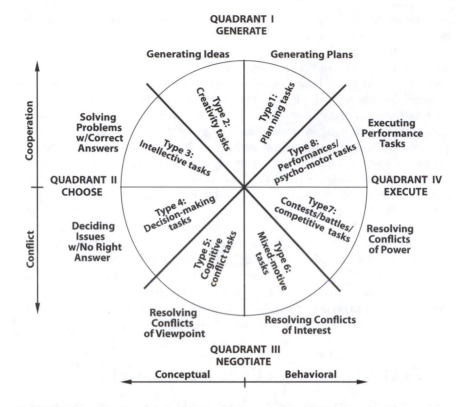

FIGURE 2.3   McGrath's (1984) task circumplex. (Reprinted with permission of Pearson Education, Inc., Upper Saddle River, NJ.)

dimension is represented along its vertical axis. Within the two-dimensional space defined by these axes, the eight task categories are arranged such that those on the left side require primarily mental activity from the group, whereas those on the right side require mainly physical activity. Similarly, the task categories shown on the top half of the figure require mainly cooperative interaction among group members, whereas those shown in the bottom half require the group to deal with competition and conflict. Further, McGrath (1984) organized the eight task types by pairs into four quadrants (top, bottom, left, and right) according to the general nature of the performance processes required by the tasks in those quadrants: Generate, choose, negotiate, and execute.

Quadrant I: Generate

Quadrant I involves tasks that are strongly generative in nature—something must be created or produced. Two types of generative tasks are considered:

planning tasks (Type 1) and creativity tasks (Type 2). As its name implies, *planning tasks* require the group to generate action-oriented plans. The objective of a planning task is to specify the sequence of steps that must be followed in order to achieve some goal (e.g., what must be done in order to successfully organized and run a charity dance marathon). The plan might be devised for later use by the group itself (e.g., if they are the dance marathon committee) or it might be prepared for use by others (e.g., if they are creating a planning packet for use by any civic-minded group interested in sponsoring such a fund-raising event). In either case, the task is simply to generate the plan, not to carry it out (carrying out the plan would be a separate task, or, more likely, a separate set of interrelated tasks).

Creativity tasks (Type 2) are also generative in nature, but here the goal is to generate ideas that do not necessarily have a strong action orientation to them. One can easily imagine, for example, generating lots of creative ideas for spending a $10,000 windfall, even though the pool of ideas, once generated, does not suggest a coherent sequence of steps that lead toward a specific goal. The brainstorming tasks that will be discussed in Chapter 3 are generally of this type. Note that because Type 2 tasks do not have as strong a behavioral orientation as do Type 1 tasks, they are positioned in the circumplex to the left of Type 1 tasks—that is, closer to the conceptual end of the conceptual-behavioral dimension. Type 1 tasks, by contrast, are positioned next to Type 8 tasks (performances), which are strongly behavioral.

Quadrant II: Choose

Quadrant II involves choice-oriented tasks. Here, the group must choose from a set of alternatives. These tasks fall into two types according to whether or not one of the choice alternatives is objectively correct. *Intellective tasks* (Type 3) are those for which there is an objectively correct answer, and the group's goal is to give a response that matches what is correct. An item from a classroom exam is a good example. It is important to recognize that, as used by McGrath (1984), the term *intellective* has a broader meaning than it does for Laughlin and his colleagues (1980; Laughlin & Ellis, 1986). Whereas Laughlin employs the term to refer to those highly demonstrable tasks that anchor one end of the intellective-judgmental continuum, McGrath (1984) uses it to refer to any choice task that has an objectively correct answer, regardless of how easy or difficult that answer might be to demonstrate. Thus, during a classroom exam, and without the aid of a reference book, it should be more difficult for solvers to demonstrate that sodium atoms contain 11 electrons than to demonstrate that 11 is the cube root of 1,331. But as McGrath employs the term, both tasks would be considered intellective, and so both would be categorized as Type 3 tasks.

Decision-making tasks (Type 4), on the other hand, are choice tasks that do not have an objectively correct answer. These are equivalent to what Laughlin calls purely judgmental tasks, and they anchor the other end of his intellective–judgmental continuum. Here the group's goal is to establish what is correct, not merely to match some external criterion, for no such criterion exists. Once again, the task faced by juries fits this type. It is the jury's duty to establish what is best, true, or just, and so determine whom should be honored, vindicated, or punished. Consistent with the previous discussion of Laughlin's intellective-judgmental continuum, it is likely that Type 4 tasks will generate more debate, argument, and controversy than Type 3 tasks, especially those Type 3 tasks that have easily demonstrated correct answers. Consequently, Type 4 tasks are positioned in the model below Type 3 tasks, closer to the conflict end of the cooperation-conflict dimension.

Quadrant III: Negotiate

Quadrant III involves tasks that require group members to negotiate with one another as their main activity. McGrath (1984) suggests that tasks in this quadrant have an even larger potential for conflict than do Type 4 tasks. Indeed, it is hard to imagine how a task that does not involve conflict could be located in this quadrant. Additionally, Quadrant III tasks have a strong inward focus. That is, the group's objective is to resolve a problem *among us*, as opposed to solve a problem *confronting us*. What differentiates the two specific task types within this quadrant is the underlying source of the conflict. *Cognitive conflict tasks* (Type 5) require the group to resolve differences in viewpoint or opinion. Such differences may arise either because members interpret the same information in different ways, assign different importance to that information, or both. Thus, for example, the members of a geological survey team may be at odds about the meaning of a set of data concerning the stability of a particular underground rock formation. Unless they can resolve this difference, it may be hard for them to agree on what recommendations to offer policy makers who would like to use the site for a hydroelectric dam.

In contrast, *mixed motive tasks* (Type 6) require the group to resolve conflicts of interests. Here, it is not so much that members disagree about either the meaning or significance of task-related information. Rather, they disagree about one or more of the underlying goals and objectives to be achieved. Thus, the reward contingencies may be such that different members gain different benefits from different courses of action, such that what is good for one member is bad for others, and vice versa. Or the various courses of action may simply align with different member values. The members of an interdisciplinary research team, for example, may be at loggerheads over the best approach for achieving a particular objective, each preferring a method that favors his or her own discipline. Again, unless the members can resolve such differences, it will be hard for them to make progress toward achieving their objective. Tasks used in research to study bargaining and negotiation obviously fit this category. So, too, does the classic prisoner's dilemma game and other similar tasks with a built-in social dilemma structure, especially if multiple rounds of play are allowed. In such tasks, members' self-interests are typically at odds with the interest of the group as a whole, such that it is difficult to satisfy both at the same time.

It should be clear that in natural settings Quadrant III tasks are most likely to arise in the context of decision making, especially in choice situations that do not have easily demonstrated, objectively correct answers. It is often the need to make a decision, to select one course of action and reject others, that brings into sharp focus both cognitive conflict and mixed motive situations. This tends to blur the distinction between Type 4 tasks, on the one hand, and Type 5 and 6 tasks on the other. Indeed, even the distinction between Type 5 and Type 6 tasks is less clear than it might at first appear. Members may interpret the same information differently, or attach different importance to that information, in part because of underlying motive or value differences. Consequently, the differences in viewpoint that suggest an activity is a Type 5 task may, upon closer inspection, turn out to be rooted in value or interest differences, suggesting that it is really a Type 6 task.

Quadrant IV: Execute

Finally, Quadrant IV involves tasks that require primarily physical action. Here, again, there are two types. *Contests* (Type 7) are tasks performed against an opponent or adversary group. The outcomes of contests are usually interpreted in win/lose terms. Competitions between sports teams fit this category (e.g., basketball, soccer, ice hockey), but so too do military and street gang battles. Because contests and mixed motive tasks (Type 6) both involve conflicts of interest, they appear in the model adjacent to one another. The difference between them is that, whereas contests involve conflicts of interest between groups (i.e., one team or group wins at the expense of the other), mixed motive tasks involve conflicts of interest within groups (i.e., one member "wins" at the expense of others).

Performances (Type 8), on the other hand, do not involve a competition against an adversary. Rather, they involve striving to meet a standard of excellence. Does the construction crew complete the building project on time, according to specifications, and within budget? Does the flight crew deliver the aircraft to its intended destination with minimum use of fuel and without incident? And is the fire brigade able to extinguish the blaze quickly, without permitting it to spread to adjacent structures?

Performances are distinguished from contests by the reward contingencies involved. In performances, outcomes accrue to the group according to whether or not the performance standard is met. If the fire is extinguished expeditiously and without further mishap, the fire brigade is congratulated. If not, they are reproached. In competitions, on the other hand, outcomes accrue to the group according to whether or not they excel relative to another group. The spoils of war go to the victor no matter how honorably the vanquished may have fought. Of course, performances are easily converted into contests by shifting the reward contingencies. Thus, if two groups that normally strive to achieve a standard of excellence are suddenly rewarded according to whose achievement is greater, a contest has been created. This is the way sporting events are structured when the tasks involved do not normally give opponents an opportunity to interfere with one another (e.g., rowing, swimming, gymnastics).

The Task Circumplex: Strengths and Weaknesses

The comprehensiveness, appealing internal structure, and aesthetic symmetry of McGrath's (1984) group task circumplex have made it a popular tool for conceptualizing the similarities and differences among group tasks. At the same time, at least two shortcomings of this model are apparent. One concerns the exclusivity criterion for classification schemes. As noted previously, a good classification scheme is one in which there exists a single appropriate class designation for every task. It appears, however, that certain portions of McGrath's circumplex may not be sufficiently well defined to permit unambiguous classification. As suggested above, this is especially true with respect to task Types 4, 5, and 6. The other shortcoming is that McGrath's circumplex clusters together certain tasks that have been shown empirically to be different from one another in ways that are important for group process and performance. Tasks that have a correct answer, but that vary in demonstrability, are an example. McGrath's circumplex places all such tasks in the Type 3 category, even though there is evidence that differences in demonstrability have a substantial impact on groups. As with many things, the simplicity of this model is both a virtue and a vice. Its simplicity makes it easy to understand, but that same simplicity likely distorts at least some of the real underlying relationships that exist among group tasks.

Steiner's Group Task Typology

In contrast to McGrath's (1984) group task circumplex, which relies heavily on surface characteristics to infer underlying structural relationships among tasks, Steiner (1966, 1972) took an approach to categorized group tasks that ignores surface characteristics altogether. Rather, he focused exclusively on those underlying task demands that determine how group member efforts are combined to yield an overall group product. Steiner differentiates group tasks in three ways: according to their subtask structure, according to the nature of their goals, and according to the combinatorial processes they permit. The last of these has been especially useful for theory and research in small group performance.

Subtask Structure: Divisible Versus Unitary Tasks

Steiner (1972) drew an initial distinction between divisible and unitary tasks. A *divisible task* is one with two or more easily separated parts that require different skills and abilities. For Steiner, a key feature of a divisible task is that its different parts are performed by different members of the group. Divisible tasks are thus more than simply tasks with a subtask structure—those subtasks must be performed by different individuals.[13] The shipboard position-fixing task studied by Hutchins (1990) is a good example. In order to fix the ship's position, two crew members take bearings (determine the compass direction) of specific charted landmarks as they appear on shore, another person records those bearings in a log book, a fourth draws lines of position on the ship's nautical chart based on the logged bearings, etc. The task of fixing the ship's position is thus divided among group members such that each acts on a different stimulus complex, with a different subgoal, and applies a different set of skills and abilities to accomplish that subgoal.

When a task comprises multiple subtasks that call for different skills and abilities, it is possible for the group as a whole to succeed even when none of its members can do the entire task alone, as long as every subtask can be performed by someone in the group. It is thus unnecessary for every member to possess all of the skills and abilities demanded by the task. Rather, it is necessary only that they collectively possess all of those skills and abilities. Under this scenario, the assignment of members to subtasks is critical to group success—who does what matters. Members must be assigned in such a way that every subtask is performed by someone who actually does possess the skills and abilities needed to do it well. These assignments might be made by an authority external to the group, or they might be negotiated among the group members themselves. If it is the latter, then assigning members to subtasks becomes an important subtask in its own right.

For some divisible tasks the boundaries between subtasks are clear. For others they are not. If subtask boundaries are clear, then how the task should be decomposed is also clear. Subtask boundaries may be inherently clear, or they may have been made clear by externally imposed rules (procedural directives). If the subtask boundaries are not clear, however, then it might be possible to decompose the task in many different ways, in which case the group is faced with yet another preparatory subtask: establishing those boundaries, and so an operative subtask structure. One way or another, subtask boundaries must be clarified before members can be assigned to them.

In contrast to divisible tasks, *unitary tasks* cannot be meaningfully sub-divided into separate activities that require different skills and abilities. Rather, unitary tasks demand that all members engage in the same activity, applying the same skills and abilities. Among the various laboratory tasks we have considered in this chapter, the tourism task (Taylor et al., 1958) and the Milkman's Quandary (Figure 2.1) are examples of unitary tasks. In each case, every member of the group is presumed to apply the same type of skills and abilities to the same stimulus complex and is trying to accomplish the same goal. A four-person team engaged in a tug-of-war against an opposing team is also performing a unitary task. Likewise, four city employees assigned to mow the grass in a municipal park would be performing a unitary task. Though each may do his or her share of the mowing, and each mows a different quadrant of the park, the four would nevertheless be doing exactly the same thing. Consequently, it should not matter who is assigned to mow which quadrant, because each calls for the same skills and abilities. Many hands often do make light the work, but they do not necessarily make that work divisible, at least not in the sense that Steiner (1972) used the term.

Task Goals: Maximizing Versus Optimizing Tasks

Crosscutting the divisible-unitary distinction is the distinction between maximizing and optimizing tasks. *Maximizing tasks* are tasks that have as their goal performing as much or as quickly as possible. Generating as many ideas as possible (e.g., for stimulating tourism) and unloading supplies from a truck as quickly as possible are both maximizing tasks. In contrast, *optimizing tasks* are tasks that have as their goal the production of some specific, most desirable product. Finding the correct answer to the Milkman's Quandary is an example; the goal is to match a specific preferred response, the one considered to be correct. The shipboard position-fixing task and the AM radio assembly task employed by Liang et al. (1995) are also optimizing tasks. The position-fixing crew is trying to place a mark on the chart that best corresponds to their true position, and the radio-assembly team is trying to produce an instrument that will actually work. As these various examples suggest, both unitary and divisible tasks can be either maximizing or optimizing.

Permitted Group Process

Unitary tasks can be further subgrouped according to the type of combinatorial process they permit; that is, according to the way members' efforts may be combined to yield a group product. Perhaps the easiest to understand are *additive tasks*. On an additive task, the group's product is determined by summing the products of the members' efforts. Thus, the amount of force applied to one end of a rope in a game of tug-of-war is the sum of the individual forces applied by the team members. Similarly, the number of ideas that a group generates for promoting tourism in America is the sum of the number of ideas generated by each of the group members. Note that additive tasks do not require members to *contribute* equally. They merely require that member contributions be *weighted* equally. Further, additive tasks may be either maximizing or optimizing. Pulling on a rope with as much force as possible is a maximizing additive task, whereas pulling on a rope with just enough force to steady a heavy load suspended by block-and-tackle (e.g., a piano) is an optimizing additive task.

Other unitary tasks restrict member contributions in different ways. *Conjunctive tasks*, for instance, require all group members to contribute identically to the group's product. Consequently, the group's product on a conjunctive task is determined by the performance of the member who individually is able to contribute the least. The classic metaphor for conjunctive tasks is a chain. A chain can withstand no more stress that can be tolerated by the weakest of its individual links, no matter how strong its other links might be. Similarly, three friends who are hiking together can travel no faster than the slowest among them. It matters little that some members can hike faster than others. If they attempt to do so, they will quickly lose sight of one another and will no longer be hiking together. In a like manner, the distance that two people can carry a heavy object (e.g., a large table) without stopping to rest is determined by how far the weaker of the two can go. And if all members of a group are required to learn a skill to criterion before the competence of the group as a whole can be certified, time-to-certification will depend on the slowest learner in the group. Note that in each of these examples every member of the group must perform the task, and member contributions (i.e., hiking speed, distance traveled carrying the heavy object, time invested prior to certification) are constrained to be equal. The member's efforts are conjoined— linked together—with the effect that the group's collective performance can be no better than that of its least capable member.

Member contributions are restricted in a different way on *disjunctive tasks*. Unlike conjunctive tasks, which require every member to contribute identically, disjunctive tasks permit just one member's contributions to determine the group's product. As Steiner (1972) notes, on disjunctive tasks, the group's product is really an individual product that is adopted or sanctioned by the group. In the game of basketball, for example, teams are awarded one or more free-throw opportunities whenever a technical foul is committed by the opposing team. Shooting these free throws is a disjunctive task for the team. The resulting point(s) (if any) accrue to the team as a whole, but only one player may actually attempt the shot. Which player that is, is up to the team to decide.

Many problem-solving tasks are similarly disjunctive in nature. An item on a multiple-choice exam taken by a group is an example. Unless every member of the group knows the correct answer at the outset, the group's performance will depend on which member's individual answer is selected to represent the group as a whole. That several members may have given that same answer individually has no bearing on how the group's response is scored—just like a free throw shot, the selected response is not made more or less accurate by virtue of the number of members who individually could have given it. This is not to say that the number of members preferring a given answer is irrelevant to the group's problem-solving process. Quit the contrary. As previously discussed, it is often highly relevant. But once a particular answer is adopted, the number of members who individually endorsed that answer is of no consequence.

It is important to note that some authors have incorrectly characterized disjunctive tasks as being the polar opposite of conjunctive tasks, suggesting that, whereas conjunctive tasks make group performance dependent on the contributions of the least capable member in the group, disjunctive tasks make group performance dependent on the contributions of the most capable member. The latter part of this statement is true only under some circumstances and is not a defining characteristic of disjunctive tasks. When tasks are organized such that all members perform the task simultaneously, and the quality of their individual products is known before one member's product is selected to represent the group as a whole, then groups will, in fact, usually be able to choose the best among their members' products to represent them. Problem-solving tasks with highly demonstrable solutions fit this description. Likewise, golfers sometimes play a "best ball" team game that, in part, has this structure. Four players form two teams. After all four have teed off on each hole, each team determines which of its members' two balls has the best lie. Thereafter, the members of each team take turns playing their team's "best ball" for the remainder of that hole, discarding the other one. Other tasks are organized such that the best member's performance is selected naturally, without a separate choice by the group. An example is when the group's speed at unscrambling an anagram is determined by the first person to shout out the correct answer. But there are also many disjunctive tasks where the group's performance does not reliably depend on its best member. Problem-solving tasks with solutions that are difficult to demonstrate fit this description. Here, groups will frequently choose the wrong answer even when one of their members individually knows the correct answer. And basketball players do sometimes miss free throws when one or more of their teammates could have made the shot.

Finally, on *discretionary tasks* no constraints of any sort are placed on how member contributions are combined. Discretionary tasks permit groups to weight member contributions in any way they want. They might give equal weight to every member's contributions (as in an additive task), give all the weight to one member's contributions and none to anyone else's (as in a disjunctive task), or weight members' contributions unequally in some other way. As Steiner (1972) notes, tasks that afford this kind of discretion most often are optimizing tasks. An example is forecasting some uncertain future event (e.g., the price of a stock at the close of business tomorrow, or the enrollment in introductory psychology next year). The group is free to weight member estimates in any way they want in order to make an accurate forecast. They might, for example, give more weight to predictions made by members with special expertise or experience, while giving less weight to extreme estimates that depart markedly from the estimates of others. The task itself permits any of these possibilities, and it is up to the group to decide (implicitly or explicitly) what specific scheme will be used.

The various limitations on permitted group process implied by additive, conjunctive, and disjunctive tasks may arise for a number of reasons. Sometimes they result from physical, temporal, or technological constraints. For example, the physics of time and space make it impossible for hikers to travel together at different rates, and a too-short rope (technology) may prevent more than one person at a time from grabbing hold and applying pressure. Consequently, hiking together is always a conjunctive task, whereas steadying a heavy load that tugs at the other end of the rope may sometimes be a disjunctive rather than additive task. Permitted group process can also be dictated by social norms and customs. Mountaineering safety conventions, for instance, prescribe that climbers be roped together when traversing certain types of terrain. Of course, once roped-in they can no longer climb at their own pace, and their task becomes strictly conjunctive. Similarly, democratic ideals dictate that member opinions (votes) be weighted equally when making certain kinds of decisions. Such tasks are therefore constrained to be additive. Finally, specific procedural directives associated with the task may dictate what combinatorial processes are permitted, quite independent of any physical or normative imperatives. Thus, a team foot race might be scored in several different ways: by summing the members' individual finishing times (an additive task), by counting only the time of the first member to cross the finish line (a disjunctive task), or by counting only the time of the last member to cross the finish line (a conjunctive task). It is easy to construct a scenario in which, given the same member performances, a different team wins under each of these scoring regimes.

Permitted Group Process and the Search of Synergy

In Chapter 1, I differentiated two types or levels of synergy. Weak synergy was defined as group performance that exceeds the performance of the typical group member when working alone, whereas strong synergy was defined as group performance that exceeds the solo performance of even the best group member. One value of Steiner's (1972) group task typology is that, better than others, it helps to identify where we might profitably search for evidence of weak and strong synergy, and what that evidence might look like.

Maximizing additive tasks are the simplest case. On such tasks, group performance can be tested for evidence of synergy by comparing it to the sum of the performances exhibited by group members when working independently. Or, to differentiate weak and strong synergy, the group's performance score can be divided by group size to obtain the average member performance when working in a group. This value might then be compared with both the average performance of group members when working alone (to test for weak synergy), and with the solo the performance of the most productive group member when working alone (to test for strong synergy).

Disjunctive tasks are only slightly more complex. Maximizing disjunctive tasks generally involve quantitative response scales, and can be tested for both weak and strong synergy in essentially the same way as is done for additive tasks (however, there is usually no need to divide the group's performance by group size). Optimizing disjunctive tasks, on the other hand, might call for either a quantitative response (as when estimating the number of students who will enroll next year) or a choice among discrete alternatives (as when answering multiple-choice exam questions).[14] If it is the former, then once again procedures similar to those employed for additive tasks can be used, although here it is necessary to focus on difference scores (i.e., between the observed and optimum response; see Chapter 5, pp. 162–165). If, on the other hand, a choice among discrete alternatives is called for, then group performance must be tested for weak and strong synergy along the lines described previously in connection with the discussion of group tasks versus performance aggregates. Specifically, weak synergy is evaluated by comparing the proportion of groups giving the optimal response to the overall proportion of members giving that response when working alone (i.e., proportions replace means as the key performance indicator). Strong synergy, on the other hand, is evaluated by comparing the proportion of groups giving the optimal response to the proportion of groups that contain at least one member who is able to give the optimal response when working alone (cf. Chapter 4, pp. 124–126). It is worth noting here that, if in a particular group there is at least one member who can give the optimal response when working alone, then strong synergy is not possible in that group (because it is impossible to do better than to give the optimal response). This is part of the more general problem that, when optimizing tasks are too easy, they create artificial performance ceilings that can obscure whatever strong synergistic performance gains might otherwise be evident.

Discretionary tasks often involve a quantitative response scale and so also can be tested for synergy in the way described above for additive tasks. However, here certain circumstances are also apt to make synergy more difficult to detect. For example, if members' individual responses are unbiased (i.e., neither systematically too high or too low), then errors will tend to offset one another when those responses are averaged, leaving that average close to the true value. Under these circumstances, it may be easier for the group to outperform its best member than to outperform its average member. Indeed, in the extreme case, the average of the members' responses will be perfectly accurate, so that no improvement at all is possible relative to that criterion. Yet the group may still perform better than its best member! Such disordinal results make conclusions about synergy more difficult to draw, a point that I take up at greater length in Chapter 5. More easily interpreted are results that occur in situations where members' individual responses are systematically biased. Here, the expectation is that their average response will depart from, rather than converge on, the true value. Indeed, the true value may be completely outside the range of individual responses (i.e., if all members are biased in the same direction, though not necessarily to the same degree). If so, then there is at least the possibility that the group can out-perform both its average and its best member. Thus, once again the specific nature of the task vis-à-vis members' individual performance is crucial in determining whether or not the effects of synergistic processes, if they exist, can be detected.

Finally, conjunctive tasks present yet another set of difficulties. First, they require a different standard for judging weak synergy. Weak synergy on a conjunctive task is defined as group performance that exceeds the performance of its *least capable* (not average) member when working alone. This is because conjunctive tasks, by definition, constrain group performance to be no better than what its least able member can produce. If there were no performance gain (or loss) whatsoever on a conjunctive task, then the group's performance would be identical to that of its least capable member when working alone. Group performance that exceeds the standard set by the solo performance of its least capable member, even though it does not rise to the level of its average member's solo performance, would thus seem a legitimate example of a performance gain that is attributable in some way to group interaction. Thus, it merits the synergy label and should be included within the range of weak synergy on conjunctive tasks. But, as usual, the group's performance would not be considered an example of strong synergy unless it surpassed the performance of its best member when working alone.

Second, conjunctive tasks appear to offer considerably fewer opportunities for synergistic performance gains to emerge, especially strong synergy. This is partly because only those synergistic processes that operate through the group's least capable member can potentially impact group performance on conjunctive tasks. Further, the magnitude of the performance gain that is needed in order to qualify as an example of strong synergy is larger for conjunctive tasks than it is for other task types. This is because the gap between the weak and strong synergy thresholds (i.e., the solo performance of the least and most capable group members, respectively) is larger for conjunctive tasks than it is for other task types (where the weak synergy threshold is set by the solo performance of the average, not least capable, member of the group). As a result, if a gain is observed in group performance on a conjunctive task, its likelihood of falling within the range defined as weak rather than strong synergy is higher than it would be for other task types. Said differently, strong synergy, which almost certainly is a rarer phenomenon than weak synergy to begin with, is apt to be rarer still on conjunctive tasks compared to other task types.

In sum, because conjunctive tasks are susceptible only to those synergistic processes that operate via the least capable member of the group, and because the magnitude of the performance gain needed to achieve strong synergy is greater, conjunctive tasks seem a less promising place to search for synergy, especially strong synergy, than do additive, disjunctive, and discretionary tasks. Yet, even here some evidence of synergistic performance gains can be found. That evidence will be considered in detail in Chapter 8.

☐ Chapter Summary

In this chapter, I have focused on the tasks that groups perform. I began by defining a group task as a set of instructions for acting on a particular stimulus complex. Instructions are directives that specify the goal(s) to be accomplished and the procedure(s) to be employed in pursuit of those goals. The stimulus complex is the sum total of all the inputs that the group is expected to work with. This definition provides a basis for differentiating group tasks from performance aggregates and so helps to better focus questions concerning synergy in group performance. It also provides a foundation for differentiating tasks and subtasks, and so for conceptualizing subtask structures and their implications (e.g., for decisions about subtask staffing and sequencing).

I then examined several systems for describing and classifying group tasks. First I considered systems that represent task differences in terms of underlying dimensions. According to this approach, tasks are viewed as occupying different positions in a multidimensional space. An important goal of research that follows this approach is to identify the properties of that space. Marvin Shaw's (1963) multidimensional analysis of group tasks is the most comprehensive exemplar in this category. It was described in detail, as was Laughlin's (1980, 1999) intellective-judgmental task continuum. Though more narrowly focused than Shaw's work, Laughlin's analysis has proved extremely useful for ordering a variety of empirical results concerned with group problem-solving.

Finally, I considered two typological approaches to conceptualizing task differences. In contrast to dimensional approaches, these attempt to organize tasks in terms of a limited number of discrete categories. McGrath's (1984) task circumplex was examined in this context, as was Steiner's (1972) task typology. The latter is particularly useful because it leads to some fairly specific suggestions about where the search for synergy might most profitably be conducted.

The impact of task variables on group process and performance is undeniably substantial, so it is not surprising that the importance of understanding group tasks and their properties has been recognized since the earliest days of research on small group performance (e.g., South, 1927; Thorndike, 1938). What *is* surprising is that so little work has actually been done toward attaining that understanding. Relative to their potential explanatory power, tasks and task attributes are among the least studied topics in the field of small group behavior. Group process and performance cannot be studied at all, of course, unless the group does *something*. But too often we pay insufficient attention to the details of what that something is. In most studies, the group's task is held constant. And even when it is varied, task is usually treated as a replication factor that at best is of only secondary interest. Seldom is the task per se the main focus of the research. Group tasks deserve much greater attention than they have received. A serious investment of intellectual capital in this direction has the potential to pay handsome dividends, both in terms of understanding group process generally and in terms of understanding where synergistic performance gains are (and are not) likely to be found. This is a point that I take up again in Chapter 10.

☐ Endnotes

1. I differ with Hackman (1969) on this point. Hackman argued that tasks sometimes have no goals. For example, he suggested that the directive "Watch this motion picture" constitutes a task with no goal. I disagree. Although this task involves no tangible product apart from the behavior of those performing the task, it still does involve a goal —to direct and maintain one's attention on the motion picture. If this is done for the duration of the film, the goal has been achieved. I do not distinguish tasks according to whether or not they result in a physical product or artifact. All tasks have goals, although in some cases those goals may be purely behavioral or experiential (e.g., to have fun).

2. To see this, consider a situation in which, after an exam is over, a question is discovered to have two equally correct answers. The instructor might decide to toss this item out, or she might opt to give students credit if they selected either of the correct answers for that item. An argument might be made for either choice, and either is likely to be acceptable as long as the rule is applied equally to all students. Yet for many students these two alternatives will yield different total exam scores.

3. Strictly speaking, "best" refers to performance, not persons. Thus, for exam items with dichotomous scoring (i.e., correct vs. incorrect), two or more members might all be considered best on a particular item if they all answer correctly; giving the correct response is in this case the best performance observed in the group. And if no one in the group answers correctly, giving the incorrect response is the best performance observed (even though best is not very good in this case).

4. In many other cases this decision will be out of the group's control and instead will be communicated to them in the form of procedural directives (e.g., "First do A, then B, then ..."). This is most likely to occur when (a) tasks and subtasks are routinized, (b) the order in which subtasks are performed is critical to the group's success, and (c) the group's success on the overall task is itself important within the larger social or organizational context in which the group is embedded (e.g., product assembly teams in a manufacturing organization).

5. Another example from the same category is the husbands-and-wives problem shown in Figure 4.1 in Chapter 4.

6. Shaw was not very explicit about how his sample of tasks was obtained. However, casual inspection suggests that certain task categories were overrepresented in his sample, whereas others were either underrepresented or missing altogether.

7. A compensatory task is one on which higher levels of participation, effort, or contribution by one member compensates for lower levels of participation, effort, or contribution by another (cf. Steiner, 1966).

8. Other kinds of juries face comparable situations, including those empaneled to sit in judgment at legal proceedings. The decisions made by petit juries in both civil and criminal cases are sometimes strongly judgmental. It is the jury's responsibility to try (establish) the facts of the case, and the jury's

verdict is taken by the legal system to be "the" answer concerning those facts. Consequently, it is the jury's verdict alone that determines whether a defendant is acquitted or convicted. This is true even when a jury returns a verdict that is widely unpopular (e.g., because it is inconsistent with the facts as others see them). This should not be taken to mean, however, that all cases tried before juries are equally judgmental, at least not in the sense that term is used here. Consistent with the conditions for demonstrability to be described shortly, cases seem most judgmental when they involve a large body of complex evidence, applicable law that is itself complex, and involve issues that speak to competing beliefs and values. These are cases for which unassailable logical, legal, and/or moral arguments are most difficult to mount, thus making the correctness of any particular verdict extremely hard to defend. Conversely, cases seem less judgmental (though not necessarily purely intellective) when they involve a small body of easily understood evidence, applicable law that is simple and well defined, and involve issues that speak to beliefs and values that all pull in the same direction. Here, convincing logical, legal, and moral arguments are more easily constructed, and the correctness of one verdict over another is more easily defended.

9. Laughlin and Ellis (1986) are not completely clear on the distinction between Conditions 1 and 3. Regarding Condition 1, they suggested that group consensus on a conceptual system, such as a language, code of law, or branch of mathematics, implies agreement on the native terms, basic vocabulary, syntax, axioms, permissible relationships or operations, etc., of that system. However, these speak to the group members' knowledge of the conceptual system. Consequently, they seem more properly the province of Condition 3. It would be cleaner to limit Condition 1 to consensus among members about what conceptual system is appropriate for understanding and solving the problem and let Condition 3 include all relevant knowledge about the content of that system. Thus, groupmates may agree that differential calculus is the proper conceptual system for finding the local maximum of a particular function (Condition 1). It is another matter altogether whether those who cannot solve the problem themselves nevertheless know enough calculus to follow a solution proposed by someone else (Condition 3). My discussion of these conditions presumes this cleaner distinction.

10. Interestingly, in courtroom jury decision making there is also a general leniency bias, such that simple majority factions favoring a not-guilty verdict are more influential than simple majority factions favoring a guilty verdict. The guilty alternative seems to require a strong majority at the outset of discussion if it is to be adopted by the jury as a whole (e.g., Kerr & MacCoun, 1985; MacCoun & Kerr, 1988, Stasser, Kerr, & Bray, 1982; Tindale, Davis, Volrath, Nagao, & Hinsz, 1990).

11. If a conceptual system for solving the problem does not exist, then the problem does not have a solution; it is the existence of a relevant conceptual system that gives meaning to a problem and to what is considered correct versus incorrect. By extension, if a conceptual system exists but is underdeveloped (e.g., permissible operations and relations are not precisely or fully specified), then there may be no uniquely correct solution; many solutions may be equally correct given the limits of the conceptual system, with no logical means of choosing among them.

12. The synergistic performance gain in bicycle racing that is due to drafting can be conceptualized in precisely this way. As discussed in Chapter 1, a pair of cyclists can travel faster and further by taking turns leading and following behind one another than either could manage by riding alone. This occurs because the lead rider is able to break the wind for the follower, thus making it easier for the follower to keep pace. But this latter benefit accrues strictly as an incidental consequence of the lead rider pursuing his or her primary subtask goal—riding as fast as possible. Importantly, the lead rider does not choose to make this benefit available to the follower. Rather, it occurs as a function of the physics of the situation.

13. Two points are worth noting here. First, although the term "divisible" speaks to the *possibility* of dividing the task, Steiner himself consistently used the term in reference to tasks that had *in fact* been divided among group members. Second, my earlier discussion of tasks with subtasks did not specify whether those subtasks are performed by individuals, by a subgroup of members, or by the group as a whole. Real-world examples of each are easy to find. It seems valuable for understanding group process to consider a task's subtask structure even when those subtasks are all performed by the group as a whole (and so would not be considered divisible by Steiner). Thus, as I use the phrase, "tasks with subtasks" is broader and more inclusive than Steiner's (1972) divisible task category.

14. As I use the term here, "choice" does not necessarily imply volition. The previously described basketball scenario, in which one or more free-throw shots are attempted following a technical foul, also fits the category of an optimizing disjunctive task that calls for a choice among discrete alternatives. This is the case even though the response is not "chosen" in the usual sense of the word. Rather, each free-throw is simply made successfully or not.

Idea Generation

Creative Thinking in Groups

In the next four chapters, I consider group performance on each of four broad categories of tasks: idea generation tasks, problem-solving tasks, judgment tasks, and decision-making tasks. These are, of course, only a subset of all the many possible tasks that groups perform. For example, they fit just three of the eight types found in McGrath's (1984) task circumplex (see Chapter 2). Nevertheless, these task categories have commanded the lion's share of attention in the small group performance literature. For each one, I describe the most important empirical research concerned with group performance on such tasks, giving particular emphasis to recent developments, and suggest where research in the search for synergy on such tasks might best be directed in the future.

I begin in this chapter with idea-generation tasks. The central question addressed here is whether or not ideational productivity benefits from group interaction. Are groups any better than individuals at generating ideas? And, more to the point, is there any evidence of synergy in collective ideation? There is a 60-year history of research on this question, and as will be seen, the evidence gathered during most of this period has been overwhelmingly negative. It points strongly in the direction of process loss, not gains. Recently, however, evidence has begun to emerge suggesting that process gains may be possible, albeit only some of the time, and only under some circumstances.

☐ The Origins of an Idea

In the fall of 1939, Europe was once again at war. Germany had mounted a bold and devastating invasion of Poland. Within two weeks of crossing the Polish frontier, German troops were in command of half the country, and within four weeks Warsaw surrendered. Newspaper and magazine accounts described the German advance as no mere "war of occupation, but a war of quick penetration and obliteration—*blitzkrieg*, lightning war" ("Blitzkrieger," 1939). Aided by relentless aerial bombardment, fast-moving armored divisions led the charge, cutting swiftly and deeply into Polish territory. Lines of communication were severed, homes, shops, and factories were destroyed at will, and the civilian population was terrorized and scattered. It was a ferocious, and ferociously efficient, operation.

Accounts of this and other similar military exploits dominated the world news that year, so it is not surprising that thoughts of storm troopers and commando raids might have come easily to those participating in the special groups assembled in America for quite a different purpose by Alex Osborn. Osborn, a founding partner in the advertising firm Batten, Barton, Durstine, and Osborn, was in search of new ways to stimulate creative ideas that could be put to use by the clients of his company. Osborn was certain that creative ideation is facilitated when criticism is avoided as ideas are being generated. He further believed that there is a direct relationship between the quantity and quality of ideas—that the first 50 ideas generated for solving a problem are usually inferior to the last 50 ideas. And, most importantly, he was convinced that group ideation is more productive than individual ideation. Thus, he began organizing his employees, and those of his clients, into small groups, challenging them to generate new ideas for addressing a wide range of problems. Among other things, these groups produced ideas for selling U.S. savings bonds (103 ideas generated in 40 minutes), reducing employee absenteeism (89 ideas in 30 minutes), improving U.S. Air Force executive officer development programs (57 ideas in 45 minutes), improving U.S. Army recruiter effectiveness (91 ideas in 12 minutes), restoring telephone service to storm-damaged long-distance lines (57 ideas in 25 minutes), opening a new drugstore (87 ideas in 90 minutes), increasing foot traffic through a specialty shop (49 ideas in 30 minutes), and improving a railroad's customer services (54 ideas in 25 minutes). The early participants in these groups were so enthusiastic about the results they were able to produce in such short periods of time that they dubbed their activity "brainstorming"—they used their brains to "storm" creative problems in commando fashion, with the "stormers" working collectively to quickly and decisively overpower their objective (Osborn, 1953, 1957).

Key to the effectiveness of these brainstorming groups was that they followed a set of procedural rules consistent with the principles of creative ideation that Osborn (1953, 1957) believed to be true. These rules are:

1. *Criticism is ruled out.* Adverse judgment of ideas must be withheld until later. The purpose of the brainstorming session is to generate many, varied, and unusual options.
2. *"Free-wheeling" is welcomed.* The wilder the idea the better; it is easier to tame down than to think up. Since criticism is temporarily ruled out, it is acceptable and desired that really wild and unusual ideas are shared.
3. *Quantity is wanted.* The greater the number of ideas, the more the likelihood of useful ideas.
4. *Combination and improvement are sought.* In addition to contributing ideas of their own, participants should suggest how the ideas of others can be turned into better ideas, or how two or more ideas can be joined into still another idea.

Although these four rules are typically cited in the literature as *the* defining characteristics of brainstorming, in the revised edition of his book Osborn (1957) specified a number of additional desirable qualities and procedures for effective brainstorming. He suggested, for example, that the optimum group size for brainstorming is 12, with the group comprising individuals of nearly equal rank or status so as not to hamper "free wheeling." He also proposed that the problem to be attacked be revealed to group members at least two days in advance so they can "sleep on it." At the start of the brainstorming session, he recommended that the group brainstorm a different, very easy problem as a "warm-up" exercise. Osborn also advocated that each group be led by someone trained in the methods of brainstorming. It was the leader's job to carefully explain to the group the four rules for brainstorming listed above and then enforce adherence to those rules during the session. For their part, the group members should offer only one idea per speaking turn, raising their hands to do so, and they should not be permitted simply to read aloud ideas taken from a prepared list. Members should be encouraged to take notes about ideas they think of while others are talking so as not to forget them. Further, anytime they come up with a new idea sparked by a suggestion made by someone else, members should both raise their hand and snap their fingers. Osborn believed such ideas were especially valuable and should be given priority by the leader when more than one hand is raised at a time. When the rate of idea production begins to drop, the group leader should be prepared either to suggest new directions in which to look for additional ideas, or to propose a new idea of his or her own (taken from a list created in advance but held in reserve for just such occasions). Every group should have a recording secretary to write down the ideas as they are mentioned, and the secretary should keep a running tally of the number of ideas produced so that the leader can set goals for generating additional ideas (e.g., "We're now up to 75 ideas; let's try for 100!"). Finally, Osborn cautioned that ideas should never be identified by the names of those who suggested them, and that those ideas should be judged, weeded out, and selected for further action by a separate group at a later session.

☐ Early Empirical Tests

This technique for coaxing creativity from groups, developed against the backdrop of a world at war, became so popular during the postwar era that the very term "brainstorming" entered the English language as a common noun. Judging by the ease with which trade books touting the virtues of brainstorming can be found today (e.g., Michalko, 2006; Souter, 2007; Sweeney, 2005; Warmke & Buchanan, 2003), its popularity remains strong nearly seven decades later. Beyond popularity, however, what evidence is there of the effectiveness of group brainstorming? In particular, what basis is there for concluding that interaction among group members *per se* contributes to the effectiveness of brainstorming groups?

   The evidence cited by Osborn (1953, 1957) for the effectiveness of brainstorming comes primarily from case examples that he presents in only slightly more detail than I did several paragraphs above. Importantly, with two exceptions, Osborn provides no basis of comparison for evaluating the results generated by the brainstorming groups he described. The two exceptions were brief summaries of unpublished "classroom experiments" conducted in the context of creative thinking courses. One involved a single group of students that generated 10 times as many ideas when critics were barred from the room as when critics were present and encouraged to voice their concerns as ideas were suggested (1957, p. 232). The other involved 20 engineers who were divided into two groups, with one working collectively to come up with creative solutions to a problem and the other working individually. According to Osborn, "[w]hen scientifically assayed, the findings showed that the 'brainstorming' method had produced 44% more worthwhile ideas than the solo method" (1957, p. 82). But no further details were given. Thus, the evidence Osborn presented is sketchy at best.

An Idea-Generation Paradigm

It was not until 1958 that the first controlled experimental study testing the effectiveness of group brainstorming was published (but see Watson,

1928). Taylor, Berry, and Block (1958) recruited 96 Yale University under-graduate students to participate in a study of creativity. Half of these students were assigned to work together in one of 12 four-person groups, whereas the other half worked individually. In both conditions, the students generated ideas for solving three problems: (a) how to stimulate greater European tourism in America,[1] (b) how to ensure that, in light of increasing birth rates and projected teacher shortages, schools can continue to provide effective instruction to children, and (c) identifying all of the practical benefits and difficulties that would arise if people born after 1960 had an extra thumb on each hand. These problems were presented verbally, one-at-a-time, and for each one of them participants had 12 minutes to generate as many ideas as they could. In terms of the task typologies discussed in Chapter 2, all three problems appear to be Type 2 (creativity) tasks, according to McGrath's (1984) task circumplex, and unitary, additive, maximizing tasks according to Steiner's (1972) classification system.

Before considering the results of this study, several methodological issues are worth noting. First, because what was of interest was the effect of group interaction, not instructional set, Taylor et al. (1958) gave research participants in both experimental conditions the same directives for performing the task, including a careful explanation of the four rules for brainstorming.[2] Second, it was important that, once generated, ideas be reported by groups and individuals in exactly the same manner, thereby ensuring the comparability of response modes (i.e., some methods of responding are more time consuming than others, and these differences should not be permitted to confound the results). Thus, Taylor et al. had participants in both conditions say their ideas out loud and made an audio recording of these ideas as they were spoken. Finally, and most crucially, it was important that the interacting brainstormers be judged against noninteracting brainstormers who had available to them the same intellectual resources for performing the task. Taylor et al. accomplished this by evaluating the performance of four-person interacting groups against that of four-person "nominal groups." The latter comprised participants who worked at the brainstorming task individually, but whose ideas were pooled for comparison purposes.[3] Specifically, the data records of the 48 participants who had done the brainstorming task alone were organized into 12 sets of four, with all the ideas suggested within a set tallied to create a single performance score for that nominal group. Redundant ideas (i.e., ideas proposed by more than one person in the set) were tallied just once in this process. These nominal groups were thus comparable to the interacting groups with respect to instructional set, response mode, and intellectual resources (four persons' worth, in each case) but differed with respect to the opportunity for interaction while performing the task. Consequently, if group interaction *per se* facilitates ideational creativity, as

Osborn (1953, 1957) proposed, then the interacting groups should outperform their nominal counterparts.

It is also useful before examining the results of this study to consider how the definition of synergy, introduced in Chapter 1, relates to its *possible* outcomes. Recall that synergy in groups is defined as a performance gain that is due to group interaction. Weak synergy refers to group performance that exceeds the performance of the typical group member, whereas strong synergy refers to group performance exceeding that of even the best group member. In the study by Taylor et al. (1958), weak synergy (at least) would be demonstrated if the mean performance of the interacting groups was significantly better than the mean performance of the nominal groups. This is because the latter fairly represents what would be expected from a nominal group made up entirely of "typical" members working alone. To gain evidence of strong synergy, on the other hand, an additional analytic step is required. The best (most productive) member of each nominal group would have to be identified, and then, extrapolating from that member's individual performance, the performance that would be expected of a nominal group composed entirely of comparably productive "best" individuals would have to be estimated (i.e., by multiplying the best member's performance by n = group size, which in this case is 4).[4] Strong synergy would be demonstrated only if the mean performance of the interacting groups was significantly better than the mean of these "best member" nominal groups.

The results actually obtained by Taylor et al. (1958) are shown in Table 3.1. They found a large and statistically significant difference between the interacting and nominal groups with respect to the average number of ideas generated per problem ($p < .001$). However, as can be seen,

---

TABLE 3.1 Results from the First Experimental Test of Group Brainstorming

Variable	Means for Interacting Groups	Means for Nominal Groups
Number of ideas per problem	37.5	68.1
Number of unique ideas per problem	10.8	19.8
Mean quality of ideas[a]	2.4	2.3

[a] Note that summed quality ratings, not mean quality ratings, were reported in the original article. Because sums are affected by the number of ideas rated as well as by their quality, the interpretation of sums is ambiguous. I have therefore divided those sums by the number of ideas suggested per problem to produce the means shown here. Higher values indicate higher quality.

From "Does group participation when using brainstorming facilitate or inhibit creative thinking," by Taylor, Berry, and Block, 1958, *Administrative Science Quarterly, 3*, 23–47.

this difference was opposite in direction to what the group brainstorming hypothesis predicts: interacting groups generated significantly *fewer* ideas—by nearly half—than nominal groups!

The results also fail to support the group brainstorming hypothesis when the quality of the ideas suggested by interacting and nominal groups is compared. Many of the ideas suggested for a given problem were proposed by more than one group (whether interacting or nominal), and a few were proposed by nearly all of them. But some ideas were unique, having been proposed by just one of the 24 groups in the study. The number of unique ideas generated by each group was used by Taylor et al. (1958) as an index of the group's creativity. As can be seen in Table 3.1, the difference between the interacting and nominal groups with respect to the average number of unique ideas generated is large, statistically significant, and again favors the nominal groups. However, the difference is mainly a function of the total number of ideas generated; when the latter was statistically controlled, the advantage for nominal groups disappeared. Indeed, for one problem (thumbs), the difference was reversed, significantly favoring the interacting groups ($p < .02$). Thus, there is at least a hint in these data that group interaction may benefit creativity (defined as originality) when attacking certain kinds of problems.[5] On the other hand, this effect is strongly overshadowed by the sheer quantity of ideas produced.

Taylor et al. (1958) also rated each of the proposed ideas on three quality dimensions (ideas for the tourism and education problems were rated on feasibility, effectiveness, and generality; ideas for the thumbs problem were rated on probability, significance, and generality). The grand mean across all of these ratings is shown separately for interacting and nominal groups in Table 3.1. Although the overall difference slightly favors the interacting groups, it is not statistically significant, and in one case (thumbs) was significantly in the opposite direction (favoring nominal groups) when the problems were analyzed separately.

Thus, there is very little in the data reported by Taylor et al. (1958) to recommend group brainstorming. Rather than pointing to a synergistic facilitation of ideational creativity, their results suggest that group interaction actually inhibited creativity, with brainstorming groups generating fewer ideas overall, fewer unique ideas, and ideas that on average were of no better quality than what was produced by nominal groups.

Further Evidence

The research methodology developed by Taylor et al. (1958), especially the use of nominal groups as a standard of comparison, quickly established itself as the modal paradigm for assessing the ideational productivity of interacting groups. During the next three decades, more than two dozen studies tested the group brainstorming hypothesis using some variant of this methodology, and in a large majority of these studies similar results were obtained. Successive reviews of this literature by Diehl and Stroebe (1987), Lamm and Trommsdorff (1973), and Mullen, Johnson, and Salas (1991) have repeatedly concluded that under a wide variety of circumstances group brainstorming is less productive than individual brainstorming. The meta-analytic integration by Mullen et al. is especially informative. It indicates that the difference in ideational productivity between interacting and nominal groups is highly significant and strong in magnitude, with an average effect size of $d = 1.4$.[6] Across studies, this effect tends to be strongest (a) in larger groups, (b) when the experimenter is physically present in the room during brainstorming, (c) when the ideas generated are audio recorded (as opposed to written down on pieces of paper), and (d) when those in the nominal groups work completely alone (as opposed to working independently in the same room).[7]

It is important to emphasize that, although much of this research was done with ad hoc groups of participants drawn from undergraduate student populations, there is no reason to think that the obtained results are in any way unique to this population. Dunnette, Campbell, and Jaastad (1963), for example, conducted an early brainstorming study using as participants both advertising staff members and (separately) laboratory workers employed by the Minnesota Mining and Manufacturing (3M) company. These are the very sorts of people that Osborn himself had worked with when developing his brainstorming technique. These participants were organized into four-person groups that brainstormed four separate problems like those used by Taylor et al. (1958)—two as individuals and two as interacting groups, in a repeated-measures experimental design that counterbalanced both the content and order of the problems addressed. Of the 24 groups in this study, only one failed to produce more ideas in the nominal condition than in the interacting condition, and in that one instance the difference was tiny (162 vs. 163 ideas, respectively). Likewise, of the 96 participants, only five failed individually to suggest more ideas when working alone than when working in a group. And when the suggested ideas were rated for quality, the means were either not significantly different between conditions or favored individual brainstorming. Other studies using organizational samples that have found interacting groups to perform more poorly than nominal groups include Gryskiewicz (1988) and Paulus, Larey, and Ortega (1995).

It is also important to stress that the results are not limited to the problems originally used by Taylor et al. (1958). Similar results have been shown for a variety of problems, including self-relevant problems having to do with the participants' place of employment (e.g., Gryskiewicz, 1988; Paulus et al., 1995) and problems concerning politically controversial topics (e.g., Diehl & Stroebe, 1987). Indeed, results consistent with those presented by Taylor et al. have been obtained, even on problems that are strongly intellective in nature. Fore instance, McGlynn, McGurk, Effland, Johll, and Harding (2004) embedded a brainstorming task within a complex but well-structured inductive hypothesis-testing task. This task will be described in greater detail in Chapter 4. It is sufficient here to say that the task required participants to determine the nature of an arbitrary rule that the experimenter used to divide a standard deck of 52 playing cards into positive and negative exemplars of that rule (e.g., if the rule were "even red cards," then the 6, 10, and queen [value = 12] of hearts would all be positive exemplars, whereas the ace [value = 1] of diamonds and the 4 and 5 of clubs would be negative exemplars). McGlynn et al. asked participants to generate as many plausible hypotheses as they could about what the rule might be, give a particular set of evidence (i.e., positive and negative examples).[8] Consistent with the results of other studies, McGlynn et al. found that interacting four-person groups generated fewer hypotheses overall, and fewer plausible hypotheses, than did four-person nominal groups (see also Casey, Gettys, Pliske, & Mehle, 1984).

Finally, it is noteworthy that the few studies conducted during this 30-year period that did not replicate the pattern of results found by Taylor et al. (1958) almost always involved two-person groups. In virtually all of these, interacting dyads generated about the same number of ideas as did two people working independently (e.g., Pape & Bölle, 1984; Paulus & Dzindolet, 1993; Paulus, Dzindolet, Poletes, & Camacho, 1993; Torrance, 1970). Thus, dyadic interaction seemed not to inhibit ideational productivity, though it did not facilitate it either. Only one of these studies provided clear evidence of higher quality ideas by interacting dyads relative to nominal dyads (Cohen, Whitmyre, & Funk, 1960). The others found either no differences, differences on indices that do not unambiguously reflect idea quality (i.e., summed ratings, cf. endnote 6), or they simply did not assess idea quality. And, of course, studies involving dyads can be found that do replicate Taylor et al. (e.g., Barkowski, Lamm, & Schwinger, 1982; Furnham, & Yazdanpanahi, 1995). So, while dyadic brainstorming sometimes yields atypical results, it is by no means a universal exception to the rule and, in fact, rarely has produced findings that are genuinely favorable to the group brainstorming hypothesis.

In sum, the early empirical literature is nearly monolithic in its repudiation of the group brainstorming hypothesis. With the possible exception of dyadic brainstorming, group interaction seems to interfere with ideational productivity, resulting in the production of fewer ideas overall, and ideas that are of no higher quality than what would be produced by the same number of persons working individually. If there is any element of synergy in group brainstorming, it is apparently overwhelmed by countervailing, inhibitory forces in ordinary interacting groups.

Reality Versus Perception in Brainstorming Groups

Synergy in groups is defined in terms of performance gains that are due to group interaction. It refers to genuine, objective performance gains, not merely to perceptions of such gains by group members. Member perceptions are irrelevant for deciding whether or not a particular group performance is an example of synergy. It is nevertheless interesting to consider the perceptions of those who have participated in a group brainstorming session. Doing so provides some insight into why group brainstorming remains popular as an idea-generating technique despite the evidence that brainstorming typically hinders rather than helps ideational creativity.

In discussing his approach to stimulating creativity, Osborn (1953, 1957) reported that those who participated in group brainstorming sessions were often quite enthusiastic about their experience and that they typically viewed the sessions as having been highly productive. Similar positive reactions were noted informally as soon as researchers began to test the group brainstorming hypothesis more rigorously (e.g., Taylor et al., 1958, p. 31). However, this phenomenon did not come under systematic investigation until much later.

Several research studies using the basic idea-generation paradigm have included post-experimental questionnaires specifically designed to assess participants' perceptions of their performance while brainstorming (e.g., Diehl & Stroebe, 1987; McGlynn et al., 2004; Nijstad, Stroebe, & Lodewijkx, 2006; Paulus & Dzindolet, 1993; Paulus, Dzindolet, Poletes, & Camacho, 1993; Paulus et al., 1995; Stroebe, Diehl, & Abakoumkin, 1992). These studies indicate that participants who brainstorm in interacting groups generally enjoy their experience more, and are more satisfied with their personal performance, than those who brainstorm individually. Further, whereas group brainstormers often report that they personally generated relatively many ideas, individual brainstormers tend to report that they personally generated relatively few. The same pattern occurs when participants are asked to judge the overall quality of the ideas they generated: group brainstormers rate the quality of their ideas higher than do individual brainstormers. And group brainstormers typically believe they would have produced many fewer and lower quality ideas had they brainstormed alone, whereas individual brainstormers believe they would have produced many more and higher quality ideas had they brainstormed in a group. Such findings signal a marked disconnect between participants' objective performance and their subjective evaluation of that performance. In a phrase, brainstormers demonstrate an "illusion of group productivity." This appears to be part of a broader syndrome of illusory perceptions about group performance found on a variety of tasks (e.g., Allen & Hecht, 2004; Heath & Jourden, 1997; Hinsz & Nickell, 2004; Jourden & Heath, 1996; Plous, 1995; see also Naquin & Tynan, 2003), but it is especially striking in the case of brainstorming because it runs so strongly counter to reality—group brainstormers perceive themselves to have performed better than individual brainstormers, even when exactly the opposite has actually occurred.

The illusion of group productivity experienced by brainstormers appears to occur for at least three reasons. First, even prior to participating in a formal brainstorming session, people evidence a naïve belief in the creative potential of groups (cf. Allen & Hecht, 2004). For example, Paulus et al. (1993) found that, after reading the standard brainstorming instructions, but before actually starting to brainstorm, 65% of respondents predicted that they personally were likely to generate more ideas brainstorming in a group than brainstorming alone. In contrast, only 30% of respondents thought they would likely generate more ideas brainstorming alone than in a group. Further, 51% of these same respondents thought they would generate better quality ideas brainstorming in a group, whereas only 24% thought they would generate better quality ideas brainstorming alone. Such expectations are highly likely to color participants' subsequent evaluations of their actual brainstorming experience.

Second, during the brainstorming session, group brainstormers gain information that supports a positive appraisal of their individual performance, whereas those who brainstorm alone do not. Specifically, group brainstormers have available to them a substantial amount of social comparison information to assist in evaluating their performance (Paulus & Dzindolet, 1993; Paulus et al., 1993). Without necessarily retaining the exact source of every idea, participants nevertheless gain a sense of the rate at which ideas are generated by their groupmates. That information should, on average, convince them that their own performance is roughly on par with others. Those who brainstorm alone, on the other hand, must forgo such comparative data. As a result, they are likely to be less confident about how well they personally have performed. This should become increasingly problematic as time goes on and it becomes more and more difficult to surface additional novel ideas. The growing difficulty of generating new ideas will be accompanied by longer and more frequent periods during which no new ideas are forthcoming. Those who brainstorm in groups typically experience fewer such "dry spells," at least at the group level. With multiple people all trying to generate ideas simultaneously, it is much more likely that at any given moment at least one of them will have something to contribute. This is true even relatively late in the session. Thus, compared to those who brainstorm alone, those who brainstorm in groups should find unproductive dry spells to be a less salient element of their brainstorming experience, and so less damaging to their satisfaction with their performance (Nijstad et al., 2006).

Finally, after the brainstorming session is over, participants have both the motive and the opportunity to unwittingly misattribute to themselves ideas that were suggested by others. Regarding motivation, like most people, those who brainstorm in groups usually want to see themselves in a favorable light. This esteem-based concern is a key driving force behind numerous self-serving perceptual and attributional biases, not the least of which is the tendency to take personal credit for the successes of one's group, while avoiding blame for group failures (e.g., Larson, 1977; Leary & Forsyth, 1987; Rantilla, 2000). But it is a structural feature of group brainstorming that allows participants to act on this motive. Specifically, and as Osborn (1953, 1957) proposed, in most brainstorming groups no record is kept of who in the group suggested which ideas, and members are often told explicitly that during their discussion they should avoid identifying ideas by their source. Thus, there is neither a formal mechanism, nor an incentive, for participants to keep track of who said what during their brainstorming session. The rationale usually offered for conducting the session in this way is to help minimize the potential for evaluation apprehension. This is presumably accomplished by making it harder for participants to recall later on who first suggested a particular idea. However, this also makes it easier for them to think that a particular idea may originally have been their own when in fact it was not. Given that every member in the group was aware of each suggested idea at least at the moment it was proposed (whether by themselves or by someone else), it is not surprising that there might be some confusion about the origin of certain ideas. Add to that the desire to maintain a positive self-image and it is easy to understand why the confusion might tend systematically to favor the self. Thus, for example, Paulus et al. (1993) found that participants in four-person interactive brainstorming groups claimed personal responsibility for 37% of the ideas generated by the group, which stands in contrast to the mathematically correct value of 25% (i.e., the average of any four values that are constrained to sum to 100%). Similarly, Stroebe et al. (1992) asked participants to examine a list of all the ideas generated by their interactive or nominal brainstorming group and to identify (a) those they had suggested, as well as (b) those suggested by others but that they had thought of independently. Interactive group brainstormers proved to be significantly less accurate than their nominal group counterparts in identifying the ideas that they had actually suggested (57 vs. 76%, respectively). Moreover, members of interacting groups claimed that 33% of the ideas mentioned by others in the group had occurred to them independently, whereas those in nominal groups claimed this was true for only 13% of the ideas. Evidence that such results stem, at least in part, from the prohibition against identifying ideas by their source comes from several studies in which brainstormers have been encouraged to think carefully about who contributed each of the ideas produced by the group (e.g., Marsh, Landau, & Hicks, 1997; see also Wicklund, 1989). When this is done, participants are significantly less likely to misappropriate the ideas of others.

Thus, there is ample reason for those who participate in brainstorming groups to think well of their experience. They enter the brainstorming session with unrealistically high expectations that are apt to predispose them to view their group activity in a positive light. During the session they tend to acquire social comparison and process information consistent with these expectations. And afterwards, their self-serving perceptual biases should encourage them to believe that they contributed more than their fair share of the ideas collectively produced by the group. All of these conspire to encourage the false impression that having brainstormed in a group was a productive, worthwhile exercise.

☐ Barriers to Brainstorming Effectiveness

It seems fair to say that most researchers working in the field of small group behavior in the 1950s and 1960s were about as naïve as the general public in their beliefs regarding the creative productivity of groups. Thus, when evidence began to mount that groups brainstorm less, not more, effectively than individuals, it undoubtedly caught many by surprise. And, as is often the case when there is a mismatch between evidence and intuition, this phenomenon drew a good bit of research attention. Initially, that attention was directed toward establishing the reliability and generalizability of the basic finding. Gradually, however, the research turned toward illuminating its underlying mechanisms. Shedding light on these mechanisms can be useful, even though our primary interest is understanding process gains, not losses, because doing so may suggest ways in which those mechanisms can be disengaged, thereby allowing the hoped-for benefits of collective ideation to emerge. In this section, I review the central findings concerning these mechanisms.

Production Blocking

The single biggest factor leading to poor performance in group brainstorming appears to be production blocking. A central premise of group brainstorming is that participants' imaginations will be stimulated by exposure to the ideas of others. This implies that during a brainstorming session group members should attend to and think about one another's ideas as they are presented. This, in turn, requires that they conduct themselves in a way that makes it possible to contemplate one another's ideas. For example, it is helpful if members adopt some sort of turn-taking procedure so that only one member speaks at a time. When two or more members speak simultaneously, none is easily understood. It was precisely to avoid the problem of simultaneous speech that Osborn (1953, 1957) originally proposed that members raise their hands and wait to be called upon by the group leader before volunteering an idea. Even without a formal leader, however, members are usually quite adept at regulating the turn-taking process during group discussion. Simultaneous speech accounts for only a tiny fraction of a group's total discussion time, and when it occurs, it is resolved rather quickly (cf., Schegloff, 2000). Thus, simultaneous speech, in and of itself, is not a major impediment to group brainstorming performance.

The impediment lies instead in what members must do in order to avoid simultaneous speech. Someone who thinks of a new idea during a brainstorming discussion can announce it immediately to the rest of the group only if no one else happens to be talking at that moment. If, on the other hand, someone else is talking, it will be necessary (to avoid simultaneous speech) for the member with the new idea to monitor the conversation for an opportunity to talk, which usually means waiting until the current speaker has finished. Indeed, it may be necessary to wait for several additional members to speak if those members have previously signaled (perhaps nonverbally) their desire to talk.

It is this waiting for a turn to speak that is at the root of production blocking. While waiting, the person with a new idea to contribute must simultaneously perform three cognitive tasks. First and foremost, he or she must hold the new idea in memory, which typically requires a certain amount of silent rehearsal. Second, he or she must continue monitoring the discussion for signals indicating when it is appropriate to begin speaking. If this task is not attended to closely, an available speaking turn may be lost to someone else, thereby necessitating an even longer wait. Finally, he or she must also listen to and think about what the current speaker has to say. This, of course, gets to the very purpose of the group brainstorming format.

The most obvious danger in all of this is that, while waiting for a speaking turn, the new idea may be forgotten. That is, the twin demands of monitoring the discussion for an opportunity to speak, while at the same time paying attention to what the current speaker has to say, may interfere with the idea rehearsal process, causing members to forget the new ideas that have come to them. And even when they do not lose the thought altogether, they may still have sufficient difficulty recovering it when a speaking turn does become available that their momentary hesitation enables another member to usurp that turn, thus necessitating an additional round of waiting and further risk of forgetting. Forgotten ideas, of course, do not count toward the ideational productivity of either group or individual brainstormers. But individual brainstormers are less at risk of forgetting their ideas because they do not have to wait for a speaking turn in order to contribute them. Thus, forgetting is one mechanism by which production blocking operates, and it is more likely to occur in group than in individual brainstorming.

Less obvious than forgetting, but potentially more powerful as a production blocking mechanism, is that, while members wait for an opportunity to contribute their current new idea, it becomes more difficult for them to generate additional new ideas. The need to rehearse their current idea in order to retain it in memory, to monitor the discussion for an available speaking turn, and to attend to what is being said by someone else, all interfere with the production of additional new ideas. These activities impose a heavy cognitive load that leaves members with insufficient resources for idea generation. This form of production blocking thus has its impact at a different point in the overall brainstorming process than does production blocking that is due to forgetting. Whereas forgetting implies that the group is blocked from capitalizing fully on the ideational efforts of its members, interfering with the generation of new ideas means that it is ideational productivity itself that is being blocked. In combination, these two processes significantly constrain the creative productivity of interactive brainstorming groups relative to the same number of individuals who brainstorm alone.

Empirical Evidence

The first clear experimental evidence of production blocking in group brainstorming was provided in a study by Diehl and Stroebe (1987, Experiment 4). In addition to standard interacting and nominal group brainstorming conditions, these authors created several special nominal group conditions in which brainstormers who worked individually in separate rooms experienced delays prior to contributing their ideas that were much like those typically experienced by members of interacting groups. In all conditions participants generated ideas for reducing unemployment in Germany (the participants were German university students) and announced their ideas aloud into a microphone connected to a tape recorder. However, in two of the special nominal conditions participants were told that they could state their ideas only when permitted to do so by the signal lights on the table in front of them. Specifically, these participants were told that they were part of a four-person brainstorming group, that each member of the group was working in a separate room, and that they were to contribute their ideas by means of an intercom that had a signal system attached to it. The signal system was driven by voice-activated sensors that detected when a member was speaking, and these sensors controlled the signal lights in the four rooms. In each room there was one green and three red lights. The green light represented the participant in that room, and the three red lights each represented one of the participants in the other three rooms. Whenever a given participant began to speak, four lights were illuminated automatically: the green light in his or her own room and the red lights representing him or her in the other three rooms. These lights were switched off as soon as that person stopped talking for 1.5 seconds. Because those who participate in standard brainstorming groups usually speak only when others are silent, participants in these two special nominal conditions were instructed to talk only when all of the red lights were off. These two special nominal conditions differed from one another only in that participants could hear the other members state their ideas in one of them (Special Nominal Condition 1) but not in the other (Special Nominal Condition 2). A third special condition was run in which participants also could not hear the ideas contributed by the others. However, in this condition, although the operation of the signal lights was explained, participants were instructed to disregard the lights and to speak whenever they had something to say (Special Nominal Condition 3). The results from this study are displayed in Table 3.2.

As can be seen, the performance of those who could state their ideas only when permitted to do so by the signal lights (Special Nominal Conditions 1 and 2) was similar to that of standard interactive brainstorming groups and significantly worse than the performance of standard nominal groups. In contrast, the performance of those who were instructed to ignore the signal lights and to state their ideas whenever they had something to say (Special Nominal Condition 3) was similar to that of standard nominal brainstorming groups and significantly better than the performance of

TABLE 3.2 Mean Number of Ideas Generated by Four-Person Interacting and Nominal Brainstorming Groups

Condition	Mean Number of Ideas
Standard Interacting Group	55.67
Special Nominal Condition 1. (Talk only when lights off; hear others' ideas)	37.67
Special Nominal Condition 2. (Talk only when lights off; do not hear others' ideas)	45.67
Special Nominal Condition 3. (Talk at any time; do not hear others' ideas)	102.67
Standard Nominal Group	106.00

Adapted from "Productivity loss in brainstorming groups: Toward the solution of a riddle," by Diehl & Stroebe 1987, *Journal of Personality and Social Psychology, 53,* 497–509 (Experiment 4). With permission of the American Psychological Association.

standard interacting groups. In other words, when individual brainstorm-ers experienced the same contribution delays as group brainstormers, they performed similarly, generating less than half as many ideas as they otherwise would have. These data provide strong support for production blocking as one reason why interactive brainstorming groups typically do not perform as well as an equal number of individuals working alone.

It is important to note that in a standard group brainstorming session participants have much less time in which to articulate their ideas than is the case in a comparable-length individual brainstorming session. For example, with four people in a group, and given that members do not speak simultaneously, each has on average only 25% of the total session time in which to express his or her ideas. This contrasts with 100% of the total session time when people brainstorm individually. Although it might be supposed that this accounts for much of the productivity differential between individual and group brainstorming, two follow-up experiments by Diehl and Stroebe (1991) suggest otherwise. In one (Experiment 1), both interacting and nominal groups generated more ideas in longer sessions than in shorter sessions, but session length did not interact with type of brainstorming. The increase in the number of ideas generated from shorter to longer sessions was roughly the same for interacting as for nominal groups. If production blocking were merely a matter of constraining the expression of already-generated ideas (i.e., interacting groups think of and remember more ideas than can actually be expressed in the time allowed), then extending the length of the brainstorming session should have ben-efited interactive groups more than nominal groups.[9] But it did not.

In a second experiment (Diehl & Stroebe, 1991, Experiment 2), some participants brainstormed individually but were allotted only 25% of the session time for expressing their ideas. This was accomplished by having a computer fitted with a voice-activated sensor track that displayed for participants the total amount of time they had spent so far stating their ideas. When their total talking time reached 25% of the session length, the tape recording of ideas was automatically terminated. This manipulation had virtually no impact on productivity. When aggregated to four-person nominal groups, these participants still generated many more ideas than did four-person interacting groups, and roughly the same number as did standard four-person nominal groups. Thus, production blocking is not simply a matter of there being insufficient time for members of interacting groups to express themselves.

Finally, one other experiment in this series (Diehl & Stroebe, 1991, Experiment 4) should be mentioned because it hints at the underlying complexity of production blocking. This experiment recreated Special Nominal Conditions 1 and 2 from Diehl and Stroebe (1987, Experiment 4). Thus, four participants brainstormed in separate rooms, could state their ideas into a microphone only when permitted to do so by signal lights, and either could (Special Nominal Condition 1) or could not (Special Nominal Condition 2) hear one another as they stated their ideas. Half of the participants in each condition were given a notepad on which to jot down their ideas while working, whereas the other half were given nothing (as is typically done). A notepad is a convenient tool that enables participants to "off-load" their ideas, and so relieves them of having to mentally rehearse those ideas while waiting for an opportunity to speak. It was found that providing a notepad did tend to improve participants' idea-generation performance, but only when they could not hear one another's ideas—that is, only in Special Nominal Condition 2. Apparently, being able to write down their ideas freed-up sufficient cognitive resources to promote further idea genera-tion. This occurred, however, only when the participants were not also burdened by having to attend to the ideas of others. This result sug-gests that the task of mentally rehearsing already-generated ideas, and the separate task of listening to and thinking about the ideas of others, may act independently to block the ideational performance of those who brainstorm in interactive groups. Later in this chapter, I address more fully the complex ways production blocking occurs when I con-sider the details of two recently-developed cognitive models of idea generation in groups.

Motivation Loss in Groups

Although available evidence suggests that production blocking is the sin-gle most significant factor constraining the performance of brainstorming groups, it is not the only factor that does so. There are in addition several features of the group brainstorming situation that, in comparison to indi-vidual brainstorming, can restrict ideational productivity by undermin-ing members' motivation to think of and contribute ideas. I consider each of these factors briefly here.

Evaluation Apprehension

One factor that can lead to motivation loss in brainstorming groups is *evaluation apprehension*. Although the rules of brainstorming clearly indi-cate that ideas are to be suggested without regard to quality, that free-wheeling and wild ideas are encouraged, and that all criticism of ideas is to be withheld, participants nevertheless may at times be reticent to offer certain ideas because those ideas may be judged negatively by others in the group. They may fear, for example, that their ideas will be viewed as silly, simplistic, impractical, irrelevant, socially or politically insensitive, or in some other way unacceptable. It has been shown, for example, that group brainstorming participants are more reluctant to contribute ideas when others in the group are perceived to be experts on the topic at hand (Collaros & Anderson, 1969). Experts are presumably better qualified than nonexperts to evaluate their groupmates' contributions. Similarly, brainstorming groups whose members demonstrate a strong dispositional concern for how they are perceived and evaluated by others (high social anxiety) tend to generate many fewer ideas than groups whose members do not demonstrate this disposition (low social anxiety). By contrast, people who are high versus low in social anxiety do not perform differently when they brainstorm alone (Camacho & Paulus, 1995).

Taking a different tack, Diehl and Stroebe (1987, Experiment 3) examined the role of evaluation apprehension in brainstorming groups by telling half of their participants that a judge was watching them from behind a two-way mirror and that a video recording of their session was being made for demonstration purposes in a social psychology course. These authors reasoned that, if low productivity in group brainstorming is due in part to evaluation apprehension, then an experimental induction of evaluation apprehension should impact individual brainstormers (who should normally have relatively low evaluation apprehension) more strongly than group brainstormers (who should already have relatively high evaluation apprehension).[10] This is just what was found, but only when participants also believed that it was their individual performance that was being evaluated. That is, telling participants that they were being observed and recorded in order to evaluate their individual performance reduced the productivity of nominal groups more than three times as much as it reduced the productivity of interacting groups. On the other hand, when they thought that it was the collective performance of their nominal or interactive group that was being evaluated, this manipulation had virtually no effect at all.[11] This pattern seems quite consistent with the presumed operation of evaluation apprehension in interacting groups, since the very concept of evaluation apprehension speaks more directly to concerns about evaluations of the self than evaluations of one's group. On the other hand, and as Diehl and Stroebe point out, group type (nominal vs. interactive) still accounted for more that 70% of the variance in this study, indicating that the effect of evaluation apprehension was comparatively small.

Social Loafing and Free Riding

A second form of motivation loss in brainstorming groups is *social loafing*. Social loafing is defined as a motivation loss that results from the inability to identify individual member contributions to the group product (Harkins, 1987; Kerr, 1983). In the case of group brainstorming, this is a likely consequence of the prohibition against identifying ideas by the names of those who suggested them. As noted previously, this feature of group brainstorming creates ambiguity about who contributed what, so much so that participants themselves find it easy to claim more personal credit than they really deserve for the ideas that have been generated. This same ambiguity also makes it difficult to link external incentives to individual performance when brainstorming in groups. That is, members who contribute relatively many ideas cannot be singled out for reward, nor can members who contribute relatively few ideas be singled out for punishment (though extreme outliers in either direction may be an exception). Thus, whereas evaluation apprehension may cause members to withhold certain of their ideas for fear that they will be judged objectionable by others, the inability to identify precisely the number of ideas that each member has contributed may lessen participants' motivation to generate many ideas in the first place. In support of this notion, a number of studies have demonstrated that when idea-generation tasks are arranged so that the number of ideas contributed by each member cannot be determined, participants generate significantly fewer ideas than when their separate contributions to the total can be determined (for reviews see Karau & Williams, 1993; Williams, Harkins, & Karau, 2003).

In contrast to social loafing, *free riding* is a motivation loss that results from the perception that one's efforts are dispensable (Harkins, 1987; Kerr, 1983). The root cause of free riding can be traced to the problem of simultaneous speech during group brainstorming, and the attendant need to adopt some type of turn-taking procedure in order to avoid it. Turn-taking adds a disjunctive feature to what is otherwise an additive task. Recall from Chapter 2 that an additive task is one in which the group's product is determined by summing the products of its members' efforts. A disjunctive task, on the other hand, is one that permits just one member's efforts to determine the group's product. It is obvious that the brainstorming performance of nominal groups is strictly additive; the group's total score is defined quite literally as the sum of all the nonredundant ideas generated by the members working separately. Interactive group brainstorming is also largely additive; the group's total score is the sum of all the ideas contributed by its members. However, because at any given moment only one member at a time can actually contribute an idea and be understood, the subtask of giving voice to ideas during group discussion is essentially disjunctive. That is, if we focus narrowly on the momentary productivity of the group (i.e., what is happening right now), as long as a new idea is currently being contributed, the group is being productive. This is true regardless of who is making the contribution.

It is precisely because only one person can speak at a time that it becomes less important that any particular member actually be prepared to do so. This is what provides the opportunity to "free ride" on the efforts of others; participants can enjoy the benefits of membership in a (momentarily) productive group without having to exert any effort at all as long as other members are both willing and able to do the work of voicing ideas. Following this line of reasoning, several studies have demonstrated that simply increasing the size of the group working on a given task can reduce the amount of physical (Kerr & Bruun, 1983) and mental effort (Harkins & Petty, 1982; Weldon & Gargano, 1985, 1988; Weldon & Mustari, 1988) that group members are willing to exert. Larger groups make members feel that their own efforts are more dispensable, and so encourage free-riding. The presence of other more-capable members in the group has similarly been shown to reduce target members' effort (e.g., Hardy & Crace, 1991).[12] I will have more to say about social loafing and free riding in Chapter 8, which deals specifically with the question of motivation in group task settings (see especially pp. 274–281).

Performance Matching

As noted previously, when people work cooperatively to generate ideas, they learn not only the substance of one another's ideas, but also the rate at which those ideas are produced. I have already suggested that such social comparison information is useful in part because it helps members gauge the adequacy of their own performance. Equally important is that it also helps them gauge the group's implicit productivity norm, that is, the rate at which ideas *should* be produced in the group. What is more, exposure to this information sets in motion a performance-matching process, whereby members gradually adjust their individual productivity rates to more closely mirror one another. In a phrase, there is a "press toward uniformity" in the group, with members gradually converging on a common rate-of-productivity (cf. Festinger, 1950). In support of this idea, it has been found that members tend to contribute ideas at fairly similar rates in interactive brainstorming groups, whereas this is not the case for those who work in nominal brainstorming groups (Camacho & Paulus, 1995; Paulus & Dzindolet, 1993). But this occurs only if members are actually aware of the rate at which others in their own group produce ideas (Munkes & Diehl, 2003, Exp. 2).

Paulus and his colleagues (Brown & Paulus, 1996; Paulus & Dzindolet, 1993) argue that this performance-matching process helps to reduce the productivity of interactive brainstorming groups relative to nominal groups. They contend that early in a brainstorming session a relatively low member productivity norm gets established, one that is well below most members' capabilities. The reason is that early on, although it may be easy to generate ideas, it is hard to express them all because others in the group also have many ideas to contribute. So, production blocking occurs, and the rate at which each member actually contributes ideas is much lower than it would be were there no competition for speaking turns (e.g., in a nominal group). This low rate of individual productivity is then maintained over time as members seek to match, or at least not deviate too far from, one another's performance (cf. Kelly & Karau, 1993). This is the case even though the likelihood that the competition for speaking turns will gradually abate, leaving more opportunities for high-ability members to put forward additional ideas at a rate that is higher than was possible previously. By sticking close to a rate of productivity that can be maintained even by low-ability members, those who would otherwise be more productive can avoid the unpleasant feeling that they are doing all the work and are being taken advantage of by their less-capable (or lazy) groupmates (cf. Kerr, 1983). And, of course, low productivity norms have the added attraction of demanding less effort.

That interactive brainstorming groups often gravitate toward a productivity norm that is below the level they would otherwise exhibit as individuals is supported by data suggesting that the overall performance of these groups is better predicted by the productivity rate of their lowest, rather than highest, performing member (Camacho & Paulus, 1995; Paulus & Dzindolet, 1993). It is also consistent with evidence from the goal-setting literature, which suggests that when asked to set their own productivity goals, groups typically set lower goals than do individuals (e.g., Hinsz, 1995; Hinsz & Nickell, 2004). It is important to note, however, that although groups may be more inclined to converge on low rather than high productivity norms, they do not always do so. The ideational productivity of brainstorming groups can be raised, implying a higher productivity norm, by (a) providing external standards that emphasize the value of high levels of productivity, (b) getting members to view the idea generation task in competitive terms, and (c) getting them to view the idea generation task as a test of their individual creativity or intelligence (e.g., Munkes & Diehl, 2003; Paulus, Dugosh, Dzindolet, Coskun, & Putman, 2002).

In sum, there are a number of factors beyond production blocking that help to explain the performance losses commonly observed in brainstorming groups. These include evaluation apprehension, social loafing, free-riding, and performance matching. In one way or another, each of these impacts the ideational productivity of groups by reducing their members' motivation to generate and contribute ideas. Taken together, they offer a more complete picture of why it is that the ideational productivity of interactive groups is consistently below that of an equal number of individuals working independently. It is important to keep in mind, however, the relative magnitude of these effects. Meta-analytic reviews indicate, for example, that the typical size of the individual-versus-group brainstorming effect is over three times as large as that of the typical social-loafing or free-riding effect (e.g., compare Mullen et al. 1991, with Karau & Williams, 1993). It can be inferred from the previously cited work by

Diehl and Stroebe (1987) that the effect of evaluation apprehension is also relatively small compared to the typical individual-versus-group brainstorming effect. And the same is likely true for the effect of performance matching. Thus, while there is good evidence that these various effects do act to diminish group brainstorming effectiveness, it seems unlikely that any of them can explain nearly as much variance as can be explained by production blocking.

☐ Cognitive Models of Idea Generation in Groups

Efforts to more fully understand the nature and origins of production blocking in brainstorming groups have led most recently to the development of several formal models of idea generation in interactive groups. At their core, these models focus on idea generation at the individual group member level. However, because they assume that individual-level idea generation is affected by group interaction, they also speak directly to collective ideational performance. Importantly, they help to explain not only the negative impact of production blocking in interactive brainstorming, but also the long-suspected stimulating effect of idea sharing.

The Associative Memory Matrix (AMM) Model

Brown, Tumeo, Larey, and Paulus (1998) proposed an Associative Memory Matrix (AMM) model of ideational creativity in brainstorming groups that takes into consideration the content and structure of members' knowledge, as well as the degree to which members pay attention to one another's ideas (see also Paulus & Brown, 2003; Coskun, Paulus, Brown, & Sherwood, 2000). The AMM model views idea generation as a concept-retrieval process. Each group member is hypothesized to have stored in long-term memory a set of ideas (concepts) that are more or less relevant to the problem at hand. During brainstorming, those ideas are retrieved one at a time, and, depending on the availability of speaking turns, are presented to the group.

According to the AMM model, long-term memory is structured as an associative network (cf. Collins & Loftus, 1975), with the basic unit of organization being the semantic category. Ideas from the same semantic category are presumed to be more strongly associated—in the sense of being better retrieval cues for one another—than ideas from different semantic categories. The strength of these associations helps to determine the order in which ideas are accessed, according to the principle of spreading acti-vation. That is, when an idea is retrieved, other ideas become activated in proportion to the strength of their association with the already-retrieved idea (cue). Ideas that are strongly associated are more strongly activated and so have a higher probability of being retrieved next. Ideas that are weakly associated are only weakly activated and so have a lower prob-ability of being retrieved next. People are assumed to retrieve first those ideas that are most strongly activated, then gradually move to less and less strongly activated ideas, until they either run out of ideas or there is insuf-ficient activation to access them, at which point idea generation stops. One implication of this architecture is that, other things being equal, people will tend to generate a string of ideas, one after another, from the same semantic category before moving on to generate additional ideas from other categories.

The strength of the connections among ideas in long-term memory can be represented at the semantic category level by means of an $n \times (n + 1)$ matrix of category transition probabilities. It is from this matrix that the AMM model derives its name. Such a matrix is illustrated in Figure 3.1 for a very simple problem that involves just four relevant semantic cat-egories (e.g., for the problem "What things might be done to improve your university?" imagine that there are only four relevant categories of ideas: those concerning [A] course offerings, [B] extracurricular activities, [C] the university's physical plant [e.g., buildings, grounds, etc.], and [D] student financial matters). Each entry in the matrix expresses the probability of the next idea being retrieved from its column ("Next") category given that the last idea was retrieved from its row ("Previous") category. For exam-ple, according to Figure 3.1, if the previous idea was drawn from Category A, then there is a .6 probability that the next idea also will be drawn from Category A, a .3 probability that it will be drawn instead from Category B, and 0 probability that it will be drawn from either Category C or Category D. Note that there is one extra column category—the "Null" category. The values in this column represent the probability that, given an idea that

		Next Category				
		A	B	C	D	Null
Previous Category	A	.6	.3	.0	.0	.1
	B	.2	.5	.0	.0	.3
	C	.1	.1	.6	.1	.1
	D	.1	.1	.0	.5	.3

FIGURE 3.1 A hypothetical category transition probability matrix for the Associative Memory Matrix (AMM) model of group brainstorming.

was just retrieved from the row category, no further ideas at all will be drawn. The matrix entries thus reflect the relative strength of association among ideas both within and between categories for a single individual. Differences among individuals can be captured by varying the pattern of matrix entries. For example, a divergent thinker, in comparison to a convergent thinker, would be represented by lower within-category (diagonal) and higher between-category (off-diagonal) transition probabilities (cf. Coskun, 2005a).

Two concepts that are crucial to the AMM model are category fluency and category accessibility. *Category fluency* refers to the probability of retrieving another idea (from any category), given that the last idea came from the category in question (e.g., Category A's fluency is the probability of retrieving another idea from any category given that the last idea came from Category A). Category fluency is thus the overall extent to which ideas drawn from a given category spark additional ideas. Each category has its own fluency, which can be determined from the transition probability matrix by summing the row probabilities for that category, excluding its null probability.[13] According to Paulus and Brown (2003), category fluency is a function of the amount of knowledge the person has about the problem and its categories; the more knowledge a person has, the more likely he or she will be able to retrieve additional ideas.

Category accessibility, on the other hand, refers to the probability of retrieving the next idea from the category in question, given that the last idea came from a different category (e.g., Category A's accessibility is the probability of retrieving the next idea from Category A, given that the last idea came from some category other than A). Category accessibility is thus the extent to which ideas from one category are sparked by ideas from other categories. Like fluency, each category has its own accessibility, which can be determined from the transition probability matrix by summing the column probabilities for that category, excluding its within-category probability. Brown et al. (1998) argue that people are less likely to examine the content of semantic categories that have low accessibility. Thus, for the example given in Figure 3.1, Categories A and B are more accessible than Categories C and D, implying that the person represented by this matrix is more likely to retrieve ideas from the former pair of categories than from the latter pair. It is important to recognize, however, that low category accessibility does not necessarily imply low category fluency. As Figure 3.1 illustrates, Category C is much less accessible (.0) than Category A (.4), yet the two have equal fluency (.9). The same relationship holds for Categories D and B, respectively. One implication of this is that, although a brainstormer may be less likely to consider certain semantic categories (due to low accessibility), when those categories are in fact considered, they may easily lead to additional ideas if they have high fluency. As discussed below, it is precisely for this reason that group brainstorming is hypothesized to facilitate idea generation.

Thus, according to the AMM model, the semantic category from which a brainstormer's next idea will be drawn is determined by (a) the category from which the previous idea was drawn, along with (b) the transition probabilities associated with that category. This is a straightforward notion when applied to individual brainstorming. When applied to group brainstorming, however, the situation is more complex. According to the model, when brainstormers work in groups, the ideas spoken by others can supplant a member's own most-recently-retrieved idea in determining the semantic category from which his or her next idea will be drawn. But this depends on the degree to which the member pays attention to what others in the group have to say. The more attention he or she pays, the greater the likelihood that his or her own next idea will be influenced by the category membership of the spoken idea. Thus, in a group brainstorming context, the term "previous category" may be interpreted as referring either to the category membership of the brainstormer's own last-retrieved idea or to the category membership of the idea just spoken by someone else. When it is the latter, brainstormers are more likely to retrieve ideas from categories that, for them, might otherwise not be very accessible. This will be true to the extent that members differ in the degree to which they can access various semantic categories. In other words, what is "stimulating" about group brainstorming, according to the AMM model, is that it increases members' use of their own low-accessibility semantic categories—categories they would have been less likely to use had they brainstormed alone.

A Computational Approach

Brown et al. (1998) breathe life into these ideas by expressing them as a computational model—a computer program. In this form, the AMM model can be "run" in order to simulate group brainstorming. The output from a large number of such simulations can then be examined to see exactly how the model's several variables interact. Their computational model organizes the brainstorming session into a series of discrete time intervals. During each interval, each member may retrieve at most one new idea from long-term memory, and may retrieve no idea at all. If an idea is retrieved, the member then competes for a speaking turn with all other members who have also retrieved an idea during that interval. That is, consistent with the observation that in real brainstorming groups members generally do not speak simultaneously, the computational model allows only one member to announce his or her idea during each time interval, with the speaker determined randomly.[14] The announced idea is counted as an idea generated by the group as a whole. In contrast, the ideas retrieved by those who lose the speaking-turn competition (listeners) are not announced, and are not counted as ideas generated by the group as a whole. During the next time interval, the semantic category from which each individual retrieves his or her next idea is then determined stochastically, based on the previous idea category and on the entries in the member's transition probability matrix.[15] For the member who just spoke, the previous category is defined simply as the category from which his or her own just-spoken idea was retrieved.[16] Thus, for the speaker, the next category is determined in exactly the same way it would be determined if he or she were brainstorming alone. For each listener, on the other hand, the previous category is defined by the category membership of the speaker's idea with a probability of a, and by the category membership of the listener's own most recently retrieved (but unspoken) idea with a probability of $1 - a$, where a is an attention parameter that can range from 0 to 1. Values of $a > .5$ imply paying more attention to the ideas spoken by others, whereas values of $a < .5$ imply paying more attention to one's own ideas. Finally, because in real brainstorming groups idea generation does not continue indefinitely, the category transition probabilities are gradually depreciated as ideas are retrieved one after another during successive time intervals, and the null category probabilities are correspondingly increased. Consequently, as the brainstorming session progresses, the probability of retrieving no idea at all during a given time interval slowly rises. Brainstorming ends when, during a given time interval, no member is able to retrieve an idea.

The results obtained from the AMM model simulations are generally consistent with empirical findings. First, they show evidence of strong production blocking in group brainstorming. Simulated brainstormers contribute (speak) fewer ideas per person when brainstorming interactively in simulated groups than when brainstorming alone. In one case, for example, simulated individual brainstormers contributed an average of 34 ideas (100% of the ideas they retrieved), whereas each member in simulated four-person interactive brainstorming groups contributed fewer than 18 ideas on average (i.e., less than 50% of the ideas they retrieved). This difference is quite consistent with the differences found between real individual (nominal) and group brainstormers (e.g., see Tables 3.1 and 3.2).

Second, the AMM model simulations also reveal compositional and convergence effects consistent with empirical findings. Regarding group composition, simulated brainstormers contribute (speak) more ideas in interactive groups when others in the group are *not* similar to them (where similarity is defined in terms of the members' transition probability matrices). This parallels the results obtained with real brainstorming groups. For example, Diehl (1992, as cited in Stroebe & Diehl, 1994) found that groups with heterogeneous composition—where different members had ready access to different problem-relevant semantic categories—generated more ideas than did groups with homogeneous composition. Regarding convergence, simulated group brainstormers who pay close attention to what others have to say (i.e., high values of a) tend to contribute (speak) ideas from fewer semantic categories than when they brainstorm alone. That is, they converge on a smaller set of categories as the sources of their ideas. A similar trend has been noted among real brainstorming groups (Brown et al., 1998; Ziegler, Diehl, & Zijlstra, 2000), although the just-cited study by Diehl (1992) suggests that this effect may be limited mainly to groups that are homogeneous in composition.

Finally, and most importantly for our purposes here, the AMM model simulations also reveal a significant cognitive stimulation effect for group brainstorming: simulated brainstormers retrieve more ideas per person (whether spoken or not) when brainstorming in groups than when brainstorming alone. For example, in the same simulation as described above, whereas brainstormers who worked alone retrieved an average of 34 ideas each, those who worked in four-person interactive groups retrieved an average of 40 ideas each, an 18% increase (though as noted, they actually contributed less than half of these). This improvement conforms to Osborn's (1953, 1957) initial belief that idea generation in groups is more productive than idea generation done individually. It also accords with the findings from real brainstormers reported by Dugosh, Paulus, Roland, and Yang (2000). They had participants brainstorm the Taylor et al. (1958) "thumbs" problem either alone in the usual manner or alone while listening to a recording of stimulus ideas attributed to prior brainstormers. This manipulation varied the opportunity for cognitive stimulation, but did so in a way that eliminated many of the production-blocking problems associated with interactive groups. It was found that participants generated more new ideas when listening to the recording than when not listening, but only when they had an incentive to pay attention to what was being said. Dugosh and Paulus (2005) performed a similar experiment, but exposed individual brainstormers to either a large or small number of stimulus ideas. They found that participants generated more ideas of their own when exposed to the larger number of stimulus ideas, particularly when those stimulus ideas were common rather than unusual. Common ideas, compared to unusual ideas, are presumed to have a stronger associative connection to other ideas.

The AMM model thus accounts for a number of findings concerning the ideational performance of individuals and interacting groups. Most importantly, it can reproduce the common finding that interacting groups perform less well on brainstorming tasks than do nominal groups of the same size. This performance gap, according to the model, is a direct result of production blocking. That the model is able to show the negative impact of production blocking at the group level, while at the same time demonstrating an individual-level cognitive stimulation effect, is especially noteworthy, because it offers hope that synergy in real group brainstorming may still be possible if the untoward impact of production blocking can be brought under control.

At the same time, at least two limitations of the AMM model can be identified. The first is its assumption that problem-relevant ideas are stored fully formed in long-term memory, and need only be retrieved in order to be useful. This seems overly simplistic. Brainstormers often come up with completely novel solutions to problems that have not previously been encountered. Although the generation of such solutions undoubtedly relies on memory processes, it is unclear how truly novel ideas might be "remembered." The second limitation of the AMM model is its narrow view of production blocking in groups. According to the model, production blocking occurs only because brainstormers are unable to contribute all of the ideas that they individually can produce. There is no hint in the model that brainstorming in an interactive context may also interfere with the very process of idea generation. Both of these limitations are addressed in an alternative model that is considered next.

The Search for Ideas in Associative Memory (SIAM) Model

Nijstad and Stroebe (2006; Nijstad, Diehl, & Stroebe, 2003) have recently introduced an alternative model of idea generation in groups called the Search for Ideas in Associative Memory (SIAM) model. Similar to AMM, SIAM assumes that idea generation is heavily dependent on the retrieval of concepts from long-term memory. Further, it also assumes that long-term memory is organized as an associative network. However, instead of semantic categories, SIAM takes "images" as the basic unit of organization (cf. Raaijmakers & Shiffrin, 1981).[17] An image consists of learned information about a topic. Thus, each image involves a central concept, plus a number of associated (learned) "features." For example, the concept "university" may have associated with it such features as "campus," "courses," "classrooms," "laboratories," "dormitories," and "dining halls."

According to the SIAM model, idea generation is a controlled, associative process that takes place in two distinct stages. In the first stage, relevant images are retrieved from long-term memory. As in the AMM model, this process is viewed as both probabilistic and dependent on a retrieval cue. However, unlike AMM, which takes as the retrieval cue the previously retrieved idea, SIAM presumes that the retrieval cue is a separate entity constructed in working memory using effortful mental processes. That retrieval cue may contain elements of previously activated images and ideas. In the case of group brainstorming, this includes ideas proposed by other group members. In addition, because the to-be-retrieved information must be relevant to the problem at hand, the retrieval cue is also presumed to contain elements of the problem definition. The SIAM model postulates that these various elements are combined to produce a retrieval cue that then triggers the retrieval of an image from long-term memory. It is this effortful construction of retrieval cues that brings the overall idea-generation process at least partially under volitional control.

Using the retrieval cue, an image is recalled from long-term memory with a probability proportional to the combined strength of the associative links between the elements of the retrieval cue and the features of the image. Thus, image accessibility depends on the nature of the retrieval cue. Once recalled, the image is available in working memory, where it is employed to generate ideas. Idea generation is thus the second stage of the model. SIAM assumes that any given image contains many different features that can be combined in numerous ways, both with one another and with elements of the retrieval cue, in order to produce new ideas (cf. Goldenberg, Mazursky, & Solomon, 1999; Mednick, 1962; Simonton, 2003). Consequently, brainstormers are expected to be able to generate multiple ideas from the same image, and to do so relatively quickly. Further, because these ideas are based on the same cluster of information, they are likely to be semantically related and so form a "train of thought."

As ideas are generated one after another from a given image, SIAM predicts that it will gradually become more and more difficult to generate additional new ideas. This is because brainstormers will slowly run out of novel ways to combine the image features. At some point, new ideas will become so difficult to generate that the brainstormer will abandon the current image and will try to restart the process by retrieving a new image using a new retrieval cue. Once retrieved, the new image will spawn a new set of ideas (a new train of thought), until it, too, gradually yields less and less fruit and so is abandoned for yet another image. Finally, as one image after another is brought into working memory and mined for ideas, the SIAM model predicts that it will become increasingly difficult to retrieve new, not previously used images (cf. Raaijmakers & Shiffrin, 1981; Smith, 2003). At some point, this will become so difficult that the brainstormer will stop trying altogether, and the entire idea generation process will come to a halt.

Thus, according to the SIAM model, idea generation involves a two-stage process: (a) a controlled, effortful, cue-dependent, knowledge-activation stage, followed by (b) an idea-generation stage in which problem solutions are produced quickly by means of relatively automatic mental manipulations of that now-activated knowledge. Like AMM, SIAM assumes an associative network architecture in long-term memory. But unlike AMM, it calls attention to the purposeful construction of retrieval cues and to the active manipulation of retrieved information in working memory. These differences lead to several novel predictions about idea generation, in both individual and collaborative brainstorming contexts.

SIAM and Individual Brainstorming

When people brainstorm individually, SIAM, like AMM, predicts semantic clustering in idea production, such that successively generated ideas are more likely to belong to the same rather than to different semantic categories. However, the basis for this prediction is rather different in the two models. In the AMM model, semantic clustering is predicted because ideas from the same category are presumed to be more strongly associated in long-term memory than ideas from different categories. In the SIAM model, on the other hand, semantic clustering is predicted because the process of generating ideas from an already-activated image in working memory (second stage) is presumed to be easier than the process of retrieving new images from long-term memory (first stage). The mental manipulation of information in working memory is thought to be a relatively automatic process that requires little in the way of conscious, effortful control. As such, it should be possible to generate several ideas from the same image in quick succession. Those ideas are apt to be semantically related simply because they are based on the same cluster of information. In contrast, ideas that are generated from different images are less likely to be semantically related. Further, in order to produce the latter, a separate retrieval cue would have to be constructed for each image, with each retrieval cue used in a separate search of long-term memory. These take both time and effort, making it more burdensome to generate successive ideas from different images than to generate them from the same image. Consequently, semantic clustering is predicted.

For exactly the same reasons, the SIAM model also predicts that semantic clustering will be accompanied by temporal clustering. Specifically, the average time lag between the production of successive ideas from the same semantic cluster is predicted to be shorter than the average time lag between the production of successive ideas from different semantic clusters. These two kinds of clustering, semantic and temporal, are illustrated in Figure 3.2. Finally, because of the expected connection between semantic and temporal clustering, the SIAM model also predicts that semantic clustering will be associated with greater overall ideational productivity. That is, it predicts a positive correlation between the degree of semantic clustering and the total number of ideas generated within a given period of time. More clustering implies quicker, more efficient idea generation, which should result in the production of more ideas per unit of time. Although the AMM model is not very explicit about temporal matters, it might make the opposite predictions: a negative relationship between semantic and temporal clustering, and a negative relationship between

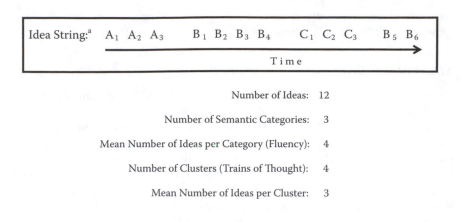

<table>
<tr><td>Idea String:[a]</td><td>A₁ A₂ A₃</td><td>B₁ B₂ B₃ B₄</td><td>C₁ C₂ C₃</td><td>B₅ B₆</td></tr>
</table>

Idea String:[a] A_1 A_2 A_3 B_1 B_2 B_3 B_4 C_1 C_2 C_3 B_5 B_6

T i m e

Number of Ideas:	12
Number of Semantic Categories:	3
Mean Number of Ideas per Category (Fluency):	4
Number of Clusters (Trains of Thought):	4
Mean Number of Ideas per Cluster:	3

[a] Different letters in the idea string refer to different semantic categories, and subscripts identify individual ideas within a semantic category. Larger gaps in the horizontal spacing between ideas indicate larger temporal lags in idea production.

FIGURE 3.2 Coding for a hypothetical string of ideas.

semantic clustering and the total number of ideas generated within a given period of time. This is because semantic clustering implies deeper sampling of fewer semantic categories, which in turn means longer and longer lag times as one struggles to retrieving more and more ideas from the same category. In contrast, retrieving a series of ideas from many different categories means not having to sample any one of those categories very deeply, which in turn suggests generally shorter retrieval times.

Empirical evidence from studies conducted with individual brainstormers working at computer terminals (so their response latencies could be recorded) supports the predictions of the SIAM model. In four separate experiments Nijstad, Stroebe, and Lodewijkx (2002, 2003) found that the sequence of ideas generated by participants displayed the predicted semantic clustering (i.e., discernable trains of thought were evident), that participants' within-cluster response latencies were shorter than their between-cluster latencies, and that the degree of semantic clustering was correlated with the total number of ideas they generated. Across experiments, these three effects were not only statistically significant, they were all descriptively large, with effect sizes ranging from $d = .9$ to 1.9 (Nijstad & Stroebe, 2006).[18]

SIAM and Group Brainstorming

The same idea-generation processes described above are also presumed to operate when people brainstorm interactively in groups. However, and

as previously discussed, two things happen during group brainstorming that do not occur when people brainstorm alone: (a) group members
often delay expressing their ideas until others have stopped talking, and
(b) members get exposed to the ideas put forth by others. Like AMM,
SIAM suggests that the first of these (speaking turn delays) is the root
cause of production blocking and so inhibits ideational productivity in
groups, whereas the second (being exposed to the ideas of others) is a
source of cognitive stimulation and so promotes ideational productivity
in groups. The two models differ, however, in how they assume these
effects are generated. The difference is clearest in the case of production
blocking. Whereas the AMM model conceptualizes production blocking
solely in terms of members' inability to contribute all of the ideas that
they individually generate, the SIAM model suggests that production
blocking can take two different forms. On the one hand, SIAM presumes
that production blocking occurs in part due to forgetting. Because some
of the ideas held in working memory during speaking turn delays are
apt to be forgotten, SIAM, like AMM, predicts that group members will
often end up contributing fewer ideas than they actually generated (i.e.,
fewer than they would have generated had they brainstormed alone).
On the other hand, and unlike AMM, SIAM presumes that production
blocking can also occur by directly interfering with the idea generation
process. When members find it necessary to delay expressing their ideas,
they must simultaneously hold those ideas in working memory, monitor
the conversation for an opportunity to speak, and listen to the ideas suggested by others. Not only do these activities put their own ideas at risk
of being forgotten, they impose a cognitive load that consumes resources
that otherwise might be devoted to constructing image retrieval cues. The
greater the cognitive load, the more difficult retrieval-cue construction
should become. Thus, within any given period of time, members should
be able to retrieve fewer images when brainstorming in groups than when
brainstorming alone, which in turn should lead them to produce fewer
ideas when brainstorming in groups.

Nijstad and Stroebe (2006) suggest that evidence of the separate operation of these two forms of production blocking can be found by examining
the semantic structure underlying the set of ideas contributed by a person when brainstorming in a group versus alone. Specifically, they argue
that because ideas created from the same image are apt to be semantically
related, any process that reduces the number of images a brainstormer
retrieves should also tend to reduce the number of semantic categories
found among the ideas he or she eventually generates. Thus, if speaking-
turn delays interfere with image retrieval, the ideas a person contributes
should fall into fewer semantic categories when brainstorming in groups
than when brainstorming alone. Further, because ideas created from the
same image are likely to be generated in relatively quick succession, any

forgetting that occurs should tend to cut short a brainstormer's train of thought. Thus, if speaking- turn delays cause forgetting, the set of ideas a person contributes should yield shorter strings of successive, semantically-related ideas when brainstorming in groups than when brainstorming alone. Nijstad, Stroebe, and Lodewijkx (2003) present empirical evidence consistent with both predictions (see also Nijstad & Stroebe, 2006). The prediction about cluster length might also be made by the AMM model. It is less clear, on the other hand, how the prediction regarding number of semantic categories could be made by that model.

Finally, although listening to others state their ideas can lead to speaking-turn delays and production blocking, the SIAM model predicts that the ideas themselves can lead to cognitive stimulation and so benefit ideational productivity. Specifically, the ideas put forth by others can be added to a member's retrieval cue and so can affect the image that is next retrieved. Consequently, SIAM predicts that brainstormers will generate more semantically diverse ideas when exposed to ideas that come from a wide range of semantic categories. The same prediction is made by the AMM model. In addition, however, because exposure to the ideas of others should make it easier for brainstormers to construct new retrieval cues, SIAM makes the unique prediction that the time lag between the end of one string of semantically-related ideas (i.e., a train of thought derived from a single image) and the start of the next string should be shorter when brainstormers are exposed to the ideas of others. This, in turn, should increase the number of ideas they generate. Again, there is empirical evidence consistent with both predictions (e.g., Diehl, 1992, as cited in Stroebe & Diehl, 1994; Nijstad, Stroebe, & Lodewijkx, 2002). It is important to note, however, that this evidence is derived from studies using research methodologies that minimized the possibility of speaking-turn delays. Had speaking turn-delays not been controlled in these studies, the benefits of cognitive stimulation would likely have been obscured by the negative effects of production blocking.

In summary, whereas the SIAM model makes many of the same predictions as does the AMM model, it makes certain additional predictions that cannot easily be derived from AMM. The latter have mainly to do with details found in the semantic structure of the ideas that brainstormers contribute and suggest a conceptual advantage for the SIAM model. However, the question of which model is superior is far from settled, and much research remains to be done. Furthermore, there is an important point of agreement between these two models: Both predict a cognitive stimulation effect in brainstorming groups. As such, they each hold out hope that, if the deleterious effects of production blocking (and motivation loss) can be controlled, the benefits of cognitive stimulation might be realized.

☐ Toward Synergy: Capitalizing On Cognitive Stimulation

The picture painted by the two cognitive models reviewed in the foregoing section is one of conflicting effects in brainstorming groups. On the
one hand, there is reason to believe that exposure to the ideas of others
can benefit ideational productivity. On the other hand, there is substantial
evidence that unstructured face-to-face interaction among group members is a flawed vehicle for delivering this benefit. The challenge, then, is
to find ways to minimize the weaknesses associated with group interaction that do not at the same time sacrifice its strengths. Here, I consider
two approaches that appear able to meet this challenge.

Electronic Brainstorming: A Technological Fix

The first approach makes use of computer technology to eliminate the
root source of production blocking that stymies the typical face-to-face
brainstorming group. Thus, rather than gathering around a common
table, group members sit at separate computer workstations, with all communication between them conducted electronically. In principle, these
computers may be located anywhere. The only requirement is that they
be networked in some fashion and that the members all engage the brainstorming task at the same time. On each member's screen are two win-
dows; one for entering ideas and another for displaying the ideas entered
by others.[19] When a member enters an idea, that idea is displayed for
everyone else in the group to see. In turn, that member is able to see all
of the ideas entered by everyone else. Importantly, these two functions
are independent of one another. Thus, each member can enter an idea at
any time, without regard to what others are doing at the moment, and the
ideas of others are displayed as soon as they are entered, regardless of
what each member might be doing. The independence of these two functions is crucial, as it effectively eliminates the main source of production
blocking in interactive groups; there is no need to wait for others to finish
contributing their ideas before contributing one's own. Rather, ideas can
be contributed the moment they come to mind, and this can occur without
fear of missing any of the ideas contributed by others. Further, because
the ideas of others are typically stored in such a way that one can scroll
back through all of them at any time, there is a greater likelihood than in
standard face-to-face brainstorming that ideas created early in the session
might stimulate new ideas much later on (i.e., because those early ideas
are less subject to forgetting when brainstorming electronically).

It is important to recognize, however, that electronic brainstorming comes with its own unique form of production blocking. Current technology requires electronic brainstormers to type their ideas into the computer using a standard keyboard. This is obviously slower than speaking one's ideas out loud, as is usually done in face-to-face brainstorming groups.[20] Thus, a legitimate question is whether electronic brainstorming is really any more productive than brainstorming in face-to-face groups, much less in nominal groups (i.e., individual brainstorming).

Published research comparing the ideational productivity of electronic brainstorming groups with that of same-sized face-to-face brainstorming groups began to appear in the early 1990s. Dennis and Williams (2005) recently conducted a meta-analytic review of this literature, identifying 22 such comparisons. With only a few exceptions, these studies found that electronic brainstorming was more productive than face-to-face brainstorming. The exceptions all involved groups that were very small (two or three persons). Thus, in groups with three or fewer members, electronic brainstorming proved to be less effective than face-to-face brainstorming. But for groups of four or more, electronic brainstorming was consistently more productive than face-to-face brainstorming. Dennis and Williams report effect sizes that average above $d = 1.5$. Indeed, for relatively large groups (size = 10 to 12) the effect sizes average about $d = 3.0$.

That the effectiveness of electronic brainstorming relative to face-to-face brainstorming might depend on group size is easily explained. The liabilities associated with having to announce ideas out loud in a face-to-face brainstorming group increase with group size; the larger the group, the greater the competition among members for speaking turns, and so the more frequent and longer the speaking-turn delays. In contrast, the liabilities associated with having to type one's ideas into a computer when brainstorming electronically do not change with group size; typing is undoubtedly slower than speaking, but this difference remains constant regardless of the size of the group. Comparing these two kinds of liabilities—those arising from speaking turn delays and those connected with typing speed—it can be inferred that the latter are greater than the former when the size of the groups is very small. However, as the size of the group grows larger, the impediments connected with speaking turn delays increase exponentially and soon surpass those associated with having to type one's ideas. Consequently, for very small groups, face-to-face brainstorming is more efficient than electronic brainstorming, but for larger groups the tables are turned, with electronic brainstorming being more efficient than face-to-face brainstorming.

A slightly different pattern emerges when the ideational productivity of electronic brainstorming groups is compared with that of same-sized nominal groups. In their meta-analytic review, Dennis and Williams (2005) identified 14 such comparisons and found that nominal group brainstorming was superior to electronic group brainstorming most of the time. Electronic brainstorming groups generated more ideas in only five studies. Importantly, however, every one of those five studies employed groups with nine or more members. Further, none of the studies in which nominal groups were superior involved groups with more than eight members (see also Dennis & Williams, 2003). In other words, for groups of up to eight members, nominal group brainstorming was found to be superior, but for groups of nine or more, electronic brainstorming was found to be superior. For the latter studies, the effect sizes favoring electronic brainstorming averaged above $d = 1.0$.

The members of nominal groups, of course, suffer no liabilities associated with speaking turn delays and should be able to contribute ideas at least as quickly, if not more so, than those who brainstorm electronically. On the other hand, nominal groups cannot benefit from the cognitive stimulation that comes with exposure to the ideas of others. In electronic brainstorming groups, by contrast, such stimulation increases with group size; the larger the group, the larger the pool of potentially stimulating ideas that each member is exposed to. Consequently, although having to type their ideas apparently puts small- and moderate-size electronic brainstorming groups at a disadvantage relative to similar-size nominal groups, larger electronic brainstorming groups apparently supply enough cognitive stimulation that they are able to overcome this disadvantage and so be more productive than similar-size nominal groups. It may be no coincidence that these larger groups approach the size originally suggested by Osborn (1953, 1957) as being optimal for effective group brainstorming.

Brainwriting: A Low-Tech Alternative

Speaking turn delays occur in standard brainstorming groups only because members are forced to share an important resource: speaking time. They are strongly interdependent in terms of their use of this resource; members can use it only when no one else in the group is doing so. Electronic brainstorming effectively removes this interdependence, allowing members to "speak" whenever they want. An alternative procedure that accomplishes much the same end but without relying on sophisticated computer technology is called *brainwriting*.

Brainwriting actually refers to a family of techniques, all of which differ from standard group brainstorming in that members are prohibited from talking with one another as they work. Instead, they must share their ideas by writing them down (VanGundy, 1981). In one version of this technique, the members of the brainwriting group are seated around a common table, and each has a supply of blank paper. The instructions given to the group include the usual four rules of brainstorming (i.e., regarding the suppression of criticism, the importance of quantity, and the desirability of both free-wheeling and improving on the ideas of others). But, instead of speaking their ideas out loud, members are asked to write each idea on a sheet of paper, then pass that paper to the person on their right. Thus, each member simultaneously passes and receives a sheet of paper. Members then read the idea written on the sheet they receive and, if possible, add a new idea to it. They then pass this piece of paper, now with two ideas written on it, to the person on their right. This process is repeated until each sheet travels all the way around the table and is again in the hands of the person who wrote the first idea. At this point, members read over all of the ideas written on the paper they are holding, set that sheet aside, and write another new idea on a fresh sheet of paper. The new sheet is then passed around as before, with each member adding a new idea. This entire process is continued until the allotted time for idea generation expires.

Paulus and Yang (2000) conducted a study that employed exactly this procedure, asking four-person groups to generate as many uses as possible for a paper clip. The performance of these brainwriting groups was compared to that of four-person nominal groups, who also recorded their ideas on paper. It was found that the brainwriting groups on average generated 41% more ideas than did the nominal groups. This effect is not only opposite in direction to what typically is found with brainstorming groups, it is both statistically significant and descriptively large (the effect size was nearly $d = 1.3$). What is more, when these participants were asked in a second session to work independently to generate additional ideas for the same problem (i.e., all participants now worked under constraints identical to the nominal group condition in the first session), those who formerly had been in the brainwriting condition generated nearly twice as many additional ideas as those who formerly had been in the nominal group condition.

These results appear to be a clear and powerful demonstration of cognitive stimulation, and, in contrast to electronic brainstorming, they were achieved with relatively small groups. Indeed, differences comparable to those just described have been reported for groups as small as two persons (Coskun, 2005b; but see also Coskun 2005a). Paulus and Yang (2000) argue that one advantage of brainwriting over electronic brainstorming is that the brainwriting procedure compels group members to attend to the ideas of others, and to do so in relatively small batches (1 to 3 ideas per sheet in their study). Electronic brainstorming, by contrast, makes the ideas of others available but typically does not force members actually to read or think about those ideas. Thus, relative to electronic brainstormers, brainwriters may spend more time considering the ideas of others, or may consider more of them.

In summary, for groups that are geographically dispersed and routinely communicate electronically, electronic brainstorming may be a convenient way to capitalize on the cognitive stimulation that members can provided one another, especially when the group is reasonably large. On the other hand, for smaller groups, and groups that typically interact face-to-face, brainwriting may be the better alternative. Although further investigation into both techniques is warranted, especially brainwriting, the evidence currently available indicates that both have the potential to help groups achieve genuine gains in ideational productivity, gains that go beyond what the members are able to achieve as individuals. These techniques, in other words, suggest a clear way forward in the search for synergy in group performance.

☐ Quality Matters

The research literature, much like this chapter, has given primary emphasis to the *number* of ideas that small groups are able to generate. Considerably less attention has been paid to the *quality* of those ideas. Indeed, many studies fail even to measure the quality of the ideas that groups generate. This is surprising, given that in most real-world settings a premium is place on the quality of the ideas produced, not just their quantity (cf. Rowatt, Nesselroade, Beggan, & Allison, 1997). In this final section of the chapter, I address two quality-related issues: the possibility that quantity leads to quality, and whether groups are any better than individuals at identifying their high quality ideas.

Does Quantity Breed Quality?

The markedly greater emphasis in the research literature on ideational quantity relative to quality appears to be driven by the assumption that quantity and quality are related—that quantity begets quality. As noted previously, this idea has roots in Osborn's (1953; 1957) original theorizing about brainstorming.

The quantity-breeds-quality hypothesis takes two distinct forms. The weaker form states that, as the total number of ideas produced by a group goes up, so too does the number of high quality ideas they produce. High quality ideas are typically defined as those that exceed some predefined threshold when rated by expert judges on such factors as originality and feasibility. There is substantial evidence in support of this weak form. Among those studies that have measured both the quality and quantity of ideas produced, the total number of ideas generated and the number of high quality ideas generated are usually very highly correlated and typically respond in the same way to whatever experimental manipulation is introduced. Diehl and Stroebe (1987, 1991), for example, reported correlations exceeding $r = .80$. Indeed, these authors conclude that the two measures (total number of ideas and number of high quality ideas) are so strongly correlated that the additional information to be gained by analyzing a set of quality ratings is too small to justify the time and effort needed to obtain them. Whether or not this conclusion is warranted, it seems evident that, if groups can be made to generate more ideas, they will also tend to generate more high quality ideas.

Osborn (1953; 1957), however, subscribed to a stronger form of the quantity-breeds-quality hypothesis. He postulated that during an idea-generation session, relatively common, low quality ideas are easy to generate and so will tend to emerge first. As time goes by, however, he presumed that the supply of common ideas would run low, and that groups would begin to uncover more unusual, high quality ideas. Thus, he contended that, among the ideas coming to light during a brainstorming session, those that emerge later in the session should tend to be of higher quality than those that emerged earlier. Consequently, if groups can be made to generate more ideas, those additional ideas should be of higher average quality than the ones that were generated before them.

The empirical evidence that speaks to this stronger form of the quantity-breeds-quality hypothesis is decidedly mixed. The earliest evidence comes from a pair of studies by Parnes (1961). He had university students work individually to generate as many uses as possible for a plain wire coat hanger. They did this for either 5 minutes (Study 1) or 15 minutes (Study 2). In both cases, participants generated significantly more high quality ideas later in the session than earlier, just as the strong form of the hypothesis predicts.

Basadur and Thompson (1986), on the other hand, obtained quite different results. They had managerial and professional employees work either individually (Study 1) or in four-person groups (Study 2) to generate potential solutions to real problems relevant to their jobs. Afterwards, participants identified the single best idea from among those they had generated. Of primary interest in this study was whether the best ideas were more likely to come from the first third of all ideas generated for that problem, from the second third, or from the final third. It was found that, among individuals, the best ideas were approximately evenly distributed across these thirds. For groups, on the other hand, there was a clear and statistically significant tendency for the best idea to emerge earlier rather than later; the best idea appeared among the first third of the ideas generated 45% of the time, the second third 31% of the time, and the final third only 24% of the time. The pattern was the same even when the best *four* ideas generated by each group were examined. These results are clearly opposite to what is anticipated by the strong form of the quantity-breeds-quality hypothesis.

Further, a number of studies have examined the average quality of all the ideas generated by each group. If the strong form of the quantity-breeds-quality hypothesis is correct, then groups that generate more ideas should tend to have higher average quality scores than those that generate fewer ideas. For example, if nominal brainstorming groups are able to generate more ideas than standard interactive brainstormers, and if the strong form of the hypothesis holds, then one would expect the additional ideas produced by the nominal groups to raise the average quality of their contributions relative to that of interactive groups. But the empirical evidence does not bear this out. Rather, even when there are significant differences between treatment conditions with respect to both the total number of ideas generated and the number of high quality ideas generated, average idea quality tends not to differ. The data shown in Table 3.1 are an example of this.

A recent exception to this general trend is worth noting, however. Rietzschel, Nijstad, and Stroebe (2007) had individuals (Experiments 1 and 2) and dyads (Experiment 2) brainstorm about what people can do to maintain or improve their health. Just prior to brainstorming, their participants were primed to think about one specific category of health related behavior (e.g., nutrition vs. hygiene), or they were not primed at all. Priming was accomplished simply by asking participants to respond to several questions about their own health-related behavior (e.g., "How much time and attention do you usually devote to healthy nutrition [hygiene]? Please provide some examples of your behavior."). This manipulation increased the number of ideas generated in the primed category; primed individuals and dyads generated more ideas in the primed category than did nonprimed individuals and dyads. Further, among dyads this effect was strongest when both members were primed to think about the same category. Moreover, the average quality (defined as rated originality) of the ideas generated in a given category tended to be higher when that category was primed. Thus, priming increased both the quantity and the average quality of the ideas produced, just as the strong form of the quantity-breeds-quality hypothesis predicts. This occurred, however, only within the primed category, suggesting perhaps an important boundary condition for that hypothesis.

To summarize, whereas most of the available evidence supports the weak form of the quantity-breeds-quality hypothesis, support for the strong form is mixed. On the other hand, considerably less research has been done to test the strong form. Further, the evidence contrary to the strong form can be challenged on methodological grounds. Much of it is indirect and relies on statistical tests that have very low power (e.g., the above-mentioned data from studies that compare the overall average quality of ideas generated by interacting vs. nominal groups). Additionally, in some cases the quality measures themselves are suspect. For example, Basadur and Thompson (1986) relied on a measure of idea quality derived from the participants themselves. As will be explained shortly, there is good reason to be suspicious of such measures. These considerations, along with the results obtained by Rietzschel et al. (2007), suggest that additional research on the strong form of the quality-breeds-quantity hypothesis is warranted.

Selecting High Quality Ideas

Another legacy of Osborn's (1953, 1957) early theorizing that survives in the research literature is the near-exclusive focus on idea generation as opposed to idea selection. In particular, very little research has concerned itself with the ability of groups to evaluate and select from among the ideas they produce. Osborn, of course, believed that groups should refrain from evaluating their ideas while generating them, and suggested that by doing so groups will produce more and better solutions to the problem at hand. There is good evidence in support of this notion, at least with regard to the quantity of ideas produced (e.g., Buyer, 1988; Lamm & Trommsdorff; 1973; Meadow & Parnes, 1959; Meadow, Parnes, & Reese, 1959; Parnes & Meadow, 1959; Price, 1985). But in the real world it is not enough simply to generate lots of ideas. Decisions must be made about which of those ideas will be developed further and put into operation. Innovation in organizations, for example, depends at least as much on the implementation of creative ideas as it does on generating those ideas to begin with (West, 2002). Given that not all generated ideas can or should be implemented, it is necessary to choose among them. The question, then, is whether the selection of high quality ideas is benefited by group interaction.

As with idea generation in groups, questions about idea evaluation and selection are best addressed by including a nominal group in the research design. Only a very few studies have done this. The first appears to be a study by Williams and Sternberg (1988). Contrary to the Osborn approach, these authors had participants perform a task that combined idea generation and idea evaluation. Specifically, participants worked either in three-person nominal or interacting groups to generate the best solution they could to each of two problems. One required them to suggest how a particular community organization might best use its powers to help resolve a land-use conflict facing a rural town in northwest Connecticut. The other asked them to design a promotional program for a new artificial sweetener that can replace sugar in a variety of foods. Both problems were fairly complex, entailing multiple issues and constraints. For each problem, participants were given 30 minutes to prepare a one-to-two page report describing their proposed solution. Thus, it can be inferred that participants had to think up various ways that each problem might be solved, then select and describe the approach they believed was best. Those in interactive groups worked together to generate a single report for each problem, whereas those in nominal groups worked separately to produce three different reports. These reports were later rated for quality by an expert judge (where quality was defined as a linear combination of creativity, persuasiveness, practicality, and overall excellence). Williams and Sternberg found that the interacting groups generated reports that were of significantly higher quality than the average report generated by members of the nominal groups.

The results from this study seem to be evidence of synergy in group performance; the quality of the ideas actually put forth as suitable for implementation apparently did improve as a result of group interaction. However, Williams and Sternberg (1988) did not analyze their data in a way that enables us to distinguish whether their interactive groups displayed weak or strong synergy. Recall from Chapter 1 that weak synergy is defined as group performance that exceeds the performance of the typical group member when working alone, whereas strong synergy refers to group performance that exceeds the performance of even the best group member when working alone. The results presented by Williams and Sternberg clearly indicate that groups performed better than the typical member (viz. better than the average of the nominal groups), which suggests at least a weak form of synergy. However, because the performance of the interactive groups was not compared with that of the nominal groups' "best" members, it cannot be determined whether the requirements for strong synergy were met. That is, a rigorous test of strong synergy in this study requires that the best individual report from each of the three-person nominal groups be identified, and that the mean quality of the group reports be compared with the mean quality of these best-member reports. Strong synergy would be indicated only if the group mean is significantly higher than this best-member mean. Judging from the effect size obtained in this study, and using an analytic approach suggested by Steiner and Rajaratnam (1961), it seems likely that the mean group quality score would have been close to, but probably not significantly above, the mean best-member quality score. Thus, an educated guess is that the interactive groups in this study demonstrated weak synergy, not strong synergy. Still, even weak synergy can be of significant practical value.

The task employed by Williams and Sternberg (1988) can be understood as one that required participants to imagine alternative ways in which each problem might be solved, then select the approach they think is best. However, because participants were not asked to document the various solution alternatives they considered, there was no way in that study to determine either the number of solution alternatives generated or how that number might relate to the quality of what was eventually chosen for inclusion in the final reports. Two more recent studies address these issues.

Faure (2004) had business students work in four-person nominal or interactive groups to generate as many ideas as they could for stimulating greater European tourism in America. Recall that this is one of the problems used in the original brainstorming study by Taylor et al. (1958). It was presented in Faure's study as a marketing problem. After working at this task for 10 minutes, participants in both the nominal and interacting group conditions individually identified their five favorite ideas from among all those generated by their group as a whole. Then the members in each group (whether originally nominal or interactive) worked collaboratively to select the three best ideas from among those identified as favorites. All of the generated ideas were rated for quality by expert judges, where quality was defined in terms of practicality and effectiveness. The idea-generation results obtained in this study were quite consistent with most traditional brainstorming studies. Faure found that, relative to nominal groups, interacting groups generated fewer ideas overall, and fewer original ideas (defined as ideas suggested by less than 10% of all groups in her study). On the other hand, among those ideas select by groups as their three best, no quality differences of any kind were found between the interactive and nominal groups. Thus, having generated a smaller number of ideas to begin with seemed not to disadvantage interactive groups when it came time to select a few high quality ideas. Contrary to Williams and Sternberg (1988), however, Faure's interactive groups did not surpass the performance of her nominal groups. Perhaps this is because Faure's nominal groups ceased to be nominal when they selected their best ideas; idea selection was an interactive process in every group, including those that formerly were nominal during the idea-generating stage of her study. Thus, there may have been no performance differences in the idea-selection stage simply because by that time all of the groups employed the same interactive process for combining member inputs.

Rietzschel, Nijstad, and Stroebe (2006) also conducted a study that assessed both idea generation and idea selection in groups, but they used an experimental design that maintained the distinction between interactive and nominal groups throughout. They had students work in three-person nominal or interactive groups to generate ideas for improving education in their university's department of psychology. Afterwards, but still as either nominal or interacting groups, participants identified (and rank ordered) what they thought were their four best ideas. Once again, interactive groups generated fewer ideas than nominal groups. And once again there were no quality differences between the ideas that interactive and nominal groups identified as their best. Thus, even when the interactive–nominal distinction is maintained until the end, interactive groups could do no better than match the quality of nominal groups.

Thus, the study by Williams and Sternberg (1988) stands alone in suggesting that interactive groups may be better able than nominal groups to identify high quality ideas. There are, of course, many methodological differences between this study and those by Faure (2004) and Rietzschel et al. (2006), and it is possible that one or more of these differences may prove to be a crucial moderating variable. Still, based on what little research is currently available, it seems reasonable to conclude that group interaction does not always benefit the selection of high quality ideas.

☐ Chapter Summary

In this chapter, I have traced the main themes in the small group performance literature related to idea generation. I have focused in particular on empirical research that sheds light on the process gains and losses that occur as a result of working collaboratively to generate ideas. It is this work that best illuminates the progress that has been made in the search for synergy in group ideational performance.

This literature is dominated by the group brainstorming approach to ideation initially proposed by Osborn (1953, 1957). Thus, I began by describing Osborn's original ideas and presented in some detail the seminal empirical research that tested the effectiveness of group versus individual brainstorming. From the outset, the research findings strongly challenged Osborn's prediction: Under most circumstances, groups demonstrated a very strong tendency to generate fewer ideas than an equivalent number of individuals working independently. This result quickly established itself as *the* central finding in the literature. This counterintuitive result captured a great deal of attention as researchers absorbed themselves in identifying its underlying causes. Chief among these is production blocking, but evaluation apprehension, social loafing, free riding, and performance matching also play a role, and I summarized the research bearing on these causes. For much of the history of this literature, the prospects for synergy seemed bleak, to say the least.

Recently, however, several cognitive models of idea generation in groups have been proposed that suggest how process gains as well as process losses can arise from collective ideation. Further, techniques have begun to emerge that help groups actually realize the process gains (via cognitive stimulation) while minimizing the effects of process loss. I reviewed the empirical evidence demonstrating the effectiveness of these techniques.

Finally, I touched on two very under-studied topics that deserve more research attention. Both of these concern the quality of the ideas suggested by groups.

From our current vantage point, now more that 60 years after research on brainstorming first began, the prospects for synergy in group ideation appear slightly brighter than they once did. It is evident that group interaction poses a set of serious challenges to ideational creativity. On the other hand, recent advances in theory, technology, and methodology offer hope that these challenges can be overcome, and that at least a modicum of synergistic benefit can be reaped from the cognitive stimulation inherent in group settings. From both a practical and theoretical standpoint, it seems worthwhile to devote greater attention in the future to finding ways to realize these benefits.

☐ Endnotes

1. Recall that this task was mentioned at several points in Chapter 2 in connection with the discussion there of group task characteristics.
2. Although they do not say so explicitly, it seems likely that in the individual condition Taylor et al. (1958) modified the fourth rule of brainstorming (combinations and improvements are sought) to emphasize how the participant's own previously contributed ideas might be turned into better ideas, and how two or more of those ideas might be joined to form still another idea.
3 Recall that the use of nominal groups as a standard of comparison was introduced in Chapter 1 (see pp. 13–14).
4. An adjustment would also have to be made to account for the redundant ideas likely to be generated in a hypothetical group of best members.
5. Unlike the tourism and teacher shortage problems, which call for suggesting steps or approaches to solve a problem, the thumbs problem requires the anticipation of consequences. It is conceivable that this distinction signals the presence of an important task variable that gives an advantage to interacting relative to nominal groups as far as originality goes. Hackman (1968) found roughly similar results: When groups were required to generate ideas or images (e.g., "Write a story about …") they were judged significantly more original than when they were asked to develop a plan to achieve a goal (e.g., "Devise a way to …"). Recall that Hackman's (1968) study was discussed in the early pages of Chapter 2. This task effect appears never to have been systematically followed-up.
6. The value reported here is the mean standardized difference between group and individual brainstorming for the number of ideas generated. Mullen et al. (1991) found an effect of comparable magnitude for idea quality. Less confidence should be placed in this latter result, however, because their analysis appears to have included findings from a number of early studies that indexed idea quality by the sum of quality ratings across ideas. Such

an index is affected at least as much by the number of ideas generated as by their perceived quality, thus confounding its interpretation (cf. Footnote a in Table 3.1). Studies that use a summed index of this sort almost always report higher quality ideas for nominal than for interacting groups. In contrast, studies that report mean quality scores that are mathematically independent of the number of ideas generated tend not to find quality differences between the ideas of interacting and nominal groups.

7. Bond & van Leeuwen (1991) reanalyzed the studies reviewed by Mullen et al. (1991), using an alternative statistical methodology, and arrived at a somewhat different list of moderators. The two studies are in agreement, however, regarding the strength and consistency of the basic group-versus-individual brainstorming effect.

8. For any given set of evidence there is an unspecifiably large number of plausible hypotheses. For instance, given the 6, 10, and queen of hearts as positive exemplars of the rule, and the ace of diamonds and the 4 and 5 of clubs as negative exemplars, the rules "hearts," "values greater than 5," and "even red cards" are all plausible. Many more such rules can be imagined.

9. This argument hinges on the assumption that idea generation becomes more difficult as time goes on, implying that the rate of production gradually slows. This assumption is consistent with available evidence.

10. This prediction assumes either that there is a functional ceiling for evaluation apprehension, such that once that ceiling is achieved no higher levels are possible, or (more likely) that it becomes increasingly difficult to raise evaluation apprehension further as the baseline level of evaluation apprehension goes up.

11. It should be noted that although the three-way interaction described here is clearly visible by inspection of the cell means reported by Diehl and Stroebe (1987, Exp. 3), their study involved a relatively small number of participants (just two interacting or nominal groups per condition), so that there was insufficient power to detect that interaction statistically. Thus, these data should be interpreted cautiously.

12. This suggests an alternative explanation for the perceived-member-expertise effect observed in the previously cited study by Collaros and Anderson (1969).

13. Equivalently, a category's fluency is $1 - p(\text{Null})$ for that category.

14. Other decision rules might be used to determine who will speak, in order to simulate status differences or stable dispositional differences among members (e.g., with regard to social anxiety or social dominance).

15. For the very first time interval, the category is selected randomly from among all relevant categories, each weighted by its relative accessibility.

16. Coskun et al. (2000) proposed an extension to the AMM model that includes a short-term memory component. According to this extension, every time an idea is retrieved and/or spoken, it is added to short-term memory. There, ideas interact to determine what the "previous" category will be. In principle, short-term memory may contain ideas retrieved and/or spoken at any earlier time during the brainstorming session. However, there is a strong decay function associated with short-term memory, which in effect gives priority to more recent ideas. Thus, the "previous" category is much more likely to be defined by a recently retrieved or spoken idea than by an idea that was

retrieved or spoken some time ago. This decay function helps to explain the finding reported by Coskun et al. (2000) that, in real brainstorming groups, category priming (i.e., giving brainstormers the names of various categories from which they might retrieve their ideas) benefits ideational productivity more when the primes are presented sequentially over the course of the brainstorming session than when they are presented simultaneously at the beginning of the session. They are less effective in the latter case presumably because they decay in short-term memory before they can be fully exploited.

17. Although the term *image* suggests a visual or spatial representation of the learned information, the model itself makes no such assumption.

18. It is worth noting that the measure of clustering used in these studies, the Adjusted Ratio of Clustering (ARC) score, takes into account, and is mathematically independent of, the total number of ideas generated (Roenker, Thompson, & Brown, 1971). Thus, it seems unlikely that these correlations are an artifact of cluster measurement.

19. Although a number of software applications have been designed specifically for electronic brainstorming, there are also now available many general-purpose software tools that can easily be adapted to support electronic brainstorming (cf. Dennis & Williams, 2003).

20. This is not an inherent impediment of electronic brainstorming, but rather a limitation of current technology. It seems likely that in the not-too-distant future electronic brainstormers will be able to speak their ideas into the computer, with voice-recognition software used to translate their spoken words into text that can then be distributed to others on the network.

Problem Solving

Performing Tasks With Correct Solutions

This chapter is about group performance on problem-solving tasks, which is to say, cognitive endeavors that have as their goal the production of an objectively correct solution. These are also sometimes called *intellective tasks*, a term that refers broadly to their location on Laughlin's Intellective–Judgmental Task Continuum. As will be recalled from Chapter 2, Laughlin (1980, 1999; Laughlin & Ellis, 1986) suggested that cooperatively performed cognitive tasks can be meaningfully arrayed on a continuum anchored at one end by those that are purely intellective, and at the other by those that are purely judgmental. A purely intellective task is one where it is possible for group members to demonstrate to one another the correctness of a proposed solution (e.g., a simple arithmetic problem). A purely judgmental task, on the other hand, has no objectively correct solution (e.g., deciding whether Bach or Mozart was the greater composer). As such, on purely judgmental tasks it is impossible to conclusively demonstrate that one response is in fact better than another. The present chapter is concerned with group performance on tasks that are at or near the left-hand (intellective) end of this continuum.

Group performance on problem-solving tasks has most often been evaluated dichotomously as either correct or incorrect. This focus reflects the principal concern people have in real-world problem-solving situations. When, for example, a team of software engineers is dispatched to resolve an anomaly in a complex computer network, it is whether or not they can pinpoint the fault and restore the network to a functional state that is of greatest consequence. Although other aspects of their performance may also be of interest (e.g., the speed or efficiency with which they complete their task), it is whether they are able to solve the problem at all that is of paramount concern. A substantial portion of the empirical literature dealing with group problem-solving effectiveness focuses on task performance that is evaluated dichotomously in this way, although recently there have been several important developments in the literature that concern problem solving efficiency.

In the first section of this chapter, I review some of the early literature on group problem solving, concentrating on research that bears most directly on the question of synergistic performance gains in groups. Virtually all of that work takes the dichotomous, correct-versus-incorrect approach to evaluating group performance. I emphasize there the conceptual and analytic development of several formal models of group performance. These models have had a major impact on the way we think about group performance gains on problem-solving tasks. After that, I turn to two more-recent streams of research that involve fairly complex, iterative problem-solving tasks, and that examine the efficiency with which groups solve problems as well as their ability simply to identify the correct solution. As will be seen, it is one of these latter programs of research that provides the most compelling evidence of strong synergy in group problem-solving performance.

□ Formal Models of Group Problem-Solving Performance

A classic problem-solving task often used in laboratory research is the husbands-and-wives transfer problem shown in Figure 4.1. The goal in this task is to transfer three couples from one bank of a river to the other without violating any of the social or physical restrictions described. When confronted with this problem, people either do or do not solve it; there is no middle ground. As such, groups and individuals are usually compared in terms of overall solution rates. Questions about synergy therefore turn on the proportion of groups versus the proportion of individuals that are able to solve the problem correctly.

The earliest research in this area compared solution rates for groups and individuals directly. For example, Marjorie Shaw (1932) found that 60% of four-person groups solved the husbands-and-wives transfer problem correctly, whereas only 14% of individuals did so. Other investigators have similarly found that the solution rate for groups is higher than that for individuals, not just on the husbands-and-wives problem (e.g., Lorge & Solomon, 1959, 1960; Marquart, 1955), but on a wide variety of other problem-solving tasks (for a comprehensive review of this early work, see Hill, 1982).

Husbands and Wives[*]

Problem: Three beautiful women (W_1, W_2, W_3) and their jealous husbands (H_1, H_2, H_3) come to a river that must be crossed by means of a small rowboat. The rowboat can accommodate no more than three passengers at once. All of the men can row, but none of the women can. How can the entire party be transported to the opposite bank if none of the men will permit his wife to be in the company of another man unless he too is present?

The problem can be solved in as few as 7 crossings. Two such solutions are give below.

Crossing	On Original Side	In Boat	On Opposite Bank
Solution A	H_1, W_1, H_2, W_2, H_3, W_3		
1	H_2, W_2, H_3, W_3	→ H_1, W_1 →	
2	H_2, W_2, H_3, W_3	← H_1 ←	W_1
3	H_3, W_3	→ H_1, H_2, W_2 →	W_1
4	H_3, W_3	← H_2, W_2 ←	H_1, W_1
5	W_3	→ H_2, W_2, H_3 →	H_1, W_1
6	W_3	← H_3 ←	H_1, W_1, H_2, W_2
7		→ H_3, W_3 →	H_1, W_1, H_2, W_2
--			H_1, W_1, H_2, W_2, H_3, W_3
Solution B	H_1, W_1, H_2, W_2, H_3, W_3		
1	H_2, W_2, H_3, W_3	→ H_1, W_1 →	
2	H_2, W_2, H_3, W_3	← H_1 ←	W_1
3	W_2, W_3	→ H_1, H_2, H_3 →	W_1
4	W_2, W_3	← H_2, H_3 ←	H_1, W_1
5	W_3	→ H_2, W_2, H_3 →	H_1, W_1
6	W_3	← H_3 ←	H_1, W_1, H_2, W_2
7		→ H_3, W_3 →	H_1, W_1, H_2, W_2
--			H_1, W_1, H_2, W_2, H_3, W_3

[*] Although often attributed to the Italian mathematician Niccolo Tartaglia (c.1499-1557), the origins of this problem are traceable at least to the medieval scholar Alcuin (c.732-804). See Pressman & Singmaster (1989).

FIGURE 4.1   The husbands-and-wives transfer problem.

The direct comparison of group and individual solution rates in this way is a reasonable first step toward understanding synergistic performance gains on dichotomously scored group problem-solving tasks. The solution rate for individuals working alone speaks in a straightforward way to the definition of weak synergy given in Chapter 1. Weak synergy was defined there as group performance that exceeds what the typical group member would be able to achieve working alone. If group members and individuals are drawn in the same way from the same population, and if groups are able to solve problems correctly more often than individuals, then it seems reasonable to conclude not only that those groups have outperformed the typical member, but that their improved performance was due in some way to group interaction.

However, surpassing the solution rate for individuals does not, by itself, tell us whether weak or strong synergy has been observed in groups. To determine this, a best-member standard is needed. It is group performance vis-à-vis this more stringent standard that has captured the most attention for the past half-century. Indeed, although never expressed in precisely these terms, it seems fair to say that during this period researchers have been engaged in a search for more than just synergy in problem-solving groups. They have been engaged in a search for *strong* synergy.

A Formal Best-Member Model

Strong synergy was defined in Chapter 1 as group performance that exceeds what even its best member is able to achieved working alone. Thus, strong and weak synergy are distinguished by reference to a best-member standard: Strong synergy is group performance that surpasses that standard, whereas weak synergy is group performance that falls short of it (but still is above the typical- or average-member standard). Lorge and Solomon (1955) were the first to offer a formal model that quantifies the best-member standard. They argued that a group that performs exactly at the level of its best member will solve a problem correctly whenever any of its members can solve that same problem working individually, and will fail to solve the problem correctly only if none of its members individually can solve it. Thus, in order to determine the group solution rate that corresponds to a best-member standard, it is necessary only to determine the probability that the group will contain *at least one* member who can solve the problem correctly when working alone. This probability—and so the expected group solution rate under a best-member model—is given by the following expression:

$$P_g = 1 - (1 - P_i)^r \tag{4.1}$$

where P_g is the expected solution rate for groups, P_i is the known solution rate for individuals, and r is group size. For example, suppose that 30% of the individuals in some well-defined population (e.g., college sophomores) can solve the Husbands-and-Wives transfer problem correctly on their own. If we were to assemble four-person groups at random from this population, then for these groups $P_g = 1 - (1 - .3)^4 = .76$. In other words, a best-member model anticipates that 76% of the groups drawn from this population will solve the problem correctly, because 76% of them are likely to contain at least one member capable of solving the problem alone.

Equation 4.1 is known as Lorge and Solomon's Model A.[1] Although easily applied without further explanation, it is instructive to examine this model's derivation more closely. It relies on two rules from elementary probability theory: (a) the complement rule, and (b) the multiplication rule for independent events. The complement rule states that if the probability of an event happening is p, then the probability of it not happening is $1 - p$. Thus, if P_i is the probability of a randomly sampled individual from the population of potential group members being a *solver*, then $(1 - P_i)$ is the probability of that same individual being a *nonsolver*. (For ease of expression, throughout this chapter, I refer to individuals who are able to solve a given problem on their own as "solvers," and to those who are not able to solve it on their own as "nonsolvers.") The multiplication rule for independent events states that the probability of two or more independent events happening jointly is the product of the probability of each one happening individually. For example, if the probability of observing "heads" in a single coin toss is .5, then probability of observing four "heads" in each of four tosses is $.5 \times .5 \times .5 \times .5 = .06$. This is equivalently expressed as $(.5)^4$, where the exponent indicates the total number of independent events (here, coin tosses). Similarly, in a problem-solving context, if r is group size—the number of persons independently sampled from the population in order to form the group—and if $(1 - P_i)$ is the probability of any given member being a non-solver, then $(1 - P_i)^r$ is the probability that *all* members of the group will be nonsolvers. Finally, the complement rule is applied one last time by computing $1 - (1 - P_i)^r$. This yields the probability of there being *at least one* solver in the group.

Understanding the derivation of Equation 4.1 helps to illuminate several of the assumptions underlying Model A. First, the model applies to disjunctive tasks only, which is to say, unitary tasks that permit just one member's contributions to determine the group's product (disjunctive tasks were discussed in Chapter 2 in connection with Steiner's [1972] task typology). Second, the model assumes that there are just two kinds of people: solvers and nonsolvers. Third, the multiplication rule for independent events carries with it the assumption that people do not perform any better or worse as a result of working together in a group compared to when they work alone—just as a coin is no more or less likely to come up heads when tossed with other coins than when tossed alone. Fourth, the model assumes that the larger the size of the group the more likely it is that at least one of its members will be able to solve the problem (although this relationship is one of diminishing returns). Finally, it assumes that when any solver proposes the correct solution, that solution will be endorsed by the rest of the group, and so adopted as their collective response. Model A thus describes a group process that would seem to be maximally efficient with respect to capitalizing on member problem-solving abilities.

Empirical Evidence

The primary challenge in applying Model A is obtaining a useful estimate of P_i. Ideally this would be done with a large-sample population study, from which a precise value could be derived. In practice, however, P_i has typically been set equal to the solution rate for a comparatively small sample of individuals run concurrently in the same study. Lorge and Solomon (1955), for example, used Model A in a re-analysis of Shaw's (1932) original data by setting P_i equal to the solution rates she reported for 21 individuals. Thus, for the husbands-and-wives transfer problem, $P_i = .14$. Substituting this value into Equation 4.1, it is found that the solution rate predicted for a four-person group is $P_g = .45$. Although the solution rate that Shaw actually obtained for groups (.60) exceeds this value, due to sampling error associated with both groups and individuals, the difference is not statistically significant. A similar analysis was applied to the results from two of the other tasks that Shaw used. On only one of these (also a transfer problem) was there a significant difference between the group solution rate predicted by Model A and the solution rate actually observed. In that one case, no individuals solved the problem (thus, $P_g = P_i = .00$), whereas 60% of the groups solved it. Interestingly, these were the same groups who had previously solved the husbands-and-wives transfer problem correctly.

Most studies that have compared actual group solution rates to those predicted by Model A report either no difference between the two, or find that group solution rates are actually below what is predicted by Model A. Only very rarely have group solution rates been found to be higher than the best-member solution rate predicted by Model A (e.g., Doise, Mugny, & Perret-Clermont, 1975; Shaw & Ashton, 1976). In other words, groups have most often been shown to perform better than their average member (P_i), but either equivalent to or worse than their best member (P_g).

Social Decision Scheme Theory

A powerful extension of the ideas embodied in Lorge and Solomon's Model A can be found in Davis's (1973) Social Decision Scheme (SDS) theory. This theory derives its name, and certain of its terminology, from its more common application in decision-making contexts. Decision-making tasks are generally found in the middle and right-hand (judgmental) portions of Laughlin's (1980; 1999; Laughlin & Ellis, 1986) Intellective–Judgmental Task Continuum, and will be examined in Chapter 6. SDS Theory is quite general, however, and can be applied as well to intellective problem solving. Thus, I introduce the theory here and refer to it again in Chapter 6.

SDS Theory is concerned with the underlying process (social decision scheme) by which diverse member response preferences are resolved into a unitary group response. In problem-solving contexts, a member's *response preference* refers to the solution that he or she would propose if he or she were to tackle the problem alone. This usage implies at least a provisional belief in the correctness of that solution. Response preferences may or may not vary from one member to the next, and may or may not be correct. A *group response* is the solution actually settled on by the group as a whole. Finally, a *social decision scheme* is a formal model of the group process by which member response preferences are transformed into a consensual group response (cf. Smoke & Zajonc, 1962). When invoked, a given social decision scheme is presumed to apply to all logically possible distributions of member preferences.

According to SDS theory, the probability that a group will solve a given problem correctly depends on (a) the nature of that problem, (b) the social, organizational, and cultural context within which the problem is presented, and (c) the distribution of members' response preferences. Regarding the last of these, SDS requires that close attention be paid to how many group members prefer each proposed solution alternative. To understand this idea, it is helpful initially to distinguish groups only according to the numbers of solvers and nonsolvers they contain, under the simplifying assumption that nonsolving members all prefer the same incorrect solution to the problem. This assumption is unrealistic in most situations, as there are usually many possible incorrect solutions that might be given to a problem. Further, the distribution of nonsolvers over these incorrect solutions may sometimes impact the group's ability to collectively identify the correct solution.[2] Nevertheless, it is useful to ignore this complexity for now and return to it later, after the basic SDS approach is more fully understood.

With this restriction in place, let us consider four-person groups. In such groups it is possible to distinguish five different distributions of solvers and nonsolvers:

4 Solvers and 0 Nonsolvers	(4, 0)
3 Solvers and 1 Nonsolver	(3, 1)
2 Solvers and 2 Nonsolvers	(2, 2)
1 Solver and 3 Nonsolvers	(1, 3)
0 Solvers and 4 Nonsolvers	(0, 4)

SDS theory holds that for any given task and social context, each of these distinguishable distributions has its own characteristic solution probability—its own likelihood of yielding a correct group answer to the problem. More important than these individual solution probabilities, however, is the *pattern* of probabilities across all (five, in this example) of the distinguishable distributions. As will be seen, it is from the pattern of solution probabilities across distributions that inferences about group process during problem solving are drawn. Simply put, different patterns suggest different underlying processes—different social decision schemes.

Truth Wins and Error Wins SDS Models

One can take either an inductive model-building approach to applying SDS theory or a deductive model-testing approach (Kerr, Stasser, & Davis, 1979; Stasser, 1999a). The former application is less common. It involves estimating from data the solution probability associated with each distinguishable distribution of solvers and nonsolvers for a given problem and group size, and then inferring from that set of probabilities the underlying group process, or social decision scheme, that best explains the entire pattern of data. This stands in contrast to the more prevalent model testing approach, which involves deducing on logical grounds the pattern of group solution probabilities that ought to be observed for a particular social decision scheme, then evaluating the degree to which that pattern fits a given set of data. This approach is most usefully implemented within a competitive framework that pits the predictions of different social decision schemes against one another (Hastie & Stasser, 2000). It is this latter approach that guides the following discussion.

Consider, for example, the husbands-and-wives transfer problem described earlier. Suppose that when four-person groups attempt this problem they use a strict best-member group process—the same process that underlies Lorge and Solomon's Model A. Within the tradition of SDS theory, this best-member group process is known as the *Truth Wins* social decision scheme model. The Truth Wins model states that groups with at least one solving member will solve that problem correctly when working collectively. The only groups that should fail to solve the problem are those that have no members who are solvers. It is thus easy to derive from this model the probability with which groups comprising different numbers of solvers and nonsolvers are predicted to produce a correct solution. These probabilities are shown for four-person groups in Table 4.1, under the Truth Wins heading. As can be seen, the probability of a correct group solution is 1.0 for all distinguishable distributions of solvers and nonsolvers except (0, 4), where it is 0. Equivalently, the probability of an incorrect

TABLE 4.1 Group Solution Probabilities for Four-Person Groups Predicted by the Truth Wins and Error Wins Social Decision Scheme Models

(r_s, r_n)	Truth Wins		Error Wins	
	C	I	C	I
(4, 0)	1.0	.00	1.0	.00
(3, 1)	1.0	.00	.00	1.0
(2, 2)	1.0	.00	.00	1.0
(1, 3)	1.0	.00	.00	1.0
(0, 4)	.00	1.0	.00	1.0

Note: r_s is the number of solvers in the group, r_n is the number of nonsolvers, C is the probability of the group giving the correct solution to the problem, and I is the probability of the group giving an incorrect solution.

group solution under the Truth Wins model is 0 for all distinguishable distributions except (0, 4), where it is 1.0.

Note that, like Model A, the Truth Wins social decision scheme reflects a group process that makes optimal use of members' individual capacities to solve the problem confronting them. However, this is not quite the same as saying that this process makes optimal use of member resources. To be sure, an individual solver must possess all the resources needed to solve the problem correctly. This is true by definition. But it is also conceivable that the requisite problem solving resources may be distributed among members in such a way that each of them is incapable of solving the problem alone, and yet the group can solve the problem collectively if the members pool those resources in an appropriate way. The latter more nearly describes an optimal use of member resources but is not what is implied by the Truth Wins model.

Table 4.1 also gives the predicted solution probabilities for a second social decision scheme, Error Wins. The *Error Wins* model holds that, if at least one member of the group is a nonsolver, then the group as a whole will fail to solve the problem correctly. Under this model, the only groups predicted to solve the problem correctly are those with no nonsolvers. If Truth Wins is a best-member model, then Error Wins can be considered a worst-member model.

Notation like that shown in Table 4.1 is unnecessarily cumbersome for representing social decision schemes such as Truth Wins and Error Wins, because the ideas they represent are relatively simple. However, that notation becomes quite helpful when considering more nuanced models that are relevant to some of the recent empirical research on group problem solving. Three such models are considered next.

Truth-Supported Wins, Proportionality, and Majority-Proportionality SDS Models

The left-hand portion of Table 4.2 gives the solution probabilities for a social decision scheme called *Truth-Supported Wins*. According to this model, the underlying group process does not permit a lone solver to prevail in the group. Even though he or she may be able to propose the correct solution, a lone solver is presumed incapable of convincing the rest of the group to adopt that solution as its collective response. Rather, the group must contain at least two solvers if it is to adopt the correct solution. Thus, in four-person groups, the Truth Wins (Table 4.1) and Truth-Supported Wins (Table 4.2) models differ only with respect to the solution probabilities associated with distinguishable distribution (1, 3). Implicitly, the Truth-Supported Wins model assumes that, although a single member may individually possess the resources needed to determine the correct answer to a problem, one member alone cannot possess all of the additional resources that may be needed in order to demonstrate the correctness of that solution to others.

Table 4.2 also gives the solution probabilities for the *Proportionality* social decision scheme model. One interpretation of this model is that every member has an equal chance of convincing the group as a whole to adopt his or her proposed solution. If so, then the probability of the group correctly solving the problem is directly proportional to the number of members who independently can solve it.

Finally, the right-hand portion of Table 4.2 gives the solution probabilities for a composite social decision scheme model labeled *Majority-Proportionality*. At the core of this model is the democratic ideal that

TABLE 4.2 Group Solution Probabilities for Four-Person Groups Predicted by the Truth-Supported Wins, Proportionality, and Majority-Proportionality Social Decision Scheme Models

(r_s, r_n)	Truth-Supported Wins		Proportionality		Majority-Proportionality	
	C	I	C	I	C	I
(4, 0)	1.0	.00	1.0	.00	1.0	.00
(3, 1)	1.0	.00	.75	.25	1.0	.00
(2, 2)	1.0	.00	.50	.50	.50	.50
(1, 3)	.00	1.0	.25	.75	.00	1.0
(0, 4)	.00	1.0	.00	.00	.00	1.0

Note: r_s is the number of solvers in the group, r_n is the number of nonsolvers, C is the probability of the group giving the correct solution to the problem, and I is the probability of the group giving an incorrect solution.

groups (and societies) should be governed by the preferences of the majority. Consequently, when a majority response preference exists, the group as a whole is predicted to adopt that preference as its collective response (Majority Wins). This means that if most members are solvers, then the group as a whole will succeed. But if the majority are nonsolvers, then the group is expected to fail.

The majority principle is a simple one, but groups do not always have clear majorities. For example, a four-person group might contain two solvers and two nonsolvers. In such cases, the Majority-Proportionality model predicts that groups will switch to a proportionality decision scheme, with the group solution probabilities being proportional to the number of solvers and nonsolvers in the group. Thus, the Majority-Proportionality model assumes that groups have two social decision schemes in their repertoire, with the Majority Wins scheme being prepotent over the Proportionality scheme.

The implications of the Majority-Proportionality model become clearer if we relax the previously imposed restriction that nonsolving members all prefer the same incorrect solution to the problem. Table 4.3 gives the solution probabilities predicted by the Majority-Proportionality model for four-person groups when nonsolvers may give different incorrect solutions. Thus, up to four different incorrect answers might be preferred by

TABLE 4.3 Group Solution Probabilities for Four-Person Groups Predicted by the Majority-Proportionality Social Decision Scheme Model when Nonsolvers May Propose Different Incorrect Solutions

$(r_s, r_{n\text{-}a}, r_{n\text{-}b}, r_{n\text{-}c}, r_{n\text{-}d})$	C	I_a	I_b	I_c	I_d
(4, 0, 0, 0, 0)	1.0	.00	.00	.00	.00
(3, 1, 0, 0, 0)	1.0	.00	.00	.00	.00
(2, 2, 0, 0, 0)	.50	.50	.00	.00	.00
(2, 1, 1, 0, 0)	.50	.25	.25	.00	.00
(1, 3, 0, 0, 0)	.00	1.0	.00	.00	.00
(1, 2, 1, 0, 0)	.25	.50	.25	.00	.00
(1, 1, 1, 1, 0)	.25	.25	.25	.25	.00
(0, 4, 0, 0, 0)	.00	1.0	.00	.00	.00
(0, 3, 1, 0, 0)	.00	1.0	.00	.00	.00
(0, 2, 2, 0, 0)	.00	.50	.50	.00	.00
(0, 2, 1, 1, 0)	.00	.50	.25	.25	.00
(0, 1, 1, 1, 1)	.00	.25	.25	.25	.25

Note: r_s is the number of solvers in the group. $r_{n\text{-}a}, r_{n\text{-}b}, r_{n\text{-}c}$, and $r_{n\text{-}d}$ are the number of nonsolvers who prefer different incorrect solutions a, b, c, and d, respectively. C is the probability of the group giving the correct solution to the problem. I_a, I_b, I_c, and I_d are the probabilities of the group giving different incorrect solutions a, b, c, and d, respectively.

members. In reading Table 4.3 it is important to recognize that the subscripts a, b, c, and d refer to *different* incorrect solutions, not to *specific* incorrect solutions. For example, if there are two solvers and two nonsolvers in a group, and the two nonsolvers prefer different incorrect solutions, this is represented simply as (2, 1, 1, 0, 0), regardless of which specific incorrect solutions they might prefer.[3] Likewise, $I_a = I_b = .25$ implies that the two incorrect solutions—whatever they may be—are each predicted to be adopted by the group 25% of the time, given that one member prefers each. Using this notation, it can be seen that there are a total of 12 distinguishable distributions of solvers and nonsolvers if we allow that nonsolvers may give different incorrect solutions. In only five of these is there a clear majority. So, the Majority Wins subscheme can be applied only in these five cases. In the remaining seven distinguishable distributions there is no majority, so the Proportionality subscheme must be applied. Thus, although the Majority Wins subscheme is prepotent over Proportionality in the Majority Proportionality model, the Proportionality subscheme may in fact apply in a greater variety of situations.

Numerous other social decision schemes might similarly be translated into predicted solution probabilities for groups with different patterns of member solution preferences. For example, using Table 4.3 as a template, one can easily specify the probabilities for a *Plurality–Equiprobability* model (Plurality Wins when a plurality exists; otherwise all solutions are equally probable). As another example, based on Latané's (1981) work, a Social Impact model might be developed in which the predicted group solution rate is a power function of the number of members preferring each solution alternative. SDS Theory can accommodate an indefinitely large number of such models.

SDS Theory thus provides a useful framework for translating a wide variety of ideas about group process into specific predictions about performance. It is important to note, however, that the predictions themselves do not always uniquely identify the ideas that generated them. In some instances, the same pattern of predicted solution probabilities may be derived from two or more very different notions about group process. The Proportionality model is a case in point. The interpretation of that model given above—that members have an equal chance of convincing one another to adopt their proposed solution—is not the only idea that implies group solution probabilities proportional to the percentage of solvers in the group. A rather different process that leads to the same prediction is that, the more members there are who can independently determine the correct solution to a problem, the more they can support one another by sharing the demands of articulating arguments, remembering and communicating relevant information, and demonstrating the correctness of that solution. This view of group process invokes strong assumptions about cooperative interdependence among members who share solution preferences and stands in contrast to the earlier interpretation (equal influence among members), which assumes instead that members present and argue for their solution preferences quite independently. Yet another process that can generate proportionality in predicted solution probabilities is turn-taking (Laughlin, 1999). Across a series of problems, the members of a group may agree, implicitly or explicitly, to take turns honoring one another's solution preferences. If so, then for any one of these problems it is equally likely that it will be each member's turn, which again anticipates solution probabilities that are proportional to the number of solvers in the group. The point is, then, that although the various social decision schemes described above lead to precise predictions about group performance, they do not always precisely identify a single underlying group process. In some cases they may reflect either the separate or joint operation of several processes (see Chapter 10, pp. 359–365 for further discussion of this point). SDS is therefore a valuable but imperfect tool for establishing the operative group process in a given situation.

SDS Models and the Search for Synergy

In order to test among any set of social decision scheme models, it is necessary first to determine the number of solvers and nonsolvers in the group. Several approaches to doing this are available. One is simply to pretest members on the target problem before allowing them to work on it as a group. There are many circumstances in which this strategy is not practical, however. Furthermore, even when it is practical, pretesting can distort the normal pattern of group interaction, as members enter the group problem-solving discussion with already-formed solutions in mind, rather than evolving a solution *de novo* during discussion.

An alternative approach is to estimate the likely composition of groups from the known distribution of solvers and nonsolvers in the population from which group members are drawn. This is essentially the same procedure as described earlier in connection with Lorge and Solomon's Model A. For example, suppose that, based on extensive prior research with individuals, it is known that the proportion of solvers in a given population for a given problem is $P_i = .3$. If groups are created by drawing members at random from this population, then the probability that a group will have each possible distribution of solvers and nonsolvers can be determined using the binomial probability function (Davis, 1973; Stasser, 1999a). These probabilities are given for four-person groups in Table 4.4. As can be seen, if 30% of the population can solve a given problem correctly, then the most common four-person group would comprise a single solver and three nonsolvers. Forty-one percent of all randomly constructed four-person groups would be expected to have this composition. About a quarter of all groups (24%) would be expected to have no solvers at all, and another

---

TABLE 4.4 Group Composition Probabilities
for Four-Person Groups, Given $P_i = .3$

(r_s, r_n)	Probability
(4, 0)	.01
(3, 1)	.08
(2, 2)	.26
(1, 3)	.41
(0, 4)	.24

Note: r_s is the number of solvers in the group, and r_n is
the number of nonsolvers.

---

quarter (26%) would be expected to have two solvers. The rarest group of
all would be one with four solvers, which would be expected to occur just
1% of the time.

Each of the previously discussed social decision scheme models, when
combined with these group composition probabilities, yields an overall
predicted solution rate across all groups of a given size. For example,
according to the Truth Wins model, if four-person groups are drawn at
random from a population in which $P_i = .3$, then 76% of them should be
able to solve the problem correctly. This value is derived by multiplying
the various solution probabilities under the Truth Wins model (given
in Table 4.1) by the corresponding composition probabilities (given in
Table 4.4), then summing over the products. Thus,

$$P_{tw} = (1.0 \times .01) + (1.0 \times .08) + (1.0 \times .26) + (1.0 \times .41) + (.00 \times .24) = .76 \quad (4.2)$$

Note that $P_{tw} = .76$ is exactly the same value as that obtained from Lorge
and Solomon's Model A (Equation 4.1). It is the same because Truth Wins
and Model A are alternative ways of expressing the same underlying ideas
about group process.

Likewise, this procedure can be used to derive the overall solution rate
predicted by each of the other social decision scheme models discussed
above. These solution rates, ranked in order of magnitude, are as follows:

Truth Wins	.76
Truth-Supported Wins	.35
Proportionality	.30
Majority-Proportionality	.22
Error Wins	.01

It should be clear from this analysis that the Proportionality model
yields exactly the same predicted solution rate in groups as exists in the

population for individuals: $P_p = P_i = .3$. This holds for all group sizes and for all values of P_i. P_i, of course, is the level of performance that can be expected of the typical group member when working alone. As such, it is one of the two defining baselines for evaluating synergy in groups; it defines the level of performance that must be exceeded in order to claim evidence of even weak synergy in groups. The Proportionality model thus implies an underlying group process (or collection of processes) that neither benefits nor harms group performance relative to individual performance. Stated differently, it defines within the SDS framework the best-performing social decision scheme that does *not* involve any sort of synergistic performance gain.

The Truth Wins model provides the other defining baseline for evaluating synergy in groups; it specifies the level of performance that must be exceeded in order to claim evidence of strong synergy. Note that in the example given above, the overall solution rate predicted by the Truth Wins model far exceeds P_i, the weak synergy baseline. The relationship $P_{tw} > P_i$ (and so $P_{tw} > P_p$) is also quite general. Note, however, that group performance conforming exactly to the predictions of the Truth Wins model would be taken as evidence of only weak synergy. It would not be considered evidence of strong synergy simply because strong synergy is defined as performance that *surpasses* what is predicted by the Truth Wins model. Performance matching the predictions of the Truth Wins model would, however, be the strongest possible case of weak synergy.

With the Proportionality and Truth Wins models as reference points, other SDS models can be evaluated for their implications regarding synergy in groups. Thus, in the example given above, the Truth-Supported Wins model predicts a weak synergistic performance gain (because $P_{tsw} = .35 > P_i = .3$), whereas the Majority-Proportionality and Error Wins models both predict performance losses—both predict group performance that falls below $P_i = .3$.

Two points concerning these latter models are worth noting. First, unlike the Proportionality and Truth Wins models, the conclusions pertaining to the Truth-Supported Wins and Majority-Proportionality models are not general across group size and P_i. With regard to group size, if in the example above we had considered three-person rather than four-person groups, then the overall solution rate predicted by the Truth-Supported Wins model would drop to $P_{tsw} = .22$. This is identical to the rate predicted by the Majority-Proportionality model and implies a net process loss, not gain (because $P_{tsw} = .22 < P_i = .30$). With regard to P_i, on the other hand, and returning to four-person groups, if a much easier problem had been employed, so that $P_i = .7$ rather than .3, then the Truth-Supported Wins and Majority-Proportionality models would predict group solution rates of $P_{tsw} = .92$ and $P_{mp} = .78$, respectively. Note that because $P_{mp} = .78 > P_i = .7$, the Majority-Proportionality model now predicts a weak synergistic gain in group performance, not a loss.[4] The point here is that certain SDS models, and the group processes they reflect, do not guarantee either a performance gain or loss in groups. Whether a gain or a loss will occur, and to what degree, is often predicted by these models to depend on additional factors, such as the size of the group and the solution rate among individuals in the population from which members are drawn. The implication of this is important. It suggests that it may be unrealistic to hope for a single set of universally applicable group processes that reliably yield synergistic performance gains across all situations.

Second, that there are no models within the SDS framework that predict group performance above and beyond what is predicted by the Truth Wins model. The reason lies at the heart of the SDS approach. SDS Theory is fundamentally a social combination theory that seeks to describe the way in which member preferences combine to yield collective group responses (Laughlin, 1980, 1999; Stasser & Dietz-Uhler, 2001). The specific models within this framework are all constrained to operate exclusively on member preferences in order to predict group responses, as opposed to, for example, operating on the information, assumptions, and background knowledge that may have given rise to those preferences. Consequently, if *no* member in the group prefers the correct solution (which is the only situation in which it is even possible to surpass the predictions of the Truth Wins model), then there is nothing beyond chance for any conceivable SDS model to operate on in order to predict that the group will adopt the correct solution. In other words, SDS Theory as a whole is incapable of predicting performance that surpasses the Truth Wins model. Despite this limitation, the SDS framework, and the Truth Wins model in particular, provides an essential baseline for evaluating observed solution rates. Thus, although the concept of strong synergy is formally outside the SDS framework, that framework itself is nevertheless capable of signaling the presence of strong synergy when it does in fact exist.

SDS Models and Demonstrability: Empirical Evidence

Laughlin and Ellis (1986) reviewed the early empirical research on social decision scheme models as applied to intellective problem-solving tasks. They observed that the best-fitting model varies according to the apparent demonstrability of the task—that is, according to how easy or difficult it should be for members to demonstrate to one another that a proposed solution is either correct or incorrect (see Chapter 2, pp. 48–51, for a fuller discussion of demonstrability). Of greatest relevance to the present discussion, their review suggests that the more demonstrable the task, the more closely group performance conforms to the predictions of the Truth Wins model. For example, the Truth Wins model better describes group performance on verbal insight problems (e.g., the husbands-and-wives transfer problem) than on general world knowledge problems (e.g., What is the longest river in Asia?). Insight problems are more demonstrable than world-knowledge problems in the sense that it is more evident when a correct solution has been proposed—even to group members who could not have solved the problem on their own. World knowledge problems, by contrast, tend to be solved by a group process that more closely resembles a Truth-Supported Wins social decision scheme.

Because the solutions to mathematical problems are also highly demonstrable, Laughlin and Ellis (1986) suggest that group performance on purely mathematical problems should best fit the Truth Wins social decision scheme. To test this hypothesis, they gave university students 10 mathematical problems presented in a multiple-choice format. The students attempted these problems first as individuals, then in five-person groups. Based on the distribution of answers given individually by group members, their performance as a group was predicted according to each of six different SDS models, including Truth Wins, Truth-Supported Wins, Simple Majority, and Majority-Proportionality.[5] As predicted, the Truth Wins model best fit the group performance data, although the Truth-Supported Wins model was a close second-best fit and could not be rejected by a statistical goodness-of-fit test. Similarly, Stasson, Kameda, Parks, Zimmerman, and Davis (1991) found that the observed performance of five-person groups on mathematical problems fell between the predictions of the Truth Wins and Truth-Supported Wins models, though it was closer to the former than the latter.

It is interesting to note that in neither of these studies did group performance *surpass* the predictions of the Truth Wins model. At best, groups only *matched* what that model predicts. It would seem, then, that groups may be capable of only weak synergistic performance gains on these highly demonstrable mathematical tasks; they clearly are able to perform such tasks better than their average member (Proportionality) but appear unable to perform them better than their best member (Truth Wins). This suggests that task demonstrability, by itself, is not the key to finding strong synergy in group performance. Rather, to find strong synergy it seems necessary to consider task attributes beyond demonstrability. Toward this end, I examine next group performance on two particularly interesting intellective tasks: one that emphasizes inductive reasoning and one that emphasizes deductive reasoning.

☐ Collective Induction

Building on the SDS framework, Laughlin and his colleagues (1996, 1999; Laughlin & Hollingshead, 1995) have pursued an extensive program of research concerned with group performance on collective induction tasks. A collective induction task is one in which problem solvers work cooperatively to induce a general rule or principle that can account parsimoniously for a given set of facts or observations. Scientists provide the prototypic example of collective induction when they work together to develop theories that can explain their data. But collective induction is not limited to science. Physicians engage in collective induction when they confer with one another about a patient's symptoms in order to diagnose his or her illness. Likewise, police detectives engage in collective induction when they team up to examine evidence and solve a crime. Laughlin has developed a challenging laboratory task that similarly involves collective induction but that requires no special expertise on the part of research participants. It is called the *rule induction task*. To fully appreciate the findings generated by research using this task, it is helpful to have a thorough understanding of the task itself. Thus, I describe the task in detail in the first section below. I then discuss the research results, their theoretical relevance, and their implications for the search for synergy in small group performance.

The Rule Induction Task

The rule induction task makes use of a standard deck of 52 playing cards. Prior to the start of a problem-solving session, the experimenter chooses a rule that logically partitions this deck into two parts: one comprising all cards that conform to the rule (positive exemplars), and one comprising all cards that do not conform to it (negative exemplars). For instance, a very simple rule is "red cards." All cards in the suits hearts and diamonds fit this rule and so are positive exemplars, whereas all cards in the suits spades and clubs do not fit this rule and so are negative exemplars. The rule thus chosen becomes the induction target for the problem-solving session; it is this rule that problem solvers will try to induce.

The problem-solving session itself is divided into a series of trials. During each, the problem solvers (whether working individually or as a group) choose a specific card from the deck of 52 and then ask the experimenter whether that card is a positive or negative exemplar. Based on the answer given, along with the answers given on all previous trials, the problem solvers attempt to infer what the rule itself is.

This all becomes clearer if we consider an example that traces the actions of a hypothetical problem solver over a series of trials. Although the example will focus on a single problem solver working alone, exactly the same actions could also be performed by a group of problem solvers working collectively. The example employs the following standard notation: *D*, *H*, **S**, and **C** identify the four suits in a deck (diamonds, hearts, spades and clubs, respectively), and A, 2, 3, 4, 5, 6, 7, 8, 9, 10, J, Q, and K identify the 13 individual cards in each suit, where the values of A, J, Q, and K are 1, 11, 12, and 13, respectively. For added clarity, all symbols for black cards are printed in bold face, whereas all symbols for red cards are printed in italics.

To begin, we must first decide what rule will be used as the induction target. The number of possibilities is nearly limitless. The rule may rely on any feature of the cards, or any combination of features, and need not partition the deck into equal-size parts. For example, the rule "even-numbered red cards" involves two features and divides the deck into a smaller set of cards that fits the rule (e.g., *2D* and *6H*) and a larger set that does not fit it (e.g., *3D* and **6C**). Further, the rule may be defined either on single events, as in the forgoing example, or on sequences of events. An example of the latter is the rule "even-numbered red cards alternating with odd-numbered black cards." The sequence *2H*, **3S**, *4D*, **7C** fits this rule and so is a positive exemplar, whereas the sequence **3S**, **7C**, *2H*, *4D* does not fit the rule and so is a negative exemplar (this is true even though exactly the same cards are involved in each case). Let us suppose for this example that the chosen rule is the last one above: "even-numbered red cards alternating with odd-numbered black cards."

The problem-solving session always starts with the experimenter placing on the table in front of the problem solver a positive exemplar of the rule. Thus, in the present example the experimenter might place *2H* on the table. This one datum does not give the problem solver much to go on; a very large number of rules might plausibly have generated this outcome, including all three of the rules given as examples in the paragraphs above. Nevertheless, it is not unreasonable that the problem solver might guess at the rule, perhaps hypothesizing that it is simply "red cards." At this point, the problem solver would be required to test her hypothesis by "playing" one card from the deck of 52. Playing a card simply means asking the experimenter whether the selected card is a positive or negative exemplar of the target rule. Any card in the deck may be played on any given trial, and the same card may be played on multiple trails. For instance, the problem solver might attempt to confirm her hypothesis by playing *8D*, a red card. The experimenter would reply that *8D* does not fit the target rule and so is a negative exemplar. As a permanent record of this, the experimenter would place *8D* below the original card on the table in front of the problem solver, as shown in the panel labeled Trial 1 in Table 4.5. In general, negative exemplars are always placed below the last-played card.

Trial 1 is now complete. Every subsequent trial follows the same pattern. Thus, on each one the problem solver (a) examines all positive and negative exemplars identified so far, (b) proposes a hypothesis about the correct rule, (c) tests that hypothesis by playing one card from the deck of

TABLE 4.5 Hypothetical Exemplar Displays for Six Successive Trials on the Rule Induction Task

Trial 0	2H			
Trial 1	2H			
	8D			
Trial 2	2H	3S		
	8D			
Trial 3	2H	3S	4D	
	8D			
Trial 4	2H	3S	4D	
	8D		9H	
Trial 5	2H	3S	4D	7C
	8D		9H	
Trial 6	2H	3S	4D	7C
	8D		9H	8C

Note: Table entries identify individual cards, using standard notation (e.g., *2H* refers to the two of hearts; see text). Boldface entries are cards from black suits; italicized entries are cards from red suits. For each trial, the underlined entry is the card "played" on that trial. Positive exemplars appear to the right of the last-identified positive exemplar (top row in each panel). Negative exemplars appear below the last-played card.

52, and (d) learns from the experimenter whether that card is a positive or negative exemplar of the correct rule.

Based on the outcome of Trial 1, the problem solver might guess that the rule is "even-numbered cards alternating with odd-numbered cards," and test this hypothesis by playing **3S** on Trial 2. The experimenter would respond that **3S** does fit the rule, and place **3S** to the right of *2H*, yielding the display shown for Trial 2 in Table 4.5. In general, positive exemplars are always placed to the right of the last-identified positive exemplar, and so always appear in the top row of the exemplar display. This makes sequential patterns of positive exemplars easier to identify, and so hypotheses defined on event sequences are easier to induce. Notice here that **3S** is a positive exemplar even though the problem solver's hypothesis is incorrect. As in science, a given card (piece of evidence) may fit multiple rules (theories), even though just one of those rules (theories) is apt to be correct. This is an important point to which I will return below.

Suppose the problem solver continues to entertain the hypothesis "even-numbered cards alternating with odd-numbered cards" and on Trial 3 plays 4D. The experimenter would respond that 4D does fit the rule, and place it to the right of **3S** (see Trial 3 in Table 4.5). Again the evidence conforms both to the experimenter's target rule and to the problem solver's incorrect hypothesis.

At this point, the problem solver has no reason to abandon her hypothesis; it is perfectly plausible, given the available evidence. On the other hand, there are many other hypotheses that are also plausible. Even so, she is apt to stay with her hypothesis. Thus, she might play 9H, anticipating that it, too, will be declared a positive exemplar. However, the experimenter informs her that 9H does not fit the rule, and places it below 4D (see Trial 4 in Table 4.5).

Now the hypothesis "even-numbered cards alternating with odd-numbered cards" is clearly implausible. It is implausible because, in effect, the entire sequence 2H, **3S**, 4D, 9H has been declared to be a negative exemplar. If this sequence fits the problem solver's hypothesis, as it does, but also is a negative exemplar of the correct rule, then the problem solver's hypothesis cannot be correct.

Forced by logic to abandon her hypothesis, our intrepid problem solver might now entertain the possibility that the target rule is "numbers increasing by 1," noting the left-to-right progression that now appears in the top row of the exemplar display. She might also change her hypothesis testing approach to a disconfirmatory strategy, which is to say, playing cards that are inconsistent with her hypothesis, expecting them to be declared negative exemplars. For example, she might play **7C**, anticipating that it will be placed below 9H in the exemplar display. The experimenter, however, would declare **7C** a positive exemplar of the correct rule, and place it to the right of 4D (Trial 5 in Table 4.5).

In the wake of two unexpected outcomes, the problem solver may at this point begin to feel a bit frustrated. Her frustration, along with the growing complexity of the exemplar display, might cause her to focus increasingly (and inappropriately) on just the top row of that display—the positive exemplars. Noting the pattern of suits observed there, she might propose the hypothesis "a repeating sequence of four different suits." What she fails to realize—because she did not sufficiently attend to the negative exemplars—is that this hypothesis was made implausible by the outcome of the very first trial (i.e., if it were correct, 8D would have been declared a positive exemplar). Nevertheless, sticking with her new disconfirmatory hypothesis testing strategy, she tests this hypothesis by playing **8C**. As expected, the experimenter declares **8C** to be a negative exemplar and places it below **7C**.

And on it goes, one trial after the next, until some fixed number of trials (typically 10–15) has been completed or time runs out, at which point a final hypothesis is elicited from the problem solver, and the session ends. The same basic procedure is followed when the rule induction task is performed by groups rather than individuals. Thus, on each trial the group collectively proposes a hypothesis and collectively chooses a card to play in order to test that hypothesis. The one procedural difference of note that typically occurs when groups perform the task is that members also propose (but do not test) their own individual hypotheses on each trial, and do so just before the group as a whole proposes and tests its collective hypothesis.

Several features of the rule induction task are worth noting. First, there are multiple dependent variables on which individual and group performance might be compared. Among these are whether or not the target rule is eventually discovered and, if so, on which trial it first appears among the problem solvers' hypotheses, the number of plausible and implausible hypotheses proposed, and the frequency with which confirmatory versus disconfirmatory hypothesis tests are performed. Second, because in the collective version of the task members typically propose their own individual hypotheses prior to the group as a whole proposing and testing its collective hypothesis, it is possible to examine the social decision schemes that groups employ when choosing collective hypotheses and to do so without having to estimate the group's composition from population parameters. Rather, the group's composition, at least with respect to the hypotheses that members generate on their own, is known directly. This has the benefit of eliminating the impact of random error associated with an estimation process. As noted previously, however, this procedure risks distorting the normal pattern of group interaction in comparison to what occurs when individual member hypotheses are not elicited. Third, the accumulating evidence over trials yields an increasingly large and complex pattern of positive and negative exemplars. On the one hand, as this body of evidence grows in size, it becomes more and more informative, in the sense that it permits a larger number of hypotheses to be discarded as implausible. On the other hand, the growing complexity of the exemplar display makes it increasingly difficult to use effectively, either to check the plausibility of an already-existing hypothesis or to induce a new one that fits all of the data. Variations on the basic procedures can add further to the cognitive demands of this task. For example, groups might be permitted to generate and test multiple hypotheses simultaneously using multiple exemplar displays (e.g., Laughlin, Magley, & Shupe, 1997; Laughlin & Bonner, 1999; Laughlin, VanderStoep, & Hollingshead, 1991).

A final feature of the rule induction task that is important to recognize is that its core problem-solving activity—proposing and testing hypotheses about the target rule—is sometimes a highly intellective undertaking and sometimes wholly judgmental. To see this, consider that every hypothesis a problem solver might put forth can be classified, at the moment it is proposed, as either plausible or implausible vis-à-vis the evidence currently available. *Plausible hypotheses* are consistent with all of the evidence provided in the exemplar display. *Implausible hypotheses*, by contrast, are inconsistent with at least some part of that evidence. Every implausible hypothesis is demonstrably incorrect; the demonstration requires only that one call attention to that portion of the evidence with which it is inconsistent. Therefore, to conclude that a given implausible hypothesis is incorrect is an intellective subtask. By contrast, there is no plausible hypothesis that can be demonstrated to be uniquely correct relative to all other plausible hypotheses. This is because all plausible hypotheses, whether ultimately correct or not, fit the currently available evidence equally well (e.g., in the foregoing example, the hypotheses "red cards alternating with black cards" and "cards with a value of 7 or less" are both equally plausible given the exemplar displays in Table 4.5). Therefore, to conclude that one particular plausible hypothesis is more likely correct than another is a purely judgmental subtask. The rule induction task is thus partly intellective and partly judgmental, depending on the relationship between the hypothesis in question and the evidence available in the exemplar display. It is intellective to the extent the exemplar display contains evidence inconsistent with the to-be-evaluated hypothesis, and is judgmental to the extent that the display does not contain such evidence. Or, expressed in terms of the ideas presented in Chapter 2, the rule induction task is a task with subtasks, where the subtasks differ in demonstrability, and so in the extent to which they are intellective versus judgmental (see pp. 40–41).

Group Performance on the Rule Induction Task

Laughlin and Shippy (1983) were the first to examine group performance on this rule induction task. They had individuals and four-person and five-person groups perform the task either once or twice, using a different target rule each time. They employed the standard procedure described above, except that instead of a fixed number of trials, they allowed participants to continue either until their group hypothesis was correct or time ran out. It was found that groups were more apt to discover the correct rule than individuals were, did so in fewer trials, and proposed a larger percentage of plausible hypotheses overall. Specifically, 55% of the groups, but only 40 of the individuals, eventually proposed the correct rule as a hypothesis. The groups required an average of 8.43 trials to do so, whereas individuals required 14.93 trials. And across all trials, groups proposed plausible hypotheses 95% of the time, whereas individuals did so only 80% of the time. The performance of four-person and five-person groups did not differ significantly. Similar results have been obtained in a number of other studies (e.g., Laughlin, 1992; Laughlin & Futoran, 1985;

Laughlin & McGlynn, 1986; McGlynn, McGurk, Effland, Johll, & Harding, 2004; see also Crott, Giesel, & Hoffmann, 1998; Hoffmann & Crott, 2004). Taken together, these findings suggest that groups are both more effective and more efficient at rule induction than is the average person working alone.

These rather simple comparisons clearly indicate the presence of a synergistic performance gain in groups. By themselves, however, they do not permit any conclusions about whether that gain is a weak or a strong form of synergy. For this, a different analytic approach is needed.

One possibility is to try to identify the social decision scheme that best describes the underlying group process occurring during collective induction. Laughlin et al. (1991) suggested just such a scheme. They argued that the operative group process can be summarized by a hybrid of the previously discussed Truth-Supported Wins and Majority-Proportionality models. It is convenient here to state their proposed model in two steps, although there is no assumption that the underlying group process actually unfolds in discrete steps. First, according to this model, if on a given trial two or more members independently propose plausible hypotheses (i.e., before the group proposes its collective hypothesis), then the group's collective response will be selected only from among those plausible hypotheses; all other (nonplausible) hypotheses will be ignored. Otherwise no hypothesis will be ignored. Thus, in this first step, truth (plausibility) wins if supported by at least one other member, where winning implies only that the hypothesis is retained in the set that will be considered further, while other hypotheses are excluded. Second, from those retained hypotheses, the group response is selected according to a majority-proportionality model.[6] Thus, according to this hybrid model, not only is a lone plausible hypothesis with a single advocate not guaranteed to be adopted as the group's collective response, it will be trumped by an implausible hypothesis that has majority support. Indeed, even if no majority exists, the proportionality subscheme suggests that a lone plausible hypothesis with a single advocate is still less likely to be adopted than an implausible hypothesis advocated by as few as two members.[7]

This hybrid model was first offered by Laughlin et al. (1991) as a *post hoc* description of the performance of 200 four-person groups previously observed in studies by Laughlin (1988) and Laughlin & McGlynn (1986). However, its validity was subsequently confirmed prospectively in studies by Laughlin (1992) and Laughlin and Shupe (1996; see also Laughlin, 1996). Laughlin (1999) provided additional support for it in an analysis that aggregated the results of seven different experiments involving a total of 616 four-person groups. The hybrid model was competitively tested against five alternative models and out-performed (i.e., fit the data better than) all of them. Finally, it is worth noting that Bonner, Baumann, Lehn, Pierce, and Wheeler (2006) have recently demonstrated that the hybrid model also predicts group responses on a task that required deductive as well as inductive reasoning.

It is important to recognize that the hybrid model is most directly concerned with what happens on a single trial of the rule induction task; it is intended to predict the hypothesis that will be proposed and tested on any one trial by the group as a whole based on the distribution of hypotheses proposed by its members on that same trial. However, this model also has implications for what is apt to occur over a series of trials. Specifically, correct hypotheses can be expected to survive from trial to trial and be tested again. This is because, by definition, correct hypotheses can never be contradicted by any present or future evidence. Incorrect hypotheses, on the other hand, will tend to be discarded, either because they can be shown to be implausible given evidence already in the exemplar display, or because they are apt to become implausible when new evidence is generated by future hypothesis testing. As a result, if any member proposes a correct hypothesis on any trial, then the group solution—the final hypothesis proposed by the group after the last trial—is likely to be correct a very high percentage of the time. For example, in his analysis of 616 four-person groups, Laughlin (1999) found that the probability of a correct final group hypothesis was .91 if at least one member proposed the correct hypothesis on at least one trial, and that it was .01 if no member ever proposed the correct hypothesis. Such data suggest that, with respect to their overall performance on the rule induction task, groups perform at or near the level of their best member (Truth Wins).

An alternative approach to assessing overall group performance on the rule induction task relies on comparisons with the performance of nominal groups. As we have seen before, nominal groups are groups in name only; they are really individuals who perform the rule induction task alone, but who are treated as a unit for statistical comparison purposes. In three separate experiments, Laughlin et al. (1991) and Laughlin, Bonner, and Altermatt (1998) had participants perform the rule induction task either alone or in four-person interacting groups. In each study, the data records of the individual problem solvers were organized into four-person nominal groups according to the order in which they participated in the study (i.e., the first four individual participants were treated as one nominal group, the next four were treated as another nominal group, etc.). For each nominal group, the number of times the correct hypothesis was proposed by each member (out of a possible 11) was used to determine who performed best, second-best, third-best, and worst. The mean performance of the four-person interacting groups was then compared to the mean performance of these best, second best, third best, and worst nominal group members. In two studies it was found that the performance of the interacting groups was on par with that of the best nominal group members, and was significantly better than the performance of the second-best, third-best, and worst members. In the third study (Laughlin et al., 1998, Experiment 1), the performance of the interacting groups matched that of the second-best nominal group members. Because participants were randomly assigned to work either alone or in interacting groups in these studies, and because the nominal groups were formed in roughly the same way that the interacting groups were formed (i.e., according to when their members participated in the study), the best, second-best, third-best, and worst of four nominal group members can, on average, be expected to be equivalent to the best, second-best, third-best, and worst of four interacting group members, respectively. Consequently, these results indicate that the interacting groups performed either as well as their best member would have performed working alone (in two studies) or as well as their second-best member would have performed working alone (in one study).

In summary, group performance on the rule induction task nearly always exceeds the performance of the average group member when working alone (the weak synergy threshold) and frequently is at or near the level displayed by the best group member when working alone (the strong synergy threshold). But no study to date has shown that groups can exceed the performance of their best member on this task. Thus, as with problem-solving tasks that are more purely intellective, on the rule induction task groups appear to show only weak synergistic performance gains.

☐ Groups Perform Better than the Best Individuals on Letters-to-Numbers Problems

So far, we have seen scant evidence in the experimental literature for strong synergistic gains in group problem-solving performance. During the last half-dozen years, however, several studies have appeared that do provide compelling evidence of strong synergy. All of these derive from a program of research concerned with group performance on a cryptography task (Laughlin, Bonner, & Miner, 2002; Laughlin, Hatch, Silver, & Boh, 2006; Laughlin, Zander, Knievel, & Tan, 2003). The focus of this work is on the efficiency with which groups and individuals are able to break a letters-to-numbers code. As before, an understanding of the task itself is helpful in order to appreciate the findings generated by this program of research. Thus, I begin again by describing the task in some detail.

The Letters-to-Numbers Task

The object of the letters-to-numbers task is to decipher a specific coding of letters to numbers that is known only to the experimenter. Prior to the start of the problem-solving session, the experimenter randomly assigns (without replacement) each of the letters A, B, C, D, E, F, G, H, I, and J to one of the numbers 0, 1, 2, 3, 4, 5, 6, 7, 8, and 9. The problem solver's task is to identify the full coding of 10 letters to 10 numbers in as few trials as possible. Like the rule induction task, letter-to-numbers is performed over a series of trials, where each trial entails several problem-solving steps that yield incremental information about the code. Unlike the rule induction task, however, letters-to-numbers emphasizes deductive rather than inductive reasoning. Below I illustrate how a problem solver might decipher the full coding of letters to number, making use of the example given in Table 4.6.

Each trial of the letters-to-numbers task comprises five steps. The first is for the problem solver to use some or all the letters A though J to form an equation that will be solved by the experimenter (as in the rule induction task, the experimenter is the source of all task-relevant information). For example, on Trial 1 the problem solver might propose the equation $A + B = ?$ Equation solutions are always given in letters, with each letter treated as a numerical digit. Thus, suppose the experimenter responds by saying that $A + B = EC$. From the experimenter's answer it can be deduced that $E = 1$ (because the only two-digit numbers that can be created from the sum of two different single-digit numbers are the integers 10 through 17). Learning the solution to the proposed equation is the second step in each problem-solving trial.

The third step in each trial is for the problem solver to propose a hypothesis about the mapping of one letter to one number. For example, after

TABLE 4.6 Hypothetical Equations, Hypotheses, and Answers for Five Successive Trials on the Letters-to-Numbers Task

Trial	Equation Proposed	Answer Given	Hypothesis Proposed	Answer Given
1	$A + B = ?$	EC	$A = 9$	False
2	$E + E = ?$	B	$C = 0$	True
3	$B + E = ?$	F	$D = 4$	False
4	$FF + EE + E = ?$	GD	$H = 9$	True
5	$DD + EE + E = ?$	IJ	$J = 7$	True

Note: The full coding of letters-to-numbers for this example is A = 8; B = 2; C = 0; D = 5; E = 1; F = 3; G = 4; H = 9; I = 6; J = 7. Equations and hypotheses are proposed by the problem solver(s), and both types of answers are given by the experimenter.

learning that A + B = EC, the problem solver might propose the hypothesis A = 9. The experimenter then provides feedback about whether or not this mapping is correct. Suppose the experimenter responds that A = 9 is false. Although not particularly helpful at the moment, this piece of information may be useful later on as additional information is obtained, and the range of possibilities is narrowed further. Learning whether the proposed hypothesis is true or false is the fourth step in each problem-solving trial.

The final step in each trial is for the problem solver to propose the full coding of 10 letters to 10 numbers. This invariably means guessing at those mappings that cannot be deduced from the experimenter's feedback so far. Thus, in the present example, after just one trial the problem solver should be confident in proposing only that E = 1, and he or she should not propose A = 9. Everything else would be just a guess. If the correct coding is given for all 10 letters, the problem is solved. If not, then the problem solver moves to the next trial without benefit of further feedback. (This final step in each trial is not represented in Table 4.6. We will assume that the full coding is not given correctly until the last trial listed).

On every subsequent trial the same five steps are repeated. Thus, on Trial 2 the problem solver might propose the equation E + E = ? If the experimenter responds E + E = B, then it is learned that B = 2 (because if E = 1, then E + E = 1 + 1 = 2). Furthermore, it can also be inferred that A = 8 and C = 0. These latter inferences are derived by combining all of the information obtained so far. Specifically, if B = 2 (deduced in Trial 2) and E = 1 (deduced in Trial 1), then A + B = EC means that A must be either 8 or 9 (because these are the only two numbers that, when added to 2, yield a two-digit number). But A cannot be 9, because of the feedback given to the hypothesis proposed on Trial 1 (A = 9 is false). Therefore, it can be concluded that A = 8, and consequently that C = 0 (because 8 + 2 = 10). At this point, the coding of four letters to numbers has been determined: A = 8, B = 2, C = 0, and E = 1. To confirm these inferences, the problem solver might now propose the hypothesis C = 0, to which the experimenter would respond C = 0 is true.

Building on the results from Trial 2, the problem solver might next propose (on Trial 3) the equation B + E = ? If the experimenter responds B + E = F, then it is learned that F = 3 (because if B = 2 and E = 1, then B + E = 2 + 1 = 3). If the problem solver then proposes the hypothesis D = 4, and the experimenter responds D = 4 is false, then on the third trial the coding of one additional letter has been learned.

Now suppose that on Trial 4 the problem solver proposes a more complex equation: FF + EE + E = ? If the experimenter responds FF + EE + E = GD, then it is learned that G = 4 and D = 5 (because if F = 3 and E = 1, then FF + EE + E = 33 + 11 + 1 = 45). Suppose that the problem solver now proposes the hypothesis H = 9 and that the experimenter responds H = 9 is true. This lucky guess means that the problem solver should now be able to give at least 8 of the 10 letters correctly when proposing the full coding of letters to numbers. If the full coding is stated correctly, then the problem is solved. Otherwise, a fifth trial would occur.

Let us assume that a fifth trial does occur. Following the same pattern as before, suppose that on Trial 5 the problem solver proposes the equation $DD + EE + E = ?$ The experimenter should respond $DD + EE + E = IJ$, so that it is learned that $I = 6$ and $J = 7$ (because if $D = 5$, and $E = 1$, then $DD + EE + E = 55 + 11 + 1 = 67$). To verify this, the problem solver might propose the hypothesis $J = 7$, to which the experimenter would respond $J = 7$ is true. Thus, the problem solver should now be able to state correctly the full coding of all 10 letters to 10 numbers.

To summarize, on each trial the problem solver (a) proposes one equation (in letters), (b) learns the answer to that equation (also in letters), (c) hypothesizes a specific mapping of one letter to one number, (d) learns whether or not that single mapping is correct, then (e) proposes the full coding of 10 letters to 10 numbers and learns whether or not that full coding is correct. If it is not completely correct, then another trial occurs. This continues until either the full coding is given correctly, a specific number of trials have occurred (typically 10), or time runs out.

The same basic procedure is followed when groups rather than individuals perform the letters-to-numbers task. Thus, on each trial the group collectively proposes one equation, learns the answer to that equation, collectively hypothesizes a specific mapping of one letter to one number, learns whether or not that mapping is correct, then collectively proposes the full coding of 10 letters to 10 numbers and learns whether or not it is correct. In addition, and paralleling what was done on the rule induction task, each group member also individually proposes one equation, hypothesizes a specific mapping of one letter to one number, and proposes the full coding of 10 letters to 10 numbers. Each of these is done just before the group collectively performs the same step. However, when the letters-to-numbers task is performed by groups, feedback is given only about the group's collective equation, collective hypothesis, and collective full coding.

Letters-to-Numbers and Strong Synergy

In the first published study to employ the letters-to-numbers task, Laughlin et al. (2002) compared the performance of 82 four-person groups to that of 328 individuals who worked on the task alone. For purposes of statistical comparison, the data records of the individual problem solvers were organized into 82 four-person nominal groups according to the order in which they participated in the study. For each nominal group, the number of trials required by each member to correctly state the full coding of 10 letters to 10 numbers was used to determined who performed best, second best, third best, and worst. The mean performance of the best, second-best, third-best, and worst members across the 82 nominal groups were then used as standards for evaluating the performance of the four-person interacting groups.

Laughlin et al. (2002) found that their interacting groups outperformed all four of these individual standards. Importantly, their four-person interacting groups performed the letters-to-numbers task statistically significantly better than even the best of the nominal group members. The interacting groups proposed significantly more complex equations, identified significantly more letters per equation, and in the end solved the full coding of 10 letters to 10 numbers in significantly fewer trials. For instance, whereas the best nominal group members identified an average of 2.25 letters per equation and solved the problem completely in an average of 5.90 trials, four-person interacting groups identified an average of 3.12 letters per equation and solved the problem completely in an average of 5.60 trials.

Because participants were assigned at random to work either alone or in interacting groups, and because the nominal groups were assembled in roughly the same way that interacting groups were (according to the temporal order in which they participated in the study), the best, second-best, third-best, and worst of the nominal group members should be equivalent, on average, to the best, second-best, third-best, and worst of the interacting group members, respectively. Therefore, these results are compelling evidence that the interacting four-person groups performed better than even their best members would have performed working alone. Said differently, the performance of the interacting groups exceeded what a best-member (Truth Wins) model would predict and clearly indicates a strong synergistic performance gain. Indeed, this appears to be one of the very few unassailable demonstrations of strong synergy in the group problem-solving literature. These findings with four-person groups have since been replicated with both three-person and five-person groups (Laughlin et al., 2003, 2006; but see also Bonner, 2004).

Letters-to-Numbers: Further Considerations

What is it about letters-to-numbers problems that permits groups to perform better than their best member? One possibility is that this task somehow allows each member individually to be a better problem solver when working collaboratively with others than when working alone. For example, it might be supposed that working collaboratively improves members' contributions by increasing their motivation to do well. Yet it is not obvious why letters-to-numbers problems should spark more motivation from members than other problem-solving tasks. To be sure, the letters-to-numbers task is very engaging, but so are many others. Further, the literature suggests that there is often a tendency for motivation to decline, not increase, when working collectively on tasks of this sort (see Chapter 8, pp. 271–281). These considerations make a motivational explanation less plausible than it might at first appear.

Alternatively, it might be suggested that working collaboratively on the letters-to-numbers task improves members' performance by boosting their individual problem-solving ability. However, this too is inconsistent with much of the extant literature. For example, the production blocking problem that occurs on idea generation tasks implies that working collectively can interfere with members' cognitive activity, and so hamper their ability to produce new ideas that might otherwise help them on problem-solving tasks (see Chapter 3, pp. 85–90). Thus, if there is a member-level benefit to performing the letters-to-numbers task collectively, it would have to be one that overcomes both the cognitive and motivational liabilities typically associated with group interaction.

Laughlin et al. (2002, 2003, 2006) did not attribute the strong synergistic performance gains they observed on letters-to-numbers problems to member-level improvements in either motivation or problem-solving ability. Rather, they attributed it to the highly intellective nature of the task itself. Unlike their earlier rule induction task, each inferential subtask that must be performed in order to solve a letters-to-numbers problem is clearly demonstrable. This is true not only with respect to rejecting incorrect inferences, but also with respect to recognizing correct inferences. By contrast, and as previously noted, within the rule induction task, only the rejection of incorrect inferences (implausible hypotheses) is demonstrable. The recognition of correct inferences—specifically, distinguishing correct from plausible-but-incorrect hypotheses—is not demonstrable. This makes letters-to-numbers problems more demonstrable overall, and so more purely intellective, than the rule induction task. Indeed, like the mathematical problems used in earlier group problem-solving research (e.g., Laughlin & Ellis, 1986; Stasson et al., 1991), letters-to-numbers problems appear to be located at or very near the highly intellective end of Laughlin's Intellective-Judgmental task continuum.

But letters-to-numbers problems have an important feature that traditional mathematical problems do not possess. As described more fully below, there are multiple strategies for deciphering the full coding of letters to numbers. Moreover, the comparative efficiency of these strategies can be gauged by problem solvers as they perform the task. That is, once a particular strategy is recognized, problem solvers can project roughly how many trials it would take to solve the full coding of 10 letters to 10 numbers using that strategy. Importantly, such projections can be made in advance of actually implementing the strategy and are themselves a demonstrable subtask. Further, the structure of the letters-to-numbers task is such that it permits problem solvers to switch from one strategy to another at will and to do so without losing any of the information they have already gained. Consequently, problem solvers can benefit from implementing a more efficient strategy even when it is belatedly recognized. However, as will be argued shortly, it may be easier for problem solvers to reap this benefit when working in groups than when attempting a letters-to-numbers problem alone. If so, this would explain why groups are able to solve letters-to-numbers problems in fewer trials than even their best members can individually, thus pinpointing one source of strong synergy in group intellective performance.

Equation Strategies

Consider first the equations that problem solvers propose on each trial of the letters-to-numbers task. Almost any equation, even a very simple one, is apt to generate at least some information pertinent to the mapping of letters-to-numbers. Still, certain types of equations can be expected to generate more information than others. One approach to solving letters-to-numbers problems is to use a two-letter substitution strategy. This involves proposing a series of equations with two single-letter terms that successively substitute letters learned in earlier trials. This strategy was employed on Trials 1 though 3 in the example given in Table 4.6. Once it was known that $E = 1$ (because $A+B = EC$), then $E + E = ?$ identified the letter that maps onto 2 ($E + E = B$). Subsequently, $B + E = ?$ identified the letter that maps onto 3 ($B + E = F$), and so forth. This method is simple, reliable, and works regardless of which letter is known initially. On the other hand, it is also rather inefficient—it requires as many as 9 trials to identify the full coding of 10 letters to 10 numbers (with 0 identified by elimination), and more if multiple trials are need to learn the identity of the first letter.[8]

A more efficient approach is to use a multiletter strategy. Here, the problem solver makes use of more elaborate equations with known, multidigit answers in order to identify several different letters simultaneously. Consider, for example, one variant of this strategy. If it is recognized that the sum of the numbers 0 through 9 is 45, then the equation $A + B + C + D + E + F + G + H + I + J = ?$ can be used to identify two letters on the very first trial—those that map onto 4 and 5. The sum of the remaining 8 numbers is $45 - 4 - 5 = 36$. Therefore, proposing an equation that sums over all letters except the two just identified will itself identify the letters that map onto 3 and 6, and so forth. This particular multiletter strategy is nearly twice as efficient as the two-letter substation approach; it requires exactly five trials to identify the full coding of 10 letters to 10 numbers (with 0 again identified by elimination). In general, strategies that involve equations with more letters and/or terms tend to identify the coding of more letters per trial than strategies that involve equations with fewer letters and/or terms. As a result, they also permit problem solvers to identify the full coding of 10 letters to 10 numbers in fewer trials overall.

As noted above, the structure of the letters-to-numbers task permits problem solvers to switch strategies without penalty. Thus, problem solvers can profit from implementing a more efficient strategy whenever it happens to be discovered. Strategy switching was illustrated in the example given in Table 4.6, where there was a switch on Trial 4 away from the simple two-letter substitution strategy to a more complex multiletter strategy (e.g., $FF + EE + E = ?$). Switching strategies at this point markedly reduced the number of trials-to-solution. An even more efficient multiletter equation would have been $E + EE + EEE + \cdots + EEEEEEEEE = ?$, which identifies all of the remaining letters (with 0 once again identified by elimination). Indeed, this equation could have been proposed as early as the second trial to yield the full coding of 10 letters to 10 numbers.

Hypothesis Strategies

Strategy is not restricted to equation formation in the letters-to-numbers task. It also plays a role when deciding what hypothesis to propose about the mapping of one letter to one number. Two strategies suggest themselves. One involves proposing hypotheses about letters that have not yet been identified. The hypotheses proposed on Trials 1, 3, and 4 in Table 4.6 illustrate this approach. In essence, each of these was a wild guess, although they become progressively less so over trials as the range of possible answers gradually narrows. The advantage of this guessing strategy is that it affords another opportunity to gain new information helpful for deciphering the full coding of letters to numbers. Potentially useful information may be gained even when the hypothesis turns out to be false (e.g., having learned that $A = 9$ is false in the first trial was helpful in the second trial for deducing that $A = 8$).

An alternative hypothesis formation strategy is to propose hypotheses that confirm the identity of letters that should already be known. This was illustrated in Trial 2, for example, where the problem solver proposed $C = 0$. As described above, prior to proposing this hypothesis, the problem solver should have been able to deduce the identity of C. Thus, learning that $C = 0$ is true yields no new information to help decipher the full coding of letters to numbers. On the other hand, problem solvers who are uncertain of their inferential powers should find affirmative answers to such hypotheses reassuring. Moreover, this confirmatory hypothesis testing strategy can serve a corrective function when deductive errors have in fact been made. Even so, this strategy is generally less efficient than simply guessing about letters whose identities are truly unknown.

Strategy Efficiency, Strategy Change, and Strong Synergy

Several strategy-related factors likely combine to promote the emergence of strong synergistic performance gains among groups attempting letters-to-numbers problems. In particular, compared to individual problem solvers, groups may (a) be better able to generate and evaluate alternative strategies and/or (b) be more willing to abandon one strategy in favor of another.

With regard to the first of these, the cognitive load imposed by the letters-to-numbers task is substantial and may be sufficiently great as to make it easier for groups than for even the best individuals to consider alternative approaches to solving letters-to-numbers problems. This is apt to be particularly true once they have discovered and begun to implement a workable strategy, even one that is less than maximally efficient. Groups may have an easier time of this because the subtask of exploring alternative strategies, which includes both conceptualizing new approaches and assessing their relative effectiveness vis-à-vis the current strategy, can be performed independent of, and simultaneously with, the subtask of implementing an already chosen strategy. Thus, for example, while some members are figuring out what the next equation should be according to the current strategy, others can consider better strategies. Simply put, strategy implementation and strategy exploration are separate subtasks that can be performed in parallel by different members of an interacting group. Individuals, by contrast, must perform both subtasks themselves, and they may not have the cognitive resources to do so in a fully effective way. Consequently, individual problem solvers may focus on the (arguably more important) implementation subtask to the relative exclusion of the exploration subtask.

Although speculative, this possibility is consistent with evidence presented by Laughlin et al. (2006), who reported that individual problem solvers are twice as likely to use the simpler two-letter substitution strategy as they are to use a more efficient, but more complex, multiletter strategy. Moreover, once they initiate it, individual problem solvers have a very strong tendency to stick with the two-letter substitution strategy to the end. They may do this simply because it is easier than marshalling the additional cognitive resources needed to identify more efficient strategies as they go along.

Also with regard to generating and evaluating alternative strategies, it is interesting to note that dyads do not display the same evidence of strong synergy that is found in larger groups. Specifically, Laughlin et al. (2006) compared the performance of two-, three-, four-, and five-person interacting groups to that of the best members in two-, three-, four-, and five-person nominal groups, respectively. They observed that, although three-, four-, and five-person interacting groups all performed significantly better than the best members in comparably sized nominal groups, two-person interacting groups did not perform better than the best members of two-person nominal groups. The results for four-person groups replicate the findings originally reported by Laughlin et al. (2002), and those for three-person groups replicate Laughlin et al. (2003). It should be noted, however, that Bonner (2004) did not find evidence of strong synergy in three-person groups. Thus, whereas groups with four or five members tend to show strong synergistic performance gains on letters-to-numbers problems, and groups with just two members do not, three-person groups sometimes do and sometimes do not show these gains.

These results suggest that a minimum of four members may be necessary in order to guarantee strong synergy in group performance on letters-to-numbers problems. Perhaps a minimum of four is needed to effectively distribute the cognitive load imposed by the task. Alternatively, it may be that group performance on this task is benefited by a certain degree of diversity among the problem-solving strategies that members individually are able to devise, and that at least four members are required to ensure such diversity. Said differently, groups of four or more may be able to perform better together than even their best members would have performed alone, not so much because of the greater quantity of problem-solving resources they bring to the task, but because of the greater heterogeneity of those resources, with greater heterogeneity facilitating the creation of novel approaches to solving letters-to-numbers problems. The issue of diversity among member resources, especially as they relate to problem-solving strategies, is a complex one that will be taken up at greater length in Chapter 9 (see pp. 331–343).

Finally, it also seems likely that problem solvers may be more confident in the soundness of their deductive reasoning when working on letters-to-numbers problems in groups compared to when working alone. Most problem solvers are apt to be somewhat uncertain about how to proceed when they first encounter this task and gain confidence only after working on it over several trials. It is likely, however, that their confidence will rise more quickly when they work on the task in groups as opposed to when they work individually (cf. Sniezek, 1989, 1992; Sniezek & Henry, 1989; Tasa, Taggar, & Seijts, 2007). Once acquired, task-specific confidence should permit (though not necessarily cause) problem-solvers to utilize more efficient problem-solving strategies. For example, those who are more confident in the accuracy of their deductive conclusions should be less prone to use confirmatory hypotheses when proposing the mapping of one letter to one number (i.e., the third step in each problem-solving trial), and should instead be more willing to employ a guessing strategy. As previously argued, although a confirmatory strategy may be comforting, it is largely unproductive. Guessing, on the other hand, can yield new information that demonstrably contributes to deciphering the full coding of 10 letters to 10 numbers. If groups do indeed gain confidence in their deductive powers more quickly than individuals, then a careful analysis of their trial-by-trial hypotheses should reveal that groups propose fewer hypotheses than individuals about letters they should already have known (e.g., as in Trial 2 of Table 4.6). Unfortunately, none of the studies published to date concerning group performance on the letters-to-numbers task report an analysis of problem-solvers' hypotheses.

In sum, the emergence of strong synergistic gains in group performance on the letters-to-numbers task is likely the result of one or more factors that enable groups to generate and adopt better task-performing strategies than even their best members would be able to do working alone. These include (a) the greater capacity of groups to exploit the inherent divisibility of certain letters-to-numbers subtasks, thus allowing them to better cope with the cognitive demands imposed by the task as a whole; (b) the greater diversity of problem-solving resources that groups possess, which enables them to more readily conceive novel strategies; and/or (c) the greater rate at which groups are likely to gain task-relevant confidence, which should permit them to abandon more quickly the comfortable-but-less-efficient strategies they are apt to employ initially.

☐ Chapter Summary

In this chapter, I have provided an introduction to the empirical literature concerned with group performance on problem-solving tasks. On such tasks, the goal is to identify the objectively correct solution. I have focused on those aspects of this literature that bear most directly on the issue of group performance gains.

The first section of the chapter focused on several formal models of group problem-solving performance. I began with Lorge and Solomon's Model A, then sketched the subsequent development and application of Davis's (1973) social decision scheme theory. The relationship between various SDS models and solution demonstrability was discussed. The overarching conclusion that can be drawn from this body of work is that groups typically perform better than an average-member model (Proportionality) would predict, and approach the performance predicted by a best-member model (Truth Wins). The latter result is especially likely as the task becomes increasingly demonstrable. However, at least on the sorts of problems historically employed in SDS research, group performance has not been shown to exceed that predicted by a best member model, even when the task in question is highly demonstrable. In other words, weak synergy, not strong synergy, typifies much of this literature.

The remainder of the chapter then examined in some detail two more-recent streams of research concerning tasks that are broadly relevant to many forms of everyday problem-solving: the rule induction task and the letters-to-numbers task. Both involve repeated cycles of reviewing evidence, formulating hypotheses, and probing the environment for new evidence. Further, both become increasingly information-rich over time. These tasks are unusual in that they are more complex than what typically is found in the group problem-solving literature. The empirical evidence regarding group performance on these two tasks was reviewed. The rule induction task is noteworthy because it yields group performance that is equivalent to (but not better than) the performance of its best member. This occurs despite the fact that the rule induction task is not fully demonstrable. The letters-to-numbers task, on the other hand, is remarkable because it is the one problem-solving task on which groups have repeatedly been shown to perform better than even their best members. Given that this result has been so difficult to find with other problem-solving tasks, some suggestions were offered concerning what it is about the letters-to-numbers task that permits the emergence of strong synergy in group performance.

☐ Endnotes

1. Lorge and Solomon (1955) also proposed a Model B, which extends these same ideas to tasks that have two or more independent stages or subtasks.
2. For example, a group may be less likely to identify the correct solution if nonsolvers all prefer the same incorrect answer compared to when each of them prefers a different incorrect answer.
3. Although Table 4.3 does not distinguish groups according to which specific incorrect solutions their nonsolvers prefer, if different incorrect solutions have different probabilities of occurring, then it is necessary to distinguish among groups in this way, too, in order to determine the overall probability of obtaining each summary distribution shown in that table.
4. However, neither model predicts a strong synergistic performance gain, simply because the Truth Wins model (which provides the criterion that must be surpassed to claim evidence of strong synergy) now yields a predicted solution rate of $P_{tw} = .99$.
5. A seventh model, simple Proportionality, was tested indirectly in this study.
6. Laughlin et al. (1991) also allow that the group's collective response might be an emergent hypothesis—one that was not previously proposed by any member individually. However, this is expected to occur only if no more

than one plausible hypothesis has been proposed and no majority hypothesis exists. Even then, emergent hypotheses are expected to be very low probability events.

7. An example in a four-person group would be a plausible hypothesis advocated by one member, pH1, an implausible hypothesis advocated by two members, iH2, and a different implausible hypothesis advocated by one member, iH1. According to the hybrid model, the group will select its response from among all three of these hypotheses (none is excluded, because only one plausible hypothesis was proposed), and iH2 is twice as likely to be adopted as either of the other two.

8. In practice, the total number of trials-to-solution employing this simple two-letter substitution strategy is apt to be less than what is suggested here, because several letters may be guessed correctly when proposing hypotheses about the mapping of one letter to one number. But this is true regardless of the type of equation proposed and does not obviate the point being made about the relative efficiency of different strategies. Thus, I ignore this detail here.

Judgment Calls

Performing Tasks With Hard-to-Demonstrate Correct Answers

This chapter and the one to follow are about group performance on judgment and decision-making tasks, respectively. They stand in contrast to Chapter 4, which focused on problem-solving tasks. Judgment and decision making can be distinguished from problem solving in terms of Laughlin's Intellective–Judgmental task continuum (1980; 1999; Laughlin & Ellis, 1986). As defined in Chapter 4, collective problem solving is a cooperatively performed cognitive activity located at or near the intellective end of that continuum. This means that in principle it should be possible for group members to convincingly demonstrate to one another whether or not a proposed task response (solution alternative) is, in fact, correct. Such demonstrations depend in part on the existence—and availability to the group—of objective evaluative criteria that are enmeshed in a nexus of well-defined rules, operations, and relationships. The latter constitute the conceptual system(s) within which the problem is solved. Thus, the letters-to-numbers task involves problem-solving because proposed solutions are readily evaluated by reference to the rules of mathematics, deductive reasoning, and natural language.

If we can say that problem solving occupies roughly the left-hand (intellective) third of the Intellective–Judgmental task continuum, then judgment and decision making occupy the remaining two thirds. Collective judgment and collective decision-making are two types of cooperatively performed cognitive activities in which it is substantially harder, if not impossible, for members to demonstrate conclusively to one another that a proposed response (judgment or decision alternative) is, in fact, correct. This may be because information that would normally be useful in such

159

a demonstration is unavailable, or because the applicable conceptual system is ambiguous about how the information that is available should be interpreted and combined.

It is more difficult to distinguish *between* judgment tasks and decision-making tasks, especially with respect to demonstrability. Arguably the most prototypic type of judgment task is quantity estimation (e.g., estimate the number of students who will apply for admission to your university next year). When an individual or group is asked to give an estimate of some quantity, the response provided is quite naturally treated as a continuous variable. Further, if an objective criterion exists (e.g., the number of students who actually do apply for admission next year), the individual or group response can be evaluated in terms of its *degree* of correctness; some estimates will be more correct than others, even if none is perfectly correct. Estimation tasks are also marked by their open-ended nature, and by the very large number of possible responses that might be given.

Decision making, by contrast, typically involves a small number of fixed response alternatives that are not easily ordered in terms of degree of correctness. Rather, one alternative is usually considered superior to the others, with the rest simply being inferior, though perhaps for different reasons. As a result, like many problem-solving tasks, performance on decision-making tasks is most often evaluated dichotomously, according to whether or not the group has chosen the alternative deemed best.

I address the issue of synergy in group judgments in the present chapter, then turn to group decision making in Chapter 6. In both chapters, the focus is on tasks for which there is some reasonable way to evaluate the quality of the responses that are given. This is an essential requirement if meaningful conclusions about performance gains are to be drawn. Consequently, I ignore judgment and decision-making tasks located at the extreme right-hand (judgmental) end of the Intellective–Judgmental task continuum. As noted in Chapter 2 and elsewhere, these are tasks where the central goal is to establish what is best, correct, or true, as opposed to just matching some externally defined standard of excellence. Because there is no way to evaluate the quality of responses given to such tasks, they are beyond the scope of empirical inquiry into synergistic performance gains in groups.

It should also be noted at the outset that the present chapter is much shorter than are the chapters on group problem-solving (Chapter 4) and decision making (Chapter 6). This reflects the fact that the empirical literature on group judgment is less well developed than are the literatures in those other two areas, and that there is consequently less material to cover.

☐ Quantity Estimation

Research that compares the quality of individual and group judgments has dealt almost exclusively with quantity estimation tasks. Such tasks require that a specific quantity or magnitude be reckoned. Real-world examples include gauging the driving distance from Zurich to Lisbon (when planning a vacation), estimating the number of households with Internet access in Mexico (when preparing a marketing plan), and judging the average salary of one's colleagues (when asking for a raise). In each case, the response scale is such that the estimate provided can be evaluated according to its absolute distance from the correct or true value, with closer estimates being more accurate.[1] Estimation tasks thus call for an optimum response—one that is as near as possible to the true value.

Estimation tasks sometimes involve reckoning present quantities, as in the examples above, but sometimes involve reckoning past or future quantities. Estimates of future quantities are often called forecasts. Examples include predicting the sales volume for a new consumer product (when making a production schedule) and estimating the completion date of a construction project (when preparing a contract).[2] Forecasts are typically made on the basis of some identifiable set of data. Often there is a temporal structure to that data, but not always. Sales volume, for example, might be forecast on the basis of historical sales information (e.g., from the past several years), where seasonal and annual trends must be taken into account. Construction project completion dates, on the other hand, are commonly estimated from the scope and complexity of the work to be done, as well as the availability of materials, equipment, and labor. Here, detecting trends over time is less relevant to the task.

Estimates and forecasts can be generated either by individuals or by groups. From a logistical standpoint, individual estimates are usually easier to obtain. Group estimates, on the other hand, are often thought to be more accurate. For this reason, when accuracy is paramount, groups rather than individuals are more likely to be assigned the task of producing the required estimate (cf. Lawrence, O'Connor, & Edmundson, 2000). But is this assumption about the superiority of group estimates justified? Are collectively generated estimates really more accurate than those produced by individuals working alone? And, more to the point, is there any evidence of a synergistic performance gain when estimation tasks are performed collectively rather than individually?

☐ Criteria for Assessing Synergy in Collective Estimation

Before addressing this question, it is useful to consider what is needed from a methodological standpoint in order to draw conclusions about the presence or absence of synergy in group performance on estimation tasks. Research that compares the performance of groups and individuals on such tasks usually proceeds by having participants estimate some target quantity twice. They do so first as individuals working alone, then again later as part of an interacting group. If any special information is provided to help participants make their estimates, that information is typically made available on both occasions. Consequently, one can look for evidence of synergy in group performance on such tasks by comparing the group's collective estimate to the estimates made individually by its members. Several different comparisons are possible.

One is to compare the accuracy of the group's estimate with the mean accuracy of the members' individual estimates. Such a comparison requires that each of the members' individually generated quantity estimates first be scored for accuracy, then the mean of those accuracy scores computed. Across a wide variety of estimation tasks, such comparisons generally show that groups are indeed more accurate than individuals, often by a wide margin. However, these comparisons are not particularly helpful for understanding synergy in groups. The reason is that they involve a performance standard—mean individual accuracy—that does not relate in a useful way to the definition of synergy given in Chapter 1. Recall that synergy refers to a performance gain that is attributable in some way to group interaction. It implies that the group has been able to accomplish something collectively that could not reasonably have been achieved by any simple combination of individual member efforts. Average member accuracy is an insufficient criterion for judging the presence of synergy in groups because it does not address the "simple combination of members' efforts" issue. Instead, it leaves members' efforts (or, more precisely, the products of their efforts) essentially disaggregated and so tells us nothing about what would be achieved by combined those efforts in some simple way that does not itself depend on group interaction.

A better approach is to compare the accuracy of the group's collective estimate to the accuracy of the average of the members' individual estimates. This requires that the members' individual estimates first be averaged, and then that the accuracy of that single average be assessed. Averaging the estimates first, before assessing accuracy, is a simple and straightforward procedure for combining individual efforts. It obviously requires no group interaction. Moreover, it is an approach that any manager or policy maker might consider when thinking about how best to combine independent estimates made by others. The accuracy of the average of the members' estimates provides a more useful—and more stringent[3]—baseline for judging the presence of synergy in group performance. If synergy denotes performance that is above and beyond what would be expected from a simple combination of member efforts, and if averaging typifies simple combinatorial processes, then group performance on a collective estimation task should be taken as evidence of synergy only if it exceeds the level of accuracy achieved by the average of its members' individual estimates. Said differently, the accuracy of the average estimate (as opposed to the average accuracy of the separate estimates) establishes a minimum criterion that must be surpassed if evidence of even weak synergy is to be claimed.

Distinguishing Weak Versus Strong Synergy

But what about strong synergy? Recall that strong synergy refers to group performance that exceeds what even the best member in the group is able to accomplish working alone. When performing an estimation task, the best member is defined as the one whose individual estimate comes closest to the true value of the target quantity. The accuracy of the best member's estimate provides a reasonable standard for differentiating between weak and strong synergy in group quantity estimation, but only if the best member's estimate is itself more accurate than the average of the members' individual estimates. To see this, consider the two possible alignments of best and average member accuracy.

The first is when the best member's quantity estimate is more accurate than the average of the members' estimates. In this case, strong and weak synergy can be clearly differentiated. If the group's collective estimate is more accurate than both the average estimate and the best member's estimate, then it seems reasonable to view the group's performance as an instance of strong synergy; they have achieved a level of performance that is beyond not only what a simple combination of member efforts would yield, but also beyond what even their best member was able to accomplish alone. On the other hand, if the accuracy of the group's collective estimate is intermediate between these two standards—better than the average estimate, but not as good as the best member's estimate—then the group's performance should be viewed as an instance of only weak synergy. And, of course, if the group's collective estimate does not exceed the accuracy of even the average of the members' estimates, then it provides no evidence of synergy at all and might even indicate a net process loss (i.e., if it were less accurate than the average of the members' estimates).

The other possible alignment of best and average member accuracy is when the best member's quantity estimate is *less* accurate than the average.[4] In this case, if the group's collective estimate is found to be more accurate than the average of its members' individual estimates, then it will also be more accurate than its best member's estimate. On the other hand, surpassing the accuracy of the best member by itself says nothing about the group's collective accuracy vis-à-vis the average estimate and so does not necessarily indicate performance that has surpassed what reasonably could have been achieved by a simple combination of member efforts. Consequently, surpassing only the accuracy of the best member's estimate is insufficient evidence for claiming a synergistic performance gain. Rather, it is necessary that the group's collective estimate also be more accurate than the average member estimate. Furthermore, there is no way in this situation to distinguish between weak and strong synergy—because there is no unambiguous criterion for doing so. Thus, when the best member's estimate is less accurate than the average estimate, and the group's collective estimate is more accurate than both, all that can be said is that some sort of synergistic performance gain has occurred. It is not possible to say whether that gain reflects a weak or strong form of synergy.

The Role of Bias in Individual Estimates

Which of the two alignments described above is more likely to occur in a given setting depends a great deal on the degree to which the members' individual quantity estimates are biased (Einhorn, Hogarth, & Klempner 1977; Reagan-Cirincione & Rohrbaugh, 1992). Unbiased estimates are estimates that are no more likely to be too high than too low. The mathematics of probability, and of expectations in particular, tells us that the expected value of a set of unbiased estimates is equal to the true value of the quantity being estimated. This means that, when unbiased estimates are averaged, the positive and negative errors in those estimates will tend to offset one another, leaving the mean closer to the true value than most, if not all, of the individual estimates. Thus, if group members are drawn at random from a population that is unbiased in its estimates of some target quantity, the average of their estimates will tend to converge on the true value of that quantity, deviating from it by chance alone. Further, the magnitude of this deviation can be expected to decrease as the size of the group increases.

This stands in contrast to what is likely to happen when members are drawn from a population that is systematically biased in its estimates. Biased estimates are consistently either too high or too low. There are a great many reasons why estimates might be biased. They might be biased, for example, because of the undue influence of one or more anchor values (e.g., Whyte & Sebenius, 1997), because critical information upon which the estimates depend is not uniformly distributed in the population (e.g., Lavery, Franz, Winquist, & Larson, 1999), or because the estimates concern the group's own future behavior (e.g., how long it will take them to complete a project; e.g., Buehler, Messervey, & Griffin, 2005). Regardless of the reason for the bias, the average of the estimates will not converge on the true value. Instead, it will tend toward a value that deviates from the true value by an amount equal to the bias. The greater the bias in the population from which group members are drawn, the greater the expected difference between the average of the members' individual estimates and the true value.

These considerations have two important implications for the search for synergy in group performance on collective estimation tasks. First, there will generally be more opportunity to observe synergistic performance gains in groups when their members' individual quantity estimates are systematically biased, compared to when they are unbiased. The mean of a set of biased estimates simply leaves more room for improvement than does the mean of a set of unbiased estimates. How much more depends on the amount of bias involved. Second, when individual quantity estimates are systematically biased, one is more likely to observe that the best member's estimate is more accurate than the average estimate. Consequently, not only is there more opportunity to observe synergy in groups whose members' individual quantity estimates are systematically biased, there is also a greater likelihood of being able to distinguish between weak and strong synergy. In short, the search for synergy in group performance on collective estimation tasks is apt to be most productive when focusing on quantities that individuals systematically either overestimate or underestimate.

□ Evidence of Synergy in Collective Estimation

Although several dozen studies have compared the performance of groups and individuals on estimation tasks, only a fraction of that number provide all of the information needed to make a full assessment regarding synergistic performance gains. The most severe problem has been not reporting the accuracy of the average of the members' individual estimates. Many studies have reported instead the mean accuracy of the members' estimates (i.e., without first averaging those estimates).[5] As argued above, this prevents any meaningful assessment of synergy at all. And among those studies that do report the accuracy of the average of the members' estimates, many either do not report the accuracy of the best member's estimate or report it in a way that leaves it unclear whether the best member is more or less accurate than the average. This, too, is problematic, because it prevents the differentiation of weak and strong synergy.

Strong Synergy

Among those studies providing sufficient information to properly gauge performance gains, very few offer clear evidence of strong synergy. Henry (1993) asked participants to estimate nine different "world knowledge" quantities (e.g., the year of Beethoven's birth; the length of the Nile River). Participants did this first as individuals, then collectively in three-person groups. It was found that the groups' collective estimates were more accurate than the average of their members' individual estimates 72% of time, and more accurate than their best member's estimates 17% of time. Using a similar procedure, Credé and Sniezek (2003) had participants estimate the number of parking tickets issued per year at their university. The group estimates were more accurate than the average of their members' individual estimates 70% of time, and more accurate than their best member's estimates 35% of time.

In a more elaborate study that took a rather different approach to assessing accuracy, Reagan-Cirincione (1994) had business and public administration students estimate either the average teacher salary in each of the 50 states of the United States or the number of regular season games won by each of 50 professional baseball teams. Participants estimating teacher salaries were provided five pieces of information about each state: its poverty rate, total expenditures on primary and secondary education, average amount of financial aid provided per student, region of the country in which the state is located, and size of the student population. Similarly, those estimating baseball team performance were given five summary statistics about each team: its overall batting average, earned run average, number of errors committed, number of bases stolen, and number of double plays turned. Participants estimated one or the other of these two sets of quantities first as individuals and then again (in a separate session) as members of either four-person or five-person groups. For both tasks, accuracy was defined as the correlation between the estimates and the true values across the full set of cases. These correlations were computed separately for each group and for the participants within each group. Thus, the dimension of accuracy being assessed in this study was how well variation in the true values was tracked by variation in the estimates. It was found that the group estimates (mean $r = .72$) were significantly more accurate than the estimates given by their best members (mean $r = .65$; $p < .01$), which in turn were significantly more accurate than the average of the member estimates (mean $r = .47$, $p < .01$). Overall, 81% of the groups performed better than their best member on these tasks.

It is worth noting that, unlike most studies, Reagan-Cirincione (1994) provided her groups with substantial process support as they made their collective estimates, and this may have played an important role in producing the effects she observed. Specifically, each group was assigned an independent facilitator who was trained to encourage equal participation and to foster both analytical and intuitive thinking. Further, both groups and individuals were given extensive statistical feedback about their observed pattern of information utilization across cases—that is, how they actually weighted the various pieces of predictor information—and they had an opportunity to reconcile this feedback with their intuitive beliefs about how that information should be weighted before finalizing their estimates. Because all groups received this elaborate intervention (i.e., there was no no-treatment control condition), it is difficult to say exactly how important it was for producing the performance gains Reagan-Cirincione observed.

Weak Synergy

The results from the three studies just described clearly suggest that groups are capable of strong synergistic performance gains when engaged in collective estimation tasks. However, they more commonly demonstrate weak synergy. For example, Laughlin, Gonzalez, and Sommer (2003) had participants estimate quantities within each of 36 different world-knowledge domains, aided in most cases by information about the true value of other quantities within the same domain (e.g., when estimating the population of Seattle, participants might be informed about the populations of San Francisco and St. Louis). Subsequently, participants were organized into three-person groups, and they collectively estimated the same quantities again under the same informational conditions. The group estimates were found to be significantly more accurate than the estimates of their second- and third-best members, but no more accurate than the estimates of their best member. Although the average of the members' individual estimates was not reported in this study, the estimate of the second-best member in a three-person group can be taken as a rough approximation of that average (assuming that members were drawn from a symmetrically distributed population). Thus, it seems reasonable to conclude that this study finds evidence of weak synergy.

Several studies have found collective group estimates to be significantly less accurate than their best members' estimates but still better than the average of their members' estimates. Sniezek (1989) found this when participants were asked to perform four different sales forecasting tasks. The collective forecasts of five-person groups were significantly more accurate than the average of their members' individual forecasts but not as good as their best member's forecast. The same pattern was observed by Rohrbaugh (1979), who had participants estimate a set of 40 student GPAs based on information about each student's standing on five personality variables. Rohrbaugh employed a methodology similar to the one used by Reagan-Cirincione (1994) described above, with accuracy defined in terms of the correlation between estimated and true values over the 40 targets.

Finally, several studies have reported group estimates to be more accurate than the average of their members' individual estimates, but without reporting the accuracy of their best member's estimate (e.g., Ang & O'Connor, 1991; Frings, Hopthrow, Abrams, Hulbert, & Gutierrez, 2008; Olsson, Juslin, & Olsson, 2006; Sniezek & Henry, 1989; Trotman, 1985).[6] These studies indicate that some kind of synergistic performance gain occurred, but it is not possible to determine whether what was found was strong or weak synergy.

No Synergy and Process Loss

It is also important to note that some studies have found collectively generated group estimates to be no more accurate than the average of their members' individual estimates (e.g., Bonner, Gonzalez, & Sommer, 2004; Fischer 1981; Gigone & Hastie, 1993, 1996, 1997a; Sniezek, 1990). Worse yet, collective estimates have occasionally been found to be significantly less accurate than that average. Buehler et al. (2005), for example, asked the members of classroom project groups (Study 1) and laboratory groups (Studies 2 and 3) to forecast how long it would take their group to complete various task assignments. These estimates were then compared to the amount of time the assignments actually took to complete. Although all of the estimates tended to be overly optimistic (lower than the true value), collective group estimates were almost always more optimistic— and so less accurate—than the members' individual estimates. Similarly, when estimating Bayesian probabilities, Hinsz, Tindale, and Nagao (2008) found collective group estimates to be more accurate than the average of the members' individual estimates under some circumstances, but less accurate under others (see also Argote, Devadas, & Melone, 1990).

☐ Synergy in Collective Estimation: Further Considerations

Thus, the empirical literature seems to suggest that, although groups are capable of strong synergy, they more often display either weak synergy, no synergy, or in some cases even a net process loss. The conditions that determine which of these is most likely to occur in a given situation are at present poorly understood.

One reason why the emergence of synergy on collective estimation tasks is difficult to predict may be that researchers have paid relatively little attention to the issue of bias in member estimates (for an exception, see Hinsz, Tindale, & Nagao, 2008). As argued previously, the presence versus absence of systematic bias is likely to affect the opportunity to observe performance gains in collective estimation. Beyond mere opportunity, however, bias may impact the very process by which collective estimates are formed. The search for synergy in collective estimation would benefit from a methodical investigation of this possibility. Indeed, our understanding of collective estimation would benefit even from such simple steps as more consistently reporting the presence, direction, and strength of members' estimation biases, and whether the true value of the estimated quantity lies inside or outside the range of estimates provided individually by group members.

The search for synergy would also likely benefit if greater attention were paid to the role of member expertise (or lack thereof) in the development of collective estimates. If synergistic performance gains do in fact occur on collective estimation tasks, then almost by definition they must be the result of an error correction process rooted in group interaction. But errors cannot be corrected unless they exist to begin with. This suggests, perhaps counter-intuitively, that there should be more opportunity for performance gains to materialize when collective estimation tasks are performed by groups of novices compared to when they are performed by groups of experts, because the estimates of novices are apt to be less accurate (further from the true value) and more biased than those of experts.

Of course, groups are sometimes quite diverse with regard to member expertise. Descriptively, it is often the case that some members are more expert than others, in the sense that their estimates are consistently closer to the true value. As such, a weak synergistic performance gain would be achieved if groups were to give greater weight to the estimates of their most expert members. This strategy would pull the group's collective estimate away from the arithmetic average and toward the true value (assuming the expert's estimate is itself more accurate than the average). In the extreme case, this approach would result in the group simply adopting the estimate of its most expert member as its collective response.

Although there is empirical evidence supporting the idea that collective estimates sometimes are formed by weighting individual estimates according to members' expertise (Baumann & Bonner, 2004; Bonner, Sillito, & Baumann, 2007; Sniezek & Henry, 1989, 1990), this same work indicates that groups have great difficulty identifying who among them is more expert than the rest. Further, the weighting-by-expertise approach usually does not permit the group to exceed the performance of its best member.[7] Nor does it explain the fact that groups sometimes produce "out-of-range" estimates. Out-of-range estimates are collective responses that lie outside the boundaries defined by the highest and lowest individual member estimates (Credé & Sniezek, 2003; Henry, 1993; Sniezek & Henry, 1989, 1990). When observed, out-of-range estimates have sometimes (but not always) been associated with higher levels of group performance. Simple weighting schemes do not account for such observations, because mathematically those schemes do not permit group responses that are beyond the range of their members' individual estimates.

It is tempting to speculate that the degree of variability members perceive among their individual estimates may play an important role in determining how their collective estimate is formed.[8] When they perceive relatively little variability, members may rely on a simple—and rather mechanical—equal-weighting scheme to resolve the differences among those estimates. This, of course, is tantamount to averaging, and so would produce no synergy at all. When there is a moderate amount of perceived variability, on the other hand, members may be more thoughtful about the way they weight one another's contributions. They might, for example, look for cues to relative expertise as a way to determine the amount of influence that each member's individual estimate should have. Or, if they are unable to judge relative expertise, they might at least give less weight to extreme estimates (cf. Davis, 1996). Thus, under conditions of moderate perceived variability we might expect to see weak synergistic performance gains, as these differential weighting schemes are apt to result in at least some improvement over weighting one another's contributions equally. Finally, when members perceive a high degree of variability among their individual estimates, they might abandon the weighting-of-member-contributions approach altogether, and instead form their collective estimate on the basis of a fresh examination of the available data. It is when this happens that strong synergy seems most apt to emerge. Rethinking the task from the beginning permits the generation of a collective estimate that does not relate in a direct way to the members' individual estimates, and may even be outside the range of those estimates. In this connection, it is worth noting that in the study by Reagan-Cirincione (1994) described earlier, groups were formed explicitly with the goal of maximizing within-group variability in member estimates. This too may have contributed to the finding from that study that groups out-performed even their best members.

In sum, although it is difficult at present to draw broad conclusions about when synergistic performance gains are and are not likely to emerge on collective estimation tasks, there is reason to believe that additional conceptual and empirical work may bring greater clarity to this literature. More attention should be paid to the effects of both member bias and member expertise, as well as to the possibility that collective estimates may be formed differently in different situations.

☐ Chapter Summary

In this chapter, I have summarized that portion of the group judgment literature that bears most directly on the question of synergistic performance gains in groups. This literature deals almost exclusively with quantity estimation tasks. An important methodological issue raised in the chapter concerns the criteria that should be used for assessing synergy on such tasks and, in particular, the importance of comparing the accuracy of a group's collective estimate to the accuracy of the average of its members' individual estimates (as opposed to the average accuracy of the members' estimates). I summarized the findings from research that employs this criterion.

With respect to performance gains on collective estimation tasks, it appears that almost any kind of empirical result is possible. Several studies show evidence of strong synergistic gains, while many others point only to weak synergistic gains. And some studies find no evidence of synergy at all, or even a net process loss. I suggested several methodological reasons why the emergence of synergy on collective estimation tasks may be so difficult to predict and speculated about directions that future research in this area might profitably take.

☐ Endnotes

1. Defining accuracy in terms of absolute (as opposed to signed) distance from the true value assumes that underestimation and overestimation are equally undesirable. Although this is not always true in the real world, collective estimation in such asymmetric situations has seldom been examined empirically. For alternative approaches to assessing accuracy, see Gigone and Hastie (1997b).

2. Although real-world forecasting always involves the estimation of truly future quantities, research on forecasting usually involves the estimation of what might best be called "historical" future quantities (for an exception, see Buehler, Messervey, & Griffin, 2005). That is, participants are asked to "forecast" an unknown quantity as it actually existed at some earlier time (e.g., sales volume for the first quarter of 2007) based on relevant information from an even earlier period (e.g., monthly sales data for the years 2003 through

2006). This approach captures the essence of forecasting but avoids the inconvenience of having to wait for the true value of the estimated quantity to materialize.

3. When the true value of the estimated quantity is within the range of the members' estimates, and accuracy is defined in terms of absolute distance from that true value, the accuracy of the average of the members' estimates will be greater than the average accuracy of their separate estimates. See Wallsten and Diederich (2001) for a broader treatment of this issue.

4. To see that the best member's estimate can indeed be less accurate than the average of all the members' estimates, consider the following. The two members of a dyad are asked, "How many urban areas in the world have a population of more than 10 million people?" Member A privately estimates 14. Member B privately estimates 26. The true value is 22 (Demographia, 2008). Member A thus missed the correct answer by 8, whereas Member B missed it by 4. Thus, Member B is the best member in the dyad. However, the average of the two estimates, $(14 + 26)/2 = 20$, is more accurate still, missing the true value by just 2. Thus, in this case the best member's estimate is less accurate than the average of their estimates.

5. In principle, it might be possible in some cases to compute after the fact the accuracy of the average of the members' estimates from the reported mean accuracy of their individual estimates. This can be done, however, only when all of the individual estimates are on the same side of the true value—when they are all either overestimates or underestimates. In practice, research reports seldom provided enough information about the distribution of individual estimates vis-à-vis the true value to make this computation possible.

6. Interestingly, Frings et al. (2008) observed that, under conditions of mental impairment (alcohol intoxication), even the private estimates that group members made in the presence of their groupmates were more accurate than the estimates made by individuals working completely alone.

7. An exception is when the best member's estimate and the average estimate are on opposite sides of the true value. But even in this case, a great deal depends on precisely how much weight is accorded the best member's estimate.

8. Operationally, perceived variability might be indexed by the degree to which members' subjective confidence intervals overlap one another. Subjective confidence intervals are created by asking each member to indicate a range of values around his or her individual point estimate that contains the true value with some specific level of confidence, say 90% (cf. Kuhn & Sniezek, 1996; Larson & Reenan, 1979). Such an interval functions subjectively in much the same way that a statistical confidence interval functions objectively. The more members' confidence intervals overlap one another, the less variability they are apt to perceive in those estimates. Conversely, the less their confidence intervals overlap, the greater the variability they are likely to perceive.

Decision Making

*Selecting From Among Discrete
Choice Alternatives*

This chapter is concerned with group performance on decision-making tasks. Collective decision making, like collective judgment (Chapter 5), is a cooperatively performed cognitive activity in which it is difficult for members to demonstrate conclusively to one another that a proposed response (decision alternative) is in fact best. This difficulty arises primarily because the conceptual systems within which such decisions are made are rather imprecise about how the information available to decision makers should be interpreted and combined (cf. Chapter 2, pp. 48–49). Indeed, those systems may be so ill-defined as to suggest only vague, and perhaps conflicting, evaluative criteria, thus encouraging disagreements among members about such basic matters as the objectives to be achieved in making their decision. A parole board, for example, may struggle with how to weight retributive versus rehabilitative goals when making early prison release decisions. And in a particular case, they may argue at length about whether or not an inmate's belated, and seemingly self-serving, admission of guilt should be factored into their ruling. Thus, although it is fundamentally a cooperative activity, group decision making can sometimes be an occasion for substantial interpersonal tension and conflict.

This chapter examines the empirical literature on group decision-making effectiveness for evidence of synergistic performance gains. As was the case in Chapter 5, this means focusing only on those tasks that provide a reasonable way to assess the quality of the decisions that are made. However, unlike judgment tasks, where there are usually objective criteria against which the performance of individuals and groups can be gauged, decision-making tasks generally lack objective performance criteria.[1] Rather, performance on decision-making tasks is typically evaluated against normative criteria.

In the first section of the chapter, I introduce two classes of normative criteria that can be employed to assess decision-making effectiveness. I do this in the context of two substantive issues. One issue is whether groups are any more or less susceptible than individuals to the impact of potentially biasing information. The other is whether groups are able to make use of information that is unevenly distributed among their members prior to discussion. Regarding the latter, a particularly problematic situation arises when decision-relevant information is distributed in such a way that members do not perceive the superiority of the best-choice alternative based on just the information they hold individually. Information distributed in this way can have a decidedly pernicious impact on group decision-making effectiveness. I summarize the research findings on this point toward the end of that first section and call attention to the very sparse evidence of synergy that exists in this literature. In subsequent sections, I then consider several lines of research investigating the underlying processes that are responsible for thwarting synergistic performance gains in these situations. The bulk of this work focuses on the content of group decision-making discussions, although the independent mediational role of members' prediscussion decision preferences is also considered.

☐ Two Challenges to Effective Decision Making

Decision making tasks generally require an individual or group to choose from among a small set of fixed alternatives that differ from one another in kind rather than degree. A straightforward approach to evaluating performance on such tasks is in terms of whether or not the alternative deemed best by the researcher is in fact chosen by the decision maker(s). The best alternative is typically defined as the one that offers the greatest number of benefits with the fewest costs, or the one with more positive and fewer negative attributes than others. Such criteria are descriptively normative in that they are assumed to reflect the way most people would understand and combine the available information (e.g., most would view attribute X as an asset rather than a liability, and most would consider a choice alternative with two assets to be better than an alternative with just one). Using this approach, it is possible to ask whether decision makers are able to respond appropriately to the implications of information that normatively *should* affect their decision.

A rather different approach, and one that does not require the identification of an a priori best alternative, is to manipulate the presence or absence of information that might—but normatively *should not*—impact a decision. Such information is a potential source of bias in decision making (e.g., information about an applicant's physical appearance when deciding who will and who will not be admitted into graduate school). Thus, one can ask whether decision makers are able to resist the biasing effects of such information. Questions of this form are useful in part because they rely on prescriptive norms (i.e., social, legal, or technical desiderata) that specify very precisely what ought to occur if decision makers are behaving appropriately: their decisions ought to remain invariant when the potentially biasing information is present versus absent.

Here I consider two issues closely tied to these methodological approaches. The first is whether groups are any more or less susceptible than individuals to the impact of potentially biasing information— information that normatively should not affect their decisions. After that I examine whether groups are able to make use of information that normatively should affect their decisions, but that might not do so because it is not uniformly held by all members prior to discussion.

The Challenge of Biasing Information

Consider a situation in which one or more pieces of information that are irrelevant to a particular decision (in the sense of being nondiagnostic), or that should be ignored for some technical or legal reason, nevertheless threatens to influence that decision. A case in point is the plight of jurors who are asked to ignore some piece of seemingly useful, but legally inadmissible, evidence that inadvertently surfaces during a criminal trial. Most studies indicate that jurors are easily biased by such evidence. Inadmissible evidence that favors the plaintiff tends to increase jurors' preference for a guilty verdict, whereas inadmissible evidence that favors the defendant tends to increase their preference for an acquittal. Judicial instructions to ignore such evidence can sometimes reduce these biases, but seldom are they eliminated completely (Steblay, Hosch, Culhane, & McWethy, 2006).

An interesting question with implications for practice as well as theory is whether groups (juries) are any more or less effective than individuals (jurors) in holding at bay the biasing influence of legally proscribed information. More specifically, does jury deliberation and collective decision making help jurors follow the law when it comes to ignoring inadmissible evidence?

Several studies have employed a mock jury methodology to examine this question (e.g., Kaplan & Miller, 1978, Exp. 3; Kerwin & Schaffer, 1994; London & Nunez, 2000). For example, London and Nunez (2000) ran two separate experiments in which university students read a six-page trial summary describing an alleged sexual assault. The defendant was accused of disrobing and fondling an 8-year-old girl while she waited at his residence for her playmate, the defendant's daughter, to return home. The trial summary included both prosecution and defense testimony. The experimental manipulation in each study involved the presence or absence of a critical piece of incriminating evidence (e.g., in Experiment 1, a set of photographs of the victim found in the defendant's home). This evidence was incorporated into the trial summary read by two thirds of the participants. However, for half of these participants (one third of the total) this evidence was later ruled inadmissible by the judge (because it was obtained during an illegal search and seizure), and jurors were admonished to disregard it. The rest of the participants who read this evidence (another third of the total) learned instead that it was ruled admissible by the judge despite objections by the defense attorney. For all remaining participants (the final third of the total), the trial summary did not include this incriminating evidence (control condition). Except for the presence or absence of this one piece of information, and the judge's ruling on its admissibility, the trial summaries were identical across conditions.

After reading the summary, participants indicated whether they thought the defendant was guilty or innocent. They then met in groups of 8 to 12 members and deliberated the case for up to an hour. Afterwards, participants again indicated privately whether they thought the defendant was guilty or innocent.

In both studies, London and Nunez (2000) found that prior to deliberation a majority of participants who read the additional incriminating evidence judged the defendant to be guilty. This was true even when that additional evidence was ruled inadmissible. This stands in contrast to the control condition, where prior to deliberation a majority of participants judged the defendant to be not guilty. Thus, prior to deliberation, the verdict preferences of participants in the inadmissible evidence condition were significantly biased by that evidence.

They were not irrevocably biased, however. Rather, after deliberation, a large number of participants in the inadmissible evidence condition changed their verdict preference, so that a majority of them now preferred the not-guilty verdict. Indeed, after deliberation, participants in the inadmissible evidence condition were statistically indistinguishable from those in the control condition with respect to the percentage preferring a not-guilty verdict. By contrast, the percentage preferring a guilty verdict in the admissible evidence condition remained just as high after deliberation as before.[2]

It is noteworthy that, in the inadmissible evidence condition, a majority of participants favored a guilty verdict prior to discussion but favored a not-guilty verdict afterwards. Such a preference shift is difficult to account for by a simple "strength in numbers" decision scheme (e.g., majority rule), as any such scheme anticipates an even higher proportion of guilty preferences after deliberation than before. Instead, these results suggest that participants were better able to follow the law (i.e., the judge's instructions) with respect to inadmissible indication after deliberating the case than before. This would seem to be clear indication of a performance gain attributable to group interaction (deliberation), which fits the definition of synergy. It is likely an instance of only weak synergy, however. Although not in the majority, some participants in the inadmissible evidence condition in these experiments did prefer the not-guilty verdict even prior to deliberation, and it is likely that most of the deliberating groups contained at least one such member. If so, this would have put an artificial ceiling on the performance gains that potentially could have been achieved through group interaction—because it is not possible to perform a task any better than someone who is already performing it perfectly (i.e., without bias, in this case). Thus, although providing clear evidence that deliberating jurors adhered to judicial instructions better than the average juror who did not deliberate (weak synergy), the likelihood of an artificial ceiling prevents these studies from telling us whether performance exceeding that of the best member (strong synergy) might also have been realized. This is apt to be a persistent methodology limitation of this kind of study.

The Challenge of Distributed Information

An unusual feature of jury decision making is that great care is taken by the courts to ensure that every juror is exposed to exactly the same case information in exactly the same way. This is done so that juries will decide their cases with every member being aware of all relevant information from the outset of deliberation. However, such uniformity across group members is uncommon in the vast majority of real-world decision-making situations. Instead, due to differences in work roles, professional training, and everyday experience, the members of decision-making groups typically possess overlapping—but not identical—sets of decision-relevant information. Thus, certain members may hold useful information that is unknown to others in the group. Indeed, a frequently stated purpose of employing groups rather than individuals to make decisions is to capitalize on the unique information that various members hold. I will refer to this uniquely held decision-relevant knowledge as *unshared information*. It stands in contrast to *shared information*, which is decision-relevant knowledge that every member of the group is aware of prior to discussion.[3] When members are in possession of unshared information that bears on the decision at hand, and when the best choice alternative can be identified only by integrating that information, the decision made collectively by the group has the potential to be far superior to the decision that would be made by any single member of the group acting alone.

The Hidden Profile Paradigm

Stasser and Titus (1985) introduced a research methodology that has proved to be very useful for studying group decision making when members do not all possess exactly the same information about a topic. It is called the *hidden profile paradigm*.

Imagine a four-person group that must decide between two mutually exclusive courses of action, A and B. They might, for example, be presented with a financial investment task where they are asked to decide whether it would be wiser (more profitable) to invest a sum of money in Company A or Company B. Each company is a small start-up venture, and each is developing a new product that it hopes to bring to market within the next year. If one invests in a company (e.g., by buying a stake in its ownership) and the new product proves successful, the value of the company is apt to rise, and the investor will reap a profit. If, on the other hand, the new product is unsuccessful in the marketplace, the value of the company is apt to fall, and the investor will lose money.

Before meeting to discuss this matter, every member of the investment group is given a packet of decision-relevant information to read. This information describes the new product that each company is developing, some of the strengths and weakness of those two products, obstacles that must be overcome in order to manufacture and sell each of them, and evidence of consumer demand for each. Importantly, however, members do not all read exactly the same information. Rather, their reading packets are carefully constructed so that each contains some information that is also in every other member's packet (shared information) and some that is in that one packet alone (unshared information). The members are cautioned that their reading packets do not contain exactly the same information, but they are not told which of their information is shared and which is unshared. After they have finished reading, the packets are collected and the group meets to discuss the information and decide which company is the better investment.

Let us suppose that there are 18 separate pieces of information that bear on this decision. Imagine that 6 of them imply that Company A's product will be more successful and that investing in Company A would therefore be the better choice. The remaining 12 items all imply that Company B's product will be more successful and that investing in Company B would thus be the better choice. For simplicity, I will refer to information implying that Company A is the better choice as "A Information" and to information implying that Company B is the better choice as "B Information." Finally, let us suppose that all 18 pieces of information are equally valid, important, and memorable. Thus, what distinguishes these two choice alternatives is the sheer volume of information favoring each. Assuming that it is wiser to choose a course of action supported by a larger body of evidence (i.e., evidence that points to more favorable and fewer unfavorable attributes), then Company B would appear to be the better choice alternative, because there is twice as much information favoring B as there is favoring A.

There are many different ways in which these 18 items of information might be distributed across the reading packets given to the four members of this group. Two such distributions are displayed in Table 6.1. In the top panel, the information is distributed so that each packet contains the same proportion of items favoring each company as exists in the total set of 18 items. Specifically, each contains six pieces of B Information and

TABLE 6.1 Hidden and Manifest Profile Information Distributions

Group Members			
1	2	3	4
Manifest Profile			
A_1	A_1	A_1	A_1
A_2	A_2	A_2	A_2
A_3	A_4	A_5	A_6
B_1	B_1	B_1	B_1
B_2	B_2	B_2	B_2
B_3	B_3	B_3	B_3
B_4	B_4	B_4	B_4
B_5	B_6	B_7	B_8
B_9	B_{10}	B_{11}	B_{12}
Hidden Profile			
A_1	A_1	A_1	A_1
A_2	A_2	A_2	A_2
A_3	A_3	A_3	A_3
A_4	A_4	A_4	A_4
A_5	A_5	A_5	A_5
A_6	A_6	A_6	A_6
B_1	B_2	B_3	B_4
B_5	B_6	B_7	B_8
B_9	B_{10}	B_{11}	B_{12}

Note: Each entry refers to a single piece of information. Letters indicate the choice alternative favored by the information. Subscripts identify the content of the information. Two entries with the same letter and subscript refer to the same information.

three pieces of A Information: a 2:1 ratio. This is accomplished by making the A and B Information shared and unshared in equal proportions. Thus, one third of the A Information (A_1 and A_2) and one third of the B Information (B_1, B_2, B_3, and B_4) is shared by all members, whereas the remaining two thirds of each type (A_3, A_4, A_5, A_6, and B_5, B_6, B_7, B_8, B_9, B_{10}, B_{11}, B_{12}) are unshared. This distribution creates a *manifest profile*, meaning that the better choice alternative—Company B—should be apparent to each group member individually prior to discussion based on just the information contained in his or her own reading packet.

Quite a different distribution is shown in the bottom panel of Table 6.1. Here, each packet contains six pieces of information favoring Company A and three pieces favoring Company B. This ratio is exactly opposite to what exists in the full set of 18 items. This is accomplished by making all of the A Information (A_1, A_2, A_3, A_4, A_5, A_6) shared, and all of the B Information (B_1, B_2, B_3, B_4, B_5, B_6, B_7, B_8, B_9, B_{10}, B_{11}, B_{12}) unshared. This distribution creates a *hidden profile*, meaning that the better choice alternative—again, Company B—is not likely to be perceived as such based on just the information presented in the individual reading packets. Rather, prior to discussion each group member should prefer the inferior alternative, Company A. In short, by making the information about the inferior alternative widely shared, and the information about the superior alternative unshared, the hidden profile distribution should bias members against the best choice alternative, at least initially.[4]

Although different in detail, it is evident that the two information distribution conditions shown in Table 6.1 are also similar in several ways. Most importantly, in both conditions each of the 18 pieces of decision-relevant information is seen by at least one member of the group prior to discussion. Thus, in both conditions the group as a whole is given all of the available information. Further, in both conditions every group member individually sees the same amount of information: nine items. Consequently, information load—the amount of material that members individually must remember as they begin their group discussion—is equivalent across conditions. The primary difference between the two conditions, therefore, has to do with what information is shared and what is unshared.

Is a group's collective decision affected by the way decision-relevant information is initially distributed among members prior to discussion? The hidden profile distribution is of particular interest, for it is here that a full and open discussion among group members can potentially do the most good. By thoroughly discussing all of the information available to them, members should be able to educate one another about information that originally was not widely shared, and so correct one another's misperceptions regarding which choice alternative is actually best. This stands in contrast to the manifest profile distribution, where a full discussion of the available information can do little more than reaffirm members' initial (correct) opinion regarding which choice alternative is best.

The Decisional Impact of Hidden Profiles

Stasser and Titus (1985) were the first to examine the effect of hidden versus manifest profile information distributions on the decisions made by groups. The task they employed involved political rather than financial decision making, and three rather than two choice alternatives, but otherwise was structured in much the same way as described above. Thus, they had four-person groups collectively decide which of three hypothetical candidates would be the best choice for student body president at their university. In preparation for this decision, members read a packet of information about each candidate. In one experimental condition, their packets each contained all of the available information. This produced a manifest profile without resorting to the use of unshared information (but did so at the cost of introducing a between-condition information-load differential). This information clearly favored one candidate over the other two. In a second experimental condition, the reading packets were constructed so as to create a hidden profile much like the one shown in Table 6.1, where every member's packet individually favored the same inferior candidate. Additionally, in a third experimental condition, a hidden profile was created in which two of the reading packets favored one inferior candidate and two favored the other.

Stasser and Titus (1985) found that 83% of the groups in the manifest profile condition chose the best candidate—the one favored by the majority of the information in their packets. By contrast, only 18% of the groups in the two hidden profile conditions chose the best candidate. This difference occurred despite the fact that groups in all conditions collectively held the same information about all three candidates. What differed among them was simply the way in which that information was distributed prior to discussion. Groups in this study clearly had great difficulty discovering the best choice alternative when the decision-relevant information was distributed among them in a way that created a hidden profile.

The adverse impact of a hidden profile relative to a manifest profile has been replicated in a large number of studies using a variety of decision-making tasks. In addition to affecting collective group choices when deciding among political candidates, hidden profiles have been shown to impair decisions about which financial investment is best (e.g., Hollingshead, 1996; Kelly & Karau, 1999; McLeod, Baron, Marti, & Yoon, 1997), which suspect is most likely to have committed a murder (e.g., Stasser & Stewart, 1992; Stasser, Stewart, & Wittenbaum, 1995; Stewart & Stasser, 1998), and which job candidate is best (e.g., Scholten, van Knippenberg, Nijstad, & De Dreu, 2007; Schulz-Hardt, Brodbeck, Mojzisch, Kerschreiter, & Frey, 2006).

The hidden profile effect has also been replicated in populations other than university students—the source of participants for all of the studies cited in the paragraph above. Christensen, Larson, Abbott, Ardolino, Franz, & Pfeiffer (2000), for example, demonstrated that trained professionals also fall prey to the effect of hidden profiles, even when making decisions within the scope of their professional expertise. These authors had three-person teams of physicians diagnose two complex patient cases, one involving Parkinson's disease (a degenerative disorder of the central nervous system) and the other lupus erythematosus (an autoimmune disease). Information about each case was presented by means of a video recording of an interview with the patient. The patient reported verbally, or visibly displayed, the relevant symptoms and other diagnostic information. However, each physician privately viewed a different version of the patient video, with each version containing some diagnostic information that was also in every other version (shared), and some that was in that one version alone (unshared). For half of these teams, the videos were constructed so that the information most crucial for making a correct diagnosis was shared across all versions. For the remaining teams, that same crucial information was unshared. Thus, in the former condition the information was distributed so as to create a manifest profile, whereas in the latter it was distributed so as to create a hidden profile. Importantly, however, in each team every piece of diagnostic information was seen by at least one member. After viewing their individual videos, the physicians met as a group to discuss the information and diagnose the case. Christensen et al. found that when the distribution of case information created a manifest profile, the team diagnoses were correct 100% of the time. However, when the information distribution created a hidden profile, the team diagnoses were correct only 71% of the times a statistically significant difference in diagnostic accuracy.

In sum, across both tasks and participant populations, groups have consistently been shown to perform worse when the decision-relevant information is distributed so as to create a hidden rather than manifest profile.

Hidden Profiles and Synergy in Group Decision Making

The difference in performance between groups working under conditions of a hidden profile and those working under a manifest profile is often substantial and deserves careful attention. But this difference is not very informative regarding the question of synergy in groups. More relevant is whether or not groups perform better than individuals when a hidden profile exists. For example, we might compare the collective decisions made by groups to the prediscussion decision preferences of their members and ask whether groups are any more likely than their individual members to select the choice alternative deemed best. It seems reasonable that they should be, given that under conditions of a hidden profile group members individually (prior to discussion) hold a pattern of information that hides the superiority of the best alternative.[5]

Surprisingly, this result occurs much less frequently than might be expected. For example, in the study by Stasser and Titus (1985) described above, 23% of participants in their hidden profile conditions individually preferred the best choice alternative prior to discussion. This stands in contrast to the previously reported 18% for groups in those same conditions that eventually chose the best alternative. Although not statistically significant, this difference is opposite in direction to what would be expected if there were even a weak synergistic performance gain in these groups.

More favorable results (from the standpoint of synergy) have been obtained in other studies, but only under some conditions. For example, Stasser and Stewart (1992) examined group performance on a murder mystery task and found that three-person groups were more effective than their individual members at identifying the one suspect (out of three) who was most likely to have committed the homicide in question. This occurred, however, only when participants believed that they collectively held enough information to solve the murder (but see Stewart & Stasser, 1998). Indeed, in this condition, even when a third or fewer of their members initially favored the best alternative, 62% of the groups nevertheless chose that alternative. In contrast, when participants were given exactly the same case information, distributed in exactly the same way, but were led to believe that they did *not* have enough information to solve the murder, groups were not more effective than their individual members. These results hint at a weak synergistic performance gain, but only when participants believe that they have been given sufficient information to successfully complete the task.

Stasser et al. (1995) used the same murder mystery task but distributed the case information in a way that made each member the de facto expert about a different suspect (by including in each reading packet shared information about all three suspects but unshared information about just one of them). Here, too, three-person groups were found to be more effective than their individual members at solving the crime. But this performance gain materialized only when members knew who in their group had the most information about each suspect. Specifically, some groups were told at the outset of discussion who among them had read extra information about each suspect (but not precisely what that information was). These groups solved the crime more effectively than their individual members. Other groups, however, were not told who had read extra information about each suspect, and these groups did not solve the crime more effectively than their individual members. (I will return to the issue of expertise in decision-making groups later in this chapter; see pp. 200–203).

Hollingshead (1996) found that face-to-face groups were more effective than individuals in deciding which of three companies was the best financial investment, but only when participants were forced to rank-order the three companies from best to worst. When they were asked instead simply to pick the best company, groups were not more effective than individuals.

Finally, Scholten, van Knippenberg, Nijstad, and De Dreu (2007) found that groups were more effective than individuals at deciding which of three job candidates was best, but only when the members initially preferred different candidates and were held accountable for their group's decision-making process (i.e., they believed they would have to explain that process later on). When there was an initial (incorrect) consensus about which candidate was best, or when members were not held accountable, groups were not more effective than individuals (see also Brodbeck et al., 2002; Schulz-Hardt et al., 2006).

The foregoing results focus mainly on the overall proportion of individuals and groups choosing the a priori best alternative, and suggest that synergistic performance gains may occur under some conditions but not others. Similar conclusions are reached when a more detailed, social decision scheme (SDS) analysis is applied to these same data. I introduced SDS Theory in Chapter 4, in connection with the research presented there on group problem solving (see pp. 126–137). This theory and analytic approach can be applied as well to group decision making. An SDS analysis focuses on the proportion of groups choosing the best alternative given a particular distribution of member prediscussion preferences, and on the pattern of such proportions across all possible prediscussion preference distributions (a la Figures 4.1 to 4.3). It is from the latter that inferences are drawn about the underlying processes giving rise to the group decisions. These processes are summarized as social decision schemes.

Paralleling what we saw in Chapter 4, two social decision schemes are of particular interest when assessing synergy in decision-making groups: Proportionality and Truth Wins. The Proportionality model predicts that a group will choose the a priori best alternative with a probability equal to the proportion of its members who prefer that alternative prior to discussion; the larger the proportion, the more likely it is that the best alternative will be chosen by the group as a whole. Proportionality is an "average-member" model, in that it predicts that groups will perform at the level of their average member. As such, it represents an important baseline for evaluating synergy in groups: it defines the level of performance that must be exceeded in order to claim evidence of even weak synergy. The Truth Wins model, by contrast, predicts that a group will choose the best alternative if at least one of its members prefers that alternative prior to discussion. Truth Wins is thus a "best-member" model, and so represents a second important baseline for evaluating synergy in groups; it defines the level of performance that must be surpassed in order to claim evidence of strong synergy.

Two studies have employed an SDS analysis to evaluate group decision-making performance when a hidden profile exists. Hollingshead (1996) did this with the data she collected from groups asked either to rank-order or to pick the best of three investment alternatives. She found that, as a whole, groups in her study performed better than predicted by the Proportionality model but not as well as predicted by the Truth Wins model. This suggests the presence of a weak synergistic performance gain. Further, she observed that, among groups choosing the best alternative when no more than a minority of their members preferred that alternative prior to discussion, most were in the condition in which face-to-face groups rank-ordered the alternatives from best to worst. This suggests once again that the performance gains she observed were concentrated primarily in that one condition.

Stasser et al. (1995) also employed an SDS analysis and also found that, across experimental conditions, groups generally performed better than predicted by the Proportionality model but not as well as predicted by the Truth Wins model (though they were much closer to the latter than the former). Interestingly, among their groups with *no* members who initially preferred the best choice alternative (i.e., the guilty suspect in their murder mystery task), 33% nevertheless chose that alternative when they knew who in their group held extra information about each suspect. In contrast, only 6% of such groups chose the best alternative when they did not know who held extra information about each suspect. Of course, the Truth Wins and Proportionality models both predict that, when no member prefers the best alternative initially, no group will select it, regardless of what members know about the mix of information they hold. Thus, these data hint at a strong synergistic performance gain in this one experimental condition.

In summary, the evidence for synergy in decision-making groups confronted by a hidden profile is spotty, to say the least. Performance gains appear in some experimental conditions but not others, and, when they do appear, they are more apt to be of the weak rather than strong variety. Still, there is an important unifying theme in this disparate set of findings. Groups seem able to outperform individuals when the prevailing experimental conditions strongly encourage them to explore their decision-relevant information thoroughly. Knowing that a murder can be solved conclusively should motivate members to examine closely everything that they have learned about the case. Knowing who in the group has privileged information about a particular suspect should encourage members to seek out and carefully consider that information. Being required to rank-order all of the choice alternatives (as opposed to simply picking the best one) should encourage members to consider more of the information they collectively hold, if only to sort out the less-favored alternatives. And accountability, along with underlying differences of opinion among members, should encourage groups to be as methodical as possible in resolving their differences. In short, groups do not seem automatically to outperform individuals on decision-making tasks that involve a hidden profile; synergy on such tasks apparently does not emerge spontaneously. Rather, it seems necessary to nurture synergy by providing conditions that encourage a fuller, more complete discussion of the available decision-relevant information (cf. van Ginkel & van Knippenberg, 2008, 2009).

Hidden Profiles and Synergy: Further Consideration

An objection might be raised at this point that the comparison of groups to individuals on hidden profile tasks is an unfair one. After all, groups have the resources (information) necessary to make the correct decision, whereas individuals do not, and synergy refers to a gain in performance that results from interaction, not simply from having more resources.

However, the hidden profile situation is not too different from the cycling scenario described in Chapter 1, where the speed and distance traveled by cyclists riding as a team, drafting one behind the other, is compared to that of cyclists riding alone. When riding as a team, the cyclists must consider one another's strength in relation to their riding position. A team will succeed in riding faster and further than any one of its members might do riding alone only by ensuring that the member who at the moment is best-rested and strongest is the one riding in the lead position. The rider who is best-rested and strongest is the one with the most resources to contribute. Further, it is the lead rider who provides others shelter from the wind, thus making their subtask less difficult. But of course, the leader's resources are gradually depleted by the rigors of breaking the wind, and so he or she must periodically be refreshed by riding for a time in one of the easier, following positions. While doing so, another rider, one who is now better rested and stronger, will take the lead. Thus, the interaction that is critical for creating a strong synergistic performance gain in cycling teams is fundamentally a matter of resource utilization. Members possess different resources at different times and rotate positions in order to take advantage of those differences.

Likewise, decision-making groups can take advantage of differences in their members' informational resources in hidden profile situations by exchanging that information during discussion. Importantly, they must do more than simply discuss their prediscussion preferences if they expect to make the correct decision. That groups often seem unable to surpass the decision-making performance of even their average member when a hidden profile exists—despite having access to a richer fund of task-relevant information—suggests that they do not automatically engage in the type of discussion needed to achieve a synergistic performance gain in these situations.

The content of discussion is thus an important point of leverage for understanding the performance of decision-making groups. Discussion content has been the focus of a good deal of follow-up research using the hidden profile paradigm. This work has yielded a number of important insights into the collective decision-making process and is examined in some detail in the next section.

☐ The Content of Group Decision-Making Discussions

The content of decision-making discussions can be coded and analyzed in many different ways. Research concerned with such content has a long and venerable history that extends back to the work of Bales (1950; Bales & Strodtbeck, 1951) and beyond. Although a complete survey of this literature is outside the scope of the present book, it is nevertheless useful to examine that portion of the literature concerned with the content of group decision-making discussions when a hidden profile exists. The goal of doing so is to better understand why it is that groups are not more effective under such conditions. The bulk of this work has focused on the relative amount of discussion devoted to shared versus unshared information and has been greatly influence by a seminal conceptual model introduced by Stasser and Titus (1987, 2003).

The Collective Information Sampling Model

Starting with the seemingly reasonable assumption that a group's decisions are governed by the content of its decision-making discussions (Burnstein & Vinokur, 1973, 1977), Stasser and Titus (1987, 2003) suggested that hidden profiles adversely impact group decisions by biasing the content of those discussions. More specifically, they argued that a group decision-making discussion can be usefully conceptualized as a sampling process, where the content of discussion is obtained by members randomly sampling from the pool of decision-relevant information that they collective hold. This sampling is accomplished by members recalling and then mentioning the decision-relevant information to which they were previously exposed. Importantly, however, because shared information is initially held by more members than unshared information, there are more opportunities for the group as a whole to sample a given item of shared information than for them to sample a given item of unshared information. As a result, shared information is more apt than unshared information to be mentioned during discussion, simply because there are more members who potentially can mention it.

These ideas were formalized by Stasser and Titus (1987, 2003) in what has become known as the collective information sampling (CIS) model. The CIS model can be expressed as follows:

$$p(D) = 1 - [1 - p(R)]^n \tag{6.1}$$

where $p(D)$ is the probability that a given piece of decision-relevant information will be discussed by the group, $p(R)$ is the probability that any member who was aware of that information prior to discussion will both recall and mention it during discussion, and n is the number of members who were aware of that information prior to discussion. Note that if the information in question is completely unshared, then $n = 1$. For completely shared information, on the other hand, n = group size. Consequently, according to Equation 6.1, for unshared information $p(D) = p(R)$, whereas for shared information $p(D) > p(R)$. By implication, $p(D_{shared}) > p(D_{unshared})$. This inequality holds for all values of $p(R)$ except 0 and 1, with the difference being greatest at a point that depends on the size of the group. For example, in a three-person group, the difference is greatest when $p(R) =$ .42. In this case, $p(D_{shared}) = .80$, whereas $p(D_{unshared}) = .42$. This means that if the members of a three-person group are able to remember and mention 42% of the information originally contained in their reading packets, they are predicted to collectively discuss 80% of their shared information, but only 42% of their unshared information.

It is important to recognize that the CIS model predicts that group decision-making discussions will be biased—they will focus more heavily on the groups' shared than unshared information—even though none of the members individually are biased. Note that Equation 6.1 uses exactly the same value of $p(R)$ regardless of whether the information in question is shared or unshared. In the example given at the end of the preceding paragraph, for instance, the same value of $p(R) = .42$ was used to calculate both $p(D_{shared})$ and $p(D_{unshared})$. The only thing that varied between those calculations was the value of n: when calculating $p(D_{shared})$, n was set to 3, whereas it was set to 1 when calculating $p(D_{unshared})$. Thus, according to the CIS model, even if members are just as likely to remember and mention the shared as the unshared information they individually hold, the group as a whole will nevertheless discuss more of its shared than unshared information.

It is also helpful to recognize that the form of Equation 6.1 is identical to that of Lorge and Solomon's (1955) Model A, which was discussed in Chapter 4 (see p. 124). Recall that Model A is a best-member model of group problem solving, and that it predicts that a group will solve a problem correctly with a probability equal to the probability that it contains at least one member who can solve the problem correctly. This same idea is adapted in the CIS model to predict the content of group decision-making discussions. In essence, the CIS model decomposes a group discussion into a series of subtasks. The goal of each subtask is to introduce a new, not-yet-mentioned piece of decision-relevant information into the discussion. These subtasks are all disjunctive, in the sense that only one member need accomplish each in order for it to be accomplished by the group as a whole. Said differently, a given piece of decision-relevant information need be mentioned by only one member in order for it to become part of the group's discussion (see Chapter 2, pp. 64–65, for a more detailed description of disjunctive tasks). Consequently, the CIS model predicts that a group will discuss a given item of decision-relevant information with a probability equal to the probability that it contains at least one member who can discuss (i.e., recall and mention) that item.

Empirical Evidence

Consistent with the predictions of the CIS model, most studies concerned with the content of group discussion in distributed information situations have found that groups discuss significantly more of their shared than their unshared information.[6] These differences have tended to be quite robust, with groups often discussing nearly twice as much shared as unshared information. For example, Greitemeyer, Schulz-Hardt, Brodbeck, and Frey (2006) had three-person groups make four different kinds of decisions, each involving 45 distinct pieces of information. For three of these, the relevant information was distributed among members so as to create a hidden profile. Across these three decisions it was found that groups on average discussed 73% of their shared information but only 41% of their unshared information. If we use .41 as an estimate of $p(R)$ in Equation 6.1, then the CIS model predicts that groups should discuss 79% of their shared information, which is not too far from what was actually observed.[7]

It is worth noting that the same pattern of discussion content was also observed in connection with a fourth decision made by groups in the study by Greitemeyer et al. (2006). For that fourth decision, the relevant information was distributed so as to create a manifest profile. Here, groups discussed 71% of their shared information and only 42% of their unshared information—very similar to the results observed for the hidden profile discussions. This similarity serves to emphasize that it is the sharedness of the individual items of information that determines discussion content,[8] not whether the overall distribution of that information creates a hidden or a manifest profile. Even so, groups selected the best choice alternative 89% of the time when making the manifest profile decision but only 7% of the time when making the hidden profile decisions.

In sum, group decision-making discussions are characterized by a strong information sampling bias, such that groups are more likely to discuss their shared than their unshared information. This bias is driven simply by the sharedness of the information, not by whether it is part of a hidden or manifest profile. Still, if their shared information is no more or less likely than their unshared information to favor the best choice alternative—the mark of a manifest profile—then groups can be expected to choose the best alternative most of the time. But if their shared information disproportionately favors a suboptimal choice alternative, while only their unshared information favors the best alternative—indicating a hidden profile—then groups are apt to select the best choice alternative much less often.

A Dynamic Perspective: Collective Information Sampling Over Time

Building on the basic information sampling idea, Larson (1997; Larson, Foster-Fishman, & Keys, 1994) proposed an extension of the CIS model that takes into account the sequential nature of a group discussion. This extension predicts not only the relative amounts of shared and unshared information that are likely to be discussed by a group, but also when during discussion that information is apt to be introduced. This extension is called the Dynamic Information Sampling Model of Group Discussion (DISM-GD).

To understand DISM-GD, consider again the hidden profile example shown in the bottom panel of Table 6.1. In this example, there is only half as much shared as unshared information. Nevertheless, the CIS model predicts that shared information will dominate discussion, at least initially. Again, this is because there are more sampling opportunities for shared than for unshared information. Specifically, at the start of discussion there are $4 \times 6 = 24$ opportunities to sample (i.e., recall and mention) an item of shared information but only $1 \times 12 = 12$ opportunities to sample an item of unshared information. Thus, assuming that members can recall all of the information from their reading packets, at the outset of discussion the probability of the group sampling an item of shared information is $24/(24 + 12) = .67$, whereas the probability of them sampling an item of unshared information is only $12/(24 + 12) = .33$.

These probabilities are not static, however. Rather, they change each time an item of information is sampled. After an item of unshared information is sampled, the pool of not-yet-mentioned unshared information shrinks by one. Further, because unshared information is held by just one member of the group, the number of opportunities to sample additional items of not-yet-mentioned unshared information is also reduced by one. Similarly, after an item of shared information is sampled, the pool of not-yet-mentioned shared information shrinks by one. In this case, however, because shared information is held by every member of the group, the number of opportunities to *sample* additional items of not-yet-mentioned shared information is reduced by four (the size of the group). In general, the opportunities to sample additional items of not-yet-mentioned shared information drop at a faster rate than the opportunities to sample additional items of not-yet-mentioned unshared information. This causes the conditional probability of collectively sampling shared information to decrease over time and the conditional probability of collectively sampling unshared information to increase.[9] For example, after sampling one piece of information, the probability that the next piece sampled will be shared information decreases to

$$[.67 \times 20/(20 + 12)] + [.33 \times 24/(24 + 11)] = .65, \qquad (6.2)$$

and the probability that it will be unshared information increases to

$$[.67 \times 12/(20+12)] + [.33 \times 11/(24+11)] = .35 \qquad (6.3)$$

These values are only slightly different from what they were at the outset of discussion (.67 and .33, respectively). However, the differences grow increasingly large as more and more information is sampled and brought into discussion.

Two illustrative sets of predictions made by DISM-GD are presented in Figures 6.1 and 6.2. Figure 6.1 gives the full set of predicted sampling probabilities for the hidden profile shown in the bottom panel of Table 6.1, assuming that members are able to recall and mention all of the information from their reading packets. The horizontal axis in the figure indicates the sequential order in which information enters discussion (i.e., the first item mentioned, the second item mentioned, and so on), with each successive position in the sequence referring to the introduction of a new, not-yet-mentioned piece of information (i.e., repetitions of already-mentioned information are ignored [but see below]). The two lines in the figure trace the probability of mentioning shared and unshared information, respectively, across the item serial positions. Thus, the first serial position on each line indicates the probability that the first piece of information sampled will be either shared or unshared information, the second serial position

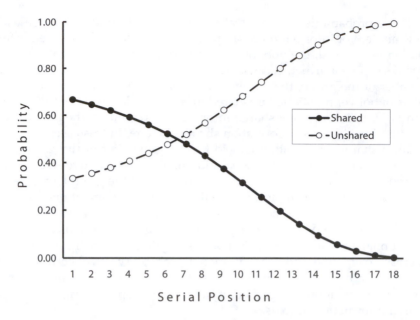

FIGURE 6.1   DISM-GD probabilities for the hidden profile shown in Table 6.1, assuming members can recall and mention all of the information from their reading packet.

indicates the probability that the second piece of information sampled will be shared or unshared information, and so forth.

As can be seen, over the course of discussion the probability of sampling additional items of shared information gradually decreases, while the probability of sampling additional items of unshared information gradually increases. Further, in this example, the first six pieces of information to enter discussion are more likely to be shared than unshared information. This is true even though the group collectively holds less shared than unshared information overall, and even though the group members are presumed to be capable of recalling and mentioning all of the information from their reading packets (i.e., $p(R) = 1.00$). Further, when members can recall and mention all of the information from their reading packets, DISM-GD predicts that $p(D_{shared}) = p(D_{unshared}) = 1.00$. That is, like the CIS model, under the special (and highly unusual) condition of perfect recall, DISM-GD predicts no *overall* discussion differential. Even so, it still does predict a differential in the *pattern* of discussion, with shared information tending to be brought out first. One implication of this is that even when members are able to recall and mention everything that was in their reading packet, if anything causes them to terminate discussion prematurely (e.g., time constraints; an early recognition by members that they all agree

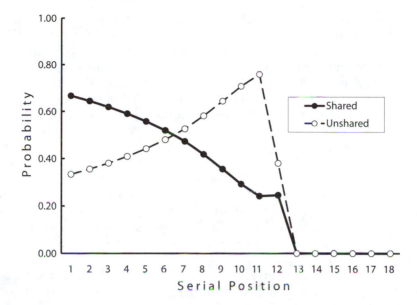

FIGURE 6.2   DISM-GD probabilities for the hidden profile shown in Table 6.1, assuming members can recall and mention only half of the information from their reading packet.

on a particular choice alternative), the group will still have discussed more of its shared than unshared information (cf. Schulz-Hardt et al., 2006).

A generally similar pattern is seen in Figure 6.2, which gives the predicted sampling probabilities for the same hidden profile, but this time assuming that members are able to recall and mention only half of the information from their reading packets. The most obvious difference between the two figures is that in Figure 6.2 members collectively begin to run out of recallable, not-yet-mentioned information after 11 items have been brought into discussion.[10] Hence, the probability of introducing new information of either type quickly drops to 0. Nevertheless, the first six pieces of information to enter discussion are still more likely to be shared than unshared information. Further, in this case, DISM-GD also predicts that groups will discuss a larger proportion of their shared than their unshared information overall. Specifically, it predicts that they will discuss 94% of their shared information, but only 50% of their unshared information. These latter predictions are identical to those made by the CIS model.[11]

Empirical Evidence

The DISM-GD predictions have been tested in four separate studies. In two of these, three-person groups of university students read written descriptions of several hypothetical candidates for a faculty position, then decided which of these would be best to hire to teach a particular college-level course (Larson et al., 1994; Larson, Foster-Fishman, & Franz, 1998). In the other two studies, three-person teams of physicians met to diagnose patient cases (Larson, Christensen, Abbott, & Franz, 1996; Larson, Christensen, Franz, & Abbott, 1998). These latter two studies employed a methodology generally similar to that described above for the study by Christensen et al. (2000). Thus, the team members each saw a different video of a patient interview, after which they met to discuss the case and decide on their collective diagnosis. It is worth noting that in all of these studies the decision-relevant information was counterbalanced across groups, such that items that were shared information in half of the groups were unshared in the other half, and vice versa. Thus, the results obtained regarding the discussion of shared versus unshared information can be interpreted independent of the content of that information.

The results presented by Larson, Christensen et al. (1998) are representative of the findings obtained in these four studies, and are shown graphically in Figure 6.3. Each of the observed data points shown there

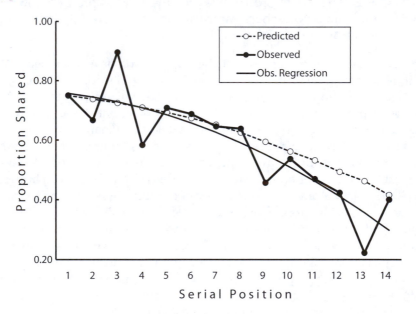

FIGURE 6.3   Predicted and observed proportion of discussions in which shared information was brought out in each item serial position. (Adapted from Larson, Christensen et al. [1998]. *Journal of Personality and Social Psychology*, 75, 93–108. With permission of the American Psychological Association.)

represents the proportion of teams in which shared information was the first, second, third, etc., piece of information introduced into discussion.[12] As can be seen, these observed proportions follow fairly closely the DISM-GD predictions. Most importantly, the proportion of groups in which shared information was introduced into discussion at each serial position steadily declined, and the proportion in which unshared information was introduced steadily increased (the introduction of unshared information is not shown in the figure, but can be easily computed by subtracting the plotted values from 1.00). Overall, the DISM-GD predictions account for 73% of the variance in the observed proportions shown in the figure. And across all four of the studies in which the model was tested, its predictions account for an average of 52% of the variance in the observed data (cf. Larson, 1997).

Thus, the CIS model, along with its dynamic extension, DISM-GD, have been very successful in forecasting the entry of information into discussion. Together they predict a sampling advantage for shared information that leads groups to discuss more of their shared than their unshared information overall and to consider their shared information first, before their unshared information.

Further Discussion: Repetition of Shared and Unshared Information

The tendency to pool (i.e., mention at least once) more shared than unshared information promotes a biased group discussion—one that disproportionately favors the group's shared information. However, there is more to this bias than just a pooling differential. Even if groups were to pool exactly equal proportions of their shared and unshared information, there is still reason to believe that they would give more discussion to their shared than to their unshared information.

The evidence for this comes primarily from research examining the frequency with which groups repeat information that members contribute to discussion. This research finds a significant tendency for groups to repeat more of their shared than their unshared information (e.g., Larson et al., 1994, 1996; Larson, Christensen et al., 1998; Parks & Cowlin, 1996; Savadori, Van Swol, & Sniezek, 2001; Schittekatte & Van Hiel, 1996; Schulz-Hardt et al., 2006; Stasser, Taylor, & Hanna, 1989; Winquist & Larson, 1998). This repetition differential occurs independently of the initial pooling differential that also favors the group's shared information. If a group's deliberation returns more often to the shared than to the unshared information that members contribute, it seems fair to say that the former is capturing more of their collective attention than the latter.

This repetition differential is less well understood than is the initial pooling differential favoring shared information. Several explanations for it have been proposed. These include the possibility that shared information is (a) easier to remember, (b) easier to validate, and (c) more rewarding to repeat. Each of these explanations is described more fully below.

Differential Memorability

First, Larson and Harmon (2007) argued that the tendency of groups to repeat more of their shared than unshared information is apt to be due in part to the likelihood that, after it is initially mentioned during discussion, shared information is more memorable than unshared information. They note that prior to the start of discussion there is no reason to believe that members can recall the shared information from their reading packet (or video) any better or worse than they can recall the unshared information. This is because experimental controls are typically in place to ensure this equivalence (e.g., by making the same items shared information for half of the groups and unshared information for the other half). However, the same cannot be said after that information is raised in discussion. Rather, a memory differential that favors shared information is apt to develop. This differential is expected for two reasons.

The first is that after it is introduced into discussion, members will have had more exposure to the shared than to the unshared information. Introducing any piece of information into discussion exposes others in the group to that information for either the first or second time. It will be their first exposure if what was mentioned was originally unshared information, because unshared information would have been only in the packet of the member mentioning the information, not in anyone else's. But it will be their second exposure if what was mentioned was originally shared information, because shared information would have been in everyone's packet. It is generally accepted that greater exposure to information makes it more accessible in memory (e.g., Anderson, 1983). This alone should make shared (two exposures) information easier to recall and repeat later on than unshared (one exposure) information.

In addition, shared information is also likely to be easier to recall than unshared information because shared information is often easier to understand. More specifically, when someone mentions a piece of complex information, but does so in an incomplete way, others in the group can often fill in the gaps with what they themselves are able to recall independently (cf. Bransford & Johnson, 1972, 1973). For example, suppose that during a discussion about whether or not to invest a sum of money in a particular company, one group member says, "I read that their product gives a bad gas, but I doubt consumers will notice." Listeners who read the same information might recall that toxic gases are a by-product of the manufacturing process used by that company, and that those gases pose a danger to production workers if not controlled. Recalling this information renders the speaker's statement more intelligible. Of course, this is possible only if the mentioned information was originally shared and so was also in the listener's reading packet. If, instead, the mentioned information was originally unshared, then the listener would have no means of supplying the missing details and would be less likely to understand the nature and implications of what was said. In short, when first introduced into discussion, shared information should often be easier to comprehend than unshared information, which in turn should make it easier to recall and use later on.

To test these ideas, Larson and Harmon (2007) had four-person groups participate in a structured discussion in which members described to one another various items of information pertaining to a financial investment decision. Beforehand, participants read all of the information that they themselves would contribute during discussion but only half of the information that they would hear others contribute. Then, after discussion, members were asked to recall as much of the contributed information as they could (i.e., whether contributed by themselves or by others). It was found that participants recalled twice as much information contributed by other members if they themselves had already read that information prior to discussion, compared to if they had not read it. This result is consistent with the idea that the tendency to repeat more shared than unshared information may be due in part to differential memorability; shared information is more readily repeated because it is more easily recalled.

Social Validation

A second explanation for the more frequent repetition of shared information is that shared information can be socially validated by the group, whereas unshared information cannot (cf. Stasser, 1992). There is often uncertainty about the veracity of particular items of information that get raised in discussion, or about the meaning or implications of that information. Members are apt to resolve such uncertainties by reference either to their own experience or to the experience of others in the group who were also exposed to that same information prior to discussion. Members are thus presumed to engage in a form of social comparison, where consensus about the mentioned information is taken as evidence of its correctness (cf. Baron, Hoppe, Kao, Brunsman, Linneweh, & Rogers, 1996; Chakin, 1987; Festinger, 1954). But this is possible only for shared information. Unshared information, by contrast, is at greater risk of being discounted or ignored simply because no one else in the group can attest to its validity and trustworthiness. If information is suspect, why bother repeating it?

Several studies have asked members after their group discussion to rate the information that was brought out (e.g., Chernyshenko, Miner, Baumann, & Sniezek, 2003; Postmes, Spears, & Cihangir, 2001; Van Swol, 2007; Van Swol, Savadori, & Sniezek, 2003; see also Greitemeyer & Schulz-Hardt, 2003). In general, these studies find that members rate the shared information brought to light during discussion to be more valid, true, and/or important than the unshared information brought to light. However, this applies only to the information that other members contributed. Members do not differently rate the shared and unshared information that they themselves contributed to discussion.

In addition to these rating data, there is also behavioral evidence consistent with the idea that shared information is repeated more often in part because it is perceived to be more valid. Parks and Cowlin (1996) distributed information among the members of four-person groups such that some of it was read by just one member (completely unshared), some was read by two members, some was read by three members, and some was read by all four members (completely shared). Consistent with other studies, information initially read by all four members was repeated more often than information initially read by just one member. More importantly for the present discussion, however, is that information initially read by either two or three members was also repeated about as often as information initially read by all four members. This is consistent with the social validation explanation for the differential repetition of shared and unshared information if it can be assumed that it takes just one additional member in the group to validate information that someone else contributes, and so for everyone in the group to have confidence in it (a type of truth-supported-wins model; cf. Chapter 4).

Mutual Enhancement

The social validation explanation for the repetition differential favoring shared information assumes that members are motivated to be accurate—that they focus more on their shared information because there is more evidence that that information it is dependable. In addition, social motives may also come into play here (cf. De Dreu, Nijstad, & van Knippenberg, 2008). For example, Wittenbaum has argued that groups tend to repeat more of their shared than unshared information because doing so is mutually enhancing for members (Wittenbaum & Bowman, 2004; Wittenbaum, Hubbell, & Zuckerman, 1999; Wittenbaum & Park, 2001). According to this view, discussing shared information may help members establish "common ground" that permits them to better understand and relate to one another. When someone volunteers an item of information during discussion, others in the group are apt not only to view the information itself as being more accurate when it is shared rather than unshared (because it can be socially validated), they are likely as well to view the member who mentioned it as someone who is competent and knowledgeable, and who contributes useful information to the discussion. In other words, the speaker's credibility and perceived value to the group should be enhanced when he or she contributes shared information. At the same time, upon hearing someone mention a piece of shared information, others in the group are apt to feel positive about their own task-relevant competence and knowledge, because the speaker has just validated their own (shared) information. Thus, communicating shared information should lead to *mutual enhancement*—members should evaluate both the speaker and themselves more positively when the speaker mentions shared rather than unshared information. Wittenbaum argues that this mutual enhancement will lead members to respond to the speaker with behavioral encouragement. That is, they are expected to display subtle verbal and nonverbal behaviors (e.g., commenting on the importance of the information, smiling, nodding, leaning forward) that are reinforcing to the speaker, and that encourage him or her to repeat additional items of shared information in the future.

Evidence bearing on the mutual enhancement idea comes from several studies in which, by experimental fiat, dyads have exchanged either mostly shared or mostly unshared information (Wittenbaum & Bowman, 2004; Wittenbaum, Hubbell, & Zuckerman, 1999). In comparison to those that exchanged mostly unshared information, the members of dyads that exchanged mostly shared information rated both themselves and their partners as more knowledgeable and competent, and viewed their collective performance more favorably. Further, under experimental conditions designed to eliminate the need for social validation, the mutual enhancement effect has been shown to disappear, as would be expected. Thus, there does seem to be support for the idea that discussing shared rather than unshared information can have mutually enhancing consequences (but see Larson, Sargis, & Bauman, 2004).

However, currently available evidence is mixed with regard to the proposition that mutual enhancement is a cause as well as a consequence of discussion content. On the one hand, taking an individual differences approach, Henningsen and Henningsen (2004) found that group members who scored high on the Marlowe-Crowne Social Desirability Scale repeated more shared and less unshared information than did members who scored low. Scores on this scale are typically interpreted as reflecting the respondent's underlying need for approval (Crowne & Marlowe, 1964). Thus, because mutual enhancement implies approval of the speaker by others in the group, those who should have been most sensitive to the mutually enhancing effects of discussing shared rather than unshared information did seem to behave as predicted.

On the other hand, there is also evidence that members do not behave as predicted when given a choice between discussing equally memorable and valid shared versus unshared information. Specifically, in two separate experiments, Schittekatte (1996, Experiment 2; Schittekatte & Van Hiel, 1996) labeled the information in members' reading packets as either shared or unshared (something that is normally not done in this area of research). If members are more motivated to repeat shared information because doing so is more mutually enhancing, then they should also be more motivated to contribute that information to begin with. This anticipates an even stronger information sampling bias when members know (vs. do not know) which of the information items they hold are shared and which are unshared. In fact, however, in both of these studies just the opposite occurred: knowing in advance what information was shared versus unshared significantly increased the amount of *unshared* information discussed (see also Kerschreiter, Schulz-Hardt, Faulmuller, Mojzisch, & Frey, 2004, as cited in Mojzisch & Schulz-Hardt, 2006; Van Swol, 2009). The discussion of shared information, by contrast, was completely unaffected by this experimental manipulation.

In light of these contradictory findings, firm conclusions are difficult to draw at present regarding the role of mutual enhancement in the repetition of shared versus unshared information. Discussing shared rather than unshared information does seem to have mutually enhancing consequences, but whether this actually motivates members to selectively repeat one type of information over the other is an open question.

Reducing the Shared Information Discussion Bias: The Role of Experts and Leaders

To this point I have treated group members in a rather homogeneous fashion, as if they were all fundamentally equivalent and interchangeable. In the real world, of course, there are many ways in which members differ one from another, some of which may impact their discussion behavior. Two differences that seem particularly germane concern (a) members' expertise and (b) their status as either leaders or nonleaders. It is likely that both play a role in helping to reduce the degree to which shared information dominates group discussion.

Subject Matter Experts

People often vary in the amount and type of expertise they bring to decision-making groups. As I use the term here, an *expert* is simply a member who has more knowledge than others in the group regarding a specific decision-relevant content area. A group may contain any number of experts, provided they each have a unique depth of knowledge in a different domain.

When groups are assembled for the explicit purpose of bringing together people who have backgrounds in different knowledge domains, each member's special area of expertise is usually known to the rest of the group. This is typically the case, for example, in interdisciplinary and cross-functional teams, where members' departmental affiliation or functional area signals their unique realms of knowledge. However, it is also possible for someone to be an expert in a particular content domain without other group members realizing it. Indeed, it is possible for a member to be an expert in a task-relevant content area without realizing it himself or herself (e.g., if he or she incorrectly assumes that others in the group have an equivalent amount of knowledge in that same area). When there is no external cue to signal a member's special expertise or skill, groups may have difficulty identifying who among them is and who is not an expert (cf. Baumann & Bonner, 2004; Bunderson, 2003; Littlepage, Robison, & Reddington, 1997; Miner, 1984).

There is reason to believe that groups do a better job of discussing the unshared information they collectively hold when members are aware of one another's special areas of expertise. A study that was summarized briefly earlier in this chapter was one of the first to examine this possibility. It is worth considering that experiment in greater detail here.

Stasser et al. (1995) gave three-person groups a murder mystery task to perform. Their goal was to decide which of three suspects was most likely to have committed a recent homicide. Prior to discussion, each member read a packet of information containing interviews collected during the crime investigation, a map of the crime scene, a note ostensibly written by one of the suspects, and a newspaper article that furnished other pertinent background details. In all, there were 24 separate pieces of case information that, in combination, implicated one of the three suspects as the person who committed the crime. This information was distributed among the reading packets so as to create a hidden profile, with some of it read by every member of the group (shared information) and some read by just one member (unshared information). Unlike the hidden profile shown in Table 6.1, however, members did not receive equal amounts of unshared information about every suspect. Rather, all of the unshared information pertaining to a given suspect was assigned to the same group member, with each member assigned to a different suspect. Thus, each member held some shared information about all three suspects, plus some unshared information about one of the suspects. The unshared information therefore defined each member's domain of relative expertise. In order for the group to choose the correct suspect, they had to combine that unshared information.

Members were given 30 minutes to study the case information individually, after which the packets were collected by the experimenter. The group was then given an additional 30 minutes to discuss the information and to decide who committed the crime. Just before starting this discussion, half of the groups were told what type of additional information each of their members held, but without revealing the specific content of that information (e.g., "Member 1 has additional information about Suspect A"). Let us call this the "expertise-identified" condition. The remaining groups were not told what type of additional information each member held. We can call this the expertise-not-identified condition.

Stasser et al. (1995) found that 61% of the groups in the expertise-identified condition chose the guilty suspect, compared to 35% in the expertise-not-identified condition. They also found that the content of the group discussions varied by condition. Groups in the expertise-identified condition both pooled (i.e., mentioned at least once) and repeated more of their unshared information than did groups in the expertise-not-identified condition. This manipulation did not, however, affect either the pooling or repetition of shared information. These results occurred despite the fact that the case information was distributed in exactly the same way in the two experimental conditions. Similar findings have been reported by others (e.g., Franz & Larson, 2002; Sassenberg, Boos, & Klapproth, 2001; Stewart & Stasser, 1995; see also Stasser, Vaughan, & Stewart, 2000). Thus, identifying members' special areas of expertise appears to reduce (though it does not necessarily eliminate) the extent to which group discussion is biased in favor of shared information.

Three factors likely contribute to this effect. First, when members realize that they are the group's subject matter expert in a domain central to the decision at hand, they are apt to feel particularly responsible for ensuring that information within that domain is brought to light and taken into account during the group's deliberations. This, of course, speaks quite directly to the primary purpose of calling together a group of experts to make a decision. It is also consistent with the results of the two previously described studies by Schittekatte (1996, Experiment 2; Schittekatte & Van Hiel, 1996). Recall that in these studies it was found that members contribute more unshared (but not more shared) information to the discussion when they knew in advance which of the information they read was shared and which was unshared.

Second, when a member is known by others in the group to have special expertise in some task-relevant domain, that member can be proactively probed for information. That is, at appropriate times during discussion, others in the group can turn to the known expert and attempt to draw from him or her information pertinent to the decision at hand. In essence, this is a "pulling" force that complements the "pushing" force arising from the expert's own felt responsibility to ensure that his or her unique task-relevant information is considered by the group. In this regard, it is interesting to note that Okhuysen and Eisenhardt (2002) found that groups discussed more of their unshared information when the experimenter's prediscussion instructions emphasized the importance of members questioning one another about their information than when those instructions simply emphasized the importance of members sharing with one another the information that they themselves held.

Third, and building on the social validation idea described above, when others in the group hear information contributed by someone whom they know independently (e.g., by reputation or via the experimenter) to be a subject matter expert, they are less apt to question the validity of that information or to be put off by the fact that they themselves cannot independently verify it. Quite the contrary, knowing that a member is an expert in a given domain should enhance the credibility of whatever information he or she contributes from that domain. This idea goes to the core of what it means to be an expert. Thus, whereas identified experts should feel more responsible for contributing their special knowledge, others in the group should be more inclined both to probe those experts for the special information they hold and trust that information when offered. In combination, these three factors should promote a more thorough discussion of unshared information in groups and so help to minimize the shared-information bias that is otherwise evident in hidden profile situations.

Group Leaders

Contributing information to the discussion, whether by experts or nonexperts, is largely a sequential process—information that gets raised during discussion is typically brought out one item at a time, though usually at irregular intervals and often in a poorly organized fashion. One consequence of this is that the full implication of information mentioned earlier in discussion may sometimes become clear only when viewed in light of facts contributed much later on by other members. This is especially true for the unshared information that is raised. Failing to make these connections between early- and later-mentioned information risks misunderstanding and suboptimal decision making.

Recognizing this problem, Maier (1967) argued that it is imperative that someone in the group take responsibility for managing the information that surfaces during discussion. He suggested that this person should keep the group focused on the decision at hand, facilitate communication, stimulate member contributions, and ensure that those contributions are "kept alive" and appropriately integrated into the decision that eventually gets made. Maier maintained that this information management role is most naturally played by the group's leader.

One way a leader might help to ensure that member contributions are "kept alive" during discussion is simply by revisiting those contributions at opportune moments. Doing so can help to keep the group mindful of facts that already have been contributed, thereby reducing the likelihood that that information will be forgotten as new ideas are considered. Such "revisitations" manifest themselves as repetitions of the information in question. Consequently, repetitions might be used to index this important information management function. If so, and if leadership in decision-making groups implies an information management role, then we might expect leaders to repeat already-pooled information more often than the other members of their group.

This idea was tested in two experiments, both done in the medical decision-making context previously described (Larson et al., 1996; Larson, Christensen et al., 1998). The study by Larson, Christensen et al. (1998) is particularly informative. They had three-person medical teams diagnose two fictitious cases, with each member seeing a different version of each patient video. Each team comprised two equally experienced interns from a teaching hospital, plus a third-year medical student. The interns had completed medical school, so held an MD degree, and were nearing the end of their first year of full-time clinical training. The students, on the other hand, had not yet completed medical school, so did not hold an MD degree, and had minimal clinical experience. In each team, one of the two interns was randomly assigned to serve as the team leader. The experimenter handed the leader a clipboard containing a team diagnosis report form. She stated that it was the leader's job to ensure that the team completed its diagnosis within the time allotted. Further, the leader was to fill out the team diagnosis report form and had ultimate responsibility for the team's performance.

As predicted, the leaders were more likely than their teammates to repeat already-mentioned case information. This was true for both shared and unshared information, although they generally repeated shared information more often. Additionally, an interesting temporal pattern emerged in the repetition of unshared information. That pattern is displayed in Figure 6.4. Each line in the figure traces the proportion of times that a particular team member was the one who repeated unshared case information in each item serial position (i.e., the first repetition, second repetition, third repetition, etc.).[13] As can be seen, early in discussion the two interns were equally likely to repeat unshared case information, and both were more likely than the medical student to repeat it. As discussion progressed, however, the intern assigned to the leader role quickly became the one who was most likely to repeat unshared information. Simultaneously, the intern not assigned to the leader role quickly became indistinguishable from the medical student with respect to repeating unshared case information. Finally, leaders in

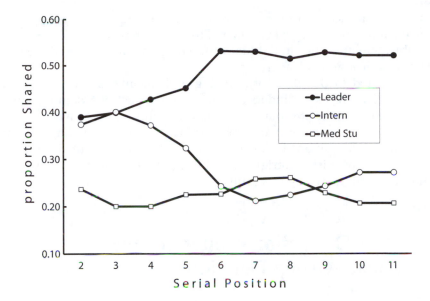

FIGURE 6.4 Proportion of discussions in which unshared information was repeated by each group member in each item serial position.
(Adapted from Larson, Christensen et al. [1998]. *Journal of Personality
and Social Psychology, 75,* 93–108. With permission of the American
Psychological Association.)

this study also asked more questions about already-pooled case information than did the other two members. Like repetitions, questions help
to keep information alive during discussion and so increase the probability that that information will be factored into the group's eventual
decision (cf. Okhuysen & Eisenhardt, 2002).

It is important to recognize that the interns participating in this study
all had the same amount of clinical experience and that the leader role was
assigned randomly. Thus, the unique repetition and questioning behavior
exhibited by leaders appears to be a reflection of their assigned position
within the group, not their relative expertise. Leaders in this study presumably felt greater responsibility than other members for guiding the
group's decision-making process, and it is this greater sense of responsibility that led them to assume a more active information management role
(cf. Scholten, van Knippenberg, Nijstad, & De Dreu, 2007).

Of course, not everyone who is assigned to lead a group will take
on the information management function with equal enthusiasm or
skill. There is evidence, for example, that assigned leaders who have a
predominantly participative style tend to encourage greater contribution of information overall but take a less active role in managing that

information once it is introduced, at least when compared to leaders who have a more directive style (Larson, Foster-Fishman, & Franz, 1998). No doubt there are other individual differences that affect the discussion behavior of assigned leaders.

Compared to the effect of knowing each member's special domain of expertise, far less is understood about the impact of assigning someone to play the role of group leader, at least with respect to whether this might reduce the tendency of groups to focus more on their shared than unshared information during discussion. Still, what limited evidence does currently exist is intriguing and suggests that this is an avenue of inquiry worth exploring more fully.

☐ Does Discussion Content Really Impact Group Decisions?

Implicit in most of the research on hidden profiles considered so far is the simple idea that group decisions depend on the content of group discussion. More specifically, it is assumed that the way in which decision-relevant information is distributed among members prior to discussion—how much of it is shared versus unshared, and which choice alternative each type favors—determines what information the group will talk about most during discussion, which in turn determines the choice they will collectively make. According to this view, group discussion is primarily a venue for integrating member information, where the group's eventual decision is shaped by the weight of evidence and argument brought to light (cf. Burnstein, 1982; Kaplan & Wilke, 2001). These ideas are represented graphically in the top panel of Figure 6.5, in what is labeled the Discussion-as-Mediator Model. This model explains that groups often select the choice alternative favored by their shared information because shared information tends to dominate their deliberations. By extension, the reason why groups perform so poorly in hidden profile situations is because in these situations their shared information tends to favor a suboptimal choice alternative (or at least does not favor the best choice alternative; cf. Endnote 4).

There is, however, another way to conceptualize the relationship between information distribution and group decisions. Gigone and Hastie (1993, 1996, 1997a) suggest that group decisions are determined by members' prediscussion preferences, not by the content of group discussion. They argue that the reason why groups more often select the choice alternative favored by their shared information is not because they spend more time discussing their shared information. Rather, it is because their

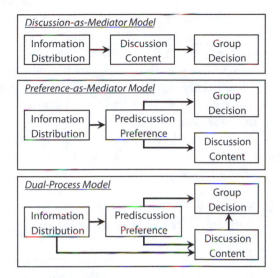

FIGURE 6.5   Three different models of the impact of information distribution on group discussion and group decisions.

shared information has a broader impact on members' decision preferences prior to the start of discussion. These authors note that, because each item of shared information is in every reading packet, it can affect every member's view of which choice alternative is best even without discussion. In contrast, each item of unshared information is in just one reading packet, which means that initially unshared information can affect only one member's opinion of what is best. Thus, according to this view, the way in which decision-relevant information is distributed among members determines their prediscussion decision preferences, which in turn determines the choice they will collectively make.

This alternative view is represented graphically in the middle panel of Figure 6.5, in what is labeled the Preference-as-Mediator Model. It assumes that member prediscussion preferences, not the informational content of their group discussion, mediates the relationship between information distribution and group decision. According to this model, groups more often select the choice alternative favored by their shared information because shared information has a broader impact on members' prediscussion preferences. Further, the reason why they perform so poorly in hidden profile situations is because under these conditions their shared information—and so their prediscussion preferences—usually favor a suboptimal choice alternative.

Two further points about the Preference-as-Mediator Model are worth noting. First, this model offers a rather different account of why group discussion tends to focus more on members' shared than unshared information. Specifically, it assumes that discussion content is driven most immediately by member prediscussion decision preferences—that members consciously choose to bring up their preference-consistent information during discussion, and that they do so to the relative exclusion of their preference-inconsistent information. Members might do this either because they are motivated to defend their prediscussion preference or because they assume that arguing in favor of their preference is what they are supposed to do. Additionally, there is evidence that group members tend to view their preference-consistent information as more credible and important than their preference-inconsistent information (e.g., Brownstein, 2003; Greitemeyer & Schulz-Hardt, 2003; Van Swol, 2007). Thus, simply by focusing on what they believe to be their most useful information, members are likely to contribute more preference-consistent information during discussion.

Unfortunately, in the hidden profile paradigm, information that is preference-consistent also has tended to be widely shared among members prior to discussion (e.g., see bottom panel of Table 6.1). Thus, groups may discuss more shared than unshared information not because they fall prey to a probability-based collective information sampling bias, but instead because members are more strongly motivated to contribute preference-consistent rather than preference-inconsistent information, and because in hidden profile situations preference-consistent information is more apt to be shared than unshared.[14]

The second point about the Preference-as-Mediator Model is that it paints a decidedly different picture of the role that group discussion plays in the decision-making process. It views discussion primarily as a venue for integrating member preferences—where members negotiate the relative weights to be accorded their various opinions about which choice alternative is best (cf. Brodbeck, Kerschreiter, Mojzisch, & Schulz-Hardt, 2007). In this respect, the Preference-as-Mediator Model has much in common with the social decision scheme approach discussed earlier in this chapter and in Chapter 4. It suggests that what matters during group discussion is the pooling of preferences, not information. Although it does not deny that shared information may be discussed more thoroughly than unshared information, the Preference-as-Mediator Model posits that these discussion effects have no direct impact on group decision making. Rather, according to this model, the informational content of group discussion, on the one hand, and the decision a group makes, on the other, are collateral phenomena that can be traced to a common source (the prediscussion distribution of information among group members) but have no inherent causal connection between them.

Empirical Evidence

The proposition that group discussion is directly influenced by members' prediscussion preferences is relatively noncontroversial; few would seriously argue against this idea. It is likely, however, that the tendency of members to contribute more preference-consistent than preference-inconsistent information occurs quite independently of whether that information is shared versus unshared. Dennis (1996), for example, reported that group members were more likely to contribute preference-consistent information during discussion than either preference-inconsistent or neutral information, even when all of that information was unshared. Conversely, studies by Greitemeyer et al. (2006) and by Lavery, Franz, Winquist, and Larson (1999) show that groups discuss significantly more shared than unshared information under both manifest and hidden profile conditions. As previously described, in a manifest profile situation the information contained in members' individual reading packets should lead them to prefer the best choice alternative even before discussion begins. This is because those packets are constructed so that the shared and unshared information they contain favors the optimal choice alternative in equal proportions (cf. top portion of Table 6.1). Consequently, in a manifest profile, the distributional status of the members' information (i.e., whether it is shared or unshared) is independent of its preference status (i.e., whether it is preference consistent or inconsistent). Nevertheless, groups still discuss more shared than unshared information in these situations.

More controversial is the proposition that the informational content of discussion has no impact on group decisions. Evidence in support of this idea comes from several laboratory experiments that all employed very similar tasks and a multi-trial "policy-capturing" methodology. Typical of these studies is the one by Gigone and Hastie (1993). They asked three-person groups to decide both individually (prediscussion) and collectively what grade each of 32 real university students was likely to have earned in an introductory psychology course offered during the previous academic year. At the start of every trial, members were each given a sheet of paper containing a small set of background information about one of these 32 students (e.g., regarding that student's high school grade point average, class attendance, self-described enjoyment of the class, etc.). Some of this information was on every member's sheet (completely shared), some was on two members' sheets (partially shared), and some was on just one member's sheet (unshared). After reading this information, but before discussing it among themselves, members reported the grade that they individually thought the student in question was most likely to have earned. Their information sheets were then collected, after which they discussed the case as a group and decided collectively what grade that student was likely to have earned. This procedure was then repeated for each of the remaining 31 students.

As in other studies, Gigone and Hastie (1993) found that, when a piece of information was more widely shared among members prior to discussion, it was more likely to be mentioned during discussion. Further, more-widely-shared information had a stronger impact on the grade decisions that groups made. However, this latter effect was not mediated by the pattern of information mentioned during dissuasion; more-widely-shared information had a stronger impact on the group decisions even when statistically controlling for the informational content of discussion. The group decisions were instead explained almost completely by members' prediscussion preferences, which in turn were determined by the particular combination of information that members each received. These results are thus consistent with the Preference-as-Mediator Model. Other studies that have used this same multitrial methodology have obtained similar results (Gigone & Hastie, 1996, 1997a; Lavery et al., 1999).

However, studies that have employed a more traditional, single-trial methodology have obtained somewhat different results. Larson, Christensen et al. (1998), for example, observed that the discussion of unshared information—but not shared information—significantly predicted diagnostic accuracy in medical teams. Likewise, Brodbeck, Kerschreiter, Mojzisch, Frey, and Schulz-Hardt (2002) found that experimental conditions that prompted greater discussion of unshared information also increased the likelihood that groups would uncover the hidden profile, which is to say, choose the decision alternative supported by the most information overall. Importantly, and unlike Gigone and Hastie (1993), this later effect became nonsignificant when controlling for the amount of unshared information discussed, a finding that strongly implicates the mediational role of discussion content. Winquist and Larson (1998) also found that the pooling of unshared (but not shared) information predicted the ability of groups to uncover a hidden profile. This effect remained significant even when controlling for members' prediscussion preferences, although those preferences did exert their own independent effect on the decisions that groups made.

In light of such conflicting findings, Winquist and Larson (1998) proposed a dual-process model of how the prediscussion distribution of decision-relevant information impacts group decision making. This model combines the main features of the Discussion-as-Mediator and Preference-as-Mediator models and is displayed graphically in the bottom panel of Figure 6.5. The Dual-Process Model posits two mediating variables: (a) members' prediscussion decision preferences and (b) the informational content of group discussion. It holds that the impact of shared information on group decision making is mediated primarily by members' prediscussion preferences, whereas the impact of unshared information is mediated primarily by group discussion. Specifically, because it is more widely distributed among members prior to discussion, shared information has more opportunity than unshared information to affect members' prediscussion preferences. Thus, even without a substantive discussion (i.e., one in which members pool their preferences but not their information), shared information should have a stronger impact than unshared information on the decision that eventually gets made. Group discussion, on the other hand, provides an opportunity to correct this initial imbalance in informational influence. When discussing unshared information, members expose one another to facts that most were unaware of originally, thus giving that information greater opportunity than before to affect the preferences of everyone in the group. This stands in contrast to discussing shared information, which, because it already had a chance to influence every member in the group prior to discussion, is less apt to have any additional impact during discussion. In other words, discussion is largely superfluous for shared information but is critical for unshared information. Thus, according to the Dual-Process Model, whereas shared information tends to exert greater influence prior to discussion, unshared information has the potential to exert greater influence during discussion.

As previously described, however, the dynamics of collective information sampling tend to limit the discussion of unshared information and so constrain its decisional impact. That is, the *potential* effect that unshared information can have on group decision making often goes unrealized simply because it is less likely to surface during discussion. Thus, the Dual-Process Model implies that shared information will often have greater decisional impact than unshared information, both because of its greater influence on members' prediscussion preferences and because unshared information is insufficiently pooled during discussion.

So why do the two sets of studies cited above generate such different results regarding the mediational role of discussion? An important feature of all the studies that found no evidence of this mediating role is that participants were required to consider a large number of cases (e.g., 32), one right after another, and were given very little time for each—often 90 seconds or less. By contrast, in the studies that did find evidence of mediation, participants were usually asked to consider just one case and were given ample time to do so—usually 20–45 minutes. It seems likely that groups run using the former methodology felt considerable time pressure to complete each case and as a result relied on easily implemented, less effortful heuristic processes, such as aggregating members' prediscussion preferences (cf., Karau & Kelly, 1992). Groups run using the latter methodology, on the other hand, had more time during discussion to think about the information members contributed, thus giving that information greater opportunity to impact the decision eventually made. The implication is that it is likely to take groups a certain amount of time to integrate into their decisions the unshared information that members contribute during discussion, especially when, as in a hidden profile, that information is contrary to the prediscussion preferences that most of their members may have. Conversely, when a decision must be made very quickly, unshared information is apt to have little impact, even when it does come to light during discussion.

In sum, current evidence suggests that prediscussion preferences and the informational content of group discussion both mediate the impact of distributed information on group decisions. However, the latter mediational process may require that sufficient time be allotted for discussion.

☐ Chapter Summary

In this chapter, I have provided an introduction to the empirical literature on group decision-making, emphasizing research that bears most directly on the question of synergistic performance gains in groups. Two broad issues were considered. One concerns the relative ability of groups and individuals to ignore potentially biasing information, which is to say, information that can, but normatively should not, affect their decisions. The other has to do with the ability of groups to incorporate into their decisions information that normatively should affect them, but that may not do so because it is not uniformly held by all members of the group prior to discussion. This latter issue has garnered far more research attention than has the former.

A particularly challenging situation that groups sometimes face is when information is distributed among members in a way that conceals from them the superiority of the best choice alternative. It is only when that distributed information is combined that the superiority of the best alternative becomes clear. Research shows that, when they exist, these so-called "hidden profiles" can have a dramatic negative effect on group decision-making performance. The empirical evidence for this was considered in some detail, as were several lines of research investigating factors that contribute to this effect. Much of this work focuses on the tendency of groups to discuss more—and more thoroughly—information that they share in common with one another than information that they hold uniquely. The reasons for this differential include an initial sampling advantage that favors the mentioning of shared information during decision-making discussions, members' greater ability to recall the shared rather than unshared information that is brought to light by others, and the ability of members to socially validate for one another the shared (but not unshared) information that gets discussed. Finally, research examining the independent impact of members' prediscussion decision preferences in hidden profile situations was also considered.

With regard to synergy in decision-making groups, the overall picture is not too different from that seen in Chapter 5 regarding group performance on judgment tasks. Across both domains, there is a small amount of scattered evidence suggesting that groups are at least capable of strong synergistic performance gains. More commonly, however, the results point to only weak synergistic gains—collective performance that exceeds the performance of the group's average member but not that of its best member. And throughout, there are numerous examples in which groups demonstrate no performance gain at all.

Clearly, synergy is not an automatic consequence of working collectively on either judgment or decision-making tasks. Rather, it seems to emerge only under a set of conditions that at present is not fully understood. Some of these no doubt have to do simply with "opportunity" factors. On quantity estimation tasks, for example, synergistic performance gains would seem to have much less opportunity to emerge when individual member estimates are unbiased, especially as the group grows large. Likewise, on decision-making tasks, a strong form of synergy is logically precluded if there is even one member in the group who prefers the best choice alternative prior to discussion. Both situations severely constrain the performance improvements that are even possible as a function of group interaction. If we are to find evidence of synergy in collective judgment and decision making, particularly strong synergy, it seems necessary to search for that evidence in circumstances unencumbered by such opportunity constraints.

Synergistic performance gains are also likely to require conditions that encourage members to examine their task-relevant information carefully and completely. This is true for both judgment and decision-making tasks. Some of these conditions undoubtedly have to do with members' motivation. Others are apt to be related to implicit assumptions (e.g., regarding the sufficiency of the available information) and heuristics (e.g., the tendency to rely on consensus as evidence of correctness) that can get in the way of a group's judgment and decision-making effectiveness. Still others are likely related to the inherent challenges associated with surfacing information that only one (or very few) group members possess. Finally, there are also hints in the literature that introducing certain special roles in groups (facilitators and leaders) may benefit the consideration of task-relevant information by members and so promote the emergence of a group performance gain. This is an under-researched topic that deserves greater attention.

☐ Endnotes

1. Although difficult to locate precisely, decision-like tasks with externally defined, objective criteria are often far enough toward the left-hand (intellective) end of Laughlin's (1980, 1999; Laughlin & Ellis, 1986) Intellective–Judgmental task continuum as to make them better fit the definition of problem-solving tasks.

2. Note that the results summarized here refer to individual participant post-deliberation responses, not to the collective responses of the groups in which those participants deliberated. London and Nunez (2000) did not report the latter. However, there is good reason to believe that the participants' post-deliberation preferences reflect fairly well the collective response made at the conclusion of deliberation by their group (cf. the literature on group polarization).

3. Shared and unshared information are actually two ends of a continuum, with various degrees of partially shared information in between. The more members there are who are aware of a given piece of information prior to the start of a decision-making discussion, the more widely shared that information is. Because relatively little research in this area has concerned itself with partially shared information, my discussion here focuses mainly on information that is either completely shared or completely unshared (but see Parks & Cowlin, 1996; Schittekatte, 1996; Schittekatte, & Van Hiel, 1996).

4. Table 6.1 displays a strong form of hidden profile, one that is designed not only to draw the individual member away from the best alternative, but also to direct him or her toward another, inferior alternative. It is possible to create a weak form of hidden profile that conceals the virtues of the best alternative without simultaneously making an inferior alternative seem more attractive. In the present example this might be accomplished by constructing the reading packets such that the A Information is distributed as in the top panel of Table 6.1, and the B Information is distributed as in the bottom panel of Table 6.1.

5. Perhaps because of this apparent reasonableness, relatively few empirical studies concerned with hidden profiles have reported member prediscussion decision preferences in sufficient detail (if at all) to permit meaningful individual-group comparisons. This explains the small number of studies cited here.

6. Among these are Devine, 1999, Greitemeyer, Schulz-Hardt, Brodbeck, & Frey (2006), Larson, Christensen, Abbott, & Franz, (1996), Larson, Christensen, Franz, & Abbott (1998), Larson, Foster-Fishman, & Keys (1994), Savadori, Van Swol, & Sniezek (2001), Schittekatte (1996), Schittekatte & van Hiel (1996), Schulz-Hardt, Brodbeck, Mojzisch, Kerschreiter, & Frey (2006), Stasser, Taylor, & Hanna (1989), Van Hiel & Schittekatte (1998), and Winquist & Larson (1998).

7. Note that although reasonably close, in this study the CIS model over-predicts the percentage of shared information that groups actually discussed. This is a fairly common result across studies. Another example can be seen in Figure 6.3 (discussed below). Over-prediction is likely the result of a small

amount of noninterdependence among the information items, which is the tendency for one item, once it is mentioned during discussion, to prompt the mention of certain other items (i.e., because of their similarity, configural relevance, etc.). For example, if someone mentions that a particular applicant for a managerial job has an MBA degree (a favorable attribute), it seems reasonable to wonder whether any of the other candidates under consideration might also have that same degree, thus increasing the likelihood that such information will be offered if anyone in the groups knows it. To the extent that dependencies of this sort exist between items of shared and unshared information, the CIS model—which assumes item independence—will over-predict the percentage of shared information that groups actually discuss (cf. Reimer, Kuendig, Hoffrage, Park, & Hinsz, 2007).

8. It is tempting to suppose that members may have a preference for discussing shared rather than unshared information, and that this accounts for the fact that groups generally discuss more of their shared than their unshared information. It is important to remember, however, that members usually are not told in advance which of the information in their reading packet is shared and which is unshared. Consequently, even if they do have such a preference, there is no way for them to act on it.

9. A conditional probability expresses the likelihood of an event happening given that some other event has already occurred. Thus, Equation 6.2 expresses the likelihood of sampling a piece of shared information given that one piece of information (whether shared or unshared) has already been sampled. It assumes that there were originally 6 pieces of shared and 12 pieces of unshared information, that group size is 4, and that sampling is done without replacement (i.e., once a piece of information has been sampled—introduced into discussion—it is removed from the pool of not-yet-sampled information). The specific terms in Equation 6.2 are as follows. The values .67 and .33 are the probabilities that the initially sampled piece of information was either shared or unshared, respectively (see text). The values 20 and 12 are the numbers of opportunities that remain for sampling shared and unshared information, respectively, assuming a piece of shared information was sampled initially (because sampling shared information eliminates 4 sampling opportunities). The values 24 and 11 are the numbers of opportunities that remain for sampling shared and unshared information, respectively, assuming a piece of unshared information was sampled initially (because sampling unshared information eliminates only 1 sampling opportunity). The terms in Equation 6.3 are similarly defined. Further examples of how these conditional probabilities are calculated by the DISM-GD computer program can be found in Larson (1997).

10. Note that there is only a .63 probability that any information at all, whether shared or unshared, will be left in the pool of recallable-but-not-yet-mentioned information after 11 items have been sampled. Thus, the probabilities shown for the twelfth serial position sum to .63, not 1.00.

11. The example shown in Figure 6.2 assumes independence of member recall, meaning that the items of shared information that one member can recall are independent of the items that others can recall. Ultimately, this is what permits them collectively to recall and mention more of their shared than unshared information. This same assumption is also made by the CIS Model.

One advantage of the DISM-GD computer program is that it permits the user to explore the predicted consequences of relaxing this independence assumption.

12. It should be noted that although the cases diagnosed by these teams each involved 25 or more pieces of information, there was a good deal of variability across teams with respect to how much of that information was actually discussed. At least 7 pieces of information surfaced in every discussion, at least 12 pieces were discussed in 54% of them, and at least 14 pieces were raised in 31% of the discussions. Thus, the proportions reported in Figure 6.3 are based on progressively fewer discussions as one moves from the 7th to the 14th items of new information mentioned. Due to sample size concerns, Larson, Christensen et al. (1998) did not analyze their discussion results beyond the 14th serial position.

13. The data plotted in Figure 6.4 reference all repetitions of unshared information, regardless of the specific items repeated. For example, Serial Position 2 refers to the second occasion on which any item of unshared information was repeated, not to the second repetition of a single item. Also, the data plotted are moving averages that combine proportions from three adjacent serial positions. For example, the data plotted for Serial Position 2 are averages across the proportions obtained for Serial Positions 1–3, the data plotted for Serial Position 3 are averages across the proportions obtained for Serial Positions 2–4, and so forth. This was done as a data smoothing technique. See Larson, Christensen et al. (1998) for further details.

14. Although the hidden profiles employed in most previous research have indeed been constructed so that shared information is preference consistent and unshared information is preference inconsistent, this is not a defining feature of a hidden profile. It is quite possible to construct a hidden profile such that members' shared information is equally likely to be preference consistent as preference inconsistent (e.g., Winquist & Larson, 1998). A weak form of hidden profile would accomplish this (cf. Endnote 4).

Learning and Memory

*Acquiring, Retaining, and Retrieving
Knowledge in Groups*

In contrast to Chapters 3 through 6, which dealt with group performance on several specific types of tasks, Chapters 7 through 9 address topics that are relevant to group performance across many task types. These topics concern learning and memory, motivation, and diversity in group composition, respectively.

At a very basic level, group performance results from the effortful application of member knowledge, skills, and abilities. Collectively, these constitute the primary resources that any group brings to its task.[1] The present chapter is concerned with the capacity of groups to acquire and use such resources, focusing on the twin issues of learning and memory in groups. In particular, it deals with the question of whether the ability to learn, retain, and retrieve task-related information is facilitated (or impaired) by group interaction. After that, Chapter 8 explores whether people are more or less motivated to apply the resources they possess when working collectively as opposed to when working individually. Finally, Chapter 9 examines the complex question of whether diversity in groups is a benefit or hindrance to performance. As will be seen, diversity can be conceptualized at different levels, one of which encompasses the distribution across members of task-relevant knowledge, skills, and abilities.

Although the present chapter is concerned with learning and memory in groups, it focuses only on learning and memory that somehow is instrumental for group performance. In particular, the chapter does not concern itself with collaborative learning groups (e.g., O'Donnell, Hmelo-Silver, & Erkens, 2006; Slavin, Hurley, & Chamberlain, 2003) or with the question of group-to-individual transfer of learning (e.g., Barron, 2003; Laughlin, Carey, & Kerr, 2008; Olivera & Straus, 2004). Collaborative learning groups are groups formed expressly for the purpose of enriching the learning of their members and are most commonly found in educational settings. Although, collaborative learning groups typically work together on various task assignments, the quality of their collective performance is seldom of concern. Rather, those group tasks are usually performed solely as a means of stimulating participation, interaction, and learning among the members of the group, with members' individual learning, memory, and performance being the outcomes of primary interest. Research on group-to-individual transfer (usually of problem-solving skills) is similarly focused on what individuals gain from their group experience. The present chapter, by contrast, is concerned with the impact of interaction on group learning, group memory, and group performance.

The first section of the chapter focuses on group learning. Group learning is a useful construct for understanding improvements in group performance over time. It is important, however, to differentiate conceptually group learning from learning that takes place at the level of the individual group member. Equally, it is important to identify empirical evidence that points to the unique contribution of group learning to group performance. The first section is devoted to these matters.

I then turn to the issue of memory in groups. To the extent that learning and memory are distinct processes, a question can be raised about whether the performance improvements displayed by groups are due exclusively to learning (an input or encoding phenomenon), or whether memory (an output or decoding phenomenon) might also play a role. The second section of the chapter addresses this question, focusing on whether collective recall is any better or worse than individual recall.

Finally, the third section of the chapter is devoted to the topic of transactive memory in groups. The term transactive "memory" is something of a misnomer, as it has just as much to do with learning as with memory. At its core, transactive memory concerns the implicit coordination of learning and memory across group members. In the third section I consider how this type of coordination comes about and how it impacts group performance.

And, of course, throughout the entire chapter my overarching concern is with synergistic performance gains in groups. Thus, at various points I call attention to the implications for synergy of what is known about learning and memory in group contexts.

☐ Group Learning

At the level of the individual group member, learning refers to a relatively permanent change in knowledge, skill, or ability that is produced by experience. Learning is conceptually distinct from performance but is typically operationalized as a performance improvement. In parallel fashion, *group learning* can be defined as a relatively permanent change in the knowledge, skill, or ability of a group that is produced by experience working together. Like individual learning, group learning is usually evidenced by a performance improvement. In this case, however, it is the collective performance of the group that improves.

Group learning is not entirely separable from individual learning. Indeed, the former depends on and is supported by the latter (cf. Larson & Christensen, 1993). At the same time, group learning can neither occur nor be demonstrated without group interaction. To illustrate, consider a group of chamber musicians who are learning to play a new composition. The members will undoubtedly spend many hours alone learning their individual parts. But they will also spend many hours rehearsing the piece as a group. Indeed, no matter how proficient the members each become at performing their individual parts, they will not perform well as an ensemble unless they spend time practicing together. By practicing together they will better learn how to coordinate their actions to achieve the desired result. Among other things, group rehearsals permit members to reach a mutual understanding about how certain passages will be played (e.g., regarding tempo and volume) and to develop ways of cueing one another that help them synchronize their actions on the fly (e.g., a subtle nod, given at just the right moment, that signals an increase in tempo; cf. Ginsborg, Chaffin, & Nicholson, 2006).[2] It is important for any group to learn to coordinate its actions in real time. Preplanned instructions (e.g., sheet music) and individual practice are seldom fully effective as a way to accomplish this. Rather, at some point the group members must interact with one another—they must actually perform their assigned task together and, in doing so, learn how best to harmonize their actions. The potential gain in performance that derives from experience working together as a group increases with the complexity of the task. The reason for this is that with more complex tasks it becomes increasingly more difficult to specifiy in advance precisely what behaviors (including their timing, intensity, duration, and contingent relationships) must be enacted in order for the group to perform optimally.

Group Learning Curves

To the extent that it occurs, group learning should improve either the quality or efficiency of a group's performance (or both), depending on the nature of the task. Efficiency can often be measured in fairly objective terms, for example by determining the amount of time it takes the group to complete a unit of work, the materials they consume, the amount of rework they must do before finally completing their task, or, more globally, their cost per unit produced. Quality, too, can sometimes be operationalized objectively, for example by measuring error rates, product defects, and other deviations from predefined performance standards.

When a group performs the same task over and over, objective measures of quality and efficiency can be used to construct a group learning curve. A learning curve is simply a plot of performance over time that illustrates the relationship between performance and cumulative task experience. To the extent that learning occurs, a learning curve should reveal improved performance as a function of experience, though often with diminishing returns. For example, as an auto racing pit crew learns to work more effectively together, the amount of time they take to service a car during a pit stop will decrease. But with every decrease in service time, further time reductions become harder and harder to achieve. As a result, their performance improvements, at least with respect to service completion times, will become progressively smaller as experience accumulates, approaching an asymptotic value.

Empirical evidence of this principle of diminishing returns in group learning first emerged during the middle years of the 20th century from laboratory research using ad hoc groups and simple problem-solving tasks (e.g., Guetzkow & Simon, 1955; Leavitt, 1951). More recently, such evidence has also been obtained from real-world groups performing highly complex and consequential tasks as part of their everyday work activities. An interesting example comes from a field study by Pisano, Bohmer, and Edmondson (2001; see also Edmondson, Bohmer, & Pisano, 2001; Edmondson, Winslow, Bohmer, & Pisano, 2003). These authors studied 16 surgical teams from hospitals in the United States as they gained experience with a new surgical procedure. These teams had recently been trained to perform a then-new minimally invasive approach to several different types of cardiac surgery, including coronary artery bypass grafting and mitral valve repair and replacement. Unlike conventional cardiac surgery, which required opening the chest cavity by splitting the breastbone and separating the ribs, the minimally invasive approach involves accessing the heart through small incisions between the ribs using specially designed instruments. The benefits to the patient of this new approach include less bleeding and risk of infection, less pain, trauma, and disfigurement, and a shorter overall recovery time. However, the new approach also poses a number of challenges. Among other things, it greatly reduces the visual access that surgical team members have to the operating field and so forces them to rely to a much greater extent than before on information read from electronic monitoring equipment in order to gauge the progress of the operation and determine what actions will be needed next. The surgeon in particular loses almost all direct visual and tactile contact with the heart and becomes much more dependent on other team members for vital information as the surgery proceeds.

Adopting the new minimally invasive procedure required that every member of the team learn new ways of acting (vis-à-vis the patient and technology) and interacting (vis-à-vis one another). The conventional, open-chest approach to cardiac surgery had evolved highly standardized roles and routines, with team members taking the majority of their cues from the surgeon's body language and from direct visual knowledge of what was occurring within the open chest cavity. Indeed, the conventional approach had become so routinized that entire surgeries could be performed with little or no discussion (Edmondson et al., 2001). Switching to the new approach demanded that these well established roles and routines be modified—subtly in some instances, profoundly in others—with explicit verbal communication becoming much more critical as a means of monitoring and coordinating team member actions.

To assess learning, Pisano et al. (2001) examined the amount of time it took these teams to complete each of a succession of surgeries using the new minimally invasive approach. Figure 7.1 displays two of the resulting learning curves they observed. Both curves trace procedure completion times (smoothed via regression techniques that control for several potential confounds) for the first 50 surgeries performed using the new technique. One curve describes the average completion times across all 16 teams. The other describes the completion times for the team that showed the best rate of learning. As can be seen, both curves exhibit the expected pattern of diminishing returns, with larger improvements appearing initially, followed by progressively smaller improvements. Across all teams, there was an average 23% improvement in procedure completion time from the first to the fiftieth surgery performed—a difference of more than an hour (from 4.73 hours for the first case to 3.67 hours for the fiftieth). The best team exhibited a 53% improvement relative to the first-case average and a 40% improvement relative to the fiftieth-case average, completing the fiftieth surgery in just 2.20 hours. This occurred despite the fact that the best team had much longer than average completion times for its first few surgeries using the new technique.

A question that can be raised about the curves displayed in Figure 7.1 is whether they actually reflect team learning, as opposed to the cumulative impact of team members individually learning to become more proficient at using the new instruments and technology associated with

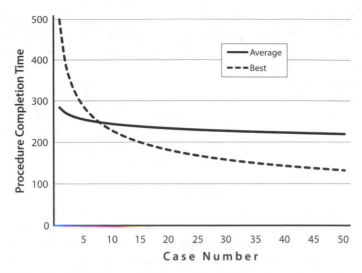

FIGURE 7.1   Surgical procedure completion time (in minutes) as a function of experience performing that procedure. (Reprinted from Pisano, Bohmer, & Edmondson (2001) with permission of the authors and publisher, copyright 2001, The Institute for Operations Research and the Management Sciences [INFORMS].)

the minimally invasive surgical approach. Pisano et al. (2001) anticipated this question and addressed it in part by subtracting from the procedure completion times the amount of time it took the surgeon to perform the middle phase of the surgery. During that middle phase, the surgeon works mostly alone to make the actual repairs to the heart. The time taken to complete that phase thus depends heavily on the surgeon's individual skill and speed. In this respect it stands apart from most other phases of the surgery, which depend much more heavily on the coordinated action of the team as a whole (e.g., to make the initial incisions that gain access to the heart, to reroute the flow of blood through a bypass machine that maintains oxygenation, pressure, and circulation, to thread a catheter and balloon from the groin into the aorta and then inflate the balloon to prevent the backflow of blood into the heart, to stop the heart, and then, after the repairs are made, to reverse all of the foregoing steps). Thus, the curves displayed in Figure 7.1 partially control for the individual learning of the one team member who is arguably most essential for accomplishing their collective task.

Other more recent studies of surgical teams have attempted to control for the individual learning of all team members, not just the surgeon's, and have yielded similar results. Reagans, Argote, and Brooks (2005), for example, assessed every member's overall experience performing a particular surgical procedure (total joint replacement) separately from his or her experience performing that procedure with each of the other members currently on the team. When summed across all members, these variables index the total amount of task-relevant individual and team experience, respectively, present in a given team at the time a particular surgery was performed. Reagans et al. found that procedure completion times decreased with increased team experience, and did so with diminishing returns, even when statistically controlling for individual experience.

Finally, the curves shown in Figure 7.1 clearly indicate that different teams learned to perform the minimally invasive cardiac surgery technique at different rates; some gained more—and more rapidly—from experience than did others. One factor that appeared to contribute to the variability in the rate at which these teams learned was the stability of their membership, especially early in their experience with the new surgical approach. Those teams with relatively stable membership learned the new approach at a faster rate than did teams with less stable membership (Edmondson et al., 2003; see also Argote, Insko, Yovetich, & Romero, 1995; Weber & Camerer, 2003).

Individual Versus Group Training

That membership stability impacts the rate at which groups learn is an important point that can be exploited to better disentangle, empirically, group learning from learning at the individual member level. One way this might be done is to compare the performance of groups whose members have been trained together to perform their assigned task with that of groups whose members have been trained separately.

Consider, for example, a laboratory experiment by Liang, Moreland, and Argote (1995). They trained research participants either individually or in three-person groups to assemble a working AM radio from the parts provided in a commercially available hobby kit. To assemble the radio, participants had to attach dozens of components (e.g., resistors, capacitors, transistors, etc.) to a special circuit board and then connect those components to one another in a prespecified manner. The kit was designed so that this could be done without using any special tools. The training began with a 15-minute, step-by-step demonstration by the experimenter on how to assemble the radio. Participants were then given 30 minutes to practice assembling a radio themselves. Those trained individually practiced assembling the radio alone, whereas those trained in groups practiced assembling the radio as a team. After 30 minutes, the experimenter examined their practice assembly, reviewed each component and connection, and pointed out any errors that had been made.

A week later, participants returned to the laboratory, and their ability to assemble the radio was formally tested. Unlike the training session, however, testing was always done in three-person groups. Those who had been trained individually the week before were randomly assigned to work with two other trainees during the testing phase. Those who were trained in groups, on the other hand, worked with the same two group-mates as before. To assess their declarative knowledge of the assembly procedure, each group was given 7 minutes to write down on a single sheet of paper all of the steps they could remember for assembling the radio. Then they were given up to 30 minutes to actually assemble a radio, with instructions to work as quickly and as accurately as possible.

The results from this study are shown in Table 7.1. As can be seen, although there was no difference in overall assembly time, groups whose members were trained together recalled significantly more of the assembly procedure, and committed fewer assembly errors, than did groups whose members were trained individually.

A follow-up study by Moreland and Wingert (1995, cited in Moreland, Argote, & Krishnan, 1996) also employed the radio assembly task, and used a procedure very similar to the one just described, but included two additional experimental conditions to test possible alternative explanations for the effects observed. In one, the group members were first trained individually, then brought together to participate in a brief team-building exercise designed to enhance their development as a cohesive work group. A week later they were tested on the radio assembly task. The purpose of this condition was to determine whether the performance differences reported by Liang et al. (1995) might be due to enhanced group development when members were trained as a group compared to when they were trained individually. In the other new experimental condition, participants were all trained in groups, but the composition of the groups was changed between the training and testing phases of the experiment, such that no two participants were ever trained and tested in the same group.[3] Here the purpose was to determine whether the effects reported by Liang et al. might be due to some sort of general knowledge gained

TABLE 7.1 Radio Assembly Performance by Three-Person Groups as a Function of Individual Versus Group Training

Performance Measure	Individual Training	Group Training
Procedural recall	16.40	25.53
Assembly errors	5.06	1.93
Assembly time	15.67	16.11

Adapted from "Group versus individual training and group performance: The mediating factor of transactive memory," by Liang et al., 1995, *Personality and Social Psychology Bulletin, 21,* 384–393. With permission of Sage Publications.

from the group training, as opposed to the specific knowledge that comes from being trained in the group in which they were eventually tested. The results of this follow-up study were quite similar to those reported in Table 7.1. Specifically, groups whose members were trained together recalled significantly more of the assembly procedure, and committed fewer assembly errors, than did groups in any other condition. By contrast, none of those other conditions differed significantly from one another.

Interestingly, in another follow-up study using the radio assembly task, individual versus group training was found to have no effect on participants' *individual* learning (Moreland, Argote & Krishnan, 1998, Experiment 3). This study used the same basic procedure as before, with the exception that during the testing phase all participants were tested individually rather than in groups. It was found that participants who were trained in groups performed no better than those who were trained individually. Importantly, compared to those who were trained individually, participants who were trained in groups remembered no more of the assembly procedure and committed no fewer assembly errors. Thus, it appears to be the group as a whole, not the individual group members, that benefited from the group training.

Two additional points are worth noting here. First, these group training effects are not limited to assembly tasks. They have been found as well on both problem-solving tasks and judgment tasks. For example, groups have been shown to perform better on Laughlin's (1996, 1999) rule induction task (see Chapter 4, pp. 138–143) when their members had previously practiced that task together compared to when they had practiced it individually (Brodbeck & Greitemeyer 2000a; Hollingshead, 1998b). Unlike the radio assembly task, however, where the benefits of group training appear to be mediated by better procedural recall, the value of group practice on the rule induction task stems mainly from improved error checking (Brodbeck & Greitemeyer, 2000b). Similarly, Olsson, Juslin, and Olsson (2006) found that dyads performed better on a multiple-cue judgment task when their members were trained together rather than individually. In this case, the advantages of training together were mediated by better recall during the study's testing phase for specific exemplars encountered during training.

Second, the gains attributable to group training and experience may often be task specific, and so not transferable to new tasks. Lewis, Lange, and Gillis (2005), for example, found that training a group together to assemble a hobby kit telephone benefited their subsequent telephone assembly performance relative to individual training. However, it did not benefit their performance when later asked to assemble a kit stereo tape player that they had never seen before. Groups whose members were trained together on the telephone assembly tasks had just as much trouble assembling the tape player as did those whose members were trained individually on the telephone assembly task.

Taken together, the findings from this line of research suggest two preliminary conclusions. One is that, when people are trained as a group, they learn something that is specific to—and useful exclusively for—the collective performance of that particular group. It is not useful in other groups. Second, the unique learning that occurs during group training is apt to be task specific and may not benefit the group's performance on other tasks, even those in the same general domain (e.g., two different assembly tasks).

Group Learning as Synergy

Groups thus learn something important as a result of working together that goes beyond what their members are able to learn by working separately. Moreover, group learning benefits their subsequent performance on that same task; it yields a performance gain. Because this gain is attributable to their previous interactions with one another, it fits the definition of synergy. What is more difficult to discern is whether the gain reflects weak or strong synergy. The reason is simply that research concerned with group training and experience has generally not compared the performance of individuals and groups. Indeed, the very idea of such a comparison seems absurd for many of the tasks studied (e.g., cardiac surgery), as it is unreasonable to expect that they might be performed at all by individuals working alone. Yet, as we have seen elsewhere, a comparison with individuals—especially the solo performance of the group's best member—is essential if questions of weak versus strong synergy are to be settled.

Insight into the matter of weak versus strong synergy can be obtained, however, by comparing individual and group performance on certain elemental tasks that are part of almost any complex group undertaking. Memory tasks are an example. On many group tasks, part of the learning that takes place is codified as declarative knowledge: knowledge that can be expressed verbally in simple declarative sentences.[4] Thus, as shown in Table 7.1, groups whose members were trained together on the radio assembly task, compared to those whose members were trained individually, were better able to recall the radio assembly procedures. Their superior performance in actually putting a radio together was presumably due in large measure to their better memory for those procedures. Because memory tasks are readily performed by individuals as well as groups, they not only can help to illuminate some of the ways in which experience working together improves group performance, they also can shed light on whether those performance improvements are evidence of weak or strong synergy. It is thus to a consideration of individual and group performance on memory tasks that I turn next.

□ Collective Recall

Learning and memory are distinct concepts that nevertheless are inextricably intertwined methodologically. Whereas learning has to do with input and encoding, memory is concerned with decoding and output. Yet, evidence of both is often derived from what is produced when individuals and groups are asked to recall a body of to-be-learned material. In this section of the chapter, I consider research that compares the recall of individuals and groups and examine it for signs of synergistic performance gains in learning as well as in memory.

Collective recall is the term applied when a group performs a memory task. Collective recall is a collaborative activity wherein group members produce a mutually agreed upon representation of some previously encountered information. Reaching consensus about what was and was not a part of that original information is central to collective recall.[5]

Collective recall stands in contrast to individual recall. A very large proportion of the recall that takes place in groups is in fact the same sort of hidden mental activity that occurs when people work at a task alone. It involves members privately recollecting and applying information as necessary to perform their part of the group's task. Importantly, on most of these occasions no help is sought when trying to retrieve the target information from memory, nor is any explicit attempt made to communicate the recalled information to others in the group. Instead, members endeavor to recall the relevant information on their own and then act on what they recall, with the action itself providing the only outward indication of what may have been remembered. This happens so often and so fluidly in conjunction with task performance that we seldom think of it as a separate activity.

On some occasions, however, assistance may be sought in retrieving a piece of information ("What did the experimenter tell us last week about this red thing?"). Or, individually retrieved information may be communicated explicitly to others in the group ("I think the experimenter told us last week that this red thing has to be connected to the radio's antenna"). When this occurs, the once-private mental product becomes open to scrutiny and modification, as well as acceptance or rejection by others. If the now-public recollection does not match what others remember, there is often spontaneous discussion intended to resolve the discrepancy and so achieve consensus about the content of the original information ("No, I think she said it has to be connected *before* the radio's antenna [is connected], not *to* the radio's antenna"). A group's collective recall is the consensually endorsed product of such interactions. As such, it is distinct from—yet depends upon—ordinary individual-level recall (cf. Larson & Christensen, 1993).

Synergy in Collective Recall: The Criterion Problem

Examples of research investigating collective recall can be found as far back as the 1950s. However, the bulk of the literature has appeared in the last 15 years. Before examining this work in detail, it is useful to consider the definition of synergy as it applies to collective recall, and in particular, what the appropriate criteria are for judging the presence of weak versus strong synergy.

A group's collective recall is most often documented by having its members work collaboratively to write down on a blank piece of paper all of the information that they believe was contained in a set of previously encountered material, with the understanding that nothing should be written unless members are in agreement about it. Following the tradition established in the problem solving literature (see Chapter 4), it is tempting to compare a group's collective recall to the recall of its members when working alone. The average member's solo recall might then serve as the criterion for judging weak synergy in collective recall, while the best member's solo recall might be used as the benchmark for judging strong synergy.

Indeed, these were precisely the standards employed in an early study by Perlmutter and DeMontmollin (1952), who found that three-person groups were able to recall a set of 19 two-syllable nonsense words better when working collectively ($M = 17.70$) than either their average ($M = 12.85$) or best members ($M = 15.55$) were able to do working alone. Similarly, Ryack (1965) found that interacting dyads recalled a set of nonsense syllables better than did both the average and best members from comparably constructed nominal dyads—dyads whose members actually performed the recall task individually, but who were randomly paired after the fact, and treated as dyads for data analytic purposes. Ryack's use of nominal dyads to establish both an average and a best member performance standard is the same strategy later employed by Laughlin and his colleagues for evaluating performance gains in interacting groups on the rule induction and letters-to-numbers problem-solving tasks (e.g., Laughlin, Bonner, & Altermatt, 1998; Laughlin, Hatch, Silver, & Boh, 2006; see Chapter 4, pp. 145–146 and 149–150).

Unfortunately, although the solo performance of the average member is a reasonable standard for drawing conclusions about weak synergy in collective recall, the solo performance of the best member is usually not adequate as a standard for drawing conclusions about strong synergy.

The reason has to do with the way recall performance is typically operationalized and what it means to be the "best" member in a group. In most research paradigms, the recall of both individuals and groups is indexed by the *amount* of information retrieved from memory. For instance, if the to-be-learned material comprises 19 nonsense words, recall performance would normally be operationalized as the total number of words correctly written down. However, this total is actually an aggregate measure; it is derived by counting the number of successes on a series of (19 in this example) different recall tasks, where retrieving each of the stimulus items is a separate task.[6] This means that the member who is "best" according to his or her total score is actually only "best on average" in terms of those separate recall tasks. Although this member is the one who most often can recall an item correctly when others cannot, there may a few items that this member cannot recall that nevertheless can be recalled by someone else in the group. For each such item, someone other than this ostensible "best" member is actually best. Consequently, an analysis that relies on members' total scores to define who is best when working alone uses a standard that is typically below the best individual's performance at the item (task) level of analysis.

As argued in Chapter 2, the search for synergy is a search for group performance gains at the task (as opposed to aggregate) level of analysis. Consequently, conclusions about both weak and strong synergy must be based on standards of comparison that faithfully represent what happens at the level of the task. With regard to collective recall, it is inappropriate to draw conclusions about strong synergy using the best member's total score as a standard of comparison, because that score often does not reflect what happened when trying to retrieve each of the separate items. Importantly, the person with the best total recall score is apt not to have been best on every single one of those items. Strong synergy is demonstrated when the group's performance *on a given task* exceeds the performance of even its best member *on that task*. It is insufficient to show that the group's performance exceeds the performance of the person who, on average, is best across tasks.

A more appropriate criterion for differentiating strong from weak synergy in collective recall is the pooled recall of *all* the members in a group when working alone. Equivalently, the pooled recall of all the members in a comparably constructed nominal group can serve this function. A nominal group's pooled recall is determined simply by giving the nominal group credit for having recalled an item if *any* of its members is individually able to recall that item. Computed in this way, a nominal group's recall score will be higher than its ostensible "best" member's score to the extent that others in the group are able to recall information that the "best" member cannot recall. In effect, the nominal group's score is a best member criterion at the task level of analysis. As such, it is a more appropriate criterion for judging the presence of strong synergy in collective recall.

To summarize, in the context of collective recall, when nominal groups provide the standard of comparison, weak synergy in interacting groups is indicated by performance that exceeds the average recall score of the nominal group *members*.[7] Strong synergy, by contrast, is indicated by interacting group performance that exceeds the average *pooled* recall score of the nominal *groups*. Alternatively, when the collective recall of an interacting group is compared to the previously-assessed solo recall of its own members, weak synergy is indicated by collective recall that exceeds the average of the members' individual scores, whereas strong synergy is indicated by group performance that exceeds the members' pooled score.

Group Learning and Collective Recall

Relatively few studies employing collective recall as a dependent measure have been designed to draw inferences about group learning (as opposed to memory). Even fewer have assessed both individual and collective recall, thereby permitting inferences to be drawn about the nature of any synergistic performance gains that might occur as a result of learning in groups.

One example from this small set is a study by Finlay, Hitch, and Meudell (2000, Experiment 1). Participants performed an embedded figures task in which they were presented with a series of 10 pictures containing hidden animals. The goal was to identify (by pointing to) the four target animals in each picture that were named on an accompanying list. Participants worked at this task either individually or in dyads. Because the two members of each interacting dyad identified the location of the hidden animals together, and so in the same order, it was expected that they would encode the list of animal names more similarly than would be the case for any random pair of participants who performed the embedded figures task alone. In other words, the researchers postulated that a group-level learning variable—encoding similarity—would be affected by working collaboratively on the embedded figures task.

The results of the study support this prediction. On a subsequent recall task, all participants worked individually to write down the names of as many of the 40 target animals as they could remember. Participants wrote these names one after another in the order they were recalled. The similarity of the order in which pairs of participants recalled the animal names was taken as an index of how similarly they had encoded that information in memory. As expected, participants who had worked together on the embedded figures task recalled the animal names in a more similar order than did random pairs of participants who had performed the embedded figures task alone. Thus, working collaboratively led members to encode task-relevant information similarly.

But that is not the whole story. After performing a brief distractor task, Finlay et al. (2000, Experiment 1) had participants recall the same list of animal names a second time. Some participants did this again as individuals, whereas others now worked collectively in dyads to recall the list. Further, in some cases the dyads were composed of the same two people who had worked together on the original embedded figures task (old dyads), while in other cases they were composed of two people who had performed the embedded figures task alone (new dyads). Thus, compared to the new dyads, old dyads consisted of members who had encoded the stimulus information more similarly. It was found that both kinds of dyads performed better than did individuals on the second recall task. However, old dyads performed better than new dyads. Specifically, old dyads recalled 19% more of the animal names than did new dyads, and in fact performed at a level comparable to that of nominal dyads—random pairs of participants who performed the second recall task alone, but whose written recall records were pooled. Thus, having similarly encoded the stimulus material benefited collective recall, permitting old dyads not only to surpass the weak synergy criterion (the average performance of individuals working alone), but to match—though not exceed—the strong synergy criterion (the average pooled performance of nominal dyads).

A slightly different way to think about the Finlay et al. (2000, Experiment 1) results is in terms of the retrieval cues produced while working collectively versus individually on the embedded figures task. Inherent in the encoding similarity idea is the notion that the temporal order in which the animals were discovered provided participants with a common set of episodic cues that they could later employ to help them recall the content of the animal name list. For example, if while performing the embedded figures task the dog, crow, fish, and snake were discovered in that order, "dog" might serve as a retrieval cue for "crow," which in turn might become a retrieval cue for "fish," etc. Thus, if one member of a dyad recalls (and announces) dog and crow, it should be easier for the other member to recall fish and snake if he or she discovered the animals in that same order. Said differently, exposure to a common set of episodic cues at the time of encoding should help members later on when they work collaboratively and so have an opportunity to cue one another. Old dyads in the Finlay et al. study were presumably able to reap this "cross-cueing" benefit, whereas new dyads were not, simply because new dyads were less likely to share the same experience-based retrieval cues.

This idea is demonstrated more clearly in a study by Andersson and Rönnberg (1997, Experiment 1). They asked participants to learn a list of 90 words. The words were presented in a booklet, one per page. During the learning phase, participants had 20 seconds per word to write down a retrieval cue—another word—that later would be used to help them recall the target word. In creating each retrieval cue, participants were instructed to write a word that seemed appropriate to them and that they had thought of when they saw the target word. Participants worked at the cue-generating task either individually or in dyads. Like individuals, dyads also generated a single retrieval cue for each target word, but the two members had to agree on what cue they would write down. Five days later, participants returned to the laboratory to recall the word list using the previously generated cues, and did this as well either individually or in dyads. Among the dyads, half had previously performed the cue generation task with the same partner (old dyads), while the rest had previously performed it individually (new dyads). For the old dyads, all of the retrieval cues employed during recall were those they had generated collaboratively. For the new dyads, half of the retrieval cues were taken from those previously generated by one member and half were taken from those generated by the other. It was found that, during collective recall, old dyads recalled 60% more of the target words than did new dyads, and, like the old dyads studied by Finlay et al. (2000, Experiment 1), performed at a level comparable to that of nominal dyads. The superior performance of the old dyads can be attributed to the common set of retrieval cues that they generated while learning the target words.

Thus, working collaboratively to learn a body of material appears to benefit a group's subsequent collective recall of that material. This seems to occur at least in part because collaborative learning helps members encode the information similarly and/or exposes them to a common set of episodic retrieval cues. These commonalties provide them with a more efficient means of working together later on to help one another retrieve from memory the target information they learned.

Individual Versus Collective Recall

The performance gains by old dyads relative to new dyads in the forgoing studies, along with the previously described results from the radio assembly experiments, clearly suggest that collective recall benefits when members work together at the time of encoding. But what about working together at the time of retrieval? Does working collaboratively to recollect a set of previously presented material benefit group performance even if the information was originally encoded individually?

There is a sizable body of empirical evidence to suggest that it does. But that benefit appears to be in the range of weak rather than strong synergy. Specifically, interacting groups nearly always recall more material than do individuals working alone, but not more than the pooled amount recalled by comparably constructed nominal groups. This is what was found, for example, in the previously cited studies by Perlmutter and DeMontmollin (1952) and Ryack (1965). The same pattern also has been observed in numerous contemporary investigations using experimental stimuli that range from simple word lists to video presentations of complex social interactions, and time delays prior to recall that range from several minutes to several months (e.g., Andersson, 2001; Andersson, & Rönnberg, 1995, 1996, 1997; Basden, Basden, Bryner, & Thomas, 1997; Hinsz, 1990; Weldon, Blair, & Huebsch, 2000; Weldon & Bellinger, 1997).[8] In these studies the total amount of information recalled by interacting groups sometimes approached—and even matched—the pooled recall of comparably constructed nominal groups. But there appear to be no studies in which the recall of interacting groups has exceeded the nominal group criterion by a statistically meaningful margin.

Weak Synergy, Strong Synergy, and Group Process in Collective Recall

Synergy, of course, is defined as a performance gain that is attributable in some way to group interaction. This is true for both weak and strong synergy. If this concept is to be usefully applied to collective recall, then some sort of identifiable group process must be involved. It is instructive to consider briefly what such a process might look like.

Asking research participants to collaboratively recall and record information that was presented to them at some previous time forces them to engage in the same sort of interactions that would normally occur only sporadically and on an impromptu basis in most real-world situations. At minimum, it requires that they exchange their individual recollections, accept as correct those recollections of others that in fact are correct, and reject recollections that are incorrect. Thus, the written record they produce is not created by mechanically combining their remembrances, but rather by actively negotiating with one another about which of those remembrances will and will not be written down. If a group were able to do this perfectly well, but no more, their collective performance would match, on average, the pooled performance score of comparably constructed nominal groups. The pooled performance of nominal groups thus reasonably defines the upper limit of weak synergy in collective recall.[9]

But the empirical record suggests that groups often are not able to do this perfectly well. A member might, for example, offer a piece of valid information that no one else in the group can remember, but do so with such hesitation and uncertainty that others are unconvinced of its authenticity. As a result, it does not get included in their consensual written record, even though that individual would likely have written it down when working alone. Or, a member might offer an invalid remembrance—something that was not actually part of the to-be-learned material—and do so with such conviction that others in the group accept it as genuine. Thus, it gets added to their written record when it should not be. Rejecting accurate recollections and accepting inaccurate ones reduces the magnitude of any synergistic performance gain that might be observed in collective recall.

But what about strong synergy? Strong synergy requires that groups do more than simply accept correct recollections and reject incorrect ones. If interacting groups are to surpass the pooled performance of nominal groups, they must also be able to recall information that *none* of their members could have recalled working alone. This might occur, for example, through some form of cross-cueing, whereby members prompt one another with semantic (as opposed to episodic) cues drawn from the content of the to-be-learned material that help them recall certain items of target information that they would not have been able to remember on their own.

Cross-cueing would seem to be essential in order to generate a strong synergistic performance gain in collective recall. Even if cross-cueing occurs, however, a group might nevertheless demonstrate only weak synergy if the beneficial effects of cross-cueing are outweighed by a deficiency in their ability to discriminate between valid and invalid recollections. Conversely, strong synergy might emerge despite a group's less-than-perfect ability to discriminate between valid and invalid recollections if this weakness is outweighed by the effects of cross-cueing. Thus, whereas strong synergistic performance gains might be taken as prima facie evidence that at least some amount of cross-cueing occurs in collective recall, the group process(es) underlying weak synergy are apt to become clear only with a more detailed analysis of the content of collective recall.

The Cross-Cueing Hypothesis

One way to test for the presence of cross-cueing in group interaction is to employ an experimental design in which participants attempt to remember the stimulus material during two successive recall sessions. During the first, all participants try to recall the information individually. Then, in the second session, half work collectively in groups to recall that same material, while the rest again try to recall the material as individuals. In this way, the content of a group's collective recall can be directly compared with the content of its members' individual recall in order to determine whether or not any new items emerged when they worked collectively that had not occurred to their members when working individually. The rate at which these "emergent" memories appear in collective recall can also be compared to the rate at which they appear when participants merely attempt a second time to recall the stimulus material as individuals.

Meudell, Hitch, and Boyle (1995) employed just such an experimental design. They presented university students with a list of 60 words, displayed on a video screen one-at-a-time for three seconds each. Included in this list were three words from each of 20 different semantic categories (e.g., birds, fruits, furniture, etc.), intermixed randomly. After a brief distraction interval, participants were asked to recall individually as many of the words as possible (first recall session). When they finished, their response sheets were collected. Then, half of the participants were assigned to work collaboratively in dyads to recall the information again (second recall session), while everyone else recalled the information a second time as individuals. It was found that interacting dyads recalled more words during the second recall session than would be expected based solely on the performance of their members when working alone during the first session (i.e., assuming they were simply pooling the words they had previously recalled individually, without recalling new ones). However, individuals working alone also recalled more words during the second session than during the first. Further, groups working collectively and individuals working alone did not differ with respect to the number of *new* words recalled during the second session. This was true even though the semantic structure of the stimulus material (i.e., the fact that the words were drawn from a large number of distinct semantic categories) provided many opportunities for cross-cueing ("Weren't there also a few birds?"). Nor did varying the typicality of the category exemplars make a difference—more words were recalled when the stimulus material comprised highly typical rather than atypical category exemplars, but within each level of typicality there were no differences between groups and individuals with respect to the number of emergent words that appeared during the second recall session. Similar findings have been reported by Finlay, Hitch, and Meudell (2000) and Meudell, Hitch, and Kirby (1992).

Thus, at present there is little evidence that cross-cueing contributes significantly to group performance on collective recall tasks when group members are first exposed to the to-be-learned material as individuals. Under these conditions, groups seem not to have access to more recollections than their members could have retrieved working strictly on their own. This conclusion stands in contrast to the one previously drawn about cross-cueing when members work interactively while learning the stimulus material (see pp. 230–232). It would appear that cross-cueing benefits group performance only when members share a common set of episodic retrieval cues—experience-based cues developed during learning that members can draw upon later to help one another recall the target material.

Interference in Collective Recall

But the absence of a cross-cueing effect when members are first exposed individually to the to-be-learned material does not by itself explain why under these conditions the recall performance of interacting groups often falls below that of nominal groups. For this, it is necessary to consider two other possibilities: interference and conservatism in collective recall.

First, collective recall may be subject to an interference effect, wherein members actually hinder one another's ability to retrieve material from memory. This possibility was first suggested in papers published simultaneously by Basden et al. (1997) and by Weldon and Bellinger (1997). Basden et al., for example, point to the robust finding in the individual recall literature that presenting at the time of recall a few of the items from a previously studies word list can inhibit a person's ability to recall items from the remainder of that list (e.g., Aslan, Bäuml, & Grundgeiger, 2007; Basden & Basden, 1995; Nickerson, 1984). This "part-list cueing effect" is said to occur because the presented items are encountered in a way that is inconsistent with the idiosyncratic organization of the stimulus material that participants developed when they first studied the word list and so disrupts their use of that organization when later trying to recall the list. Basden et al. argue that essentially the same thing happens when group members are exposed to the spontaneously generated recollections of their groupmates; once announced, those recollections disrupt other members' retrieval strategies and so interfere with their ability to call forth additional memories of the stimulus material.

Basden et al. (1997) conducted a series of experiments designed to test for interference in collective recall. Their stimulus material in each case consisted of a single word list containing multiple exemplars from a number of different semantic categories. After an initial study period, and after performing a distractor task to reduce recency effects, participants were asked to recall as many words from the list as they could. They did this either individually or in three-person groups. However, the group condition involved a highly constrained form of collective recall. Specifically, members took turns recalling the words, with each mentioning one word per turn. Members were cautioned not to help one another recall the words or to speak out of turn. If a given member could not recall a new word from the list within 10 seconds, the turn passed to the next member. This continued until there were three consecutive turns without a member recalling a new word. Parallel time constraints were imposed on individuals recalling the words alone.

It was found that, when the number of semantic categories was large, collective recall was better than individual recall, but not as good as the pooled recall of three-person nominal groups. Additionally, the recalled words were retrieved from fewer semantic categories in the collective compared to the individual recall condition, and the sequential order in which they were recalled was semantically less well organized. These latter findings both suggest that members' retrieval strategies were disrupted in the collective recall condition. Interestingly, collective recall was just as good as nominal group recall when members were forced either to retrieve nonoverlapping subsets of the stimulus material (i.e., all members studied the entire list, but they were later restricted to recalling words from different semantic categories) or to retrieve the words by category (i.e., exhausting one category before moving to the next). Comparable findings have been reported by others (e.g., Finlay, Hitch, & Meudell, 2000; Wright & Klumpp, 2004). Taken together, these results seem to suggest that the recollections announced by one group member can indeed impair the retrieval of additional recollections by others.

This interference effect in collective recall is reminiscent of certain of the explanations described in Chapter 3 for production blocking in brainstorming groups (see especially pp. 95–106). Recall that the task of a brainstorming group is to generate as many ideas as possible for solving a given problem (e.g., increasing tourism). The typical finding in this literature is that brainstorming groups produce more ideas than individuals working alone but fewer ideas than similar-size nominal groups. The reduced ideational productivity of brainstorming relative to nominal groups has been attributed in part to the adverse effect of group interaction on members' ability to retrieve from memory the raw materials from which new ideas are formed (e.g., Brown, Tumeo, Larey, & Paulus, 1998; Nijstad & Stroebe, 2006) and seems very much the same sort of thing as the interference identified in the context of collective recall.

Conservatism in Collective Recall

In addition to interference, collective recall may also be subject to a conservatism bias—groups may be more cautious than individuals when deciding which of their recollections will be consensually endorsed. Collective recall, by definition, requires that group members come to an agreement about which recollections will and will not be recognized and included as part of their group recall. This, in turn, depends on their perceptions of the validity of those recollections. A given recollection might be judged valid because the member who recalled it is confident of its accuracy and is able to communicate that confidence to the rest of the group ("I'm sure 'cardinal' was one of the words on the list, because it first made me think of the baseball team, not the bird."). Or, it might be judged valid because others in the group can independently recall the same information ("Yeah, I remember seeing 'cardinal,' too"). The latter, of course, bespeaks the same sort of social validation process as discussed in Chapter 6 in connection with group decision making (see pp. 197–198). Conversely, a recollection might be judged invalid if the member mentioning it does so hesitantly, or if it cannot be independently confirmed by others.

Individuals who perform the recall task alone must similarly decide which of their recollections will and will not be reported, and here, too, the decision turns on judged validity. But individuals, of course, have only their own internal experiences on which to base their validity judgments. Importantly, unlike groups, they cannot test the validity of their recollections against the memory of others.

It is precisely because interacting groups have at their disposal multiple sources of validity cues (whereas individuals have just one) that groups are apt to be more cautious in deciding which of their member recollections will be endorsed. Because accurate remembrances can often—but not always—be socially validated by others, groups routinely put member recollections to this additional social comparison test. But increasing the number of criteria against which a recollection is evaluated also increases the chances that it may fail one of those tests and so be judged invalid. Thus, a member who recalls information with enough confidence to write it down when working alone may nevertheless be overridden by the rest of the group when no other member is independently able to recall that same information.

One implication of this line of reasoning is that, compared to nominal groups, interacting groups should tend to make not only more errors of omission—failing to list items that actually were part of the stimulus material—but also *fewer* errors of commission. that is, listing items that in fact were not part of the stimulus material. Of course, making more errors of omission should lead to poorer performance to the extent that performance is defined by the total number of stimulus items found in the recall record. Making fewer errors of commission, on the other hand, should lead to *better* performance to the extent that performance is defined by the total number of *intrusion errors* found in the recall record. An intrusion error is a "recalled" item that actually was not part of the original stimulus material.[10]

Takahashi (2007) examined these ideas in a series of three experiments. He asked nominal and interacting dyads to remember five lists of word that contained 15 items each. These lists were specially constructed so as to induce a high rate of intrusion errors. This was done by including in each list words that were all closely related to one central word, but without listing that central word itself. For example, the words in a given list might all be closely related to the game of baseball (e.g., pitcher, batter, strike), but the word "baseball" itself does not actually appear. At recall, both the proportion of listed words correctly recalled (out of 75) and the proportion of central but not listed words falsely recalled (out of 5) were recorded. Table 7.2 displays the results from one of these experiments. As

TABLE 7.2 Mean Proportion of Correctly Recalled Words and Intrusion Errors as a Function of Recall Condition

Recall Condition	Correctly Recalled Words	Intrusion Errors
Individuals	.23	.51
Interacting dyads	.29	.59
Nominal dyads	.37	.73

Note: The correct recall values are based on n = 75 stimulus words, whereas the intrusion values are based on n = 5 central-but-not-presented targets. Adapted from "Does collaborative remembering reduce false memories?" by Takahashi, 2007, *British Journal of Psychology, 98*, 1–13 (Experiment 3). With permission of the British Journal of Psychology© The British Psychological Society.

can be seen, the data for the proportion of words correctly recalled follow the typical pattern, with the mean for interacting dyads lying between the means for individuals and nominal dyads. Thus, for correctly recalled words, the performance of interacting dyads was clearly below that of nominal dyads. At the same time, and as can be seen in the table, interacting dyads generated fewer intrusion errors than did nominal dyads, though somewhat more than individuals working alone.

The findings from an interesting field experiment by Ross, Spencer, Linardatos, Lam, and Perunovic (2004) also point to a conservatism bias in collective recall. They tested a sample of 60 older married couples (mean age = 73) on a personally relevant recall task performed in its natural setting: remembering items from a previously constructed shopping list while at the grocery store. Each of the participating couples was first met in their home, shown a grocery catalog containing 70 generic items (e.g. butter, rice, glass cleaner), and asked to jointly select from it 25 items that they would purchase if they were to go shopping that day. They circled each of the items they selected. The researcher then confiscated the list, and drove the couple to the grocery store where they normally shopped. Without benefit of the list, participants wheeled a shopping cart through the grocery isles to collect those items that they remembered circling, and did so either alone or with their spouse. Recall measures were derived from the final content of their shopping cart.[11] Ross et al. found that couples who shopped together were significantly more cautious than nominal couples (spouses who shopped independently but whose shopping cart contents were pooled in the usual way) about putting items into their cart. They made more errors of omission and so performed more poorly than nominal couples in terms of the total number of circled items actually gathered while shopping. However, they also made fewer errors of commission (intrusion errors) and so performed better than nominal couples in terms of the total number of items placed into their cart that in fact had not been circled (see also Clark, Abbe, & Larson, 2006; Johansson, Andersson, & Rönnberg, 2005; Van Swol, 2008; Ross, Spencer, Blatz, & Restorick, 2008).[12]

The strength of the conservatism bias in collective recall, at least with respect to its benefits for minimizing intrusion errors, may depend on the size of the group. As seen in Table 7.2, Takahashi (2007) found that, although interacting dyads committed fewer intrusion errors than did nominal dyads, they committed more than did the average individual who worked alone. Similarly, Clark, Hori, Putnam, and Martin (2000) found that dyads had a higher false alarm rate on a recognition memory test than did their average member when working individually. On the other hand, Clark et al. also found that the false alarm rate for three-person groups was *lower* than that of their average member when working alone (cf. Clark, Stephenson, & Kniveton, 1990; Vollrath, Sheppard, Hinsz, & Davis, 1989; Weldon & Bellinger, 1997). Thus, groups may become better able to reject false recollections with increasing group size.[13]

It should be clear that the criteria for judging weak and strong synergy in collective recall must be revised when the focus is on intrusion errors. Here, weak synergy is defined as improving on the pooled intrusion error rate of nominal groups, whereas strong synergy is defined as improving on the intrusion error rate of the best (not average) nominal group members—those with the lowest intrusion rate in their respective nominal groups. Equivalently, if group members' individual recall is assessed prior to testing their collective recall, then their own pooled and best individual intrusion rates might serve as the weak and strong synergy standards, respectively. According to these criteria, the studies cited above all suggest that groups exhibit at least weak synergistic performance gains in rejecting false recollections. On the other hand, no study has yet shown that groups can produce a strong synergistic gain. The one that comes closest is the study by Clark et al. (2000), cited above, where it was found that the intrusion error rate for three-person groups was not only lower than that of their average group member, it was comparable to (but not lower than) the intrusion error rate of their best individual member. This means, of course, that their three-person groups were still performing within the range defined as weak synergy. Whether larger groups might be able to demonstrate strong synergy in rejecting false recollections is presently unknown but seems worth investigating.

Finally, the relative costs and benefits of conservatism, vis-à-vis rejecting valid and invalid recollections, respectively, are apt to vary across situations. Although endorsing valid member recollections and rejecting invalid ones may be equally important to group performance in many situations, it seems likely that there are some circumstances in which erring in one direction or the other is more problematic. Thus, whereas the costs and benefits of conservatism may often offset one another, there are almost certainly occasions in which conservatism results in either a net gain or net loss in performance for the group. A better understanding of these circumstances would help to put the impact of conservatism in collective recall in better perspective.

Collective Recall: Summary

In sum, groups have consistently been shown to demonstrate weak rather than strong synergistic performance gains when working collectively at recall tasks. This applies both to the amount of stimulus material that they are able to remember correctly, as well as to the intrusion errors that they make. There is evidence that cross-cueing benefits collective recall, but only when members work collaboratively while initially learning the stimulus material. Interference, on the other hand, is an impediment to collective recall, with members sometimes disrupting one another's retrieval strategies. Further, groups appear to be more conservative than individuals when performing recall tasks; they endorse fewer of their members' valid recollections, but fewer of their false recollections as well. The latter may be especially beneficial in situations where errors of commission are more costly than errors of omission. In short, whereas collaboration at the time of encoding can benefit collective recall, collaboration at the time of retrieval yields a mix of costs and benefits.

☐ Transactive Memory

Implicit in most of the foregoing research on collective recall is the assumption that group members initially have equal exposure to the to-be-learned material. Likewise, it is presumed that members are unaware of any systematic differences among themselves that might lead different members to attend to different parts of the stimulus information. Thus, although members may indeed learn somewhat different subsets of that material, they are presumed to have no way of knowing who in the group actually learned what until they begin to recall it collectively. In these studies, it is only through the collective recall process itself that such differences are discovered and resolved.

In most naturally occurring groups, however, the situation is quite different. Particularly in groups that have existed for a period of time, members typically are aware of numerous ways in which they and their groupmates differ one from another. These differences often have to do with their respective domains of expertise, experience, and interest, as well as differences in the group, organizational, and societal roles that members play. All of these are factors that can lead to systematic differences in the information that members attend to and learn, even when everyone is exposed to exactly the same stimulus array.

As a concrete example, consider the members of a faculty search committee who are reviewing a job applicant's curriculum vitae in order to make a preliminary determination about his or her suitability for a job in their department. There is a good chance that the committee members will all learn somewhat different things from the vitae. The member whose own research is closest to that of the applicant may learn certain details of the applicant's listed publications that others do not. The member who is most keenly interested in increasing the diversity of the department may pay more attention than others to clues that signal the candidate's gender and ethnicity. And the department chair, the committee member who is most attuned to financial matters, may be the one who looks most carefully for indicators of the applicant's likely salary expectations. In other words, each committee member's own expertise, interests, and roles are apt to lead him or her to pay particular attention to a different aspect of the curriculum vitae.

At the same time, each member's understanding of the expertise, interests, and roles of the *other* committee members is also likely to guide his or her reading of the vitae. Realizing, for example, that there is someone on the committee whose own research is closer to that of the applicant, other members may be inclined to pay less attention to certain details of the applicant's publication record, preferring instead to skim that material but "leave the details to the expert." Similarly, knowing that the department chair will eventually be the one to handle the financial aspects of the hiring process, others may feel less obliged to search for clues to the applicant's salary expectations. In short, whereas the committee members' own expertise, interests, and roles should lead them to pay more attention than they otherwise might to certain aspects of the curriculum vitae, their understanding of the expertise, interests, and roles of their fellow committee members should cause them to pay less attention than they otherwise might to certain other aspects of that same vitae. Importantly, their decisions about what information to pay more versus less attention to are apt to be made without consulting one another and so reflect a process of *tacit coordination*. Tacit coordination refers to the synchronization of members' actions based upon unspoken assumptions about what others in the group are likely to do (Wittenbaum, Stasser, & Merry, 1996; Wittenbaum, Vaughan, & Stasser, 1998). In this example, the "actions" in question are the implicit decisions that members make regarding what they will and will not attend to in the curriculum vitae.

Tacit coordination, as it applies to learning information from a stimulus array, is one part of a much broader phenomenon in the mental life of groups. As they evolve, groups develop an informal system for dividing the cognitive labor associated not only with acquiring task relevant information, but also with storing and retrieving that information later on. It is known as a *transactive memory system* (Wegner, 1987; Wegner, Giuliano, & Hertel, 1985). At its core is an implicit process of assigning responsibility for learning and retaining bits of information based on members' shared understanding of one another's expertise, interests, and roles. Members who have one or more unique areas of task-related expertise, or who have special interests or roles pertinent to specific aspects of the task, often take responsibility for learning and retaining information in those areas. Further, they typically assume that others in the group will do the same, thus relieving them of responsibility for learning and retaining information that falls within the purview of other members' expertise, interests, and/or roles. Members are increasingly able to do this as they gain familiarity with one another and so come to recognize one another's special talents, interests, etc. This is the case even though members may never speak directly about who will be accountable for learning what. As a result, different members are apt to learn different subsets of the stimulus information. The main benefit of this is that it increases the group's collective memory capacity. That is, assuming that each member can absorb only so much information within a fixed period of time, the group as a whole should be able to retain more information overall if different members attend to different things than if every member attends to the same things. It is the group's transactive memory system that provides the mechanism for sorting out who will learn what.

Equally important, the group's transactive memory system also provides the means by which members can retrieve information that they personally did not encode but that was encoded by someone in the group. That is, the same knowledge that encourages different members to learn different things—their shared understanding of one another's expertise, interests, and roles—can be used by members later on to seek out information held by others, because that knowledge signals where in the group the desired information is likely to reside. For example, realizing that one member of the faculty search committee is an expert in the job applicant's area of research, other committee members will know who to go to first for additional details about the applicant's publications when they do not have ready access to the curriculum vitae itself. Thus, beyond the task-relevant information that members are able to retrieve from their own personal memories, the transactive memory system permits them to retrieve certain kinds of information from the memories of others.

It is worth emphasizing that an effective transactive memory system requires that members share an *accurate* understanding of one another's expertise, interests, and roles. It is their shared understanding that guides their allocation of attentional resources initially, and then later on permits them to know whom to consult for information that they themselves did not encode. If members do not have a shared understanding about the distribution of expertise and interests within their group, or if they share an incorrect understanding, then their initial information acquisition efforts will be poorly coordinated, and information sought from one another later on will be harder, if not impossible, to find. The shared understanding that group members have of one another's expertise, interests, and roles is part of what has been referred to as the group's shared mental model of itself (cf. Brandon & Hollingshead, 2004; Rico, Sanchez-Manzanares, Gil, & Gibson, 2008).

Transactive Memory: Empirical Evidence

A number of experimental studies provide evidence of the operation of transactive memory in small task-performing groups. These studies can be separated into two types according to their focus. One is concerned mainly with tacit coordination and tests whether group members actually do attend to and learn different things contingent on their understanding of one another's expertise, interests, and roles. The other type addresses the idea that group members use their shared understanding of one another's expertise, interests, and roles to help them retrieve and utilize the unique information learned by others. Below I describe several illustrative studies of each type.

Tacit Coordination and Differentiated Learning

Hollingshead (2000) conducted an interesting experiment with a nontraditional sample of participants: secretaries, clerks, and administrative assistants recruited from the office staff of various academic departments within her university. These individuals participated in the study during their lunch hour. Their task was to learn the content of a long list of words drawn from distinct knowledge categories all related to office work. They learned the words with a partner and competed for a $20 prize based on the number of words they were able to learn as a team. Importantly, however, they did this without actually meeting or interacting with their partner. Rather, participants were told that their partner would be someone from another department who was also participating in the study, and whose performance would later be combined with their own to determine whether or not they won the prize. Participants were told that their team would earn one point for each word correctly recalled from the list, regardless of whether the word was recalled by one or both partners, and that the team with the most points would win the prize.

The to-be-learned word list consisted of 80 words organized into 10 categories, eight words per category. The categories were office supplies, computers, accounting, mailing, word processing, ordering desk copies, instructional resources, grades and enrollment, photocopying, and inventory. For example, "invoice," "paystub," "transfer," and "purchase order" are all words from the category "accounting." The list was formatted such that each category name appeared above the words from that category. Participants were given just three minutes to learn as many of these 80 words as they could. Because of the difficulty of learning so many words in such a short period of time, the category structure of the list encouraged participants to focus on words from some of the categories to the exclusion of others.

Prior to starting the task, participants were given a separate sheet of paper that listed only the 10 category names, and were asked to circle those categories that represented their own personal areas of work-related expertise. On average, participants claimed expertise in six of the ten categories. Half of the participants were then told that they would be paired with someone who was very similar to them with respect to their work-related expertise (similar-expertise condition). The rest were told that they would be paired with someone who was very different from them (different-expertise condition). The three-minute learning period then began. When it was over, and after a short delay, participants were given a recall sheet that contained all of the category names but none of the to-be-learned words from those categories. Participants were asked to write down on that sheet all of the words they could remember.

Not surprisingly, participants recalled more words within than outside their areas of expertise. However, and as can be seen in Table 7.3, they recalled 43% more words within their areas of expertise, and 60% fewer words outside their areas of expertise, when they expected to be paired with a partner whose expertise was different from rather than similar to their own. These results are consistent with the idea that group members take greater responsibility for learning information that is within their areas of expertise when they believed that the expertise of their

TABLE 7.3 Proportion of Words Learned Within and Outside the Participant's Areas of Expertise as a Function of the Similarity of the Partner's Expertise

| | Partner's Expertise | |
Word Category	Similar	Different
Within areas of expertise	.21	.30
Outside areas of expertise	.15	.06

Adapted from "Perceptions of expertise and transactive memory in work relationships," by Hollingshead, 2000, *Group Processes & Intergroup Relations, 3,* 257–267.

groupmates is different from their own, and that they assume others in the group will do the same, thus relieving them of responsibility for learning information that is outside their areas of expertise.

A similar study was conducted by Hollingshead (2001) using a different participant population (undergraduate students) and a different set of knowledge domains (e.g., music, alcoholic beverages, campus buildings, the library). Once again, however, participants' understanding of how their partner's expertise related to their own influenced what they learned during the study period. Furthermore, when nominal teams were actually formed at the end of the study by pairing the data records of participants who in fact claimed different domains of expertise, their total (nominal) recall was 13% better when both members believed that they would be paired with a different-expertise partner compared to when one of them believed instead that he or she would be paired with a similar-expertise partner. Thus, tacit coordination by members not only resulted in their personally learning different information when they expect to be paired with a different-expertise partner, it also resulted in their team as a whole learning more information.

Results comparable to these have also been obtained in studies that have used naturally occurring bases for surmising the distribution of expertise within the group. Hollingshead and Fraidin (2003), for example, had participants learn words from gender-stereotypic categories (e.g., professional sports and cosmetics) in an experimental set-up where the partner's gender was the only clue to his or her expertise. Using a different approach, Wegner, Erber, and Raymond (1991) and Hollingshead (1998a) both compared dating couples to randomly paired opposite-sex strangers. Dating couples undoubtedly know more about one another's expertise than do strangers, and so should be better able to coordinate their learning of new information when they do not have (or take) an opportunity to communicate with one another about what they each will learn. In all of these studies participants demonstrated clear evidence of tacit coordination when they had a basis for knowing how their partner's expertise was apt to differ from their own. Under these conditions, partners were more likely to learn different things, and as a result they collectively learned more overall.

Tapping the Differentiated Store of Information

A functioning transactive memory system is of value in part because of the greater store of task-relevant information that it implies and the ability of those who hold that information to use it in service of task accomplishment. Additionally, it is also of value because it permits group members who did not originally encode the information themselves nevertheless to access and deploy it later on. As noted above, members' shared understanding of one another's expertise, interests, and roles—the very thing that leads them to learn different information to begin with—is also the key to unlocking this store of information and making it more broadly useful to the group as a whole.

This point is illustrated in a recent study that used a participant sample quite similar to the one employed previously by Hollingshead (2000). Littlepage, Hollingshead, Drake, and Littlepage (2008) had pairs of administrative and secretarial coworkers from 18 different university departments complete a 30-item multiple-choice test. The test covered six work domains that clerical staff in those departments might reasonably encounter on the job (e.g., "Where on the Internet can you check reimbursement rates for lodging, meals, and incidental expenses incurred during out-of-state travel?"). Both members of each coworker pair independently completed the entire test. In addition, for each item in the test, both members also indicated whether they or their partner was more likely to answer it correctly. Further, in order to derive a team score, members were asked to allocate each test item either to themselves or to their partner, with the understanding that only the answer provided by the designated member would count toward their team score. It was found that coworkers agreed substantially on who would best answer each test item, indicating a well-developed transactive memory system. Moreover, team performance scores based on the members' preferred item allocations were consistently superior to performance scores based on a random allocation of items. This was true even when the item allocations were made privately, without discussion. Thus, having a well-developed transactive memory system permitted the members of these coworker pairs to deploy their partners' specific, task-relevant knowledge more effectively than they would otherwise have been able to do.

A similar conclusion is reached with respect to members directly accessing one another's unique information. Consider, for example, group decision making under conditions of distributed information, a topic that I covered in depth in Chapter 6 (see especially pp. 187–195 and 200–203). As will be recalled, decision-making groups display a pervasive tendency to discuss more of their shared than their unshared information; they discuss more of the decision-relevant information that every group member was aware of initially than information that only one member or another was aware of. This tendency is reduced, however, when the unshared information pertains to several different knowledge domains, each member of the group has specific expertise (more information than others) in at least one of those domains, and members are all aware of one another's area(s) of expertise.

For example, Stasser, Vaughan, and Stewart (2000) asked university students to study privately a packet of information containing brief position statements about campus issues allegedly written by three hypothetical candidates for student council president. After reading this information, participants met in three-person groups to recall collectively as much of the candidate information as they could and to decide which candidate would be the best person for the job. All told, there were 54 position statements, 18 by each candidate. However, each group member read only 42 of those statements. Further, the information packets were constructed such that every member read six statements by one of the three candidates that others in the group did not read. As a result, each member held 50% more information than others in the group about one of the candidates, making him or her the de facto expert on that candidate. By distributing the candidate information in this way, a pattern of differentiated learning was created that mimics what otherwise might occur naturally as a result of tacit coordination.

Participants had 15 minutes to study the information packets, after which the packets were collected and removed. Half of the groups then learned about the distribution of expertise among their members; they were told by the experimenter who in their group had read extra information about each candidate, but without signaling which specific position statements were involved. In the remaining groups the experimenter said nothing about the distribution of expertise among members. Thus, whereas members in half of the groups had a shared understanding of roughly who knew what, those in the remaining groups did not.

The groups then participated in an exercise in which they were to recall as a group as many of the position statements as they could. It was found that telling members about the distribution of expertise within their group affected the amount of information they collectively recalled. Specifically, in comparison to groups that were not told, those that were told about the distribution of expertise recalled 18% more of their unshared information (see also Sassenberg, Boos, and Klapproth, 2001; Stasser, Stewart, & Wittenbaum, 1995; Stewart & Stasser, 1995). Furthermore, this study showed that it was important for members to know the entire distribution of expertise within their group, not just that they themselves had special expertise. An experimental condition in which members learned about their own domain of expertise, but not those of others, did not yield an improvement in the group's collective recall. This overall pattern of results thus suggests that learning the distribution of expertise in their group improved collective recall by enabling members to coax from their groupmates unshared information that would not otherwise have been forthcoming.

Note that in this and several of the other studies cited above, rather strong measures were taken to instantiate the perception of distributed expertise within the group. In the present study, for example, the experimenter explicitly described each group member's special domain of expertise. Hollingshead (2000, 2001) had participants describe their own expertise vis-à-vis the stimulus material and then assured them that they would be paired with someone who had either very similar or very different expertise. And, although Hollingshead and Fraidin (2003) did not tell participants explicitly about their partner's expertise, they did reveal their partner's gender, which was a fairly obvious clue to relative expertise, considering the strongly gender-stereotypic information that participants were asked to learn.

In the real world, too, there are sometimes clear indicators of the distribution of expertise within a group (cf. Bunderson, 2003). An example is in cross-functional project teams, where members are drawn from different functional areas within their organization (e.g., accounting, engineering, marketing). Here, each member's functional affiliation signals his or her domain of expertise. However, in a great many other situations there are apt to be few, if any, external cues to members' unique areas of task-relevant expertise. In these circumstances, it is only through experience working together that members gradually come to understand who in the group is good at, interested in, and/or has experience at what. Consequently, a fully functioning transactive memory system may sometimes take a good bit of time to develop. In this regard, it is worth noting that the members of the administrative and secretarial coworker pairs that participated in the previously described study by Littlepage et al. (2008) had worked together in the same departments for an average of nearly four years.

Transactive Memory and Group Task Performance

Except for the purposes of behavioral research, groups are seldom convened simply to remember information. Instead, their recall is usually in service of some larger task that they are trying to accomplish. An important question, therefore, is whether or not transactive memory actually impacts group task performance.

Laboratory Studies

One line of evidence suggesting that it does comes from the several laboratory experiments described earlier in this chapter concerning group performance on the AM radio assembly task . Recall that in these studies participants worked collectively in three-person groups to put together a hobby kit radio that they had been trained to assemble the week before. Manipulated in these studies was the nature of that earlier training. For example, in the original study by Liang et al. (1995), some groups were composed of members who had been trained individually, whereas others were composed of members who had been trained collectively in the same three-person group as was now being tested.

Liang et al. (1995) made video recordings of the groups as they assembled the radio during the testing phase of their experiment and then coded those videos for behavioral evidence of transactive memory. Specifically, coders rated the extent to which different members (1) specialized in different aspects of the assembly process, (2) worked together in a smooth, coordinated fashion, and (3) seemed to trust one another's knowledge of the assembly process. It was found that groups whose members were trained together exhibited significantly higher scores on these transactive memory measures compared to groups whose members were trained individually. Moreover, in combination, these measures fully mediated the effect of the training manipulation on the number of assembly errors committed. Thus, groups that were trained together rather than individually displayed a more efficient transactive memory system, and this appears to have been the proximal cause of their superior performance on the radio assembly task. Similar findings have been reported in other studies employing the radio assembly task (e.g., Moreland & Myaskovsky, 2000; Moreland & Wingert, 1995, cited in Moreland et al., 1996).

An interesting follow-up analysis sheds light on the behavioral processes through which transactive memory systems develop. Rulke and Rau (2000) analyzed videos made during the *training* phase of the experiment by Liang et al. (1995) and found that, when groups were trained together, transactive memory was created by means of small encoding cycles. These cycles typically began with (1) either a question or statement indicating a lack of expertise (e.g., Member A: "I'm not sure where this red thing goes"), followed by (2) a declaration of expertise by another member (e.g., Member B: "I know," as she inserts the red piece), and (3) one or more evaluations of expertise (e.g., Member C: "Yeah, that looks right"), and ended with (4) an attempt to coordinate who would do what in the group (e.g., Member A: "Ok, so maybe you [Member B] should put in all the pieces that go on that part of the board"). The four elements of this cycle describe the key behaviors by which members learned who in their group knew what and so developed appropriate coordination strategies. These transactive encoding cycles tended to occur earlier rather than later during the training phase of the experiment. Further, the more frequently they occurred, the higher were the three transactive memory scores coded from the videos made of these same groups a week later during the testing phase of the experiment (described above).

A somewhat different approach to assessing the role of transactive memory in group task performance was taken by Moreland and Myaskovsky (2000). Like Liang et al. (1995), they employed the radio assembly task and trained group members either individually or collectively. In addition, just prior to the testing phase of the experiment, half of the groups whose members were trained individually were told how their members ranked relative to one another on each of five separate radio-building skills (i.e., who was best, second best, and worst with regard to the placement of resistors, capacitors, transistors, and other components, as well as wiring) based on their actual performance during the training phase of the experiment. Let us call this the individual-training-plus-feedback condition. It was found that groups in this condition performed very similarly to groups whose members were trained together, and significantly better than groups whose members were trained individually but who got no feedback about their members' relative performance during training (call this the individual-training-only condition). Compared to groups in the individual-training-only condition, those in the individual-training-plus-feedback condition collectively recalled more of the steps in the assembly procedure and committed fewer assembly errors. Further, on a post-experimental questionnaire, participants in the individual-training-plus-feedback condition, compared to those in the individual-training-only condition, reported that the members of their group were less similar to one another in their radio-building skills, that they knew more about the radio-building skills of their groupmates, and that their groupmates knew more about their radio-building skills. These are all signs of better transactive memory development among groups in the individual-training-plus-feedback condition compared to groups in the individual-training-only condition and provide further support for the importance of transactive memory in group performance.

Conceptually similar results have been obtained when, instead of an assembly task, groups perform a decision-making task under conditions of distributed information. As discussed previously, if group members each have unique expertise regarding some to-be-decided issue, and they are all informed of one another's expertise by the experimenter (comparable to giving members feedback about one another's skills in Moreland and Myaskovsky's (2000), individual-training-plus-feedback condition), their group is apt to discuss more of the unshared information that they collectively hold. Moreover, when a hidden profile[14] exists, such groups are more likely than groups whose members are not informed of one another's expertise to choose the decision alternative that is objectively best (e.g., Stasser et al., 1995). Thus, in decision making, too, understanding who in the group knows what facilitates group performance.

One final point is worth making here. A transactive memory system, once developed, is apt to benefit group performance only so long as the group's membership remains stable. A change of membership is likely to bring with it a change in the distribution of expertise and so necessitate a modification of the transactive memory structure. That is, the pattern of responsibility for learning, retaining, and retrieving particular types of task-relevant information will have to be changed in order to accommodate the new distribution of expertise among members. Failure to make this change risks overlooking important bits of task-relevant information, and subsequent decrements in group performance.

This point is well illustrated in an experiment by Lewis, Belliveau, Herndon, and Keller (2007). Following the general outlines of the radio assembly studies described previously, all participants in this experiment were trained in three-person groups to perform an assembly task. However, the composition of some groups was changed just prior to the testing phase of the experiment. Of particular interest here are groups in which one member was replaced with someone who had been trained in a different group, so that they now each comprised two old-timers and one newcomer. Lewis et al. found that these groups made significantly more assembly errors during the testing phase of the experiment than did groups in any other condition, including those made up exclusively of newcomers. Ancillary evidence from this study suggests that the two old-timers in these groups tended to act in accordance with the transactive memory structure established in their training group, even though that structure was no longer fully appropriate, given the expertise that the newcomer had developed as a function of his or her own (separate) training experience. Although not tested in this study, it seems reasonable to speculate that, if these groups had been given an opportunity to renegotiate their transactive memory system, taking into account the new distribution of expertise that now existed among them, their task performance might have improved. The renegotiation of transactive memory systems in light of membership change seems a worthwhile direction for future research.

Field Studies

Several field studies of natural work groups in organizational settings also point to the importance of transactive memory for group performance. Each of these studies employed one or more questionnaire measures to assess transactive memory development. Austin (2003), for example, assessed transactive memory in 27 work groups in a large apparel and sporting goods company. Among other things, he asked participants to identify who in their group was the most expert in each of 11 different skill or knowledge domains. These nominations were then compared to the nominees' self-assessments of their expertise, with greater agreement taken to be an index of better transactive memory. When aggregated to the group level, this agreement measure was significantly correlated ($\beta = .53$) with an external evaluation of the groups' performance conducted two months later.

Using a questionnaire designed to tap the same constructs found in the transactive memory coding scheme originally employed by Liang et al. (1995), Lewis (2004) examined the emergence and impact of transactive memory in 64 teams of MBA students. These teams each completed a semester-long consulting project with a client organization in their community. It was found that teams whose members had more widely distributed expertise tended to develop a stronger transactive memory system, and that this occurred primarily during the planning phase of the project. Further, the quality of their transactive memory predicted team performance as rated by the client organizations ($\beta = .37$).

Finally, a translation of the questionnaire used by Lewis (2004) was employed by Zhang, Hempel, Han, and Tjosvold (2007) to assess transactive memory in 104 work teams from high-technology firms in China. They found that task interdependence, cooperative goal interdependence, and support for innovation all predicted the development of a stronger transactive memory system, and that transactive memory in turn predicted group performance as rated by their leader or manager. It should be noted that this study is one of the few to consider how features of the group's task might impact transactive memory. Its results suggest that tasks vary in the extent to which they prompt the development of transactive memory. It is likely that the performance benefits of transactive memory, once developed, also hinge in part on the nature of the task being performed (i.e., task demands). More research investigating the relationship between task characteristics, transactive memory, and group performance is clearly needed (cf. Edmondson, Dillon, & Roloff, 2007).

Transactive Memory and the Search for Synergy

A point made earlier in this chapter is that groups learn something important as a result of working together that goes beyond what they can learn by working separately. A good portion of that "something" appears to be bound up with the concept of transactive memory. Transactive memory is an emergent phenomenon in groups. It is not a property of the group members themselves, nor is it a resource that they individually contribute to the group. Rather, if it is a resource at all, it is one that arises out of, and is crucially dependent upon, members' experience working together. How responsibility for learning task-relevant information gets distributed among group members, and what different members can be trusted to recall later on, depends on the particular mix of people in the group, what those people know about each other a priori, and what they learn about one another as a function of working collectively together.

Transactive memory would thus seem to be an important mechanism that underlies many of the performance gains that are attributable to group learning. As I argued earlier, because group learning is rooted in member interaction, it qualifies as an example of synergy. By extension, the development of transactive memory would appear to be an important mechanism that underlies synergistic performance gains in groups.[15] One promising avenue forward in the search for synergy, therefore, is to better understand transactive memory. This includes delineating those task characteristics and membership dynamics that moderate its development and impact. Said differently, the circumstances under which transactive memory development makes a difference are also likely to be circumstances in which synergistic performance gains will be found.

☐ Chapter Summary

In this chapter, I have examined the empirical literature concerned with learning and memory in groups, with an eye toward understanding how these processes might contribute to synergistic performance gains. In particular, I have focused on whether the ability to learn, retain, and retrieve task-related information is facilitated (or impaired) by group interaction.

The first section of the chapter dealt with group learning. Group learning refers to a relatively permanent change in the knowledge, skill, or ability of a group that is produced by interaction. Group learning is distinct from—yet depends upon—learning that occurs at the level of the individual group member. Evidence of group learning can be found in group learning curves that have been adjusted to control for the impact of individual learning. Learning curves are simply plots of performance over time. They show the relationship between performance and cumulative task experience and typically reveal a pattern of diminishing returns; as performance improves, further improvements become progressively harder to achieve. These points were illustrated with data from surgical teams as they gained experience using a new surgical technique. The unique contribution of group learning to group performance was also demonstrated in a series of controlled laboratory studies that employed a radio assembly task.

The middle portion of the chapter focused on several questions having to do with collective recall in groups, especially whether collective recall is any better or worse than individual recall. Collective recall is a collaborative activity wherein group members work together to remember some previously encountered information. Thus, like group learning, interaction is central to the definition of collective recall.

Empirical evidence suggests that collective recall is benefited when group members work together to learn the material that subsequently they are asked to remember. This appears to occur because working interactively while learning the to-be-recalled material helps members encode the information similarly and/or provides them with a common set of episodic retrieval cues. These in turn allow them later on to more efficiently prompt one another.

Evidence also suggests that collective recall is nearly always better than the recall of single individuals. However, collective recall is generally not better than the pooled recall of an equal number of individuals working independently. Importantly, there is little evidence for a cross-cueing effect in collective recall when group members are first exposed as individuals to the to-be-learned material. Further, under these circumstances, members can interfere with one another's retrieval of information from memory. And collective recall tends to be more conservative than individual recall. Conservatism leads groups to commit more errors of omission, though fewer errors of commission.

Finally, the last section of the chapter addressed the topic of transactive memory in groups. Transactive memory refers to an informal system for dividing the cognitive labor associated with acquiring, storing, and retrieving task-relevant information. The development of an effective transactive memory system depends on members having a shared (and accurate) understanding of one another's expertise, interests, and roles, and can occur even without explicit discussion of who will be responsible for learning what. As a result, different members in the group often learn somewhat different aspects of the task-relevant information. I reviewed the empirical evidence for the development of transactive memory in groups, as well as the impact of transactive memory on group performance.

Taken as a whole, the material covered in this chapter suggests that group task performance benefits more from group learning than from group memory. Collective recall at best seems to yield only a weak synergistic performance gain relative to individual recall. Group learning, on the other hand, seems to have at least the potential to generate strong synergistic gains. Weak and strong synergy are admittedly difficult to distinguish when it comes to learning. Yet it is hard to see the sorts of performance gains described early in the chapter in any other light. Experience working together adds to a group's performance capabilities in ways that go beyond what any one member can supply, even the best member of the group. Thus, group learning would seem to be a legitimate source of strong synergistic performance gains in groups and as such represents a useful direction for future research.

☐ Endnotes

1. Taking a broader view, we might also consider as resources the task-relevant tools that members have at their disposal, as well as the external ties they have to persons outside the group who might in some way facilitate the group's performance. The latter is commonly referred to as social capital (Coleman, 1988). I do not address these additional resources here simply because they are not the sorts of things that we typically think of as being acquired via learning.

2. The sheet music from which chamber ensembles work usually provides a great many instructions that help members coordinate their behavior and so can be viewed as a mechanism for preplanning member interactions. But even the most fully elaborated sheet music cannot specify completely every detail of what members need to know in order to play well together. Further, there are matters of artistic interpretation, which sometimes involve deviations from the composer's written instructions, that must be worked out to mutual satisfaction. Thus, even in the highly scripted world of chamber music, there is no substitute for practicing together

3. For example, suppose nine participants were trained in three groups as follows: (1, 2, 3), (4, 5, 6), and (7, 8, 9). Those same participants might then be re-organized and tested in groups (1, 4, 7), (2, 5, 8), and (3, 6, 9).

4. Although some sort of cognition is undoubtedly involved in all forms of learning, not all of what is learned is equally accessible at a conscious level. In particular, on group tasks that demand very precise temporal coordination of physical actions, much of what is learned may be, for all practical purposes, irreducibly behavioral. This would seem to be the case, for example, in many sports situations (e.g., rowing, pairs figure skating), where team members learn subtle ways of adjusting to one another's behavior that allow them to better perform their collective task. Although essential to their performance, the nature of what is learned may be nearly impossible for members to put into words or demonstrate by any means other than actually performing the task in question.

5. In other fields, the term *collective recall*, and especially its variant, *collective memory*, are used in somewhat different ways than I used them here. For a discussion of these alternative meanings, see Harris, Paterson, and Kemp (2008).

6. A similar point was made in Chapter 2 regarding the total score on multiple-choice classroom exams (see pp. 33–41J).

7. It is worth noting that although this seems a reasonable approach to operationalizing weak synergy in collective recall, it may not be satisfactory in other performance contexts where aggregate measures are used. For example, it would likely be inappropriate when applied to certain types of idea generation tasks, especially those that employ some variant of the brainstorming technique. As discussed in Chapter 3, the rules of brainstorming are designed to encourage the contribution of any and all ideas, no matter how strange or unusual. Toward that end, evaluation of the ideas put forth by members is explicitly prohibited. In other words, brainstorming attempts to eliminate the very interactions that otherwise would be important for producing a consensually endorsed group product. Consequently, brainstorming groups cannot be said to have demonstrated even a weak synergistic performance gain unless they generate more ideas than the total (pooled) number produced by all of the members in comparably constructed nominal groups.

8. The conclusion regarding Perlmutter and DeMontmollin (1952) derives from a reanalysis of their data that makes use of Lorge and Solomon's (1955) Model A. I discussed Model A in detail in Chapter 4 in connection with group problem solving (see pp. 124–126). Model A is also well suited for use in connection with the study of collective recall, and yields a criterion

that is functionally equivalent to the one derived by pooling the recollections of nominal group members. Model A predicts that interacting groups in Perlmutter and DeMontmollin's (1952) study should have been able to recall M = 18.36 of the 19 nonsense words, which is higher than the value of M = 17.70 actually reported. Hoppe (1962) performed a similar reanalysis, but inexplicably used only half of the available data. The study by Hinsz (1990) relied on a social decision scheme analysis. This approach, too, was discussed in Chapter 4 (see pp. 126–136), and yielded results consistent with the conclusion that groups' collective recall surpassed the weak, but not the strong synergy criterion.

9. This applies when recall is operationalized in terms of hit rates. As I explain in greater detail below, different criteria for establishing weak and strong synergy are necessary when the focus is on false alarm or intrusion rates.

10. Errors of commission are usually referred to as intrusions in free recall situations, and as either false alarms or false positives in recognition memory situations.

11. Participants were not required actually to purchase the selected items.

12. It is worth calling attention here to the intrusion error rates reported in the previously cited study by Basden et al. (1997). As noted, very tight constraints were placed on group interaction during the recall phase of that study. Specifically, whereas group members were permitted to hear one another recall the stimulus words, they were not permitted to discuss those recollections in any way. Rather, just like what is done for nominal groups, the experimenter constructed indices of collective recall by counting all of the words mentioned by members. This procedure thus eliminated any effects that might be due to members' collectively endorsing or rejecting one another's recollections. Interestingly, and in contrast to virtually every other study in which intrusion error rates have been reported, in this study the intrusion error rate was higher (8%) in the collective recall condition than in the nominal group condition (4%). Had groups been permitted to interact naturally in this study, the pattern of intrusion error rates would almost certainly have been reversed.

13. The stronger claim—that the effect of group size on false alarm rates is due to a general increase in conservatism, not to a change in memory sensitivity—is supported only indirectly in this study. Clark et al. (2000) performed a signal-detection analysis of their data, and found that memory sensitivity (as indexed by d') did not vary by group size. However, they did not report a measure of response bias (which a signal-detection analysis normally provides). Such a measure would allow for a more straightforward test of the conservatism hypothesis.

14. Recall that hidden profiles were discussed at some length in Chapter 6 (see especially pp. 178–181).

15. It might seem logically inconsistent to argue that transactive memory can lead to synergistic performance gains in groups. After all, synergy is defined as a performance gain that is attributable in some way to group interaction. Transactive memory, on the other hand, can develop at least in part through tacit coordination; that is, even without members speaking directly about who will be accountable for learning what. This is not the same, however, as saying that transactive memory can develop in the absence of interaction.

In Chapter 1, I defined interaction broadly as "any observable behavior exhibited by a group member that is directed toward, performed in concert with, and/or enacted in the presence of others in the group." This definition acknowledges that the mere presence of other members may be enough to spark a response that affects the performance of the group as a whole. One such "response" is tacit coordination and the ensuing emergence of transactive memory.

Motivation

Energizing and Directing Behavior in Groups

A group's performance on almost any type of task depends not only on the knowledge, skills, and abilities of it members, but also on their motivation. Insufficient motivation can spell disaster for a group, no matter what level of skill or ability its members may possess. In this chapter, I address the question of whether people's task motivation might be enhanced when they work collectively in groups as opposed to when they work alone, and, if so, under what conditions their enhanced motivation translates into measurable group-level performance gains.

Motivation is a hypothetical construct used to explain the direction, intensity, and persistence of behavior. Intensity and persistence both are tied closely to the expenditure of energetic resources. Other things being equal, both accomplishing more during a fixed period of time (intensity) and working longer at a given task (persistence) require putting forth more effort. In contrast, the direction of a person's behavior—that is, the choices he or she makes about which goal(s) will be pursued—may or may not have implications for the expenditure of energy. Choosing between more difficult and less difficult goals—goals that require either more or less effortful behaviors—clearly does relate to the amount of energy that must be expended, whereas choosing between equally difficult goals clearly does not. Thus, motivation concerns more than just expending energy. It has to do, as well, with deciding *how* that energy will be spent.

The first three sections of this chapter are all concerned with motivational topics that focus on either the intensity or persistence of behavior and so bear in a fairly direct way on the amount of energy put forth. By contrast, the final section of the chapter is devoted to topics concerned primarily with the directional influence of motivation on behavior, and so are less closely tied to the expenditure of energy.

259

In the first section, I consider one of the oldest questions in social psychology: whether working on a task in the company of others, by itself, affects motivation and performance. This question is at the root of a long line of research on social facilitation and inhibition and applies equally to individual, coactive, and collective performance situations. Because of its historical and foundational significance, this research is examined in some detail. The remainder of the chapter is concerned with motivational issues that apply to collective action more exclusively. In the second section, I examine conditions that diminish members' motivation when working collectively, whereas in the third section I consider factors that intensify their motivation. The latter, of course, are also factors that potentially can generate significant synergistic performance gains. As will be seen, the identifiability and indispensability of member contributions to the group play a central role in both diminishing and intensifying motivation. Finally, in the last section of the chapter, I consider how implicit and explicit task goals can either support or undercut the translation of member motivation gains into group-level, synergistic performance gains.

□ Social Facilitation: Working in the Company of Others

A fundamental issue of longstanding interest concerns the minimum conditions necessary for generating motivation-based performance gains in groups. In particular, a question can be raised about whether or not the mere presence of others arouses member motivation. When a group of individuals work collectively on a task, they are, at the very minimum, present together in the situation.[1] Their presence before one another—and their awareness of one another's presence—is intimately bound up with what it means for them to be a group (cf. Chapter 1, pp. 20–21). Thus, we might ask whether the simple fact of their being in one another's company while performing a task impacts their motivation. Specifically, do people put forth any more (or less) effort when others are merely present in the situation compared to when they work completely alone?

Research investigating the motivational effects of working in the company of others can be traced back more than a century to Triplett's (1898) seminal study of pacemaking and competition. A portion of that work was described in Chapter 1. As will be recalled, Triplett conducted an archival analysis of professional bicycle racing records, focusing on the results achieved by riders competing under several different racing formats over distances of up to 25 miles. Among other things, he found that the record times achieved by individual cyclists who raced against the clock while being paced by a faster, multirider vehicle were on average 23% faster than the record times achieved by cyclists who raced against the clock alone without a pace vehicle. Indeed, the times achieved by paced cyclists racing individually were only slightly slower than those achieved by paced cyclists racing head-to-head (i.e., multiple competitors in the same race).

It is tempting to interpret these results as evidence of a motivation-based performance gain that occurs in the paced-racing format. Specifically, it might be argued that the presence of the riders on the pace vehicle, and of the other competitors in the head-to-head races, aroused additional motivation beyond that generated by the cycling competition itself (i.e., in the unpaced individual races). But as discussed in Chapter 1, there is a plausible alternative explanation that calls this motivational interpretation into question. The paced racing format offers a distinct aerodynamic advantage over the unpaced format, in that racers are able to draft closely behind the pace vehicle—and behind one another in head-to-head races—and so gain significant shelter from the wind. This reduces drag, which enables them to ride both faster and further without fatigue. Thus, before drawing any conclusions about motivation-based performance gains in this situation, it is necessary first to account for the gains that otherwise would be expected simply as a function of physics.

Triplett (1898) dealt with this problem by creating a laboratory task that has the same motivational properties as paced bicycle racing, but without the aerodynamic confound. That task employed the apparatus shown in Figure 8.1. It consisted of two fishing reels (marked A and B in the figure) mounted at one end of a 2-meter-long wooden framework, with a pair of pulleys (marked C and D in the figure) mounted at the other end. Between each reel and one of the pulleys was strung a band of twisted silk cord. The reel served as a winch; when its handle was turned, the silk band moved around the pulley and reel, much like the motion of an old-fashioned clothesline. The task was to turn the handle on Reel A as

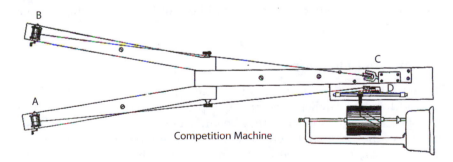

FIGURE 8.1 An overhead view of Triplett's competition machine.

fast as possible until a small flag sewn into the band made four complete circuits of its 4-meter course. The time required to do this was recorded by means of a stopwatch. Additionally, the rate of rotation of Pulley D was recorded on the paper drum of a kymograph. Reel A could be operated with or without a second person independently performing the same task using Reel B.

Triplett (1898) performed several experiments with this apparatus, mostly with children. He found that they wound the reel faster, and so took less time to complete a trial, when working alongside another child compared to when they worked alone. However, the differences he observed were not great; on average there was less than a 2% improvement in performance when working in the presence of another child.[2] Still, in terms of their direction, these findings are consistent with the bicycle racing results and suggest that the latter may not have been due exclusively to the aerodynamics of drafting. At least a fraction of the performance gain demonstrated by cyclists competing in the paced-race format may have been due instead to the mere presence of other riders on the course, independent of their ability to provide shelter from the wind.

The Early Years

A quarter century after the publication of Triplett's seminal paper, Allport (1924a) labeled this phenomenon *social facilitation*. He defined social facilitation as an "increase in response merely from the sight or sound of others making the same movement" (p. 262). Two features of this definition are worth noting. First, it clearly refers to the effect on performance of others who are independently engaged in the same activity. Such individuals are commonly referred to as *coactors*, and are, of course, more than merely present in the situation. Second, Allport's (1924a) definition sets social facilitation apart from competition.[3] Social facilitation is not the result of a conscious attempt to out-perform a rival. It is instead a direct effect of the "sight or sound of others," regardless of how well or poorly those others might be performing.[4]

An Emergent Definition

However, two trends in the empirical literature appeared very early on that indicated researchers were using in practice a rather different definition of social facilitation. First, they began to employ a wide range of tasks in their studies. Not only were participants asked to perform a variety of physical tasks, they also performed many tasks that demand predominantly mental activity, such as word association tasks (e.g., Allport, 1920; Travis, 1928), arithmetic computation tasks (Allport 1924a; Dashiell, 1930), and tasks that required answering items taken from standardized intelligence tests (e.g., Farnsworth, 1928; Weston & English, 1926). Unlike bicycle pedaling and reel winding, most of the important activity that takes place while performing such tasks occurs inside the performer's head. At the very least, it becomes a challenge with such tasks to identify the "movement" of others to which the focal person might be responding.

Second, many researchers began to examine the facilitating properties of noncoacting others—individuals who are present in the situation but who are clearly not engaged in the same activity as the person whose "response" is being measured. Such individuals are usually referred to as an *audience*, whether or not they actually attend to the performer. An attentive audience is one that closely observes the performer's behavior and so is in a good position to evaluate his or her performance. A theatre audience is an example, but so, too, is a lone experimenter observing the behavior of a research participant. Alternatively, an audience might be rather inattentive. In this case, the performer works at his or her assigned task in the presence of others who take little notice of him or her, perhaps because they are absorbed in other, quite different tasks of their own. In contrast to an attentive audience, an inattentive audience is presumably not in a good position to evaluate the focal person's performance. Thus, although neither kind of audience is "making the same movement" as the performer, an inattentive audience comes closest to being merely present in the situation.

Although the study of audience effects might at first seem relevant only to groups that perform in front of spectators (e.g., sports teams, theatre troupes, musical ensembles), it is important to keep in mind that, even when there are no spectators per se, the members of the group are themselves an audience for one another. Moreover, depending on the nature of the group's task, they may be either an attentive or relatively inattentive audience. They are apt to be most attentive when working either on unitary tasks or on tasks with subtasks that require closely coordinated action. Working together on the same unitary task quite naturally makes members attentive to one another's contributions to the group's performance (e.g., the rate at which members contribute ideas and arguments during a decision-making discussion). And when working on tasks with subtasks that require closely coordinated action, members are apt to be keenly aware of one another's contributions, even though they may each be engaged in very different activities. An example is the task of turning a racing sailboat from one tack to another. This usually requires the carefully coordinated action of the helmsman (who steers the boat) and one or more sail trimmers (who adjust the set of the sails). Each must pay close attention to what the others are doing in order to execute effectively his or her own part in making the course change. Thus, like any attentive audience, each should be in a good position to evaluate the others (e.g.,

Was the helmsman's turn too fast or slow? Was the headsail released too early or late?). Members are likely to be considerably less attentive to one another when working on tasks with subtasks that can be performed independently. Here, they may be more nearly an inattentive audience and so less able to evaluate one another, at least in the moment. It seems improbable, however, that there will never be an opportunity for evaluation, even when members work on completely independent subtasks. Eventually, their subtask products must be combined and acted upon, at which point a certain degree of evaluation seems inevitable. Thus, although the members of naturally occurring groups may at times be a less attentive audience for one another, they are seldom apt to be inattentive for the entire duration of their task performance.

These two empirical trends—the use of tasks involving mental as well as physical activity and the study of audience as well as coactor effects—suggest a definition of social facilitation that is rather different from the one originally offered by Allport (1924a). As it was actually used in research, the term social facilitation quickly came to mean an "increase in response merely from the presence of others," without the added requirement that those others be "making the same movement."

Empirical Findings

From the 1920s through the mid-1960s, empirical research on social facilitation proceeded at a slow but steady pace (cf. Guerin, 1993). Yet, an analysis of that literature yields a rather confusing pattern of findings. In particular, whereas some studies found that working at a task in the presence of others improved performance, other studies found just the opposite—that working at a task in the presence of others worsened performance (e.g., see the reviews by Dashiell, 1935; Kelley & Thibaut, 1954). The latter has been termed *social inhibition*, which can be defined as a decrease in performance due simply to the presence of others. Because they both seem prompted by the presence of others, social inhibition and social facilitation have generally been treated as a single topic. The fact that both coactors and audiences sometimes facilitate and sometimes inhibit performance, and that they often do so on mental as well as physical tasks, stymied researchers for a considerable period of time. Explaining these seemingly contradictory findings became the central challenge in this area of research.

Theoretical Explanations

A large number of theories have been proposed to account for social facilitation and social inhibition effects. However, the empirical literature is dominated by just a handful of these. Here, I focus on the theories that have received the most empirical attention and where motivation, in one form or another, plays a prominent role.[5]

Drive

Zajonc (1965; 1980) was the first to offer a parsimonious theoretical account that simultaneously explains both the facilitating and inhibitory effects produced by the presence of others (but see Thibaut & Kelley, 1959). I will describe his theory in its general form first, for it is in this form that its relationship to other theories of social facilitation is easiest to see. I will then address one specific feature of Zajonc's theory: his mere presence hypothesis.

Zajonc (1965; 1980) proposed that both social facilitation and social inhibition effects can be explained by an increase in drive that is generated when coactors or audiences are present. Drawing on the Hull–Spence drive theory of motivation (Spence, 1956), Zajonc argued that the presence of others induces a nondirective drive state in the performer that enhances his or her general readiness to respond. According to the Hull–Spence theory, drive combines multiplicatively with the habit strength of various task-related behaviors (i.e., how well practiced each behavior is) to determine which one will actually be emitted. A crucial implication of this idea is that increases in drive will enhance the likelihood of dominant (high habit strength) responses relative to nondominant (low habit strength) responses. If a task is well learned, almost by definition the correct response(s) will be dominant. Consequently, when performing well-learned tasks, the drive generated by the presence of others should increase the performer's tendency to emit correct rather than incorrect responses and thereby produce a performance gain relative to performing alone. By contrast, when a task is not well learned, incorrect response(s) will tend to dominate. As a result, when working on such tasks, the drive generated by the presence of others should increase the performer's tendency to emit incorrect rather than correct responses, thereby producing a performance decrement relative to performing alone.

This drive × habit strength framework seemed to Zajonc (1965; 1980) to be consistent with the empirical evidence available to him at the time. Many of the earlier studies that showed a performance improvement in the presence of coactors or audiences involved relatively simple tasks that could reasonably be assumed to have been well-learned by research participants (the reel-winding task used by Triplett, 1898, is a good example). In contrast, studies that showed a performance decrement in the presence of coactors or an audience often involved more complex tasks that could be assumed not to have been well-learned by participants (e.g., negotiating unfamiliar finger mazes and learning nonsense syllables; Pessin, 1933; Pessin & Husband, 1933).

Moreover, a number of studies done since Zajonc (1965) first proposed his drive theory analysis have manipulated task learning directly and have obtained results consistent with the general drive formulation. An illustrative experiment is one by Blascovich, Mendes, Hunter, and Salomon (1999) that was conducted in two phases. During an initial learning phase, participants were randomly assigned to learn one of two equally-difficult tasks: either a number categorization task or a pattern recognition task. They practiced the assigned task by themselves over successive blocks of 25 trials until they were able to perform it correctly at least 80% of the time. Then, during a subsequent testing phase of the experiment, participants performed either the task they had just learned or the alternative unlearned task, and they did so either alone or in the presence of two observers who sat near them (i.e., an attentive audience). Blascovich et al. found that the presence of observers during the testing phase either facilitated or inhibited the participant's performance, depending on which task was performed. Specifically, compared to the alone conditions, the presence of observers yielded an average 6% increase in accuracy when participants performed the previously-learned task but a 39% decrease in accuracy when participants performed the unlearned task.

There is another interesting feature of this study worth mentioning. In addition to performance data, Blascovich et al. (1999) also collected a number of physiological measures during the testing phase of their experiment. They did this in order to evaluate the applicability of a biopsychosocial model of challenge and threat to social facilitation phenomena. The biopsychosocial model (Blascovich, Mendes, Tomaka, Salomon, & Seery, 2003; Blascovich & Tomaka, 1996) is concerned with how people evaluate goal-directed performance situations and links different patterns of cardiovascular reactivity to different motivational states. According to this model, important performance situations can be experienced as either challenging or threatening. They are experienced as challenging when individuals perceive that they possess the resources needed to meet the demands of the task. They are experienced as threatening, on the other hand, when individuals perceive that they do not possess the resources needed to meet the demands of the task. These two experiences—challenge and threat—are conceptualized as distinct motivational states, and each is marked by a unique pattern of cardiovascular reactivity. Challenge is associated with an increase in cardiac activation, and by a concomitant decrease in vascular tension (vasodilation). The result is increased blood flow with little or no change in blood pressure. This pattern is the same as that observed during aerobic exercise and is thought to represent an efficient mobilization of energy for coping (Blascovich et al., 1999). By contrast, threat is associated with a smaller increase in cardiac activation and either no change or an increase in vascular tension. The result is a smaller increase in blood flow and a noticeable increase in blood pressure.

Blascovich et al. (1999) argue that this model provides a meaningful physiological index of the motivational states (i.e., challenge and threat) that underlie social facilitation effects. Specifically, they suggest that, because the presence of others usually increases the importance of performing well, it should be a source of physiological arousal (cf. Cacioppo & Petty, 1986). However, the nature of the arousal varies as a function of whether the performance situation is experienced as a challenge or a threat. When the task is well learned, performing in the presence of others is apt to be experienced as challenging, and performers should exhibit the cardiovascular pattern associated with challenge. However, when the task is not well learned, performing in the presence of others is likely to be experienced as threatening, and performers should display the cardiovascular pattern associated with threat.

This is just what Blascovich et al. (1999) found. The presence of observers during the testing phase of their experiment produced the pattern of cardiovascular reactivity associated with challenge when the task was the same as that performed during the learning phase. On the other hand, observers produced the pattern of cardiovascular reactivity associated with threat when the task was not the same as that performed during the learning phase. Finally, there was no change in cardiovascular reactivity (relative to baseline) when participants worked alone during the testing phase, regardless of which task was performed. Thus, not only does this study replicate the pattern of performance facilitation and inhibition typically found in this literature, it also provides physiological evidence of the underlying motivational states associated with these effects.

The Mere Presence Hypothesis

The drive explanation for social facilitation is elegant in its simplicity and in its ability to organize a once-confusing literature. Perhaps because of this, its introduction sparked a dramatic surge in social facilitation research (Guerin, 1993), much of which was devoted to tracking down the specific reasons why the presence of others increases drive.

Easily the most controversial idea was Zajonc's (1965; 1980) own *"mere presence" hypothesis*. He argued that the mere presence of others, independent of what they might be doing or thinking, will heighten a performer's drive state. Thus, performers should show increased drive even in the presence of inattentive others who are unable to evaluate them and who do not serve as sources of imitation, competition, or reward. According to Zajonc, this is an unlearned reaction that enhances the performer's readiness to respond to others present in the situation in whatever way may be necessary. This arousal occurs not because positive or negative outcomes are anticipated, but because "one never knows ... what sort of responses ... may be required in the next few seconds" (Zajonc, 1980, p. 50). But because the provoked arousal is nondirective, it impacts all kinds of responses, not just those involved in reacting to others. This includes task-related responses. As such, and following the Hull–Spence formulation, mere-presence-induced arousal is presumed to combine multiplicatively with habit strength to enhance the likelihood of dominant relative to nondominant task responses, thereby facilitating performance on well-learned tasks and inhibiting performance on tasks that are not well learned. It is important to recognize that the Zajonc's hypothesis suggests a very automatic response to the bodily presence of others. Performers do no intentionally choose to react with increased drive; they simply do react.

Unfortunately, it has proven quite difficult to cleanly test the mere-presence hypothesis, primarily because of the requirements associated with creating situations in which other persons are truly merely present. Among other things, it is necessary to ensure that those who are merely present have no possibility of being able to evaluate the performer and that the performer understands this. In his review of several hundred social facilitation studies, Guerin (1993) identified just 18 that satisfy the stringent methodological requirements for testing the mere-presence hypothesis. Although the majority of these studies appear to support that hypothesis, there is a sizable minority that do not. Thus, despite a recent fall-off of empirical research addressing this question, the matter seems not yet completely settled.

However, even if we assume that the "mere presence" of others is a bona fide source of arousal, it is likely just one part of any social facilitation effect that may occur in real-world task-performing groups. The reason is that, when working in a group, one's groupmates are typically more than merely present in the situation. At the very least, and as noted above, groupmates can usually evaluate one another's contributions, which also makes them important sources of social rewards and punishments. There is considerable evidence that the presence of *evaluative* others is an important source of arousal, especially when there is a potential for negative social outcomes (e.g., disapproval, Geen, 1989, 1991). Such arousal is often experienced as *evaluation apprehension.*

Evaluation Apprehension

Evaluation apprehension models of social facilitation are of two general types. One type posits that the threat of evaluation by others is a learned source of drive, which interacts with habit strength in the usual way predicted by the Hull–Spence theory (Cottrell, 1972; Henchy & Glass, 1968). The learning presumably occurs during child rearing, where the presence of evaluative others (e.g., parents and older siblings) is associated with receiving positive and (especially) negative consequences. This learning then generalizes to all potential evaluators who are present while a task is performed. Importantly, according to this view, the presence of others is drive-inducing only to the extent that those others are able to evaluate the performer. Persons who are present but who cannot evaluate the performer should not induce drive and so should neither facilitate nor inhibit performance, all else being equal. On the other hand, persons who can evaluate the performer are hypothesized to elicit a fairly automatic drive response. According to this view, drive increases involuntarily as soon as the performer realizes that evaluative others are present in the situation.

Harkins (2001a, 2006) recently reported a set of experimental results that seem generally consistent with this automatic view of the role of evaluation apprehension. He had participants perform a Remote Associates Task (RAT) that contained either easy or difficult items. As noted in Chapter 2 (see p. 50), the objective of this task is to determine the remote verbal association that is shared by a set of three stimulus words. An example of an easy RAT item is the stimulus triad birthday–line–search, to which the correct response is "party." An example of a difficult RAT item is the stimulus triad sore–shoulder–sweat, to which the correct response is "cold." Participants performed this task with the understanding that the experimenter either would or would not be able to evaluate their performance at the conclusion of the experimental session. Harkins found that, when given the easy version of the RAT, participants' performance was facilitated by the potential for evaluation; they performed better in the evaluation condition than in the no-evaluation condition. By contrast, when given the difficult version of the RAT, participants' performance was inhibited by the potential for evaluation; they performed worse in the evaluation condition than in the no-evaluation condition. Importantly, Harkins (2006) found that both effects were due to the greater effort elicited from participants in the evaluation condition relative to the no-evaluation condition. Specifically, in the evaluation condition participants generated more solution candidates that were closely related in associative memory to at least one of the stimulus words, and did so regardless of whether the RAT items were easy or difficult. But, because the correct response is less apt to be a close associate of all three stimulus words on difficult compared to easy RAT items, generating more close associates hindered performance on the difficult items but benefited performance on the easy ones. Thus, just as the learned-drive version of the evaluation apprehension model predicts, the potential for evaluation sparked the production of dominant responses (close associates). This facilitated task performance when those responses were apt to be correct (easy RAT items) but inhibited task performance when they were apt to be incorrect (difficult RAT items).

Finally, the other type of evaluation apprehension model posits a more deliberative reaction to the presence of others, one that engages thought processes that in turn regulate task-directed effort. There is evidence, for example, that the presence of evaluative others prompts self-presentational concerns (Bond, 1982; Carron, Burke, & Prapavessis, 2004) and induces a more critical appraisal of both the self and the situation (e.g., Carver & Scheier, 1981, 1998; Geen, 1981; Paulus, 1983; Sanna & Shotland, 1990). To illustrate, working in the presence of others may lead performers to consider more realistically their prospects for success at a task. If they judge success to be reasonably likely, then they are apt to respond by striving even harder (compared to working alone), because doing so can help to ensure not only that they succeed, but also that they gain the social approval that success is apt to bring. On the other hand, if performers judge success to be rather unlikely, then they are apt to withhold effort (compared to when working alone), because there is little to be gained from working hard; not only are they unlikely to succeed at the task, there is now a reasonable chance for social disapproval and embarrassment. Thus, according to this view, working in the presence of others improves performance on easy or well-learned tasks because performers make a conscious decision to exert more effort. By contrast, working in the presence of others worsens performance on difficult or poorly-learned tasks because performers make a conscious decision to exert less effort.

Summary and Integration

Thus, there appear to be several routes by which the bodily presence of others can impact performance. Some of these involve intensifying the performer's nondirectional drive state. The empirical evidence suggests that drive may be aroused rather automatically by the mere presence of others as well as by their ability to observe and evaluate the performer. In addition, the presence of evaluative others can also elicit in performers an intentional, goal-directed motivational response (i.e., to gain social approval and/or avoid disapproval). Often this implies an increase in task-directed effort, but in some cases it can mean a decrease. These evaluation-related processes, whether automatic or consciously controlled, are the ones that seem most relevant for understanding motivation and performance in collective work settings, for the members of task-performing groups are almost always in a position to evaluate one another's contributions to the collective product.

Equally important, this line of research emphasizes that working in the presence of others sometimes facilitates and sometimes inhibits task performance, depending on how easy, familiar, or well-practiced the task at hand is. All of this suggest that, in collective performance contexts, the simple fact of working in the company of others does not by itself guarantee a performance gain at either the individual or group level. Instead, much depends on the task being performed.

A final point worth making here, and one that is particularly relevant as we consider the research covered in the next two sections of the chapter, has to do with assessing motivation as a dependent variable. Like many other variables that we study, motivation is a hypothetical construct and as such cannot be observed directly. Rather, it must be inferred from behavior. Researchers who study motivational processes in group performance contexts often draw inferences about motivation from the behavioral choices their research participants make, from how much those participants are able to achieve during a set period of time, and from how long they persevere at their assigned tasks. If such inferences are to be accurate, it is essential to know the precise relationship between motivation and performance as it applies to the task at hand. For example, when motivation is inferred from behavioral measures of intensity or persistence, there must be good reason to believe that the specific measures employed are linearly (or at least monotonically) related to the amount of effort exerted (cf. Hertel, Deter, & Konradt, 2003). It is precisely for this reason that researchers who rely on measures of intensity and persistence as indicators of motivation typically use simple, well-learned tasks that can be performed by almost anyone.

☐ Collective Action and Motivation Loss

Research on social facilitation and inhibition focuses on the motivational and performance implications of other people being present in the situation. However, that research is largely unconcerned with what those other people are doing, except perhaps to the extent that what they are doing affects their ability to observe and evaluate the performer (but see Muller & Butera, 2007). Thus, the same facilitation and inhibition effects are usually predicted to arise from the presence of coactors as from the presence of a passive audience. That social facilitation researchers have more often employed audiences than coactors in their studies has, for the most part, been a decision based on methodological rather than theoretical concerns.[6]

There is good reason to believe, however, that what is being done by other people who are present in the situation can make a great deal of difference for a target performer's motivation. Of particular interest in this section of the chapter is the possibility that when others are working collectively with the performer, rather than simply being an audience or coactors, a significant loss of motivation may occur.

It is important at this point to make clear the distinction between coaction and collective action. *Coaction* refers to two or more persons working simultaneously on separate (though often identical) tasks. Two children working side-by-side on Triplett's (1898) reel-winding task are a good example, as are four swimmers competing in the same 100 m freestyle event. These individuals are coactors not only because they perform exactly the same activity simultaneously and side-by-side, but also because they are evaluated independently; each child and each swimmer generates his or her own separate product[7] and so earns his or her own performance score. This stands in contrast to *collective action*, where two or more individuals contribute to the *same* product. If, for example, Triplett's apparatus had been constructed so that it was necessary to turn both reels in order to move a single silk band strung between them, then the children performing this task would be acting collectively, not coactively. Similarly, if the four swimmers had been competing as a team in a relay race, where their team score was the total elapsed time taken by all four members to swim the assigned distance, then they would be performing collectively, not coactively. When people work collectively, there is a danger of motivation loss compared to when they work either alone or coactively.

An early empirical example of motivation loss in collective action situations is found in a study by Ringelmann (1913; Kravitz & Martin, 1986).[8] Ringelmann had individuals and groups of various sizes perform one of several physical tasks that all involved pulling or pushing against a resistance (e.g., pulling on a rope, pushing a heavy wheeled cart). In each case, his research participants were asked to pull or push as hard as they could, with the total force applied measured by means of a recording dynamometer. As might be expected, Ringelmann observed that, as the number of people working together on the task increased, the total force applied increased. However, he also observed that the average amount of force per person (i.e., total force divided by the number of persons working) decreased. For instance, in a sample of 28 men who performed a rope-pulling task alone, the average force applied to the rope was 85.3 kg. When these same individuals were organized into seven-person groups and then pulled on the rope together, the average force applied per person dropped to 65.0 kg. And when 14 people pulled together, the average dropped further to 61.4 kg. Similarly, in a sample of 20 men who performed a cart-pushing task alone, the average force applied was 160.3 kg. But when they pushed the cart in two-person teams, the average dropped to 143.2 kg.

Ringelmann (1913) attributed the decrement in average force applied per person to increased coordination problems with increasing group size; as the size of the work group went up, it became more and more difficult for every member to apply his or her efforts at precisely the same moment and in precisely the same direction. According to this view, the research participants may well have individually generated the same force when working collectively as when working alone, but some of it was wasted. Although plausible, this is unlikely to be the whole story. Studies that have used rope-pulling tasks similar to Ringelmann's have replicated his basic findings even when controlling for the possibility of coordination difficulties (e.g., Ingham, Levinger, Graves, & Peckham, 1974; Kugihara, 1999).[9] Thus, the results obtained by Ringelmann seem likely to reflect, at least in part, decreased member motivation with increasing group size. Similar effects have been observed on a host of other physical tasks designed specifically to eliminate the coordination problems that might otherwise arise with increasing group size (e.g., Kerr & Bruun, 1983; Kokubo, 1996; Latané, Williams, & Harkins, 1979; Williams, Nida, Baca, & Latané, 1989).[10]

Motivation loss when performing collectively has also been observed on a variety of cognitive tasks, including idea-generation tasks, judgment tasks, and vigilance tasks. For example, when asked to think up as many novel uses as possible for a simple object (e.g., a brick, knife, or wire clothes hanger), participants typically generate more ideas per person than when working alone than when working collectively as part of a group (e.g., Harkins, 1987; Harkins & Petty, 1982; Karau & Williams, 1997). This occurs even when the production-blocking problems usually associated with performing such tasks in interacting groups are eliminated (e.g., when members register their ideas by writing them down rather that speaking them aloud; see Chapter 3, pp. 85–90, for a discussion of production blocking in idea-generating groups).

Most of the tasks used to study motivation loss in collective action situations can be classified as additive-maximizing tasks. It will be recalled from Chapter 2 (see pp. 62–66) that an additive task is one in which the group's product is determined by summing the products of its members' efforts (e.g., the amount of force applied by a group to one end of a rope is the sum of the individual forces applied by each of those who are pulling). Maximizing tasks are those in which the goal is to perform as much or as quickly as possible (e.g., when the group is instructed to pull as hard as they can on a rope). They stand in contrast to optimizing tasks, where the goal is to produce some specific desired product (e.g., when the group is instructed to maintain a specific amount of pressure on the rope). Because of the predominant use of additive-maximizing tasks, research on motivation loss in collective work situations speaks mostly to the deleterious effects of withholding effort on the *quantity* of member contributions to the group.

There is some evidence, however, that withholding effort in collective work settings can also impact the *quality* of member contributions to the group. Consider, for example, an interesting set of studies by Weldon (Weldon & Gargano, 1985, 1988; Weldon & Mustari, 1988). In each study, university students evaluated the acceptability of a series of part-time jobs based on brief written descriptions of them. Each job was characterized in terms of five attributes assumed to be important to students when choosing a part-time job: flexibility of work hours, closeness of supervision, friendliness of co-workers, task significance, and task variety. Participants evaluated a total of 70 different jobs, assigning each one an overall rating, from very bad to very good, on a seven-point scale. They did this either individually or in groups. More specifically, in some experimental conditions, participants were told that they alone would rate this particular set of jobs. In other conditions they were told that as many as 15 other participants would rate the same jobs, and that their ratings would all be averaged together in order to arrive at a final score for each. Further, in some experimental conditions participants were asked to rate as many of jobs as they could, whereas in other conditions they were required to rate all 70 jobs. Consistent with other research in this area, when participants were asked to rate as many of the jobs as possible, they rated fewer of them when they believed that others would be rating the same jobs. Moreover, using a regression technique to determine the number of different job attributes (up to five) that each participant used when formulating his or her evaluations, Weldon found that participants relied on fewer attributes when they believed their ratings would be averaged with those of others compared to when they believed that they alone would be rating this particular set of jobs. This was true both when participants were asked to rate as many jobs as possible and when they were required to rate all of the jobs. If it can be assumed that ratings based on a larger number of job attributes are more accurate than those based on fewer attributes, and if it can be assumed further that it requires more mental effort to take more job attributes into account when making these ratings, then these studies indicate that participants exerted less effort, and as a result made lower quality contributions, when performing the evaluation task as part of a group than when performing it alone.

The Roots of Motivation Loss in Groups

Numerous factors influence the degree to which collective action produces a motivation loss (Williams, Harkins, & Karau, 2003). However, two stand out as being particularly important: identifiability and dispensability.

Low Identifiability

One key factor is the degree to which member contributions are identifiable. Identifiable contributions are contributions that can be unambiguously attributed to one member in the group. When a member's contributions are identifiable, his or her performance relative to others can be evaluated and can be rewarded or punished accordingly. In most cases those rewards and punishments are social in nature and very subtle (e.g., fleeting signs of approval or reproach by others). Even so, they can have a powerful impact on motivation (Darley, 2003). The work of coactors (and of those who work alone) is almost by definition identifiable; each generates his or her own separate product and earns his or her own performance score. By contrast, the contributions of those who work collectively sometimes are easily identified and sometimes are not. On tasks with subtasks, for example, the contributions of individual group members are typically quite identifiable (recall my earlier example of the crew turning the racing sailboat). However, when the task cannot be divided, individual contributions can occasionally be harder to identify. In Ringelmann's (1913) seminal research, for example, it was likely very difficult for members to gauge exactly how much force their groupmates were applying as they pulled and pushed. Consequently, it was easy for members to lessen the effort they exerted, and to do so without others noticing. Indeed, not only were members unable to evaluate one another's contributions, they could be fairly certain that the researcher could not evaluate their contributions either. But if their contributions cannot be evaluated, then neither can they be singled out for reward or punishment, from either inside or outside the group. More formally, the contingency between performance and outcomes, at least at the individual level, is damaged, if not broken altogether, under conditions of low identifiability. As a result, there is less incentive to perform well and so less motivation to contribute. In short, compared to working alone or to working coactively, there is a danger that working collectively with others will result in a withdrawal of effort because member contributions cannot be identified. A loss of motivation that occurs for this reason is referred to as *social loafing*.[11]

There is ample empirical evidence of this form of motivation loss. For example, in two separate experiments, Williams, Harkins, and Latané (1981) had participants perform a physical exertion task (shouting as loudly as possible) either alone or in groups of two, four (in Experiment 2), or six (in Experiment 1). Like Ringelmann (1913), they found that participants exerted less effort (they shouted less loudly) when working in groups of two than when working alone, and exerted less effort still when working in groups of either four or six. However, this pattern of diminishing effort with increasing group size occurred only when participants believed their individual contributions (how loudly they each shouted) could not be separately assessed. On the other hand, when participants believed that their individual contributions could be assessed (because they wore separate microphones), there was no significant drop in motivation with increasing group size.

Similar findings have been obtained on physical tasks that are more personally meaningful to participants. For instance, Williams, Nida, Baca, and Latané (1989) created a special intrasquad competition for the members of an intercollegiate swim team. The competition was held several weeks after the conclusion of the team's competitive swimming season and compared team members' performance in two 100 m freestyle individual races with their performance in two 4 × 100 m freestyle relay races (with suitable rest periods between races). When the swimmers' individual times in the relay races were publicly recorded and announced, they swam faster in the relay than when they swam individually. By contrast, when the swimmers believed that their individual times in the relay race were not being recorded, they swam slower in the relay than when they swam alone.

Of course, it is the potential for evaluation, not merely the identifiability of member contributions, that protects against motivation loss in collective performance situations (Harkins & Jackson, 1985). Still, low identifiability guarantees that there can be no evaluation. Even the potential for self-evaluation (e.g., knowing that one will later be able privately to compare one's own contributions with those of others) can reduce motivation loss, though this tends to be less effective than the potential for evaluation by external sources (e.g., Harkins, 2000; 2001b; Harkins, White, & Utman, 2000; Szymanski & Harkins, 1987).

High Dispensability

A second important factor that influences the degree to which collective action produces a motivation loss is whether or not the performance context leads participants to feel that their contributions are dispensable. Dispensable contributions are contributions that are not essential for successful group performance; the group can achieve its performance objectives without them. If a member's contributions are dispensable and the benefits of group successes may be enjoyed regardless of how much one actually contributes, there would seem little reason to exert the effort required to make those contributions. Indeed, members benefit most when they can reap the rewards of group success without having to pay the costs of contributing to that success, just as in a public goods dilemma (Kerr 1983; Olson, 1965). A loss of motivation that occurs because one's contributions are dispensable is referred to as *free riding*.

One obvious situation in which there is a potential for free riding is when the task is disjunctive. Recall from Chapter 2 that disjunctive tasks permit just one member's contributions to determine the group's product. If one member is able to satisfy the requirements for group success, then it seems quite unnecessary—and even inefficient—for others to expend effort toward achieving that end. Conjunctive tasks also provide an opportunity for free riding. Conjunctive tasks require that all group members contribute identically to the group's product, which implies that the group's performance is effectively determined by the member who individually contributes least (e.g., a team of mountain climbers who are roped together can climb only as fast as their slowest member). Here, even if asked to contribute as much as possible, it makes little sense for members to do so on a conjunctive task if they suspect that others will contribute less.

Kerr (1983) demonstrated the free-rider effect by asking his research participants to work with a partner on a disjunctive physical task (partners were always confederates of the experimenter whose individual performance was experimentally controlled). The task required both the participant and the partner to grasp in each hand a small rubber-bulb-style air pump (like those found on manual sphygmomanometers). Hoses from the pumps were connected to an airflow measuring device. The objective was to pump at least 350 ml of air through that device during each of nine 30-second trials. Feedback from a short series of practice trials led participants to believe that, with effort, they could successfully meet this criterion. Further, depending on the experimental condition, they learned that their partner either was or was not as capable as they were at the pumping task. Finally, the task was scored disjunctively for the team as a whole: If on a given trial either the participant or the partner met the volume criterion, then the trial was scored a success. But if neither met the criterion, then the trial was scored a failure. Participants were aware of both their own and their partner's trial-by-trial performance, and they were aware that the experimenter was recording both. Kerr found that participants exerted significantly less effort—pumped less air—when they believed they were working disjunctively with an equally capable partner compared to when they performed the task alone. This occurred despite the fact that their individual contributions were completely identifiable. By contrast, when they believed they were working with a less capable partner, the effort that participants exerted was not significantly different from the level they exerted when performing the task alone. In other words, working with a capable partner on a disjunctive task provided an opportunity for free riding, and participants took that opportunity. Working with a less capable partner, however, provided much less opportunity to free ride, so participants continued to work hard. Kerr and Bruun (1983) replicated this finding, and demonstrated as well that a parallel result occurs for conjunctive tasks, though here, as would be expected, the motivation loss occurs when working with less-capable others.

Free riding is not limited to disjunctive and conjunctive tasks. It can also occur on additive tasks if members have reason to believe that their contributions are dispensable. The previously described studies by Weldon (Weldon & Gargano, 1985, 1988; Weldon & Mustari, 1988) provide an example. The task used in those studies—judging the acceptability of part-time jobs—was additive when it was performed in groups, in that each participant's independent evaluations were to be combined with those of others in order to derive a single score for each job. As any beginning statistics student should know, the standard error of the mean decreases as sample size increases, but the magnitude of that decrease itself decreases with increasing sample size. This means that any single score will have less of an impact on the mean when it is averaged with a large number of scores than when it is averaged with a small number of scores. Even without formal statistical training, group members are apt to have a sense of this; they are likely to realize that their own judgments will have less impact on the mean rating assigned to a given job when the size of the group rating that job is large compared to when it is small. Consequently, they are apt to feel that their contributions are more dispensable when the size of the group is large compared to when it is small. And this is exactly what Weldon and Mustari (1988) found. Not surprisingly, when they felt their contributions were more dispensable, participants in these studies were more likely to free ride; they put less effort into the task, and so took fewer job attributes into account when making their evaluations.

Finally, there is evidence that high dispensability and low identifiability may combine interactively to generate motivation losses. A recent field study illustrates this point. Price, Harrison, & Gavin (2006) studied 144 student project teams recruited from 13 different graduate and undergraduate courses. These teams worked together on class projects that lasted for up to 14 weeks, and they completed a research questionnaire at the end of the project period. Among other things, the questionnaire asked the members to report how indispensable they each felt they were to their team and to rate the degree to which each of their teammates worked hard on the project. Both ratings were reverse-scored so, that higher values indicated greater dispensability and more free riding, respectively. In addition, the free-riding scores were averaged across raters to yield a single index for each team member. It was found that dispensability and free riding were significantly and positively correlated; higher levels of self-reported dispensability were associated with more free riding (as perceived by others in the group). Further, this correlation was significantly stronger when the course instructor did not have a means of identifying and evaluating each member's individual contributions to the team's product. By contrast, when each member's contributions could be identified and evaluated, the correlation between dispensability and free riding was reduced—though even here it was not eliminated completely.

Integrating Social Loafing and Free Riding with Social Facilitation

Before concluding this section, it is worth taking note of an important relationship between the two kinds of motivation loss considered here, social loafing and free riding, and the social facilitation phenomena considered previously. As we saw earlier, theories of social facilitation attempt to account simultaneously for both performance improvements and performance declines when others are present in the situation compared to when performing alone. Motivation plays a key role in most (but not all) such theories. Further, among the motivation theories, some emphasize a controlled, cognitively-mediated arousal of motivation in response to others. That is, the presence of evaluative others is presumed to cause performers to think more carefully than they otherwise might about their prospects for success at the task. If the task is relatively easy, then they are apt to expect success and so respond with greater vigor when others are present compared to when working alone. Applying more effort to an easy task should help to ensure a favorable outcome, which includes gaining the approval of those who are present in the situation. On the other hand, if the task is relatively difficult, then performers are less likely to expect success and may respond with less vigor when others are present compared to when working alone. Here, the prospect of an unfavorable outcome, including the disapproval of others present in the situation, should serve as a disincentive for expending effort. Thus, whereas on easy tasks performers are likely to exert more effort in the presence of evaluative others than when working alone, on difficult tasks they are apt to exert less effort in the presence of evaluative others than when working alone.

A related set of ideas has been used to account for social loafing and free riding effects when working collectively with others compared to when others are merely present in the situation. For example, arguing from an expected-value framework, Karau and Williams (1993) and Shepperd (1993, 2001) suggest that group members will be motivated to work hard on collective tasks to the extent that they expect their individual contributions to directly impact the group's collective performance, and the group's collective performance to directly impact their individual outcomes. Motivation should be considerably lower, they contend, when members either do not expect their individual contributions to have much effect on the group's collective performance, when they do not expect the group's collective performance to impact their individual outcomes, or both. These ideas are conveniently represented as follows:

$$\text{Motivation} = f\,(\text{MC} \to \text{GP} \to \text{MO}),$$

where MC refers to member contributions, GP refers to group performance, MO refers to member outcomes, and the symbol "$\to$" is read as "can be expected to lead to." According to this model, high dispensability yields low member motivation because it signals a weak connection between members' individual contributions and group performance ("Why should I work hard to contribute if my contributions won't affect the group's performance?"). Similarly, low identifiability produces low member motivation because it implies a weak connection between group performance and member outcomes ("Why should I work hard to contribute if my contributions won't be rewarded?"). Thus, when they occur, high dispensability and low identifiability are each expected to result in a voluntary withholding of effort.

Recognizing the similarity among these ideas, several investigators have shown that social facilitation, social loafing, and free riding can be accommodated within the same broad theoretical framework (e.g., Griffith, Fitchman, & Moreland, 1989; Harkins, 1987; Paulus, 1983; Sanna, 1992). For example, Sanna (1992, Experiment 1) included alone, coactive, and collective working conditions in a single study. Participants performed a vigilance task in which they were to press a response key each time a small dot flashed on a computer screen. The dots appeared infrequently and at irregular intervals. Participants performed the task during an initial 4-minute practice trial, and then during two 9-minute test trials. Following the practice trial they received false feedback about their individual performance. Half were told that they had performed at the 80th percentile on the practice trial compared to a normative sample, whereas the other half were told that they had performed at the 20th percentile. In this way, participants were led to expect that they would do either well or poorly on the test trials. Additionally, during the test trials, participants performed the task either (a) alone, (b) alongside a coactor who worked independently at the same task, or (c) collectively with another participant whose score was to be added to their own by the computer to form a single overall performance score for the pair. Finally, participants were told that, although norms existed for the 4-minute practice task, no norms were yet available for the 9-minute trials they were about to begin. Thus, participants in the alone condition were led to believe that, although identifiable, their performance could not be evaluated. By contrast, those in the coactive condition were led to believe that their performance was both identifiable and could be evaluated—by comparison with the coactor. Finally, those in the collective conditions were led to believe that their performance was not identifiable (because the computer would report only the dyad's combined score) and so also could not be evaluated.

The mean performance across the two test trials is shown for each experimental condition in Table 8.1. As can be seen, when comparing the alone and coactive conditions, Sanna (1992) found a facilitation effect (better performance when working coactively than alone) for those participants with a high expectancy of success, but an inhibition effect (worse performance when working coactively than alone) for those with a low expectancy of success. Additionally, when comparing the coactive and collective conditions, Sanna found a social loafing effect (worse performance when working collectively than coactively) for those participants with a high expectancy of success, but an "anti-loafing" effect (better

TABLE 8.1 Mean Performance on a Vigilance Task as a Function of Work Condition and Own-Performance Expectancy[a]

Working Condition	High Expectancy	Low Expectancy
Alone	6.94	6.06
Coactive	8.62	4.81
Collective	6.85	6.15

[a] Sanna originally reported the mean number of errors that participants committed, with lower values indicating better performance. To enhance readability, those means have been reflected here by subtracting each from the same arbitrarily high number (10.1), so that higher values indicate better performance.

Adapted from "Self-efficacy theory: Implications for social facilitation and social loafing," by Sanna, L. J., 1992, *Journal of Personality and Social Psychology, 62*, 774–786 (Experiment 1). With permission of the American Psychological Association.

performance when working collectively than coactively) for those with a low expectancy of success. This later effect is a novel one but is consistent with the idea that a realistic threat of negative evaluation (in the coactive condition) can lead to a withdrawal of effort. In this case, withdrawing effort implies being less vigilant and so committing more errors. Thus, to the extent that evaluative concerns play a role in producing both social facilitation and social loafing effects, these seemingly different phenomena can be understood in very similar ways.

The "anti-loafing" effect observed by Sanna (1992) suggests that people do not inevitably experience a motivation loss when working collectively, relative to when they work coactively. Rather, under the right circumstances, it is possible that they may experience instead a motivation gain. In the next section I explore this possibility more systematically.

☐ Collective Action and Motivation Gain

For reasons of experimental control, it has been standard practice in social loafing research to minimize the information that participants have about either the actual or anticipated performance of others in their group. Thus, researchers have typically gone to great lengths to prevent members from seeing or hearing their (usually fictitious) groupmates as they work and to control expectations about groupmate performance prior to the start of the experimental session. It is likely, however, that such expectations and real-time performance information play a critical role in regulating the amount of effort that group members commit to their task. Of particular concern in this section of the chapter is the motivational impact of expecting that one's groupmate(s) will perform either well or poorly. Two lines of research have explored this issue, each focusing on a different type of group task.

Social Compensation

The first line of research is concerned with unitary additive tasks. As noted previously, beginning with Ringelmann (1913), such tasks have been the mainstay of social loafing research. What is the motivational impact of anticipating that others in the group will likely contribute either much or little to the group's product on an additive task?

Williams and Karau (1991, Experiments 2 and 3) were the first to address this question. They had research participants work for 12 minutes on an idea-generation task. Participants were to think of as many different uses as they could for a simple object (e.g., a knife) and to write each use on a separate slip of paper. They worked on this task either coactively or collectively with a confederate of the experimenter who posed as another participant. In the coactive condition, participants and confederates placed their slips into two separate boxes (sealed so that neither could gauge the number of uses generated by the other). In this condition the experimenter emphasized that it was the number of uses they each generated individually that was of interest, and that each participant's performance would be evaluated separately. By contrast, in the collective condition, participants and confederates placed their slips into one common box (though again, it was sealed so that neither could see what the other had produced). Here, the experimenter emphasized that it was the total number of uses that the two of them generated together that was of interest, and that their performance as individuals could not be separately evaluated (which was not actually true). Finally, based on comments made by the confederate prior to the start of the 12-minute work period, participants were led to believe that the confederate was likely to generate either many or few ideas because he intended to exert either high or low effort while performing the task (in Experiment 2) or because he had high or low ability for doing that sort of task (in Experiment 3).

As can be seen in Table 8.2, Williams and Karau (1991; Experiments 2 and 3) found that, when the confederate was expected to do well, the usual social loafing effect was observed—participants generated fewer ideas when working collectively than when working coactively. On the other hand, when the confederate was expected to do poorly, the opposite occurred—participants generated more ideas when working collectively than when working coactively. The authors termed this latter result a *social compensation* effect, arguing that in the collective condition, partici-

TABLE 8.2 Mean Performance on an Idea-Generation Task as a Function of Work Condition and Expected Partner Performance

	Expected Partner Performance	
Working Condition	High	Low
Coactive	32.85	23.88
Collective	25.96	30.80

Adapted from "Social loafing and social compensation: The effects of expectations of co-worker performance," by Williams, K. D., and Karau, S. J., 1991, Journal of Personality and Social Psychology, 61, 570–581 (Experiments 2 and 3). With permission of the American Psychological Association.

pants were attempting to compensate for the expected poor performance of the confederate.

The basic social compensation effect has been replicated in several subsequent laboratory experiments (e.g., Hart, Bridgett, & Karau, 2001; Karau & Williams, 1997; Plaks & Higgins, 2000; Todd, Seok, Kerr, & Messé, 2006), as well as in at least one field study (Liden, Wayne, Jaworski, & Bennett, 2004; see also the extensive literature on organizational citizenship behavior). Further, this effect has been observed even when the expectation of poor partner performance is based on evidence that the partner will not work very hard at the task. On the other hand, the effect disappears, and indeed is replaced by social loafing, when an unmotivated partner simultaneously is perceived to have high task-relevant ability (e.g., Hart et al. 2001; Jackson & LePine, 2003; Kerr & Bruun, 1983; see also Abele & Diehl, 2008). Apparently, people will work hard to compensate for others only to the extent that they feel those others are not themselves socially loafing.

It is important to note that, unlike social facilitation, social compensation effects do not necessarily promise a net improvement in performance for the group as a whole.[12] This is because, except under highly unusual circumstances, the same overarching conditions that encourage social compensation among some group members are apt to encourage social loafing among others. To see this, consider again the data reported in Table 8.2. Suppose that two individuals of disparate ability work collectively on an additive task and that both are aware of the ability difference between them. Although the more capable member (who expects low partner performance) may increase his or her effort in an attempt to compensate for the partner's shortcomings, the less capable member (who expects high partner performance) is apt to loaf. Thus, whereas one member should behave in accordance with the right-hand (social compensation) column in Table 8.2, the other should behave in accordance with the left-hand (social loafing) column. At least for the data presented in Table 8.2, these two tendencies—social compensation and social loafing—offset one another almost perfectly and so yield no net increase (or decrease) in performance at the group level when shifting from a coactive to a collective work arrangement. In other words, social compensation reflects a motivation gain at the individual level that does not necessarily yield a performance gain for the group as a whole.

This stands in contrast to social facilitation, which, when it occurs, is apt to occur in a similar way for all group members. The conditions that promote social facilitation—members being able to identify and evaluate one another's contributions—are usually symmetric; each member is aware of what the others contribute. Thus, each serves as an audience for the others and so can prompt more striving as a result of evaluative concerns. Consequently, when it occurs, social facilitation at the individual level should have a better chance of translating into a group-level performance gain.

The Köhler Motivation Gain Effect

A second line of research concerned with the motivational impact of expecting one's groupmate(s) to perform either well or poorly focuses on unitary conjunctive tasks, where all members must contribute identically to the group's product. An important feature of such tasks is that the group's collective performance can be no better than that of its least able member. Consider, for example, the previously mentioned team of mountain climbers who are roped together while making their ascent. Although providing a measure of safety, this tethered climbing arrangement also means that the team can proceed at a pace that is no faster than its slowest member can maintain. Thus, on conjunctive tasks it is the motivation of the least-able member that has the greatest impact on group performance. Particularly interesting in the present context is whether the least-able member exerts any more or less effort on the task as a result of this work arrangement.

The earliest known empirical evidence bearing on this question was obtained in a set of experiments by Otto Köhler (1926, 1927). He had male participants perform one of several difficult physical persistence tasks. For example, one was a weight-lifting task not unlike the sort usually performed in a gym or health club. Participants were required to grasp a heavily weighted metal bar in both hands, lift it 75 cm, then lower it, and do so repeatedly every 2 seconds for as long as possible. Participants did this either alone, in dyads, or in triads. The bar was weighted with a 41 kg load (approximately 90 lb) in the alone condition and with either an 82 kg or 123 kg load in the dyad and triad conditions, respectively. Thus, the

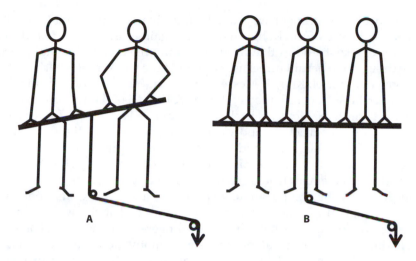

FIGURE 8.2   Köhler's (A) dyadic and (B) triadic weightlifting task.

per-person load on the bar was the same in all three conditions. When working either in dyads or in triads, participants stood side-by-side, each grasping one half (dyads) or one third (triads) of the bar (see Figure 8.2). Further, when working in triads, the strongest and weakest members were always placed at opposite ends of the bar. This, along with the proportionally greater weight involved, meant that in the two collective conditions the group could continue only so long as every member contributed. If any one of then quit, the group as a whole had to quit.

Köhler (1926) found that when groups comprised members who were moderately discrepant in their lifting ability (as indexed by their performance at the task when working alone), their collective performance was significantly better than the average of their individual performances: Dyads preformed 15% better than their members did working alone, and triads performed 5% better. Because group performance on this task depends so heavily on the persistence of the weakest member, these results imply that the weakest member was more motivated to do well when working as part of a group than when working alone.[13] However, this result obtained only when the members were moderately discrepant in ability. When members were either extremely discrepant or very similar in ability, collective performance was not better than individual performance. Thus, the motivation gain observed by Köhler was an inverted U-shaped function of the discrepancy in members' ability.

As was true of Ringelmann's (1913) early research, Köhler's (1926, 1927) findings lay nearly forgotten for more than six decades. They were reintroduced by Witte (1989). Subsequently, Stroebe, Diehl, and Abakoumkin (1996, Experiment 1) performed a near-exact replication of Köhler's weight-lifting experiment with dyads and obtained comparable results. Further evidence of the Köhler motivation gain effect can be found in a number of recent studies that have used a modified experimental procedure designed to permit direct assessment of the weaker member's contributions (e.g., Hertel, Kerr, & Messé, 2000; Kerr, Messé, Park, & Sambolec, 2005; Kerr, Messé, Seok, Sambolec, Lount, & Park, 2007; Lount, Kerr, Messé, Seok, & Park, 2008; Messé, Hertel, Kerr, Lount, & Park, 2002). In these latter studies, each participant individually grasped a much lighter (2 kg or less) metal bar in one hand and held it at arms length over a table for as long as they could. They did this either alone or in dyads. When working in dyads, each member held a separate bar, and their collective score was determined by the first person to let his or her arm drop. Consistent with Köhler's original findings, these studies showed that the weaker member exerted more effort—held the bar up longer—when working conjunctively than when working alone. This sort of motivation gain seems not to depend on the members being able to monitor one another's performance while working, as it has been demonstrated to occur even when members work out of sight of one another (e.g., Kerr et al., 2005; Lount, Park, Kerr, Messé, & Seok, 2008). Nor is it limited to physical tasks: Motivation gains by less capable group members have been documented when the task—and so the effort exerted—is primarily mental rather than physical, such as processing customer orders in a simulated retail sales situation (Hertel et al., 2003; Hertel, Niemeyer, & Clauss, 2008) and doing arithmetic calculations (Lount & Phillips, 2007). On the other hand, the magnitude of these effects do appear to be stronger when members are able to monitor one another as they are working and when the task is primarily physical as opposed to mental (Weber & Hertel, 2007).

There is, however, one aspect of Köhler's (1926, 1927) original results that has proven difficult to replicate. It is the inverted U-shaped function he reported—that the motivation gain observed when working conjunctively was largest when members were moderately discrepant in ability and smallest (or absent altogether) when members were either extremely discrepant or only slightly discrepant in ability. Just three studies have replicated this result (Messé et al, 2002, Experiments 1 and 2; Ruess, 1992, Experiment 5, as cited in Stroebe et al., 1996; but see also Hertel, Kerr, & Messé, 1999). This may indicate that the curvilinear relationship is relatively ephemeral. Alternatively, it could reflect an important methodological difference between the modern studies and Köhler's original work. In most of the modern studies, dyads have been composed of individuals who were unacquainted with one another and so had little basis for judging one another's ability vis-à-vis the task to be performed. Köhler, on the other hand, enlisted the members of a rowing club to participate in his research. Rowing ability is dependent on the same sort of physical strength demanded by Köhler's weight-lifting task, and indeed his research was conducted in the context of the club's winter weight training program. Thus, not only is it likely that these participants were well acquainted with one another, it is also likely that they could estimate relatively accurately one another's' physical strength. The inverted U-shaped function may thus manifest itself only when members are reasonably well calibrated in their estimates of one another's ability vis-à-vis the task (cf. Messé et al., 2002). Otherwise, when members are not well calibrated, the Köhler motivation gain effect may manifest itself simply as a main effect of work condition (i.e., conjunctive vs. alone).

Underlying Causes of the Köhler Effect

Several factors appear to be important in producing the Köhler motivation gain effect, and these tend to be polar opposites of the factors previously discussed as precursors to social loafing and free riding in groups.

One concerns the *indispensability* of the weakest member's effort. On a conjunctive task, more than any other task type, the efforts of the least capable member are critical to the group's success—the harder that member works, the better the group as a whole will perform. Thus, it is essential that the weakest member recognize the conjunctive nature of the task. It is also essential that the weakest member recognize—or at least suspect—that he or she may in fact be the group's least capable member. A member might come to this view based on past experience with the same groupmates on the same (or closely related) task. Or, it may arise via subtle cues observed as the group engages its present task. The contributions of other members might, for example, come a little more quickly, surely, and vigorously, or be made with greater precision, consistency, and confidence than one's own, and so convey a sense that those others are more able than oneself. This should be especially true if over time one's own contributions become more and more difficult to make (e.g., as one becomes fatigued when performing the weight-lifting task). One way or another, the Köhler motivation gain effect depends on the least capable member realizing that his or her own efforts are indispensable to the performance of the group as a whole (e.g., Gockel, Kerr, Seok, & Harris, 2008; Hertel et al., 2008; Wittchen, Schlereth, & Hertel 2007).

A second contributing factor, and one that is likely to operate in conjunction with other variables, is the *identifiability* of member contributions to the group. When performing conjunctive tasks in the real world, it is often apparent to everyone in the group who is slowest, quits first, finishes last, etc., and so who ultimately determined the group's overall performance. If this information is not available to group members, the weakest member is apt to exert no more effort when working conjunctively than when working alone, in which case no motivation gain will appear (cf. Kerr et al., 2005).

The combination of identifiability and perceived indispensability has two important consequences for the weakest member of the group. The first is that it exposes him or her to at least the possibility of a negative evaluation by others in the group. The prospect of a negative evaluation—and of the subtle untoward social consequences attendant on such an evaluation—is apt to loom particularly large when the task is highly meaningful and important. The weakest member can hope to lessen such unpleasantness only by performing his or her very best, matching as closely as possible the level of performance that others in the group seem (more easily) able to achieve. Thus, as was true for several of the other motivational phenomena discussed earlier in this chapter (social facilitation; reducing social loafing), evaluation apprehension is apt to play a key role in producing the Köhler motivation gain effect.

Equally important, identifiability also permits the weakest member to self-evaluate—to judge the adequacy of his or her own task-relevant contributions in relation to others. In terms of underlying abilities, this will by definition be an upward comparison and so is apt to yield evidence that he or she is indeed less competent than others in the group. To the extent that members prefer to see themselves favorably in most ability domains (Buunk & Gibbons, 2007; Wood, 1989, 2000), they should be motivated to minimize the size of the discrepancy between themselves and their more competent groupmates by working hard to perform their very best. Minimizing this discrepancy can do more than just mitigate the sting of an unflattering comparison. It can create a genuinely favorable comparison. This is true even though the weakest member cannot outperform his or her more able groupmates. Knowing that, with effort, one can at least keep up with groupmates who are more capable than oneself can sometimes be a great source of pride and personal satisfaction, particularly when the task is a meaningful and important one (Hertel, Kerr, & Messé, 1999).

Conjunctive tasks are not the only context in which potentially invidious social comparisons are thrust upon people. The same can happen in coactive working conditions—for example, when one must work alongside others who are known to be more capable than oneself. Here, too, the desire to evaluate oneself favorably in relation to others can prompt a motivation gain relative to working alone (e.g., Kerr et al., 2007). Phenomenologically, this may be experienced by the less capable individual as an informal competition with those more competent others—to see just how closely he or she can match their performance. This competitive orientation need not be driven by a concern for the evaluations that others might make. Rather, it can arise solely form the desire to evaluate one's self favorably.

It is important to note, however, that informal competitions of this sort cannot fully explain the Köhler motivation gain effect that is observed in conjunctive task situations. Kerr et al. (2007, Experiment 1), for example, directly compared the motivation gain exhibited by the weaker of two participants when working either coactively or conjunctively and found that, although participants increased their effort in both conditions relative to when they worked alone, the gain in the conjunctive condition was nearly twice that observed in the coactive condition. This suggests that the Köhler motivation gain effect is driven by more than just an informal competition between group members.

Finally, the inverted U-shaped relationship that sometimes has been observed between motivation gains by the least capable group member, on the one hand, and the size of the ability discrepancy between members, on the other, can be understood by introducing one additional concept. That concept has to do with the weakest member's expectation about whether or not he or she *can* perform at a level commensurate with that of his or her more able groupmates (cf. Hertel, Kerr, & Messé, 1999, 2000; Shepperd, 1993, 2001; Vroom, 1964). Such expectations should be an inverse function of the size of the ability discrepancy between members. Specifically, when that ability discrepancy is small, the weakest member should have a relatively high expectation of being able to keep pace with his or her (slightly) more capable groupmates. All that is required is a modest boost in effort. When the ability discrepancy is somewhat larger, the weakest member may still have a reasonable expectation of performing to the level of those more capable groupmates, as long as he or she perceives that, with enough effort, he or she can compensate for the (now moderate) ability discrepancy. In this case, however, substantially more effort is apt to be required. But suppose the ability discrepancy is so large that the weakest member cannot compensate by means of effort alone. Here, the weakest member is apt to have a low expectation of performing on par with his or her groupmates. Consequently, he or she has little incentive to work hard—because working hard is unlikely to help him or her escape a negative evaluation (by self or others). Thus, as the ability discrepancy changes from small to moderate to large, the motivation gain displayed by the weakest group member should be, respectively, small (because only a little extra effort is required to achieve a favorable evaluation), large (because substantially more effort is required to achieve a favorable evaluation), and small (because no amount of effort is likely to yield a favorable evaluation).

Conjunctive Tasks and Synergy

Although it centers on the efforts of just one member, the Köhler motivation gain effect nevertheless yields a genuine group-level performance gain. When the weakest member works harder conjunctively than alone, the group as a whole does better than would be expected given that member's individual performance. And because this performance gain ultimately is attributable to the particular way in which members work together, it fits the definition of synergy in groups.

Less obvious is whether the Köhler motivation gain effect should qualify as evidence of weak or strong synergy in groups. This is because the scheme for differentiating weak and strong synergy introduced in Chapter 1 is not wholly appropriate for classifying performance gains on conjunctive tasks. Recall that weak synergy was defined there as group performance that exceeds the performance of its average member when working alone, whereas strong synergy was defined as group performance that exceeds the solo performance of even its best member. It is certainly conceivable that when working conjunctively the weakest member of the group could exert sufficient additional effort to permit the group as a whole to perform above the level predicted by the solo performance of its average member. Thus, a group might persist at a conjunctive weight-lifting task longer than its average member would persist alone. This is precisely what Köhler (1926) found under conditions of moderate ability discrepancy. It is also possible—though less likely—that when working conjunctively the group might perform even beyond the level predicted by its best member's solo performance. Such results would qualify as clear evidence of weak and strong synergy, respectively.

But what should be made of conjunctive group performance that, while better than predicted by its weakest member's solo performance, is still below the level predicted by its average member's performance? On other sorts of tasks this might be dismissed as a net process loss. However, because conjunctive tasks constrain the group's performance to be no better than what its weakest member can do, it seems more appropriate to use the solo performance of the weakest member, not the average member, as the criterion for judging whether or not weak synergy has occurred. Thus, as argued in Chapter 2 (see pp. 67–68), in the special case of conjunctive tasks, weak synergy is defined as group performance that exceeded the level predicted by its least capable member when working alone, whereas strong synergy is defined as group performance that exceeded the level predicted by the solo performance of even its most capable member.

Almost all contemporary research concerned with the Köhler motivation gain effect focuses exclusively on the weakest-member criterion and so provides no indication of how the conjunctive performance of groups stands in relation to other potential criteria (an exception is Stroebe et al., 1996). For example, Messé et al. (2002) report that across studies performance gains of 10 to 50% are typical, and in a meta-analytic review Weber and Hertel (2007) found an average effect size of $d = .73$. However, because these gains are relative only to the solo performance of the group's weakest member, it is unclear whether they reflect a weak or strong form of synergy.

Still, it seems most likely that when they are observed, Köhler motivation gain effects will be within the range of weak synergy. In part, this is because, independent of task type, strong synergy is inherently more difficult to achieve than weak synergy; the performance criterion for strong synergy is always higher. Additionally, strong synergy should be particularly difficult to achieve on conjunctive tasks because the strong synergy criterion is so much further above the weak synergy criterion for those tasks (i.e., the difference between the solo performances of the best and worst members is by definition greater than the difference between the solo performances of the best and average members). Nevertheless, in future research it would be useful to report the solo performance of both the best and average member, along with that of the weakest member, in order to better gauge the strength of whatever gain is observed.

Motivation Gains on Divisible Tasks

Research on the Köhler motivation gain effect has focused almost exclusively on unitary tasks. As described in Chapter 2, unitary tasks are those that cannot be meaningfully subdivided into separate activities requiring different skills and abilities. Rather, they demand that all members engage in the same activity and so apply the same skills and abilities. When such tasks also require that group members contribute identically—that is, when they are conjunctive—the implication is that the group's product will be determined by the performance of the member who contributes least. Under such conditions, the empirical evidence suggests that synergistic performance gains are reasonably likely to appear.

Conjunctivity is not limited to just unitary tasks, however. It is also a property of many divisible tasks, and in particular tasks with subtasks (cf. Hertel, Konradt, & Orlikowski, 2004; Kelley, Holms, Kerr, Reis, Rusbult, & Van Lange, 2003). As discussed in Chapter 2, when a task involves two or more subtasks, those subtasks, by definition, each have their own stimulus complex, their own goal and procedural directives, and result in their own measurable product. Further, there are often significant interdependencies between subtasks, such that the product of one subtask becomes part of the stimulus complex for other subtasks. Returning to the racing sailboat example, a sail trimmer's job is to trim (adjust the position and shape of) the sail to which he or she is assigned so that it is maximally efficient as an airfoil and thus propels the boat forward as fast as possible. The optimal sail trim depends in part on the direction of the wind relative to the boat's current heading, with the latter being determined by the helmsman (who steers the boat). A task frequently performed aboard a racing sailboat is turning the boat around a buoy that marks part of the race course. This requires not only that the helmsman steer a new heading, but also that the sail trimmer(s) trim the sail(s) for that heading. Although these two subtasks are often initiated simultaneously, a sail trimmer cannot finish his or her subtask until the helmsman's subtask has been completed; the boat must settle on her new heading before the final sail adjustments are made. It is this interdependence between subtasks that creates conjunctivity. Thus, if each member of a group performs a different subtask, and the speed or effectiveness with which one subtask is performed depends in part on the speed or effectiveness with which one or more other subtasks are performed, then it is quite possible that the task as a whole will be completed no faster or better than the group's slowest or least capable member can manage.

Despite their often conjunctive nature, tasks with subtasks present special challenges that make performance gains difficult to predict. The reason is that, when different subtasks demand different skills and abilities, it becomes harder for members to determine who in the group is in fact least capable. Further, subtasks often vary both in difficulty and in the amount of time required to complete them. This makes some subtasks more sensitive to variations in member ability than others. Finally, subtasks can differ in their inherent criticality to overall task success; some subtasks may simply matter more that others. All of this can make it rather unclear whose efforts are in fact most indispensable. Significantly, group performance on tasks with subtasks does not necessarily hinge on the efforts of its least capable member, at least not to the degree it does on unitary conjunctive tasks. This is particularly true when members are assigned to subtasks according to ability, which is a common practice in real-world settings. This strategy reduces (but does not eliminate) the group's dependence on the contributions of its least capable member and increases its dependence on the contributions of those who are more capable—especially those assigned to the most difficult, time consuming, and/or critical subtasks. To the extent this is recognized by group members, those who are most capable should feel more indispensable when working on tasks with subtasks than when working on unitary conjunctive tasks. This heightened sense of indispensability, along with the high level of identifiability that naturally attends most tasks with subtasks, seems likely to promote in the group's most capable members the same sort of motivation gain that has been observed among the least capable members in groups working on unitary conjunctive tasks.

An illustration of a task situation in which this might occur is the bicycling example described earlier in this chapter and in Chapter 1. Two or more cyclists who ride as a team by taking turns drafting behind one another are working conjunctively; they can ride together no faster than the lead cyclist is able to pedal. The efforts of the lead cyclist are thus inherently indispensable and readily identifiable. These two conditions are exactly the ones needed to produce the Köhler motivation gain effect on unitary conjunctive tasks. In this case, however, it is the most capable member of the team, not the least capable member, who should exhibit the motivation gain. That is, the lead cyclist is (or should be) the member who at the moment is best rested and strongest. His or her teammates will be able to keep up only because their subtask is less difficult. Most importantly, they do not have to fight the wind nearly as much as the lead rider does.[14] Of course, the lead rider will gradually tire, to the point where he or she is no longer the strongest member of the team. When this happens, he or she will (or should) relinquish the lead, turning it over to the one teammate who is currently best rested and strongest. Thus, each member of the team takes a turn at the lead position and so temporarily becomes indispensable to the group. Based on what is known from unitary conjunctive tasks, it seems reasonable to predict that, while in that lead position, group members will tend to pedal faster, and with greater persistence, than they otherwise might (i.e., when riding alone). Further, and as noted in Chapter 1, this would appear to produce a genuine example of strong synergy; by riding together as a team these cyclists can travel faster and further that even the best of them would likely be able to do riding alone.

In sum, when a task involves two or more subtasks, the nature of those subtasks and their relationship to one another can strongly impact who in the group is most indispensable and so who is most apt to display a motivation gain. This suggests that under the right set of circumstances, a motivation gain might be observed by the group's most capable member, its least capable member, or by anyone in between. When they occur, these motivational effects should translate into an overall performance gain at the group level, with the group performing better than would be predicted by the (indispensability-weighted) individual performances of its members. To date, few studies have investigated member motivation gains on tasks with subtasks (but see Hertel et al., 2003). However, given the growing body of evidence for the existence of motivation gains on unitary conjunctive tasks, and the arguably greater real-world prevalence of divisible group tasks, it would seem that a systematic exploration of motivation gains on tasks with subtasks would be a worthwhile direction for the future in the search for synergy in groups.

☐ Goal Setting: Supporting Group Motivation Gains

As should be evident by now, most research demonstrating motivation gains in groups has examined group performance on relatively simple tasks. The reason is straightforward—performance on such tasks is governed more by effort than by ability, thus making motivation gains easier to document when they occur.

It is important, however, not to lose sight of the fact that real-world groups typically perform a range of tasks that are substantially more complex than those studied in the laboratory. Further, members often juggle multiple subtasks, with some subtasks being the joint responsibility of several group members and others being their responsibility alone. The interdependencies among these subtasks can be quite intricate. However, members seldom can attend to all of their various subtasks simultaneously. Instead, at any given moment they must choose which particular subtask they will work on, and how much energy they will devote to it. These choices are informed by the goals that members have. Goals channel member energies in one direction or another, and can dramatically affect whether motivation gains sparked among individual group members actually yield group-level synergistic performance gains. In this final section of the chapter, I briefly consider the impact of goals on group performance.

Explicitly Set Goals

As discussed in Chapter 2 (see pp. 31–33), every group task involves one or more goal directives. These are instructions that indicate what the group is expected to produce or achieve. Goal directives may be either implicit or explicit, and explicit goals may be more or less specific.[15] An example of a specific explicit goal is asking a group to complete a piece of work "by 11:00 a.m. on Wednesday." Much less specific is asking them to finish that work "as soon as you can." The latter is commonly referred to as a *do-best goal*. Do-best goals are usually less effective than specific goals in guiding behavior, because they do not provide clear criteria for judging either the progress that has been made toward the goal, or when the goal has been achieved. If a group given a do-best goal actually finishes its work at 4 p.m. on Wednesday, how are we (or they) to know that they could not have finished sooner? A specific goal, by contrast, makes it plain to everyone whether or not the goal has been met. Not surprisingly, specific, difficult (but attainable) goals have consistently been shown to result in better performance than do-best goals (e.g., Locke & Latham, 1990, 2002, 2006). This holds for groups as well as for individuals and for assigned as well as self-set goals. Thus, a broad recommendation for maximizing group performance is to set goals that are specific, difficult, but attainable.

Yet goal setting can sometimes go awry. For instance, although assigned goals tend to yield better group performance than self-set goals,[16] an assigned goal is apt to be effective only to the extent that it is accepted by the group. When a specific assigned goal is not accepted—perhaps because it is perceived to be beyond the group's capacity to attain—groups will tend to perform no better than when they are given a do-best goal (e.g., Klein, Wesson, Hollenbeck, & Alge, 1999; Locke, Latham, & Erez, 1988).

Another way in which goal setting can misfire is when multiple goals are assigned that conflict with one another. Goals can often be set at both the individual and group level. This is possible whenever member contributions to the group are individually identifiable. The rationale often given for setting both individual and group performance goals is that, because members have more direct control over their own performance than over the performance of the group as a whole, individual goals can be more effective than group goals at guiding behavior. Further, individual goals can serve as a safeguard against social loafing (e.g., Karau & Williams, 1993; Matsui, Kakuyama, & Onglatco, 1987).

But individual goals can sometimes conflict with group goals, particularly when members are highly interdependent. Consider, for example, the performance of a basketball team. The team's score at the end of a game is the sum of the points scored by all of its members. But because the game is played with just one ball, only one person can shoot (and so score points) at a time. If a player tries to maximize his or her own individual scoring performance by attempting as many shots as possible, this will take shooting opportunities away from his or her teammates. Furthermore, at any given moment during a game, that player may not be the one who is in the best position to successfully make a shot. If another player is better positioned, it would be more beneficial for the team's collective performance to pass the ball and let that other player attempt the shot. In other words, shooting is not the only behavior that contributes to the team's collective performance. Passing, when done at the right time and to the right player, also contributes. Thus, setting high scoring goals for individual players can create a situation where those goals not only conflict with one another, but also conflict with the group's collective goal.

A laboratory analog of just this type of situation was created by Mitchell and Silver (1990). They had three-person groups work on an interdependent tower-construction task. Each group was to build a single tower by placing small wooden blocks one on top of another. Members were each given a supply of 20 blocks, all painted in the same color, but different in color from the blocks given to the other members. In this way, each member's contributions to the tower could be identified. Group performance was defined simply as the height of the tower that the group was able to construct in 15 seconds. In one condition, members were assigned difficult individual performance goals (to each place at least 7 blocks on the tower). In a second condition, the group as a whole was assigned a difficult goal (to build a tower consisting of at least 21 blocks). Across 10 trials, it was found that the average height of the towers constructed by groups in the group goal condition was significantly higher ($M = 11.2$ blocks) than the average height of the towers constructed by groups in the individual goal condition ($M = 8.2$ blocks). It is important to note that there were no between-condition differences in either goal acceptance or commitment; members reported being just as accepting of, and committed to achieving, the individual goals as the group goals. Thus, the observed difference in performance between conditions cannot easily be attributed to differences in the intensity of the members' motivation. Rather, groups in the group goal condition were observed to engage in significantly more cooperative turn-taking than groups in the individual goal condition, and this appears to explain why groups in the former condition performed better. Much like the game of basketball, the tower-construction task permits only one person at a time to place a block on the tower. Given this constraint, turn-taking is an important coordination strategy that permits every member to contribute blocks and so facilitates the group's collective performance.

More generally, setting specific individual-level goals can be expected to impair the collective performance of a group to the extent that (a) those goals do not encompass all of the different ways in which members contribute to the group's collective product and (b) pursuing them is mutually exclusive with contributing in other ways. Thus, in the game of basketball, players can contribute to the team's overall performance both by shooting the ball and by passing it. But they cannot do both simultaneously. Furthermore, which action is more appropriate depends on the situation; sometimes it is better to shoot, and sometimes it is better to pass. If a high-scoring goal is set for individual players, that goal will tend to channel their efforts toward shooting and away from passing (because as individuals they can score points by shooting but not by passing), even when passing would be better for the team as a whole.

This analysis suggests, however, that individual goals are not *inherently* detrimental to a group's collective performance. Rather, to the extent that individual goals take into account the full range of member contributions to the group, then such goals should facilitate rather than hinder the group's collective performance. Once again, the game of basketball provides an example. Teams often keep records of the "assists" that their players make. A player is credited with an assist whenever he or she passes the ball to a teammate and that teammate immediately moves toward the basket, shoots, and scores. Setting individual player goals that emphasize both assists and scoring points directly should result in better team performance than setting player goals that focus exclusively on scoring. Individual goals that address a broader range of member contributions— especially those that are collaborative in nature—are said to be "group-centric," whereas individual goals that focus on just a narrow range of noncollaborative contributions are said to be "egocentric."

A study by Crown and Rosse (1995; see also Crown, 2007a, 2007b) provides direct experimental evidence of the benefits of groupcentric goals on collective performance. They had seven-person groups perform a sentence-construction task in which members individually created words from sets of letters they held (a la the game of Scrabble), and the group collectively created sentences from the members' words. At the beginning of the 30-minute work period each member was given a different set of 27 letters from which to form words, where each letter could be used just once. The design of the study included three conditions in which a specific, difficult group-level goal was assigned (construct five sentences, each with at least one word created by each member). In two of these conditions, a specific, difficult individual-level goal was also assigned to each member. In one case, the individual goal was relatively groupcentric (contribute at least 17 letters to the group's final sentences). In the other it was relatively egocentric (construct at least seven words, each consisting of three or more letters). Note that the 17-letter goal allows for a greater range of potential member contributions to the group (e.g., it can be achieved by forming either short or long words) than does the seven-word goal (which requires mostly short words). Hence, the groupcentric goal permits more flexibility in constructing words specifically designed to work with words already created by others (i.e., more collaboration). Consistent with this, it was found that in comparison to the group-goal-only condition, groups performed significantly better when members were also assigned groupcentric individual goals, but performed significantly worse when members were also assigned egocentric individual goals. Indeed, groups in the latter condition performed worse even than those in a separate control condition where only a do-best goal was assigned.

Thus, setting goals for individual group members can either augment or undercut the benefits of setting a goal for the group as a whole, depending on whether those individual goals are groupcentric or egocentric, respectively. Egocentric individual goals are detrimental primarily because they encourage members to ignore actions that do not benefit them directly, including actions that would benefit the group as a whole. Groupcentric individual goals avoid this problem, but are generally harder to set. This is because finding an appropriate groupcentric individual goal requires a very detailed understanding of the group's task, including all of the various ways in which group member actions can contribute to successful group performance.

Implicit Goals

The problems associated with explicitly-set egocentric individual goals can also arise when members must infer their performance goals from the task environment. These might be called *implicit goals*. Implicit goals are not expressly communicated, but instead are deduced from cues embedded in the broader social or organizational context within which the group's task is performed. Two particularly potent cues have to do with the orientation of the applicable reward system and the structure of the performance feedback that is available.

Regarding the reward system, two broad orientations can be distinguished: individually-oriented reward systems and group-oriented reward systems. Individually-oriented rewards are positive outcomes that accrue to group members contingent upon their individual performance. In the tower-building task used by Mitchell and Silver (1990), for example, rather than setting an explicit goal, members might have been offered a small amount of money for each block they contributed to the tower. When members are rewarded individually, different members often receive different outcomes. Group rewards, by contrast, are positive outcomes that accrue to members contingent upon the group's collective performance, with every member receiving the same outcome. In the case of group rewards, member outcomes are partly contingent upon how well or poorly their teammates perform. Thus, in the tower-building task, each member might have been offered a small amount of money for every block placed on the tower, regardless of who contributed it.

The orientation of the reward system can significantly impact group performance on complex, interdependent tasks. On such tasks, groups perform significantly better when the reward system is group oriented rather than individually oriented (Deutsch, 1949; Stanne, Johnson, & Johnson, 1999; Wageman, 1999, 2001; see also Homan, Hollenbeck, Humphrey, van Knippenberg, Ilgen, & Van Kleef, 2008). It seems reasonable to speculate that this effect is mediated by the implicit performance goals that members infer from the reward system. Specifically, members are apt to infer egocentric performance goals from an individually-oriented reward system and groupcentric performance goals from a group-oriented reward system (cf. De Dreu, 2007).

Members can also infer implicit goals from the structure of the performance feedback they receive. Paralleling the two reward orientations just described, members might receive feedback either about their individual performance or about the group's collective performance. In iterative performance situations, such feedback has been shown to affect how members direct their efforts and so how well or poorly the group as a whole performs.

An example is a study by DeShon, Kozlowski, Schmidt, Milner, and Wiechmann (2004). They had participants work in three-person teams on a multitrial airspace surveillance task. Team members were each given primary responsibility for monitoring and making decisions about aircraft entering a different sector of airspace represented on a simulated radar screen. Additionally, at their own discretion, members could also monitor the airspace assigned to their teammates and assist them as needed. The task was designed so that the average workload was equivalent across sectors, but from time to time different sectors became unexpectedly overloaded. At those times, discretionary assistance from others was beneficial to the team's collective performance. It was found that, when members were given feedback only about their own performance on the one sector for which they were primarily responsible, the team's collective performance suffered in comparison to when they were given feedback only about the team's aggregate performance (i.e., regarding all three sectors combined). Further, the authors demonstrated that these performance effects were mediated by members' goals and by their effort-related behavioral decisions. Specifically, the type of feedback that members received (individual vs. team) affected the performance goals they informally set for themselves and for their team, which in turn affected the effort-related choices they made while working on the task (i.e., regarding how much effort to expend in their own sector vs. other sectors), which finally impacted the team's overall performance effectiveness.

In sum, even when task goals are not communicated explicitly, members may nevertheless infer their goals from the structure of the reward and/or performance feedback systems. Indeed, such inferences are likely even when goals are communicated explicitly, thus suggesting another potential source of goal conflict that can impede group performance. For example, even when only a group-level goal is set explicitly, members may nevertheless infer individual-level goals if either the reward or feedback system focuses on their individual performance. Those inferred individual goals are apt to be rather egocentric to the extent the reward and/or feedback systems emphasize noncollaborative aspects of their individual performance. Thus, as a practical matter, those who set goals for groups in applied settings (e.g., work supervisors) should take care to ensure that their well-intentioned, explicitly-set goals are not undercut by the implicit individual-level goals that group members may infer from other cues in the broader task environment.

□ Chapter Summary

In this chapter, I have examined some of the main themes in the empirical literature concerned with motivation-based performance gains in groups. Starting from a minimalist perspective, the chapter began by considering whether working on a task in the company of others, by itself, can affect motivation and performance. This is one of the oldest questions in social psychology, and it is one that has attracted a steady stream of research for over a century. The available evidence suggests that the presence of others, especially evaluative others, can elicit in performers a rather automatic increase in nondirectional drive. In addition, the presence of evaluative others can prompt intentional motivational responses that are ultimately directed toward gaining social approval and/or avoiding disapproval. Often this means an increase in task-directed effort. Under some conditions, however, it can mean a withdrawal of effort. Furthermore, even when drive or motivation increases, increased performance does not necessarily follow. Indeed, performance is sometimes facilitated and sometimes inhibited by increased motivation, depending on how easy, familiar, or well-learned the task at hand is.

The chapter next addressed the problems of social loafing and free riding, two examples of motivation loss that arise when people work collectively in groups. Social loafing and free riding occur when performers work collectively rather than coactively, and are due to conditions of low identifiability and high dispensability, respectively. Low identifiability exists when members' individual contributions to the group's product cannot be individually distinguished. High dispensability exists when their individual contributions have little impact on the group's eventual success or failure. Because they are closely tied to issues of group member evaluation, social loafing and free riding can be understood within a broader motivational framework that also includes certain forms of social facilitation.

Motivation loss is not an unavoidable consequence of working collectively in groups. Rather, under conditions that eliminate problems of low identifiability and high dispensability, motivation gains can be expected. The third main section of the chapter examined this possibility in some detail, focusing in particular on unitary additive tasks, when members work with less capable groupmates, and on unitary conjunctive tasks, when they work with more capable groupmates. The former can yield a social compensation effect and the latter a Köhler motivation gain effect. The Köhler motivation gain effect in particular is likely to translate into genuine synergistic performance gains at the group level. Further, the conjunctiveness inherent in many tasks with subtasks suggests that Köhler-like motivation gains—and the group-level performance gains that attend them—may be more common than is currently surmised.

Finally, the last section of the chapter considered how goal setting can either support or undercut the translation of member motivation gains into synergistic group-level performance gains. Goal-setting can benefit the performance of both individuals and groups as long as the goals that are set for individual members do not conflict with one another or with the goals that are set for the group as a whole. Importantly, individual goals should take into account the full range of contributions that members make to their group's collective product. This is true not only for explicitly-set goals, but also for the implicit goals that members may infer from important situational cues, such as the structure of applicable reward and performance feedback systems.

Twenty years ago, the prospects for motivation-based group perfor-mance gains appeared quite bleak. The scholarly literature was dominated by research demonstrating the untoward impact of social inhibition, social loafing, and free riding in groups. These effects seemed quite compatible with the then-current research highlighting serious problems in other areas of group functioning, such as idea generation, problem solving, and decision making. Even the potential benefits implied by the earlier social facilitation research were eclipsed by this darker view of striving in col-lective performance settings.

The situation has changed dramatically in the past two decades. A growing body of evidence indicates that genuine motivation-based per-formance gains in collective work settings are quite possible. Indeed, some authors have suggested that performance decrements due to such factors as social loafing and free riding may be the exception rather than the rule (e.g., Erez & Somech, 1996). It is premature at this point to draw firm conclusions about the relative prevalence of motivation-based per-formance gains versus losses in groups, as there is yet much to be learned about both. Still, the prospects for synergistic performance gains that are rooted in increased member motivation when working collectively in groups seem much brighter now than they once did.

An important direction for the future in the search for synergy would seem to be the use of more complex—and arguably more realistic—group tasks, especially tasks with subtasks that vary in their interdependence. This can potentially teach us how different forms of subtask interdepen-dence impact member motivation and group performance. Additionally, more needs to be learned about the time course of various motivational phenomena. A very large percentage of the research concerned with moti-vation in groups has focused on tasks that last for no more that a few minutes. In the real world, of course, group tasks frequently last for con-siderably longer, often spanning days and weeks. Any serious attempt to predict synergistic performance gains in the real world will require that we begin to understand how collective motivational phenomena play out over these longer intervals.

☐ Endnotes

1. In the case of geographically dispersed groups that work collaboratively but interact electronically, the members are "virtually" in the presence of one another. There are undoubtedly important differences between such groups and groups that interact face-to-face (Baltes, Dickson, Sherman, Bauer, &

LaGanke, 2002; Hollingshead, 2004; Martins, Gilson, & Maynard, 2004; but see also Aiello & Douthitt, 2001; Dashiell, 1935). I do not address such differences here, however. Instead, I focus exclusively on groups whose members are colocated and so are physically present before one another.

2. Triplett (1898) did not present any tests of the statistical significance of the performance differences he reported. This is hardly surprising, as the methods for performing such tests had not yet been invented (e.g., Gosset would not publish his seminal paper on the t-test for another 10 years; Student, 1908). Still, it is interesting to note that a contemporary analysis of Triplett's data reveals rather slim statistical support for the conclusions he drew (Strube, 2005). Stronger support can be found in many of the studies that replicate and extend Triplett's basic procedures. Even so, the magnitude of the effect observed in those subsequent studies was on the whole quite consistent with what Triplett originally observed (e.g., Bond & Titus, 1983).

3. This, despite the fact that Triplett (1898) clearly labeled his apparatus a "competition machine" (see Figure 8.1).

4. Allport strove to eliminate competition as an alternative explanation in his own social facilitation research by explicitly instructing study participants not to compare themselves with one another, even when working side-by-side at the same table (Allport, 1920). The efficacy of this approach was questioned even by Allport's contemporaries (e.g., Williamson, 1926), and by today's standards it seems quite naïve. It is highly doubtful that such instructions can in fact eliminate the kinds of informal competition that often arises between individuals. It is partly for this reason that many researchers began to consider audience effects in social facilitation terms (see below).

5. For more comprehensive treatments, see Aiello and Douthitt (2001) and Guerin (1993).

6. Not only are audience conditions easier to implement (e.g., the experimenter can easily serve that function), they eliminate such confounding factors as competition and cueing effects.

7. In both cases, that product is movement of an object through space. Specifically, it is movement of the flag sewn into the child's own silk band on Triplett's apparatus, and it is movement of the swimmer's own body through the water in a swimming race.

8. Although his published report did not appear until 1913, Ringelmann's research was actually conducted between 1882 and 1887 (Kravitz & Martin, 1986), thus pre-dating Triplett's (1898) social facilitation research by a decade.

9. This is not to say, however, that coordination difficulties and motivational problems are completely independent of one another. On the contrary, there is evidence that when group members expect to have coordination problems for technical reasons, their motivation to contribute to the group declines (e.g., Larson & Schaumann, 1993). Thus, coordination difficulties can negatively impact group performance both directly and indirectly (i.e., via motivation loss).

10. It should be noted that in most cases these have all been relatively easy or well-practiced tasks. Thus, they are tasks that, under coactive (or audience) conditions, would be expected to yield a social facilitation effect. The

possibility that both facilitation and inhibition effects might be observed on the same task, depending on how the work is organized (i.e., as coaction vs. collective action), is taken up below (see pp. 278–281).

11. The term *social loafing* has often been applied more broadly to refer to any sort of motivation decline that occurs when shifting from either individual or coactive performance to collective performance. Thus, for example, what is defined below as a free-rider effect has often been labeled social loafing. However, there is value to maintaining the distinction between these labels, using the term social loafing to refer to motivation loss in groups that is attributable to a lack of identifiability and so the potential for evaluation, while using the term *free riding* to refer to motivation loss in groups that is attributable to a felt dispensability of one's contributions (cf. Harkins, 1997).

12. I use "social facilitation" here in the narrow sense of improved performance resulting from the presence of others. I do not mean it in the broader sense used previously, which also includes social inhibition effects.

13. Unfortunately, the precise magnitude of this motivation gain is difficult to gauge from Köhler's (1926) data. This is because he compared the participants' collective performance to the average of their individual performances, rather than to the individual performance of just their weakest member. By definition, the solo performance of the weakest member must have been less than that average. Consequently, the actual performance gain attributable to the weakest member's enhanced motivation in the collective condition must have been greater than what is reported here, but how much greater is not known. For the same reason, it is difficult to say whether the difference reported here between the dyadic and triadic conditions is indicative of a smaller motivation gain in the latter condition relative to the former.

14. That the lead rider must contend with the wind to a much greater extent than do his or her following teammates speaks to an important difference in the stimulus complex they face. Additionally, the lead rider has primary navigational responsibility for the team. This includes avoiding pedestrians, potholes, and other hazards in the road. Those riding behind, by contrast, do not have to deal with navigational matters beyond following the leader's every move as closely and as precisely as possible. These goal differences, along with differences in the stimulus complex, clearly indicate that riding as a team is a task with distinct subtasks.

15. The specificity of a goal should not be confused with its relative position within a hierarchy of goals. See Chapter 2 (pp. 32–33) for a discussion of the latter.

16. That assigned goals often yield better group performance than self-set goals is likely due to the fact that the goals groups set for themselves tend to be less challenging than the goals that are assigned to them (e.g., Hinsz, 1995; but see Wegge & Haslam, 2005).

Group Composition

The Impact of Diversity Within Groups

This chapter deals with a set of topics that cut across many of those addressed previously. It is concerned with the characteristics of group members, and in particular with how the distribution of member characteristics impacts group performance. The central question to be tackled is whether a group's performance is helped or hindered by diversity among its members. Is a group more effective when all of its members are similar to one another, or is there value in variety? As will be seen, this is not a simple question to answer. In this chapter, I synthesize the main themes in the literature concerned with diversity and performance in small groups and suggest how diversity among members is apt to factor into the search for synergy. I also introduce, by means of a detailed example given in the last section of the chapter, a computational approach to modeling the impact of certain types of diversity on group performance. This approach is well suited for capturing the complex dynamics of group interaction and, thereby, the performance gains those interactions may sometimes yield.

Before proceeding, I should make clear that, although this chapter is fundamentally about the composition of task performing groups, there are many compositional issues that are not addressed. Group size, staffing levels, and the average standing of group members on particular variables are three examples. I ignore these not because they are uninteresting or have no bearing at all on group performance, but because they seem less likely to shed light on the question of synergy in groups. A case in point is the average cognitive ability of group members. There is good evidence that a group's performance is related to the mean cognitive ability of its members; the higher their average cognitive ability score, the better their collective performance. This effect holds across a wide range of tasks and is mediated by such factors as group learning and the development of shared mental models (e.g., Day et al., 2004, 2005; Devine & Philips; 2001; Edwards, Day, Arthur, & Bell, 2006; Ellis et al., 2003). However, effects like this reveal relatively little about what might be occurring during group interaction. As argued in Chapter 1, synergy is an emergent phenomenon rooted in the interactions of group members as they perform their task together. To the extent that synergy is manifest at all in a particular group's performance, it is more apt to be conditioned on the way variables are distributed across members than on the central tendency of those variables. Measures of dispersion and variability are inherently relational and so quite naturally lead us to focus on the group's internal dynamics and interaction processes. As such, the study of diversity, more than the study of average member characteristics, has the potential to illuminate factors that either promote or inhibit the emergence of synergy within groups.

☐ The (Relative) Scarcity of Diversity

To put the study of diversity in perspective, it is useful to begin by noting that diversity within small groups is more the exception than the rule. Naturally occurring groups are more readily distinguished by their homogeneity than by their heterogeneity. Specifically, groups tend to be more homogeneous than would be expected on the basis of the distribution of individuals in the population from which their members are drawn (e.g., Lazarsfeld & Merton, 1954; Ruef, 2002; Ruef, Aldrich, & Carter, 2003). Or, to put it in statistical terms, within-group variance tends to be smaller than between-group variance, where "group" refers to interacting task-performing groups, not merely to collections of individuals who have been treated in a similar way.

That there might be less variance within than between groups is hardly surprising when the focus is on certain task-relevant attributes. Professional basketball teams, for example, are populated by uniformly tall players, and the members of software engineering teams typically possess very similar programming skills. What is perhaps more surprising is that there also tends to be less within- than between-group variance on such factors as member age, race, and personality, variables that in most cases have little to do with performing the group's task. Smaller within- than between-group variability on such characteristics exists despite the fact that people today are more socially and physically mobile then ever before, despite technological advances that enable us to accomplish collaborative tasks more easily with people at great distances, and despite organizational, economic, and political pressures that encourage dissimilar people to work together toward common goals. In spite of all this, it is relative homogeneity, not diversity, that is the norm in groups.

There are both structural and psychological explanations for the relative scarcity of diversity within small groups. These explanations tend to complement rather than compete with one another; each adds something that the others do not. I briefly outline three of these explanations in the paragraphs that follow.

Selective Exposure

First, from a sociological perspective, homogeneity within groups can be explained in part by the selective contact that groups have with prospective members. Groups frequently attract new recruits through the social networks of their existing members. This is perhaps more prevalent among informal groups than groups embedded within formal work organizations, but even in organizational contexts social networks are an important conduit through which new members are acquired (e.g., Barber, Wesson, Roberson, & Taylor, 1999; Brown & Konrad, 2001; Granovetter, 1973; Leung, 2003). When the opportunity arises, existing members approach and recommend people from their social network for inclusion in their group and are an important channel through which prospective members become aware of and learn about the group.

A pervasive characteristic of social networks is that they demonstrate substantial homophily; on a host of dimensions, friends and acquaintances tend to be more similar to one another than strangers are (e.g., McPherson, Smith-Lovin, & Cook, 2001). Consequently, to the extent that groups rely on the social networks of their members as a source of new recruits, the recruits they attract will reflect the collective homogeneity of those social networks. Conversely, to the degree that people rely on their social networks for information about the groups they might join, the groups they will find most visible and accessible will be those whose existing members are relatively similar to them.

In short, a sociological perspective suggests that small groups tend to be more homogeneous than would be expected by chance, partly because the social networks in which their members are enmeshed are themselves more homogeneous than would be expected by chance. This implies a pattern of selective exposure and opportunity; those who are similar to the group's current members have the greatest exposure to the group and so the greatest opportunity for membership.

The Attraction–Selection–Attrition (ASA) Model

Selective exposure is not the only factor contributing to the relative homogeneity of small groups. There also appear to be motivational reasons why group composition is characterized more by homogeneity than by diversity. Some of these are captured in the attraction–selection–attrition (ASA) model proposed by Schneider and his colleagues (1987; Schneider & Smith, 2004; Schneider, Smith, & Paul, 2001).

Schneider (1987) introduced the ASA model to explain the composition of whole organizations and, in particular, the type of persons found in an organization's senior management ranks. This work is relevant to the present discussion because the basic ideas apply equally well at the small group level of analysis (e.g., George, 1990; Wageman & Gordon, 2005).[1] Schneider argues that organizations can be differentiated one from another on the basis of the personalities of their founders and senior managers. Specifically, he suggested that an organization's top managers tend to be similar to one another in personality and different from their peers in other organizations. Thus, it should be possible to characterize every organization in terms of its own unique personality profile—a profile that reflects the most prevalent attributes of its senior personnel. It is the common personality of these managers that, according to Schneider, ultimately determines the nature of the organization, its structure, processes, and culture. This homogeneity of personality is presumed to come about as the result of a three-layered process of attraction, selection, and attrition.

First, Schneider (1987) argued that people are attracted to particular careers and organizations as a function of their values, interests, and personalities. People with similar values, interests, and personalities tend to be drawn to the same organizations, while those with different values, interests, and personalities tend to be drawn to different organizations. This should be true as well at the level of the small group. When considering the various groups they might join, people evaluate the degree to which those groups fit their values, interests, and personalities and are most strongly attracted to the ones that appear to fit best (cf. Chapman, Uggerslev, Carroll, Piasentin, & Jones, 2005). If it can be assumed that similar people evaluate fit in similar ways, then the result should be an initial restriction of range in the type of people who are interested in gaining entrance into any particular group.

Second, Schneider (1987) argued that the personnel selection decisions made by an organization are similarly driven by perceptions of fit. Individuals who are selected for inclusion in the organization (i.e., hired) must not only have the skills require to perform their job (person–task fit), they must also have a set of values and a personality that fits the organization's culture (person–organization fit). Similarly, at the small group level, given two prospective members who are equally qualified on technical grounds, there is apt to be a consistent preference for selecting the one whose values and personality seems best to fit in with the rest of the group. Or, as novelist Tom Wolfe might put it, groups seek members who have "the right stuff." Thus, the already-restricted range of values, interests, and personalities represented in the pool of individuals who are attracted to the group is apt to be narrowed further by the selection process. This should be especially true to the extent that (a) the group's current members have a strong, shared sense of what the ideal member personality is, (b) more of them must agree on an applicant before he or she is admitted, and (c) the group is able to be highly selective, admitting only a small fraction of those who might be interested in joining (cf. Dalessio & Imada, 1984; Platt, 1992).

Finally, the attraction and selection processes are not presumed to result in a perfect fit all of the time. Rather, there are apt to be cases in which, after joining an organization or small group, a new member comes to recognize that the fit with his or her values, interests, and/or personality is less than what was hoped for. Schneider (1987) argued that those who do not fit well will leave, a prediction supported by empirical observation both with respect to person-organization fit and person-group fit (e.g., Arthur, Bell, Villado, & Doverspike, 2006; Hoffman, & Woehr, 2006; Kristof-Brown, Zimmerman, & Johnson, 2005; see also Hart & Van Vugt, 2006). The result is that those who remain will be even more homogeneous than the attraction and selection processes alone would imply, and much more homogeneous than would be expected by chance, given the range of values, interests, and personalities found in the population at large.

The Moreland and Levine Model

Moreland and Levine (1982, 1992, 2003) have also proposed a model that can explain homogeneity within groups. In certain respects, theirs is much like Schneider's (1987) ASA model. For example, like the ASA model, Moreland and Levine explain group homogeneity by psychological processes at play as groups acquire and lose members. Further, and also like the ASA model, a central component of the Moreland and Levine model is evaluation; individuals and groups are both presumed to be constantly evaluating one another. However, whereas this evaluation process is framed in the ASA model in terms of the perceived fit between individuals and groups with respect to values, interests, and personality, Moreland and Levine frame it more broadly in terms of the perceived "rewardingness" of the individual–group relationship. For the individual, rewardingness is simply the extent to which the group is able to satisfy his or her personal needs. For the group, it is the extent to which the individual is able to help the group achieve its goals. Thus, a prospective member will estimate how rewarding membership in the group is apt to be, and the group will estimate how rewarding it is likely to be to have that individual as a member. According to Moreland and Levine, the outcomes of these evaluations determine the commitment that the individual and group feel toward one another. Positive evaluations boost commitment, whereas negative evaluations diminish it. Finally, the rise or fall of this mutual commitment impacts the role transitions that members make. Importantly, when a prospective member's commitment to the group, and the group's commitment to the prospective member, rises beyond a certain threshold value, the prospective member transitions to the role of new member and so begins to partake in the group's activities.

Quite unlike the ASA model, however, Moreland and Levine (1982) emphasize that, once membership has been attained, both the member and the group become active in trying to maximize the rewardingness of their relationship. For its part, the group will try to shape the behavior of its new member in order to improve his or her value to the group. This includes bringing pressure to bear on him or her to conform to the group's norms. In a word, the group will attempt to socialize its new member. Conversely, the new member will attempt to shape the behavior of the group, and to gain accommodations from it, in order to make membership maximally satisfying to him or her. To the extent that each party is successful in shaping the behavior of the other, the perceived rewardingness of the individual's membership in the group will rise further.[2] This will result in even stronger mutual commitment and ultimately allow the new member to transition to the role of full member. On the other hand, the perceived rewardingness of the relationship is apt to fall if the desired degree of socialization (of the individual) and/or accommodation (by the group) is not achieved. To the extent this occurs, the mutual commitment of the two parties to one another will also fall, with the result that instead of transitioning to the role of full member, the individual is apt to leave the group and seek rewards elsewhere (i.e., he or she will transition to the role of past member).

Based on this model, Moreland and Levine (2003) argue that homogeneity within groups occurs for three reasons. First, perceived similarity between prospective members and the group should lead to expectations of greater rewardingness. Consequently, recruits who perceive themselves to be similar to the group should be more committed to joining than those who perceive themselves to be dissimilar, and groups should be more committed to admitting recruits they perceive to be similar rather than dissimilar. Second, during the socialization process, pressure is brought to bear on new members to conform to the rest of the group. To the extent this effort is successful, the group will be more homogeneous, at least behaviorally. Finally, those who do not conform sufficiently will find the group less rewarding and so are more apt to leave. This should increase the homogeneity of those who remain, not only with respect to their behavior, but also with respect to their values, interests, and personality, just as the ASA model predicts. This latter prediction is a straightforward derivation if one considers that values, interests, and personality exert a strong influence on behavior that can be very resistant to change. If so, then it is precisely those members who stand out from the rest of the group in terms of their values, interests, and personality who are also likely to be the most different behaviorally. These members are the ones who are apt to be most consistently targeted for socialization, but they may also be the ones least likely to conform. Consequently, it can be predicted that those members who are most different from the rest of the group in terms of their values, interests, and personality will be the ones most likely to leave because they perceive the group to be less rewarding than anticipated.

Summary

The natural history of small groups appears to be marked by a consistent press toward homogeneity. This arises in part out of the ecology of small groups—specifically, the homophilious social networks from which groups draw their members. But it also arises from the motivation of people to seek situations that suit them personally. These are situations that mesh with their values, interests, and personality and so are rewarding for them. These structural and psychological factors conspire to make small groups more homogeneous than would otherwise be expected.

But, of course, the scarcity of diversity in small groups is relative. No one would argue that small groups tend to be homogeneous in any absolute sense. At the very least, the unavailability of better alternatives is apt to prevent some members from leaving voluntarily even when they perceive that they do not fit well. Similar considerations may prevent the group from pushing such members out. And even when better alternatives do exist, the costs associated with membership change can sometimes be substantially more than the costs of maintaining the status quo. Thus, the consistent pressure toward homogeneity notwithstanding, the membership of small groups often remains diverse, at least to a degree. The question, then, is what impact does this lingering diversity have on groups? In particular, what effect does it have on their task performance? It is the literature bearing on this question that I consider next.

☐ Diversity and Group Performance

Groups can be diverse in many different ways, and different types of diversity can have different effects. In order to understand how diversity impacts group task performance, it is therefore necessary to be specific about the kind of diversity in question. It is also necessary to be specific about the nature of the group's task, as the impact of diversity on group performance cannot be understood apart from the task being performed. Thus, I discuss below several different types of diversity as they relate to performance on several different types of group tasks. To help organize this discussion, I begin by presenting an overarching model of diversity effects in small groups.

A General Framework

In the broadest sense, diversity within small groups refers to variation among members on any attribute that can be used to differentiate people, whether innate or acquired. Most commonly, we think of diversity in terms of demographic variables, such as age, race, gender, religion, and ethnic or national background. When the focus is on groups in organizations, it is also customary to consider the degree to which members vary on such factors as educational and functional background (e.g., finance vs. marketing vs. engineering), tenure in the group or organization, and organizational status. Differences among members on most of these characteristics are either readily observable or easily learned. For example, the gender composition of a group will be apparent to all as soon as that group meets face-to-face for the first time. Less easily seen are differences among members on such attributes as personality, values, attitudes, knowledge, skills, abilities, beliefs, assumptions, and perspectives. In contrast to the highly visible demographic variables, differences on these latter characteristics often become evident to group members only with extended interaction, and in some cases may go completely undetected. Variation on these harder-to-observe characteristics has been referred to as *deep-level diversity*. This stands in contrast to *surface-level diversity*, which is variation on the more easily observed demographic variables (Harrison, Price, & Bell, 1998; Harrison, Price, Gavin, & Florey, 2002; Pelled, 1996).

The distinction between deep and surface-level diversity is a useful one, as diversity at these two levels tends to impact group performance in rather different ways. Deep diversity, compared to surface-level diversity, implies differences among members that exist at a level more nearly commensurate with that of the underlying demands of their group task. Recall from Chapter 1 (see pp. 15–18) that task demands refer to the resources that members must possess in order to complete their group assignment (e.g., their knowledge, skills, and abilities) and how those resources must be applied in order to achieve the best possible outcome. Thus, deep diversity denotes differences among members that have at least the potential to affect group performance in a rather direct manner.

Surface-level diversity, by contrast, very rarely involves differences that relate in a truly direct way to the demands of the group's task. Rather, to the extent that surface-level diversity impacts group performance at all, it almost always does so indirectly. One obvious possibility is that surface-level diversity might affect performance through its association with diversity at a deeper, task-relevant level. An example is when differences in age or professional background predict underlying differences in skill or perspective that somehow are important for accomplishing the task at hand. Via this route, the effect of surface-level diversity can be either positive, negative, or nil, depending on whether the corresponding deep-level diversity is beneficial, harmful, or irrelevant to the group's task performance, respectively. Alternatively, surface-level diversity might affect performance through its impact on the group's social integration—roughly, the quality of the members' interpersonal relationships with one another. An example is when differences in age or professional background make it hard for members to relate to one another, thereby increasing the likelihood of poor communication, misunderstanding, and interpersonal friction. Via this route, the impact of surface-level diversity on group performance is apt to be either negative or nil (but not positive), depending on the amount of interpersonal friction actually generated and on the degree to which such friction interferes with task performance. The reason why surface-level diversity is not expected to have a positive effect on group performance via this second route is because it seldom benefits social integration, a conclusion anticipated by our earlier discussion of group homogeneity and the associated tendency of members to leave groups that do not fit them well (e.g., Moreland & Levine, 2003; Schneider, 1987).

These various effects of surface- and deep-level diversity are represented graphically in Figure 9.1. As can be seen, whereas deep diversity among members is predicted to have both direct and indirect effects on group task performance, surface-level diversity is predicted to have only indirect effects. I discuss each of these effects in greater detail in the following sections.

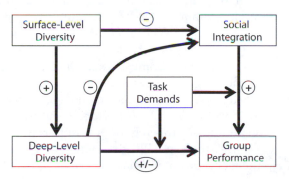

FIGURE 9.1   A general model of the impact of surface- and deep-level diversity on social integration and group performance.

Deep Diversity

Consider first the impact of deep diversity. As suggested, deep diversity has the potential to affect group performance in a rather direct way. Sometimes that effect will be positive and sometimes it will be negative, depending both on the specific dimension of diversity in question and on the nature of the group's task. Further, certain types of deep diversity are apt to affect group performance indirectly through their impact on social integration. This indirect effect may be either in addition to or instead of a direct effect.

Skill, Ability, and Informational Diversity

Diversity with respect to members' skills and abilities can mean an increased range of available member resources.[3] Holding constant the number of skills possessed by any one person, a group whose members each possess a different (though perhaps overlapping) set of skills collectively has more resources at its disposal than does a group whose members each command exactly the same skills. If those various skills are all germane to performing the task at hand, then we might expect better performance from the former, deeply diverse group than from the latter, deeply homogeneous group.

A diversity of task-relevant skills should be beneficial, for example, when the group's task is divisible. Recall from Chapter 2 (see pp. 61–62) that a divisible task is one that can be broken down into two or more subtasks that require different skills and abilities, and that can be performed by different group members. On such tasks it is not necessary that every member be able to perform all of the subtasks. It is necessary only that each subtask be performed by someone in the group. Such tasks can be conceptualized as allowing certain skills—those that are uniquely associated with the individual subtasks—to be distributed among members, as opposed to being duplicated in every member. In other words, they permit skill diversity within the group, which, as a practical matter, is often much easier to achieve than skill homogeneity. Of course, when members have diverse skills, the assignment of members to subtasks becomes critical. The group will succeed on the task as a whole only to the extent that its members perform those subtasks for which they do in fact have the requisite skills and abilities. In this regard, it is important for members to recognize whatever task-relevant skill diversity may exist among them, as this will help them choose an optimal pattern of subtask assignments. It is this recognition of deep, task-related diversity that is at the heart of the tacit coordination and transactive memory processes discussed in Chapter 7 (see pp. 241–244).

A diversity of task-relevant skills can also be beneficial when the group performs certain types of unitary tasks. Unlike divisible tasks, unitary tasks cannot be meaningfully subdivided. Even so, unitary tasks vary widely with respect to how member efforts combine to yield a group product and so the degree to which performance is affected by member skill diversity.

Disjunctive unitary tasks are one type that can benefit from skill diversity among members, particularly when several such tasks must be performed by the group. Disjunctive tasks permit just one member's contributions to determine the group's product. A good example is found in the classroom exams taken in courses that use a team-learning approach to instruction. As described in Chapter 2, students usually take course exams twice in team-learning classrooms: first working individually, then again working together in small groups (Michaelsen, Knight, & Fink, 2004). Regarding the latter, if any single member can answer a particular exam item correctly, then the group as a whole should be able to answer it correctly. Thus, like divisible tasks, disjunctive tasks permit skill diversity. It is not necessary that every member have the skill to answer a given item correctly. It is necessary only that one of them have that skill. To the extent that it increases the likelihood that at least one member of the group actually can answer a given item correctly, skill diversity should be beneficial. Indeed, skill diversity is the primary reason why the total test scores achieved by team-learning groups are routinely better than the total test scores attained by their members when taking the same exams as individuals (see Chapter 2, pp. 33–38, for a fuller discussion of this issue).

There are other types of unitary tasks, however, where diversity in member skill and ability it is apt to be a liability. In particular, it should be a liability when the group works on a conjunctive task. In contrast to disjunctive tasks, conjunctive tasks require that all members contribute identically to the group's product. An example is a guitar trio attempting to play the same piece of music together. Each member of this group is expected to play all of the notes and all of the chords in exactly the same order, at exactly the same time, and in exactly the same way. This ensemble will perform the piece well only if every member possesses all of the requisite guitar-playing skills; the group should be homogeneous with respect to those skills. If, on the other hand, different members possess different skills (e.g., one knows all the chords [a left-hand skill] but has trouble with certain fingerpicking patterns [a right-hand skill], whereas another knows all the fingerpicking patterns but has difficulty with certain of the chords), the music they produce together will be less than harmonious. This will be true despite the fact that all of the needed skills might be represented within the group as a whole. Because this task demands that every member contribute identically to the group product, no amount of skill on the part of other group members can compensate for any one member's lack of skill.

For decision-making tasks, a critical resource is decision-relevant information. To the extent that members possess, or have access to, rather different sets of decision-relevant information, the group collectively will have a larger pool of resources to draw upon while making its decision (again, holding constant the amount of information possessed by any one member). It seems reasonable to expect that decisions made in light of a larger pool of information will be better informed and generally superior to decisions based on a smaller pool of information. In many cases, however, this apparent benefit of informational diversity is likely to be offset by the fact that groups have difficulty accessing the unshared (diverse) information that members hold, particularly when they are unaware of one another's special areas of expertise (Stasser, Stewart, & Wittenbaum, 1995; Stasser, Vaughan, & Stewart, 2000; Stewart & Stasser, 1995). As described in Chapter 6 (see pp. 187–206), there is a strong tendency for the content of unstructured group decision-making discussions to be dominated by information that most or all members shared in common prior to discussion, with substantially less attention paid to the diverse, unshared information that members possessed uniquely. Consequently, whereas a diversity of information across group members represents a potentially valuable decision-making resource, groups often have difficulty tapping that resource, with the result that their decision-making performance is often less than optimal.

It will be recalled that a similar sort of issue applies when groups perform idea-generation tasks. As described in Chapter 3 (see pp. 95–101), there is good reason to expect that groups composed of members who are dissimilar (diverse) in their knowledge base should be able to generate a larger number of creative ideas than groups whose members all share the same knowledge base (e.g., Brown, Tumeo, Larey, & Paulus, 1998). At the same time, freely interacting groups are typically plagued by production blocking problems. As a result, even interacting groups whose members are diverse with respect to the knowledge they bring to the task are apt to be less productive than nominal groups whose members work independently (e.g., Diehl, 1992, as cited in Stroebe & Diehl, 1994).

Attitude and Preference Diversity

Although difficult to conceptualize in terms of resources, attitudinal and preference differences among group members are additional forms of deep diversity that become relevant when groups perform decision-making tasks. It has often been suggested that groups that are initially divided in their decision-relevant attitudes and preferences should tend to make better decisions than groups that are homogeneous on these variables (e.g., Simons, Pelled, & Smith, 1999; van Knippenberg, De Dreu, & Homan, 2004). The rationale usually given for this prediction is that such diversity is apt to generate significant task-focused conflict and vigorous debate (e.g., regarding how best to interpret a particular set of facts, what the costs and benefits are of various solution alternatives, etc.). This, in turn, is presumed to lead members to think more carefully and creatively about the issues, surface unstated assumptions and hidden constraints, integrate more of the information available to them, and perhaps uncover new and better solution alternatives. All of this would seem to presage more effective decision making.

However, the research evidence provides little consistent support for this line of reasoning. Indeed, a meta-analytic review of 28 published studies by De Dreu and Weingart (2003) found that task-oriented conflict tends to be negatively, not positively, associated with performance in decision-making groups. Part of the problem is that, in addition to task conflict, attitudinal and opinion diversity also tend to spark substantial interpersonal conflict among members (e.g., De Dreu and Weingart, 2003, found an average correlation of $r = .54$ between measures of task and interpersonal conflict in groups). Interpersonal conflict seems especially likely when the to-be-made decision is strongly judgmental (i.e., close to the right-hand end of Laughlin's intellective–judgmental task continuum; see Chapter 2, pp. 47–49), and when members' divergent attitudes and preferences are tied to deeply seeded personal values. Under these conditions, diversity in member attitudes can generate significant rancor, making a consensus decision hard to achieve. In sum, the negative consequences of interpersonal conflict often override the critical-thinking benefits that diversity-induced task-oriented conflict might otherwise confer. This is one of the reasons for the negative relationship shown in Figure 9.1 between deep-level diversity and social integration. Interpersonal conflict is a hallmark of weak social integration within groups.

Diverse Personalities

Finally, and following up on the previously discussed implications of Schneider's (1987) ASA model, diversity in member personalities may also impact a group's task performance. In most cases, this will be an indirect effect via social integration within the group. Further, the net effect is more apt to be negative than positive. This prediction is consistent with the results of a meta-analytic review by Halfhill, Sundstrom, Lahner, Calderone, & Nielsen (2005). Across 31 studies, they found that greater variance among members' personality traits was typically associated with lower group effectiveness. Building on Schneider's idea that people prefer situations that fit their personality, this result can be understood as suggesting that personality differences imply a lack of fit, promote interpersonal friction, and make it harder for members to work effectively together to accomplish their assigned tasks.

This interpretation should be approached cautiously, however. There are many personality traits, and it seems rather unlikely that diversity functions in the same way for all of them. In particular, it seems possible that diversity on relationship-related traits (e.g., agreeableness, emotional stability, helpfulness) may impact group performance differently than diversity on task-related traits (e.g., conscientiousness, goal orientation). Unfortunately, the review by Halfhill et al. (2005) does not differentiate among different kinds of traits and so does not shed light on this possibility (but see Humphrey, Hollenbeck, Meyer, & Ilgen, 2007). This is an area that merits a great deal more research.

Implications for Synergy

It is deep, task-relevant diversity, rather than surface-level diversity, that most directly affects the prospects for performance gains in small groups. Depending on the task, deep diversity can often be expected to foster modest performance gains, that is, gains within the range defined as weak synergy in groups. Occasionally, deep diversity may foster large gains—strong synergy—but such gains; are apt to be much less common, as the research literature to date clearly attests. And there are many situations in which deep diversity will likely foster no performance gains at all and perhaps even lead to a net process loss.

Evidence of weak synergy in deeply diverse groups should be relatively easy to find on divisible tasks. Here, performance gains should be a function of the explicit decisions that groups make regarding who will perform which subtasks—a planning activity—as well as the implicit decisions their members make about which subtask(s) they personally will devote more attention to. The latter is a tacit coordination process, and depends on a well-developed transactive memory system (see Chapter 7, pp. 244–254). However it is accomplished, pairing members and subtasks in a way that takes into account the diversity of members' skills and abilities should result in better overall group performance than would occur if members and subtasks were paired randomly. A random pairing provides the equivalent of an average-member performance baseline. By contrast, an optimal pairing provides a best-member baseline; each subtask is performed by the member who is best suited for it. Of course, a group can do no better than to achieve an optimal pairing of members and subtasks. Therefore, deep, task-relevant diversity among members is apt to foster no more than weak synergy on divisible tasks. The inherent nature of such tasks would seem to preclude the emergence of strong synergy.

In contrast, strong synergy is at least possible when groups work on unitary tasks that involve idea generation, problem solving, and/or decision making. In each case, task-relevant deep diversity can increase the pool of resources available to the group and so the number of different ways those resources might be combined and applied. Strong synergy should be evident on such tasks to the extent that members are able to utilize their collective resources in ways that no individual could do working along.

But as we saw in earlier chapters, empirical evidence for strong synergy on such tasks is actually quite rare, even when the groups being studied are clearly diverse. Groups often seem unable to access and effectively utilize all of their members' resources. Decision-making groups, for example, routinely surface too little of the diverse (unshared) information that members possess, and idea-generation groups are typically thwarted by production-blocking problems associated with their attempts to avoid simultaneous speech. Even on problem-solving tasks, the modal finding is one of performance gains within the range of weak, not strong, synergy.

Part of the reason why more evidence of strong synergy has not materialized in the literature may be that very few theoretical models have so far been developed that specify precisely how performance gains emerge from group interaction and, in particular, how deep diversity among members promotes such gains. Most of the models to be found in the literature are no more specific than the one shown in Figure 9.1, which, of course, hardly deals with group interaction at all. Two notable exceptions, both of which concern idea generation in groups, are the Associative Memory Matrix (AMM) model (Brown, Tumeo, Larey, & Paulus, 1998), and the Search for Ideas in Associative Memory (SIAM) model (Nijstad, Diehl, & Stroebe, 2003; Nijstad & Stroebe, 2006). These were discussed at length in Chapter 3. These models are helpful not only because they suggest the intrapersonal and interactional processes at play when groups perform idea-generation tasks, but also because they specify the diversity conditions that must be met if synergistic performance gains are to be attained by groups. Later in this chapter, I will introduce another equally detailed model that explores the prospects for weak and strong synergy when diverse groups perform problem-solving tasks.

Finally, it should be clear from the foregoing that deep diversity is not always expected to produce a performance gain. For example, it obviously should not benefit performance when the group's task is a conjunctive one. Conjunctive tasks require every member to contribute identically to the group's product and so demand that all members have the same task-relevant skills and abilities. On such tasks, skill diversity should be a significant impediment to effective performance because there is no way for members to compensate for one another's lack of skill. Deep diversity should also be an impediment to performance when it weakens social integration within the group. This can occur both when the type of deep diversity in question is task-relevant (e.g., attitude and preference diversity in decision-making groups) as well as when it is not (e.g., personality diversity). Weak social integration makes it harder for group members to work effectively together and so reduces the likelihood that their performance will show any signs of synergy, weak or strong.

Surface-Level Diversity

In contrast to deep diversity, surface-level diversity involves differences among members that affect group performance only indirectly, if at all. This section considers, in turn, the two indirect paths shown in Figure 9.1: via deep-level diversity, and via social integration within the group.

Via Deep-Level Diversity

Perhaps the most obvious possibility is that surface-level diversity may affect group performance via its link to diversity at a deeper, task-relevant level. Thus, observed differences in age, gender, educational background, or profession might be related to underlying differences in skills, abilities, or perspectives that somehow are important for accomplishing the task at hand. The use of cross-functional teams in organizations is an explicit attempt to capitalize on this idea (Kanter, 1988; Keller, 2001; Williams & O'Reilly, 1998). A cross-functional team is a small group of employees from diverse functional areas (e.g., engineering, operations, marketing, information technology) who are brought together for a limited period of time expressly for the purpose of solving a particular problem or achieving a specific objective. Such teams might be assembled, for example, to evaluate alternative methods of delivering services to their firm's clients, or to investigate a new product or market that their company might exploit. In practice, decisions about the composition of a particular cross-functional team are usually made according to the intuitions of the person or group that creates it, although highly analytical approaches to optimizing team composition have been suggested (e.g., Zakarian & Kusiak, 1999). The expectation when using such teams is that they will generate better and more innovative solutions to problems than would teams with less diverse membership. However, the reasons for this expectation rarely have to do with the diversity of the members' organizational affiliations per se. Rather, they lie in the assumption that those diverse affiliations signal a greater range of available task-relevant skills, information, attitudes, and points of view, and that it is the latter deep diversity that actually benefits performance.

In some contexts, and for some types of surface-level diversity, it may be reasonable to assume the existence of a congruent pattern of deep, task-relevant diversity. But it is not always so (e.g., Harrison et al., 2002; Lawrence, 1997). The degree of surface-level diversity that exists among group members often is not a reliable index of the diversity that lies at a deeper level. And even when it is, that deep-level diversity is not necessarily task relevant (cf. Wegge, Roth, Neubach, Schmidt, & Kanfer, 2008). For example, there are apt to be very few tasks for which an increase in either gender or racial diversity can be counted upon to broaden the range of task-related knowledge, skills, or perspectives that group members possess. This does not mean that gender and racial diversity are not linked in a meaningful way to *any* deep-level differences among people. Rather, it simply means that whatever deep-level differences they do imply are likely irrelevant for a very large proportion of the tasks that a group might perform.[4] Consequently, in most cases we should not expect either gender or racial diversity to influence group performance in the same way that, for example, functional-area diversity might when working on certain organizational problems. Indeed, even when the type of surface-level diversity seems quite pertinent, as is often the case for cross-functional teams in organizations, there is still no guarantee that the deep-level diversity it signals will in fact be relevant to the specific tasks the group must perform. The unique knowledge that comes with a background in software engineering (one member) and supply chain management (another member) may be usefully combined when applied to some organizational problems but not to others. Surface-level diversity is usually a matter of broad distinctions among people, whereas deep, task-relevant diversity is always a matter of specifics. As such, it is not surprising that even functional-area diversity within organizations has been shown, across studies, to be inconsistently related to group performance (Webber & Donahue, 2001).

Via Social Integration

The second, and arguably more common, route by which diversity on salient surface-level variables may affect group performance is through its deleterious impact on social integration within the group. Social integration refers to the quality of the interpersonal relationships that exist among group members and to the strength and breath of the psychological bonds that tie members to one another. Social integration is intimately bound up with the level of affective cohesion in the group—strong social integration implies a high level of cohesiveness, whereas weak social integration suggests less cohesiveness. Diversity on salient and meaningful demographic variables can impede social integration within a group by making it more difficult for certain members to establish strong psychological ties with one another. The evolution of this phenomenon can be traced as follows.

When a group is brought together for the first time, its members very quickly, and rather automatically, take stock of the social landscape within which they find themselves. Guided by a strong identity-driven desire to locate their position in social space, members are motivated to create a mental map of the group that identifies the important relationships among its members. At first, this will be largely a matter of perceptually partitioning the group into meaningful subgroups on the basis of readily observable demographic characteristics. That is, in the absence of other useful information, members can begin to understand the group as a whole, and their place in it, by analyzing its demographic structure. For example, a professor who is appointed to a university committee on campus safety is apt to recognize at the very start of the committee's first meeting that she is one of just three faculty members on the committee of eighteen, that the two numerically dominant subgroups are administrators and students, that women out-number men by a three to one margin, and that among the faculty, two, including herself, are substantially older than the third. In other words, as a first step toward understanding this group, the professor might categorize its members on the basis of university status (faculty vs. administrator vs. student), gender, and age. That these particular variables, rather than other possibilities, might be used as the basis for subdividing the group has to do with their relative visibility, their likely centrality to the professor's own self-identity, and their capacity for yielding a set of categories that minimize the observable differences between members within the same category while simultaneously maximizing the observable differences between members of different categories (cf. Turner & Haslam, 2001; Turner & Oakes, 1989). The presence of meaningful surface-level diversity within the group greatly facilitates this process, simply because it provides one or more ready bases for categorization.

Once accomplished, the resulting categorization of members has several rather immediate consequences. First and foremost, it suggests the subgroup to which each member most clearly "belongs." In the example above, the professor is apt to think of herself not merely as a member of the campus safety committee, but as one of the three faculty members on the committee, or perhaps more narrowly as one of its two older faculty members.[5] The category to which the faculty member perceives she belongs defines her *ingroup*. This stands in contrast to those *outgroups* (administrators and students) to which she perceives she does not belong.[6]

Second, there is a tendency for members to perceptually assimilate others toward their respective subgroup prototypes (Hogg, 2003). That is, having categorized members in such a way as to minimize easily observed within-category differences and maximize easily observed between-category differences, there is a further propensity for members to assume a correspondent pattern of underlying homogeneity within these sub-groups on a host of variables that are more difficult to observe. This is true with respect to both ingroups and outgroups. Thus, members tend to presume that others within their ingroup are generally similar to them in their attitudes, beliefs, preferences, and experiences, and to assume that the members of identifiable outgroups are both different from the ingroup on these variables and similar to one another (e.g., Brewer, 1979; Chen & Kenrick, 2002; Dasgupta, Banaji, Abelson, 1999; Wilder, 1984; Yzerbyt, Judd, & Corneille, 2004).

Third, as a result of the perceived similarity of ingroup members, and the perceived dissimilarity of outgroup members, there is a tendency for stronger interpersonal affinities to develop among members within rather than between subgroups. That is, members are more apt to be attracted to, and establish positive affective bonds with, other ingroup members than with outgroup members (cf. Byrne, 1971; Chen & Kenrick, 2002; Rosenbaum, 1986). These bonds predisposes them to have relatively open, cooperative, trusting relations in their dealings with ingroup members, while approaching outgroup interactions with greater reserve and circum-spection. As a consequence, outgroup interactions are more prone to be sources of interpersonal friction and tension than ingroup interactions.

Surface-level diversity should thus be an impediment to social inte-gration within the group as a whole to the extent that it leads members to perceive and treat more of their groupmates as outgroup members. The more salient and socially significant the surface-level differences are among members, the easier it is for outgroup perceptions—and the frac-tious interactions that sometimes attend them—to develop. Consistent with this, surface-level diversity has been shown in numerous field stud-ies to be associated with multiple indicators of weak social integration, including greater interpersonal conflict, less effective communication, less cohesiveness and commitment to the group, and less stable group membership (e.g., Harrison, et al, 2002; Jehn, Northcraft, & Neale, 1999; Mesmer-Magnus & DeChurch, 2009; O'Reilly, Caldwell, & Barnett, 1989; Pelled, Eisenhardt, & Xin, 1999; Smith et al., 1994; Tsui, Egan, & O'Reilly, 1992).

Faultlines: Correlated Versus Crosscutting Diversity

Surface-level diversity often exists with respect to multiple demographic variables simultaneously. When this happens, the relationship among these variables can affect their joint impact on the group. Consider, for example, a four-person group comprising two men and two women. Add to this gender diversity a difference with respect to nationality: Two mem-bers are German and two are Canadian. These two demographic variables, gender and nationality, might either be perfectly correlated or completely crosscut one another. They would be perfectly correlated if the two men were German and the two women Canadian (or vice versa), and would crosscut one another if one person of each gender were German and the other Canadian. The key difference between these two situations is that in the correlated diversity example there is little ambiguity about how members are likely to be perceptually categorized; members will fall into the same subgroups regardless of whether they are categorized on the basis of gender or nationality. Thus, diversity on multiple, correlated demographic variables should encourage rather stable perceptions of others as either ingroup or outgroup members, because it creates stronger perceptual faultlines within the group. By contrast, when the various dimensions of diversity crosscut one another, someone who is perceived as an outgroup member with respect to one variable might be perceived as an ingroup member with respect to another. Consequently, the perceived composition of both the ingroup and outgroup depends on which dimension of diversity is being considered at the moment. If the two dimensions are about equally salient, it should be relatively easy for members to switch back and forth between alternative categorization schemes, with no one scheme gaining the perceptual dominance that it might have attained had there been just one source of surface-level diversity within the group. Crosscutting demographics should thus discourage the development of stable ingroup-outgroup perceptions (Brewer & Gaertner, 2003).

Based on such considerations, it has been suggested that multiple dimensions of surface-level diversity should pose less of an impediment to social integration the less strongly correlated those dimensions are within a group (Lau & Murninghan, 1998). Empirical evidence in support of this hypothesis comes mainly from field studies (e.g., Bezrukova, Thatcher, & Jehn, 2007; Li & Hambrick, 2005; Molleman, 2005; but see also Lau & Murninghan, 2005; Thatcher, Jehn, & Zanutto, 2003). One of the few laboratory experiments to test this idea is a study by Sawyer, Houlette, and Yeagley (2006). They examined the impact on decision-making groups of being diverse with respect to both job function and race. In one experimental condition these variables crosscut one another (crosscutting-diversity condition). In another condition they were correlated (correlated-diversity condition). And in a third experimental condition groups were diverse with respect to job function alone (single-diversity-dimension condition). Evidence derived from both behavioral and self-report measures suggests that social integration was significantly stronger in the crosscutting-diversity condition than in either the correlated-diversity or the single-diversity-dimension conditions, with the latter two not differing from one another. These results presumably occurred because a crosscutting pattern of diversity discourages the development of stable ingroup-outgroup perceptions relative to what happens when there is either a correlated pattern of diversity or when there is diversity on just one salient surface-level dimension.

Time, Interaction, and Social Integration

Figure 9.1 is overly simplistic in that it does not directly take into account the effect of interaction among members on the development of social integration within the group. It seems reasonable, however, that social integration should depend in part on the degree to which members find actually working together to be mutually rewarding (cf. Moreland & Levine, 1982, 2003). As members work together, they gradually gain personalized information about one another, are exposed to a growing sample of one another's behavior, and accumulate a history of interactions that can be evaluated for their rewardingness. To the extent this history reflects mostly satisfying experiences, social integration should improve. It should not improve, however, when that history is marked by numerous dissatisfying experiences.

Extending this line of reasoning, Harrison and his colleagues (Harrison et al., 1998, 2002) suggest that, over time, surface-level diversity should gradually become less important as a determinant of social integration within the group, and deep-level diversity should gradually become more important. They found support for this idea in an investigation of 144 student project teams that worked on course assignments lasting 9 to 14 weeks. Diversity within each team was assessed with respect to both sur-face-level (age, gender, race/ethnicity, and marital status) and deep-level variables (conscientiousness, values, and task attitudes). As expected, the negative impact of surface-level diversity on social integration was lower in teams that interacted with one another more frequently (e.g., held more frequent team meetings), whereas in those same teams the negative impact of deep-level diversity was stronger (see also Sacco & Schmitt, 2005; Watson, Kumar, & Michaelsen, 1993; Zellmer-Bruhn, Maloney, Bhappu, & Salvador, 2008).

The rate at which the impact of surface-level diversity diminishes over time, and the impact of deep-level diversity intensifies, is likely to depend on several factors. One is the nature of the group's task. Tasks that are very stressful and that demand a high level of tightly coordinated inter-action among members create more opportunities for interpersonal fric-tion. When performing such tasks, the effects of surface-level diversity on social integration are apt to diminish more slowly, and the effects of deep diversity to intensify more quickly (cf. Jehn et al., 1999; Pelled et al., 1999). It also seems likely that the negative effects of surface-level diversity will diminish more slowly when that diversity involves multiple, correlated dimensions compared to when it involves only crosscutting dimensions.

Surface-Level Diversity and Group Performance

To the extent that surface-level diversity hampers social integration within a group, it also has the potential to damage the group's collective performance. Weak social integration encourages miscommunication, misunderstanding, and poor coordination and makes it harder for the group to recruit a high level of member effort. All of this threatens the group's ability to work together effectively. This is exactly what was found, for example, in the previously discussed experiment by Sawyer et al. (2006). The groups in that study performed a decision-making task where, prior to discussion, the decision-relevant information provided by the experimenter was distributed among members so as to create a hidden profile; members could not all appreciate the superiority of the objectively best alternative based on just the information in their reading packets. Rather, to perceive the superiority of that alternative, it was necessary for them to exchange their uniquely held information during discussion. (Recall that hidden profiles were discussed at length in Chapter 6; see especially pp. 178–187). Groups that displayed the weakest social integration were also least able to make use of one another's unique information and so least likely to choose the decision alternative that was objectively best. Specifically, whereas groups in the crosscutting-diversity condition chose the correct decision alternative 68% of the time, those in the correlated-diversity and in the single-diversity-dimension conditions chose correctly only 35% and 33% of the time, respectively.

It is unlikely, however, that surface-level diversity is always harmful to group performance, even when it demonstrably affects social integration. Rather, whether or not surface-level diversity leads to poorer performance should depend at least in part on the nature of the group's task. Surface-level diversity is most likely to impact performance when the group's task involves a high degree of member interdependence (because high interdependence implies a greater need for effective communication and closely coordinated action) and when it is very difficult or complex (because such tasks demand a greater commitment of effort by members). Conversely, surface-level diversity is least likely to impact performance when the group's task involves very little member interdependence or is relatively easy (Beal, Cohen, Burke, & McLendon, 2003; De Dreu & Weingart, 2003; Gully, Devine, & Whitney, 1995).

The moderating role of task type is clearly demonstrated in an interesting archival study by Timmerman (2000). He examined the effects of both age and racial diversity on the performance of professional basketball and baseball teams. Professional sports teams provide a unique opportunity to study the performance of real groups in their natural environment, as these are groups for which a wealth of objective performance information is publicly available. The sports of basketball and baseball are of particular interest because they differ rather markedly in the degree to which players are interdependent and so the level of coordination that is required in order for the team as a whole to perform well (Keidell, 1987). Specifically, basketball involves substantially greater player interdependence than does baseball and so demands far more coordinated interaction. A player's ability to score when shooting from the floor in the game of basketball, for example, depends not only on his or her receiving the ball at just the right moment, but also on the synchronized movements of his or her teammates to thwart the defensive action of the opposing team. By contrast, a batter's ability to hit safely in the game of baseball depends very little on what his or her teammates are doing at the moment. Thus, it is not surprising that team performance is less strongly predicted by individual player ability in the game of basketball than in baseball (Jones, 1974). Success in basketball depends more heavily on tightly coordinated player interaction.

Timmerman (2000) made use of these facts to examine the moderating role of task coordination requirements on the relationship between racial and age diversity, on the one hand, and team performance on the other. He analyzed the performance of all National Basketball Association and Major League Baseball teams that played in the U.S. between 1950 and 1997. Teams and team performance were defined by year (e.g., the Chicago Cubs fielded 48 different baseball teams during that period, with the performance of each defined by their win/loss record at the end of one regular season). This resulted in a total sample size of 871 basketball teams and 1,023 baseball teams. Timmerman found that, after controlling for the effects of mean age and ability, measures of player age and racial diversity were both significantly and negatively correlated with basketball team performance. By contrast, neither diversity measure was a significant predictor of baseball team performance.[7] These results are consistent with the idea that whatever interpersonal friction may arise as a product of surface-level diversity within groups, it is more likely to impact performance when the group's task requires closely coordinated action by members. Although Timmerman demonstrated this point with tasks that are highly physical in nature, the same should be true for group tasks that are predominantly mental (De Dreu & Weingart, 2003; van Knippenberg, et al., 2004).

Even when the task requires group members to work closely together, however, it may still sometimes be possible to neutralize, or at least dampen, the negative effect on performance that surface-level diversity might otherwise have via its untoward impact on social integration. It has been shown, for example, that mixed-gender laboratory groups asked to perform a decision-making task with distributed information perform better when they are led to believe that their gender diversity is an asset that can help them succeed (Homan, van Knippenberg, Van Kleef, & De

Dreu, 2007a). Along similar lines, a charismatic or inspirational style of leadership—also called *transformational leadership*—has been found in field settings to be associated with better group performance in research and development teams characterized by substantial nationality and educational specialization diversity (e.g., Kearney & Gebert, 2009; Shin & Zhou, 2007). Still, the fact that surface-level diversity is more commonly found to impede performance suggests that its negative impact via interpersonal friction is not easily managed.

Member Expectations About Surface and Deep Diversity

As suggested previously, surface-level diversity often is not associated with a congruent pattern of diversity at a deep, task-relevant level. Nevertheless, group members may expect such congruence. I have already noted that groupmates who share a common set of surface-level demographic characteristics (i.e., ingroup members) tend to assume that they are also relatively similar to one another in terms of such deep-level attributes as attitudes, beliefs, and experiences, at least in comparison to groupmates who do not share a common set of demographic characteristics (i.e., outgroup members). Consistent with this, members are apt to expect their demographically similar groupmates to have perspectives on the group's task that are similar to their own, while anticipating that demographically dissimilar groupmates will have somewhat different perspectives.

Interestingly, there is evidence that group performance may benefit when such expectations are confirmed. Consider, for example, a study by Phillips (2003). She had groups of university students perform a murder mystery task similar to the one employed by Stasser et al. (1995; see Chapter 6, pp. 201–202). Her participants were recruited from several campus dormitories. During the experiment, steps were taken to heighten the salience of their dormitory affiliations, and so make their campus residence a conspicuous basis for social categorization. For example, when participants first arrived for the experiment, they sat in a separate waiting area specifically designated for those living in their own dormitory, and then throughout the experiment wore color-coded nametags that identified their dormitory. At the beginning of the session, each participant received a packet of information about a fictitious murder (i.e., a list of suspects, witness interviews, a map of the crime scene, etc.). Participants were given 20 minutes to study this information privately and so to form an opinion about which suspect was guilty. They were then assigned to three-person groups, and asked to come to a consensus decision about who committed the crime. The groups were formed on the basis of both the participant's dormitory residence and their pre-discussion opinion about which suspect was guilty. Specifically, every group consisted of two students from one dormitory and one student from another. But groups varied in their opinion composition. In one condition, the two students from the same dormitory agreed with one another about which suspect was guilty and disagreed with the student from the other dormitory. Thus, in this condition the opinion (deep) diversity among members was congruent with their residential (surface) diversity. In a second condition, the two students from the same dormitory disagreed with one another about which suspect was guilty, and one of them agreed with the student from the other dormitory. Here, surface and deep-level diversity were incongruent. Importantly, however, the *degree* of diversity, both surface and deep, was identical in these two conditions.

Phillips (2003) found that after controlling for members' prediscussion opinion accuracy, significantly more groups with a congruent (60%) than incongruent (40%) pattern of diversity identified the correct suspect. Behavioral evidence from the group discussions suggested that this difference occurred because minority opinion holders expressed themselves more forcefully in the congruent than in the incongruent diversity condition. Apparently, the salient residential (surface-level) diversity among members not only triggered expectations for a congruent pattern of opinion (deep) diversity among them, it made members more tolerant of congruent differences of opinion when they emerged. Incongruent differences of opinion, by contrast, were met with surprise and irritation. This likely was uncomfortable for those expressing the incongruent opinions, making them reluctant to present their ideas very energetically.

In addition to opinion diversity, group performance also appears to benefit from a congruent alignment of informational diversity. This was demonstrated in a study by Phillips, Mannix, Neale, & Gruenfeld (2004, Exp. 1). They organized several classes of executive MBA students (students with an average of 10 years work experience) into three-person groups, such that two members in each group knew one another very well (the ingroup members), and neither knew the third member (the outgroup member). As in Phillips (2003), groups were given a murder mystery to solve. Here, however, the 12 critical clues needed to solve the case were divided into two subsets. One subset was given to two of the members, and the other subset was given to the third. In the congruent diversity condition, it was the two ingroup members who were given the same subset of clues, whereas in the incongruent diversity condition one ingroup member and the outgroup member were given the same subset of clues. Although there was no difference between these conditions with respect to the number of clues discussed (62%), the congruent diversity groups appeared to discuss the clues more thoroughly, as evidenced by the fact that they repeated them more often. Further, and again controlling for members' prediscussion opinion accuracy, congruent diversity groups chose the correct suspect 75% of the time, whereas incongruent diversity groups chose correctly only 25% of the time. Thus, with respect to both opinions and information, congruence between surface-level and deep diversity seems to benefit group decision-making performance.

However, even an incongruent pattern of surface- and deep-level diversity may sometimes be beneficial. There is evidence that groups with salient demographic differences among their members may be better able than demographically homogeneous groups to uncover and integrate the unique (diverse) task-relevant information their members possess, despite that information being incongruently distributed (Phillips & Loyd, 2006; Phillips, Northcraft, & Neale, 2006; Thomas-Hunt & Phillips, 2004; but see Homan, van Knippenberg, Van Kleef, De Dreu, 2007b). Surface-level diversity at the very least can sensitize members to the possibility of diversity at a deeper, task-relevant level. This would appear to be of value even though the surface- and deep-level diversity may be unexpectedly incongruent. Thus, while groups may profit most from their deep, task-relevant diversity when it is accompanied by a congruent pattern of surface-level diversity, incongruent surface-level diversity may still be better than surface-level homogeneity. Sensitizing members to the possibility of differences among them at a deep, task-relevant level may therefore be one way that surface-level diversity can benefit group performance.

Summary and Implications for Synergy

The effect of diversity on group task performance is anything but simple. Although Figure 9.1 reflects reasonably well the current state of knowledge in this domain, it is almost certainly incomplete. On the one hand, deep diversity can benefit group performance, and so spark synergy, by providing members a rich fund of task-relevant resources with which to work. This will be helpful for only some kinds of tasks, however, and even then the expected performance gains may not materialize if the deep diversity simultaneously weakens social integration within the group. Surface-level diversity, on the other hand, is more apt to threaten than benefit performance, because it more consistently weakens social integration. Crosscutting dimensions of surface-level diversity may be less problematic in this regard, because these do not easily support strong ingroup–outgroup perceptions and so pose less of a barrier to social integration. But even when ingroup–outgroup perceptions are strong, a congruent rather than incongruent pattern of deep, task-relevant diversity may be easier to exploit, in part because it is more likely to be expected and tolerated. These latter conditions seem to make it easier for genuine performance gains to emerge and so warrant further consideration in the search for synergy in group performance.

☐ Deep Diversity and Group Problem-Solving Performance: The ValSeek Model

As suggested previously, one reason why so little evidence of strong synergy in group performance has been found to date may be that the theoretical models driving the research have failed to specify in a sufficiently precise manner the mechanisms by which performance gains are expected to emerge from group interaction. Greater theoretical specificity would help to pinpoint not only the critical interactional processes presumed to be at play during group performance, but also the critical conditions that need to be met in order for synergistic performance gains to emerge.

To illustrate this point, in this final section of the chapter, I describe a computational model that predicts the impact of a particular type of deep diversity on group problem-solving performance. Specifically, it examines the effect of diversity in member problem-solving strategies. It is called the ValSeek model, after the value-seeking problems with which it is concerned (Larson, 2007a). Although instantiated as a computer program, ValSeek serves the same function as does any theory of group behavior and performance expressed in traditional verbal or mathematical form (Simon, 1992). One advantage of this algorithmic approach to theorizing is that a computer program can be a powerful deductive tool for making predictions that would be extremely difficult to derive by any other means. When it is expressed as a computer program, one can "run" the theory and see in its output the behavioral and performance implications of even very complex interactions among elemental model components. These "results" are the model's predictions about behavior and performance that later can be tested against empirical observation of real interacting groups.[8]

Below I explain what value-seeking problems are and how they are represented generically in the computer program that instantiates the ValSeek model. I also describe how strategies for solving value-seeking problems are represented and how both individual and group problem-solving proceeds. I then summarize a set of simulation results using the ValSeek program. These results compare the performance of groups whose members have either the same (homogeneous) or different (diverse) problem-solving strategies. As will be seen, the performance gains that are predicted by the model depend not only on whether a group's problem-solving strategies are homogeneous or diverse, but also on how closely its members interact with one another. Somewhat surprisingly, the model predicts that closely coordinated interaction between members is detrimental to the problem-solving performance of homogeneous groups, but benefits the problem-solving performance of diverse groups.

Value-Seeking Problems

A value-seeking problem is one in which the problem solver searches for a solution from among a set of alternatives that vary in their underlying worth or desirability. The goal is to find the solution with the highest possible value. Real-world value-seeking problems typically involve solutions that have multiple elements. An example is the problem of creating a promotional package that will attract new members to your local health club. Among other things, it will be necessary to decide what membership fees will be charged, for what period of time, and what amenities will be offered. The chosen solution—the specific combination of fees, time period, and amenities actually written into the promotion materials—has value in proportion to its costs and benefits. Packages that would generate higher revenue (the primary sought-after benefit) at lower cost (e.g., by offering less expensive amenities) have more value than those that would generate less revenue at higher cost. Other examples of value-seeking problems include planning a menu, arranging a travel itinerary, designing an automobile, and building a shopping center. Indeed, almost any product of human invention, whether physical or abstract, can be seen as a solution to a value-seeking problem. Each exists because the problem-solver believed that its particular combination of elements would yield greater value than any other combination that might reasonably have been put forth.

Value-seeking problems often involve a very large number of possible solution alternatives, to the point that it is impractical to evaluate all of them. This is well illustrated by the value-seeking problem that lies at the heart of the popular word game Scrabble. This game requires players to take turns forming words using one or more of the (usually) seven letter tiles that each has drawn at random. There are 13,699 ways in which seven letters can be arranged to form 1-, 2-, 3-, 4-, 5-, 6-, and 7-letter strings. Each of these, in combination with one or more letters already on the playing board, is a possible solution to the word-formation problem. Although the majority of these strings will not be useful in forming legitimate words, and so have no value at all, it is likely that a few of them will be useful. Furthermore, among the useful strings, some are apt to have more value than others (because they are longer, or involve letters with higher point values). Because the goal in Scrabble is to score as many points as possible, players should select the string with the highest value. But it is quite unlikely that any player will consider each and every one of the 13,699 possible letter strings when trying to form a word. Rather, players are apt to use simplifying strategies to help them sift through the large number of possibilities. These might be based on the frequency with which certain letter patterns typically occur ("t" and "h" go together more often the "s" and "f"), or on what is cognitively easiest to manage (e.g., build longer words from smaller ones). Although helpful, the use of such strategies will undoubtedly cause players to ignore a great many strings, some of which may have more value than the one actually played. Thus, although players may choose the string with the highest *discovered* value, they will not necessarily choose the one that is objectively best, simply because it is too big a task to systematically evaluate every possibility.

To understand how value-seeking problems are represented in the computer program that instantiates the ValSeek model, it is helpful to imagine the relationship among the possible solutions to such problems in terms of an *n*-dimensional space, where each dimension represents a different solution element. For simplicity, the ValSeek program only deals with problems that have binary solution elements—that is, elements that can assume just two possible states (e.g., high vs. low). Thus, for example, when there are three solution elements, there are $2^3 = 8$ different ways those elements might be combined and so 8 possible solution alternatives. The relationship among these can be depicted in three-dimensional space as illustrated in Figure 9.2, with each corner of that space representing a different solution alternative. The task for the problem-solver is to move through this space in search of the solution with the greatest value.

Note that each solution alternative depicted in Figure 9.2 is identified by its own three-digit binary code (e.g., 1-0-1 identifies the solution in the front lower-right corner), and each has been assigned a different value (shown in parentheses, where value is expressed in arbitrary units). It is also important to see in this example that the solution values do not bear a simple linear relationship to the state of the solution elements. In the real world, solution elements sometimes contribute additively to the total value of a solution alternative, but sometimes contribute in more complex ways. In the game of Scrabble, for instance, individual letters contribute their separate values to the value of the string as a whole only when that string forms a legitimate word. Thus, the letter C (worth three points) adds value in the string C-A-T but not in the string C-B-E.

The ValSeek computer program creates generic value-seeking problems by constructing systems of binary codes like those shown in Figure 9.2 to represent sets of abstract solution alternatives and randomly assigns a different value to each. Different random mappings of values to solution alternatives create different value-seeking problems. By averaging results across many such problems, conclusions about the performance of simulated problem-solvers can be drawn that are independent of the way particular solution elements contribute to overall solution value.

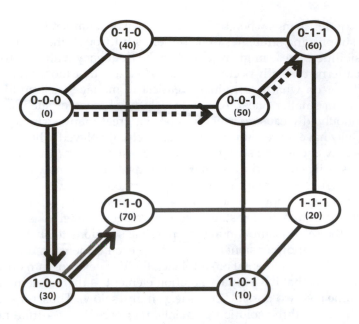

FIGURE 9.2 The solution space for a value-seeking problem whose possible solutions have three elements that each can assume just two possible states. (Reprinted from Larson (2007a) with permission of Sage Publications.) Each corner of the cube represents a unique solution alternative. Note: Each alternative is identified by its own three-digit code, and its value is given in parentheses. Arrows are explained in the text.

Problem Solving

The ValSeek model is centrally concerned with the strategies that problem-solvers use to guide their movements through an n-dimensional space in search of high-value solutions. Under conditions that make it impractical to examine every conceivable solution alternative, these guiding strategies help to determine which solution alternatives will be considered, and consequently what value problem solvers will uncover. Within the ValSeek model these guiding strategies are implemented in a generic way that nevertheless permits an assessment of their similarities and differences. This is an essential requirement if the effects of strategy diversity are to be studied.

Member Problem-Solving Strategies

Problem-solving strategies are expressed in the ValSeek computer program as *flipset heuristics*. A flipset heuristic is a general instruction for changing the binary codes that identify solution alternatives and so for shifting the simulated problem-solver's attention from one alternative to another. An example of a flipset heuristic is: "On each problem-solving step, flip one randomly selected element of the binary code," where "flip" means change that element to its other possible state.[9] Let us call this Flipset Heuristic A. According to Flipset Heuristic A, the code 0-0-0, which identifies one of the eight solution alternatives depicted in Figure 9.2, might be changed to the code 1-0-0 (by flipping its first element), to the code 0-1-0 (by flipping its second element), or to the code 0-0-1 (by flipping its third element). Each of these is equally likely according to Flipset Heuristic A, and each would result in a shift in the problem-solver's attention from the solution alternative identified by the original code (0-0-0) to the one identified by the resultant code.

For every location (binary code) in the n-dimensional solution space, the problem-solver's flipset heuristic defines a set of other locations (codes) that can be reached in a single move; that is, by applying his or her flipset heuristic once. These other locations constitute the *perceived solution neighborhood* for the location in question. Every location sits at the center of its own neighborhood, with the neighborhood's composition depending solely on the problem-solver's flipset heuristic. Thus, for a problem-solver who uses Flipset Heuristic A, the neighborhood that can be "seen" from location 0-0-0 in Figure 9.2 consists of locations 1-0-0, 0-1-0, and 0-0-1. This stands in contrast to the solution neighborhood that can be seen from that same location by a problem solver who uses a very different flipset heuristic: "On each problem-solving step, flip *all except one* randomly selected element of the binary code." Let us call this Flipset Heuristic B. For a problem-solver who uses Flipset Heuristic B, the neighborhood that can be seen from location 0-0-0 consists of locations 0-1-1, 1-0-1, and 1-1-0. Note that Flipset Heuristics A and B define completely nonoverlapping neighborhoods. This is true not only for the neighborhoods surrounding location 0-0-0, but also for every other location in the solution space. The degree of similarity between any two flipset heuristics—and so problem-solving strategies—is indexed by the degree of overlap in the perceived solution neighborhoods that those heuristics define. Because Flipset Heuristics A and B define completely nonoverlapping neighborhoods, they imply maximally different strategies for navigating a solution space.

The ValSeek computer program models problem solving by individuals as an activity that takes place in a series of discrete steps. In the very first step, a starting location (binary code) within the n-dimensional solution space is selected at random, and the value of the solution found there is determined.[10] By default, this solution becomes the "current best alternative," which is to say, the alternative encountered so far that has the highest value. The current best alternative is the standard against which subsequently encountered solution alternatives are evaluated.

Then, in every problem-solving step after the first one, two things happen. First, the simulated problem solver moves from the location of the current best alternative to some new not-yet-evaluated location. This happens by executing his or her flipset heuristic once. Second, the problem solver compares the value of the solution alternative found at that new location to the value of the current best alternative. If the new alternative has a higher value, then it replaces (i.e., becomes the new) current best alternative, and the next problem-solving step starts from that new location. If, on the other hand, the new alternative does not have a higher value, then it is abandoned, the problem solver retreats to the previous location (i.e., that of the still-current best alternative), and the next problem-solving step starts again from that location. This move-and-evaluate process is repeated in each subsequent problem-solving step until no alternative is encountered that has a higher value than the current best alternative, at which point the current best alternative becomes the chosen solution, and problem-solving terminates.

Note that this algorithm does not stray more than one move from the current best alternative. In other words, it simulates problem-solvers who search for value only in the solution neighborhood that they can see from the vantage point of their current best alternative. That search proceeds in random order but stops as soon as a neighbor is found that has more value than the current best alternative. That neighbor then immediately becomes (i.e., replaces) the current best alternative, and its perceived solution neighborhood is searched, again in random order. This is a form of constrained stochastic behavior not unlike that shown to characterize scientific creativity (cf. Simonton, 2003). A notable feature of this problem-solving algorithm is that if, in a given neighborhood, an alternative is discovered that has more value than the current best alternative but less value than some other not-yet-examined alternative in that same neighborhood, that better-but-not-yet-examined neighbor will be overlooked, at least for the moment. This would occur in the problem shown in Figure 9.2, for example, if a problem solver using Flipset Heuristic A were to start at location 0-0-0 (value = 0) and flip the first element of the binary code. This would take the problem solver to 1-0-0 (value = 30), which would immediately become his or her current best alternative and lead him or her to begin searching the perceived solution neighborhood surrounding 1-0-0. In this scenario, location 0-0-1 (which is the objectively best alternative in 0-0-0's neighborhood) would be ignored completely, and the problem-solver would instead travel the path defined by the solid arrows in the figure. Had the same problem-solver flipped the third element of the binary code when starting from location 0-0-0, he or she would have traveled the path defined by the dotted arrows.

The arrows in Figure 9.2 describe just two possible routes through this particular solution space. Both start from the same initial location, and both reflect the actions of problem-solvers who use Flipset Heuristic A. Yet one discovers the solution alternative that is objectively best (1-1-0), while the other does not. Two different paths were taken because the two problem-solvers searched the perceived solution neighborhood surrounding their starting location in different random orders. It should thus be evident that, even when endowed with identical problem-solving strategies (flipset heuristics), two simulated problem-solvers will not necessarily end up choosing the same solution. It should also be clear that, as in the Scrabble example, having chosen a particular solution is no guarantee that another, higher-value solution alternative does not exist. (For a more detailed description of flipset heuristics and the problem-solving algorithm employed in the ValSeek model, see Larson, 2007a).

Collective Problem Solving

Working collectively in a group to solve a problem implies interacting with other members to discuss ideas and information relevant to that problem. In the case of value-seeking problems, an important category of information that members are apt to discuss is the value of the solution alternatives they individually examine. This is especially like whenever a member discovers a solution that is more valuable than his or her current best alternative, for these are the moments where it is most evident that progress is being made toward the goal of finding the solution with the highest value.

The ValSeek computer program can simulate up to six people working together to solve the same problem. Prior to running the program, each simulated group member is endowed with his or her own problem-solving strategy (flipset heuristic). Members might all be given the same strategy, or they might be given very different strategies. Regardless, during the simulation each one follows the problem-solving algorithm outlined above. Thus, each member enters the solution space at an independently chosen, random start location, and each employs his or her own flipset heuristic to guide his or her move-and-evaluate search process. The only difference is that in a group problem-solving context simulated members can communicate with one another whenever one of them replaces his or her current best alternative with a newly discovered, higher-value solution. Whenever such a communication occurs, others in the group can immediately compare that same new solution to their own current best alternative. If any given groupmate finds that that new solution has a higher value, then that groupmate's own current best alternative is also replaced with the new one, and he or she too begins searching the solution neighborhood surrounding that new location. If, on the other hand, the new solution does not have a higher value than that groupmate's current best alternative, it is ignored by that groupmate, and he or she continues his or her search as before. Thus, communicating about a newly discovered solution alternative may or may not impact a given groupmate's path through the solution space, depending on the value of that groupmate's own current best alternative.

In the real world, of course, groups differ widely in how much communication actually takes place between members. At one extreme are groups whose members verbalize every step of their problem-solving activity and who capitalize immediately on even the slightest value improvement that any one of their members might identify. At the other extreme are groups whose members work in complete silence until each has reached the conclusion of his or her own search process, at which point they simply announce to one another their separately-found best alternatives and agree to adopt as their group solution the one with the highest value. Between these extremes are groups whose members verbalize some, but not all, of their incremental successes and attend to some, but not all, of what others have to say. The ValSeek computer program can simulate group interaction at any of these levels. This is done prior to running the simulation by setting the probability that each newly found, better solution alternative will be communicated to others in the group.

Simulation Results: The Impact of Problem-Solving Strategy Diversity

Problem-solving strategy diversity within groups is defined in the ValSeek model by the similarity of the members' flipset heuristics. A diverse group is one whose members have been endowed with very different flipset heuristics and so have very different problem-solving strategies, whereas a homogeneous group is one whose members have been endowed with exactly the same flipset heuristic and so have exactly the same problem-solving strategy. By separately simulating the performance of diverse and homogeneous groups, the predicted impact of problem-solving strategy diversity on group problem-solving effectiveness can be deduced.

This was the approach taken in the simulation reported below. For the sake of simplicity, this simulation examined the performance of two-person groups (dyads) on five-dimensional problems. With five dimensions, there are $2^5 = 32$ unique solution alternatives. The simulation was run 100,000 times for each of 18 conditions representing all combinations of three types of dyad composition and six levels of interaction (communication), with the results cumulated across runs. At the beginning of each run, three things happened. First, the to-be-solved problem was specified by randomly assigning to each solution alternative one of 32 values that ranged from 0 to 310 in increments of 10.[11] Second, each dyad member was endowed with one of the two previously described flipset heuristics: A or B. The assignment of heuristics to members created three types of dyads. In one type, both members were endowed with Flipset Heuristic A. These are referred to below as "A-A Dyads." In a second type, both members were endowed with Flipset Heuristic B and are referred to as "B-B Dyads." In the third type, one member was endowed with Flipset Heuristic A, and the other was endowed with Flipset Heuristic B. These are referred to as "A-B Dyads." Thus, A-A and B-B Dyads are homogeneous with respect to their members' problem-solving strategies, whereas A-B Dyads are diverse. Finally, the third thing that happened at the beginning of each run was that the degree of interaction (communication) permitted in the dyad was fixed at one of six levels: 0, 20, 40, 60, 80, or 100%. The first, 0%,, implies that members never communicated about the better solution alternatives they encountered while navigating the solution space (except at the very end, when they each announced their separately-found best alternative and agreed to adopt as their group solution the one with the higher value). At the other extreme, 100% implies that members always communicated about those better solution alternatives.

Figure 9.3 displays the percentage of dyads in each condition that found the solution with the highest value (310). To interpret these results, it is useful to begin by considering the two closely spaced dashed lines near the bottom of the figure. These indicate the value-seeking performance of a single problem-solver endowed with one of the two flipset heuristics described above. These are labeled "A Alone" and "B Alone," respectively. (Because the concept of group interaction has no meaning for individual problem-solvers, no interpretation should be given to the fact that these lines are flat. Each simply indicates the percentage of individual problem-solvers that found the highest value solution). As can be seen, the two types of individuals perform almost identically, with about 26% of them finding the highest value solution. Because these results indicate the performance predicted for the average member when working alone, they provide a useful baseline for assessing dyadic performance. Specifically, they establish the minimum criterion that must be exceeded if a dyad's performance is to be taken as evidence of even weak synergy.

Next consider the performance curves for the two types of homogeneous dyads, the A-A and B-B Dyads. Here the concept of group interaction is meaningful and, as can be seen, the degree of interaction between members significantly affects the performance of these dyads. At extremely high levels of interaction, where members communicate about all or nearly all of their newly discovered higher-value solution alternatives (80% and above), the collective performance of homogeneous dyads is hardly any better than that of the average member working alone. This relatively poor performance occurs because communication often causes members to converge on the same location within the solution space, and

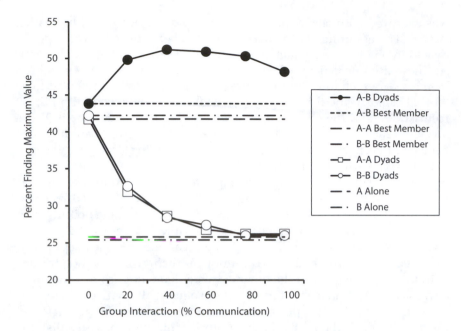

FIGURE 9.3 Percentage of simulated diverse (A-B) and homogeneous (A-A and B-B) dyads finding the maximum solution value on 5-dimensional value-seeking problems. Note: All A members are endowed with the Flipset Heuristic A; all B members are endowed with the Flipset Heuristic B.

because members with identical flipset heuristics will see and begin to explore exactly the same solution neighborhood surrounding that location. It is only when the level of interaction within these dyads diminishes that their collective performance improves. This happens because the lower rate of communication allows each member greater opportunity to explore independent regions of the solution space and so to find high-value solution alternatives on his or her own, before hearing about a new high-value solution alternative discovered by his or her partner. This implies that when communication about a new solution alternative does occur, both the communicated solution and the member's own current best alternative will tend to have higher values, leaving the dyad better off even if both members subsequently do start to explore the same set of paths through the solution space.

As can be seen in Figure 9.3, the A-A and B-B Dyads perform best when they do not interact at all (0%). These dyads are most likely to choose the highest value solution alternative when their members work through the entire problem independently, communicating only at the very end in order to determine which of their separately-found solutions is best and so will be chosen as the group solution. Performance achieved in this way, without interaction except at the very last moment, in effect establishes the level of performance that can be attained by the best member of the dyad working alone. Even when differences in performance across members are due simply to random variation, as is certainly the case for the noninteracting homogeneous dyads in the present simulation, it is still essential to know what that variation is, and so what the highest level of performance among the individual members is likely to be (cf. Steiner & Rajaratnam, 1961). A best-member baseline determined in this way establishes the level of performance that must be exceeded by interacting dyads (i.e., when the interaction parameter is greater than 0%) if the product of their collective effort is to be taken as evidence of strong synergy. Said differently, any demonstration of strong synergy requires that dyadic interaction yield benefits that are greater than what would be obtained simply by picking the best individually-identified member solution. For clarity, the best member baselines are marked in the figure by the dashed horizontal lines that intersect the dyadic performance curves when the interaction parameter is set at 0%.

Of greatest interest in Figure 9.3 is the performance curve for the dyads with diverse member problem-solving strategies, the A-B Dyads. As can be seen, and in contrast to what occurs for homogeneous dyads, interaction does not worsen the performance of the diverse dyads relative to their best-member baselines. Rather, it tends to improve their performance, with intermediate levels of interaction being best. For example, when the interaction parameter is set to 40%, there is a 17% *increase* over the best-member baseline in the percentage of A-B Dyads that eventually chose the solution alternative with the highest value. This stands in contrast to the A-A and B-B Dyads, where the same amount of interaction results in a 32% *decrease* relative to the best-member baseline.

The reason why interaction improves the performance of diverse dyads, while worsening the performance of homogeneous dyads, lies in the members' flipset heuristics and in the perceived solution neighborhoods that those heuristics define. At every location in the solution space, problem solvers that use the same flipset heuristic will see the same solution neighborhood, whereas problem solvers that use different flipset heuristics will see different solution neighborhoods. Thus, even when communication causes members to converge on the same location within the solution space (i.e., to adopt the solution at that location as their current best alternative), it will lead them to search the same solution neighborhood surrounding that location only if they share the same flipset heuristic. The members of diverse dyads, by definition, have very different flipset heuristics, which means they will continue their search by exploring very different solution neighborhoods. The more different paths they explore between them, the larger the percentage of the overall solution space they will examine, and the more likely it is that they will find an even better solution if one exists. The members of diverse dyads are therefore able to build upon one another's incremental successes because, unlike in homogeneous dyads, knowledge of those successes does not narrow the range of additional solution alternatives they are likely to consider.

However, even in diverse dyads, high levels of interaction still imply that members have a tendency to follow one another through the problem space. That is, although the members may not search the same solution neighborhood surrounding a given location, there is nevertheless a dependency between the neighborhoods they do search. As a consequence, certain regions of the solution space are likely to be systematically ignored. This problem is much less severe for diverse than for homogeneous dyads, but it is still present to a degree, and at high levels of interaction it tends to offset the benefits of being able to build on one another's incremental successes. This explains why the performance of diverse dyads does not increase monotonically with increased interaction.

Summary and Implications for Synergy

The results reported here concern dyads. Parallel findings are obtained when simulating the performance of three-person and four-person groups (Larson, 2007a, 2007b, in press). Further, the results are substantially the same when assessing the mean value of the solution alternatives eventually chosen across all groups, rather than the percentage of groups choosing the alternative with the highest value (Larson, 2006). In each case, the ValSeek model predicts that groups will outperform their average member on value-seeking problems most of the time (e.g., most of the dyadic results shown in Figure 9.3 are above the average-member baselines). However, to the extent that groups are homogeneous in their problem-solving strategies, their performance is predicted not to exceed what their best member is able to achieve working alone. Group performance that is better than the performance of their average member, but not better than the performance of their best member, fits the definition of weak synergy given in Chapter 1. On the other hand, to the extent the members' problem-solving strategies are diverse, the ValSeek model predicts that their collective performance will be better than that of even their best member, which fits the definition of strong synergy.

The results described here represent predictions based on rather extreme forms of homogeneity and diversity: homogeneous dyads had identical flipset heuristics, whereas diverse dyads had maximally different heuristics. Most real-world situations are apt to lie between these extremes. Intermediate levels of diversity should yield intermediate results. One implication of this is that, judging by Figure 9.3, group performance on value-seeking problems should more often fall below the best-member baseline than above it. In other words, weak synergy is more likely to be the rule than strong synergy. This fits well with the extant empirical literature on group problem solving, where, as described in Chapter 4, clear evidence of strong synergy has been obtained in only a very few studies.

The ValSeek model is useful because it specifies not only a set of conditions under which strong synergy is predicted to occur, but also the circumstances that should be present in any empirical test of the model's predictions. What appears to be required, according to the model, is a high level of diversity among member problem-solving strategies and a moderate amount of interaction among members. Further, the problem-solving strategies themselves should be open to external input so that members can take advantage of the gains made by others in the group. The model does not require, however, that members be aware of the diversity in their problem-solving strategies. Indeed, awareness might lead members to try to resolve such differences, thereby converting an otherwise diverse group into a homogeneous one. Thus, a final condition that would appear to be required in any empirical test of the ValSeek model is that the strategies examined involve rather stable habits of mind.

☐ Chapter Summary

This chapter has addressed a number of issues related to the distribution of group member characteristics. It began by considering diversity within groups as a dependent variable. There is good evidence that groups "in the wild" are more homogeneous than would be expected on the basis of the distribution of individuals in the population from which their members are drawn. This goes well beyond similarity on task-relevant attributes; it extends as well to similarity with respect to such things as values, attitudes, and personality. I described both structural (homophilious social networks) and psychological factors (perceived fit and rewardingness) that generate a constant press toward homogeneity within groups.

But groups seldom become homogeneous in an absolute sense; substantial diversity often remains, and this has been shown in many circumstances to impact group performance. The impact of this lingering diversity depends on whether it exists at a surface or deep level. Surface-level diversity refers to easily observed demographic differences among group members, whereas deep-level diversity refers to differences in harder-to-detect underlying attributes. Deep diversity can impact group performance either directly or indirectly. Its direct impact is highly task contingent. Whereas some types of tasks may permit strong synergistic gains in group performance as a consequence of member diversity, others are apt to permit no more than weak gains. And in some cases diversity may actually be damaging to performance. Deep diversity has its indirect impact on group performance through its (typically negative) effect on the group's social integration. Surface-level diversity, by contrast, appears to affect group performance almost exclusively by indirect means, either via its association with underlying deep-level differences among members, or via its (again typically negative) impact on social integration within the group.

Finally, I described in some detail a computational model designed to predict the impact of diverse problem-solving strategies (a form of deep diversity) on group problem-solving effectiveness. An important prediction made by this model is that groups whose members have very similar problem-solving strategies are apt to show only weak synergistic performance gains on value-seeking tasks. In contrast, those whose members have very diverse strategies should be capable of strong synergistic gains. Computational models like this one have a significant advantage over models expressed in more conventional, natural-language forms, in that they are well-suited for representing highly dynamic phenomena. The predictions made by this model would be extremely difficult to derive had it been expressed in any other form. Because of such advantages, it is likely that computational modeling will become increasingly important in the future as a means of understanding group behavior, and that it will be especially useful in the search for synergy in group performance.

☐ Endnotes

1. Further, as Schneider, Goldstein, and Smith (1995) note, it is a mistake to imagine that most organizations are large corporations listed on one of the major stock exchanges. In reality, most organizations are quite small. For example, Axtell (2001) found that the mean number of people employed by tax-paying businesses in the United States in 1997 was just 22, with a median of only 4 (i.e., the distribution is severely right-skewed). These figures exclude those businesses comprising only self-employed individuals with no other employees. Thus, the typical organization not only shares more in common with small groups than is generally envisioned, the typical organization *is* a small group!

2. In most cases the group will have a much stronger impact on the behavior of the new member than the new member will have on the behavior of the group (Latané, 1981). Members are apt to be sensitive to this fact, however, which should temper their expectations for accommodation. Thus, new members may well perceive that the group has satisfactorily accommodated to their needs even though the new members have changed their behavior much more substantially in order to suit the group.

3. For skill and ability diversity, it is useful to distinguish between "type" diversity and "level" diversity. Type diversity refers to differences in the kinds of skills and abilities that members possess (e.g., language skills, engineering skills, negotiation skills, etc.), whereas level diversity refers to differences in how proficient members are at a particular skill or how much of a particular ability they possess (e.g., strong vs. weak mathematical skills; cf. Harrison & Klein, 2007). Although type diversity implies level diversity, level diversity does not necessarily imply type diversity. My discussion here is limited to type diversity.

4. An exception might be circumstances where dealing with gender or racial issues is an integral part of the task (e.g., Sommers, 2006; see also Hollingshead & Fraidin, 2003).

5. Such subgroup identities are most likely to be called forth when the committee members interact with, or contemplate interacting with, one another. By contrast, their identity as members of the committee as a whole is most likely to become salient when the committee interacts with its larger organizational environment (e.g., when it announces to the campus community a plan to improve campus-wide safety at night).

6. The term "outgroup" is most commonly applied when discussing intergroup relations, especially when the "group" in question is actually a broad social category (e.g., women, Hispanics, Australians). Here, however, I wish to focus on intragroup relations within relatively small task performing groups whose members are nevertheless diverse with respect to one or more easily-observed demographic variables. Thus, in the present context, the terms "ingroup" and "outgroup" both refer to subgroups within the same task-performing group.

7. Timmerman (2000) treated these two dimensions of diversity separately and did not examine their correlated versus crosscutting pattern.

8. For further reading on computational modeling, see Davis, Eisenhardt, and Bingham (2007); de Marchi (2005); Epstein (2007); Hastie and Stasser (2000); Ilgen and Hulin (2000); Prietula, Carley, and Gasser (1998); and Smith and Conrey (2007).

9. The stochastic feature of this flipset heuristic ensures that no special priority is given to any one element of the binary code. This is consistent with the generic nature of the value-seeking problems being modeled, where there is no inherent priority among the solution elements themselves.

10. The value of a solution alternative is determined by consulting a look-up table. ValSeek does not attempt to model the mental or physical processes that may be involved in determining solution values. Rather, it is concerned only with the outcome of these processes.

11. There are $32! = 2.63 \times 10^{35}$ unique ways in which these values might be assigned. Thus, it is highly unlikely that the same value mapping occurred more than once across the 100,000 runs of each condition.

Conclusion

Prospects for the Future in the Search for Synergy

My goal in this book has been to systematically review the empirical literature on group task performance. The central question I have tried to address is whether or not there is an inherent benefit to collaborative work arrangements. In its barest form, this question asks whether or not interaction among members adds anything to a group's task performance that would not be provided simply by combining the separate (noninteractive) efforts of its individual members. I have considered this question in the context of a range of tasks (idea generation, problem solving, judgment, and decision making), as well as from several different process perspectives (learning and memory, motivation, and member diversity).

Where they exist, I have highlighted those segments of the empirical literature that compare the observed performance of interacting groups to the performance that would be expected of them based solely on the individual efforts of an equal number of persons working alone. The latter might be estimated from a comparably constructed nominal group—individuals selected in the same way from the same population, but who work at the task completely independently of one another—or from the group's own members when working at the task individually at an earlier time. Either way, such comparisons yield the most direct evidence concerning performance gains (and losses) that are due to interaction among group members.

In addition, in order to help gauge the results obtained from such comparisons, I introduced the concept of synergy and drew a distinction between weak and strong synergy. Synergy refers to a gain in performance that is attributable in some way to group interaction. A group is said to exhibit synergy when it is able to accomplish collectively something that could not reasonably have been achieved by any simple combination of individual member efforts. Weak synergy refers to group performance that exceeds expectations based on the performance of typical group members when working alone. Strong synergy, on the other hand, refers to group performance that exceeds expectations based on the performance of even the best group member when working alone.

Applying the synergy framework to the findings reported in the literature, it is evident that there is no simple answer to the question of whether or not there is an inherent benefit to collaborative work arrangements. Much depends on the nature of the group's task and on factors prevailing in the situation while the group executes that task. Many studies that compare the performance of individuals and groups yield clear evidence of weak synergy. In a few cases there is compelling evidence of strong synergy. And, of course, studies can also be found that report either no performance gain at all in interacting groups relative to individuals, or even a net process loss—group performance that falls below what would be expected based on the performance of the typical group member working alone.

In this final chapter of the book I provide a summary assessment of the overall synergy framework, examine its strengths and weakness, and consider the value that it adds to our understanding of groups and group performance. In addition, I offer three broad suggestions about future directions that the search for synergy in small group performance might profitably take.

☐ Does the Synergy Framework Work?

It seems appropriate to ask whether the synergy framework, and in particular the distinction between weak and strong synergy, is effective. Does it help clarify the extant empirical literature? Does it suggest where research might best be directed in the future? And most importantly, does it advance our understanding of small group performance?

A Balanced Perspective

One benefit of the synergy framework is that it offers an objective set of criteria for evaluating group performance. Synergy is not determined by assessing members' feelings or emotional reactions to their group experience. Nor does it depend on subjective ratings of group process. Instead, it is determined by comparing a group's observed performance to standards derived from the performance of individuals who work alone at the same task. Although conclusions about weak versus strong synergy rely on different standards, those standards are established in the same objective manner.

At the same time, the synergy framework is unbounded; it does not depend on a conceptual upper (or lower) limit to group performance, either explicitly or implicitly. This stands in contrast to, for example, Steiner's (1966, 1972) model, which was discussed at length in Chapter 1 (see pp. 15–20). As will be recalled, that model conceptualizes a group's actual productivity as its potential productivity minus any losses that may arise due to faulty group process. "Potential productivity," of course, is the hypothetical upper limit of what a group is capable of achieving; it is logically impossible for a group to exceed its potential. As noted in Chapter 1, there are at least two difficulties associated with this model. One concerns the substantial challenges inherent in operationalizing potential productivity. The other—more pertinent to the present discussion—is that because it uses potential productivity as its sole point of reference, Steiner's model provides no way of talking about process gains. The very concept seems incompatible with that model. Rather, Steiner's model necessarily couches in negative terms any and all group performance that falls short of what the group is maximally capable of achieving. Thus, even what I refer to as strong synergy would be seen within Steiner's model from a process loss point of view, assuming the group potentially could have done better still.

This is not a mere quibble about labels. Rather, it is a matter of fundamental importance that shapes how we think about and investigate group performance. Among the very wide array of possible behaviors that members might enact while working together as a group, some will no doubt facilitate their performance while others will impede it. It seems essential to understand both. But how can this be accomplished if performance is framed exclusively in terms of process loss? To the extent possible, we should strive to differentiate gains from losses. Doing so will enable us to recognize the weaknesses of groups while at the same time acknowledging their strengths.

The synergy framework is helpful in this regard because it distinguishes net process gains from net process losses. Unlike Steiner's (1966, 1972) model, the synergy framework employs two benchmarks that lie in the mid-range of the performance continuum. A net process gain is what I refer to as synergy in group performance, whether weak or strong, whereas a net process loss is group performance that falls below the benchmark used to establish weak synergy. Thus, the synergy framework segments the full spectrum of group performance into three distinct regions: a lower region of net process loss, a middle region of weak synergistic performance gains, and an upper region of strong synergistic performance gains.

Segmenting the performance continuum in this way is beneficial because it creates a common metric for comparing group performance across otherwise incommensurate tasks. It allows us to compare, for example, the performance of groups on problem-solving tasks to their performance on idea-generation tasks. As seen in Chapter 4, the predominant (though not exclusive) finding in the problem-solving literature is one of weak synergistic performance gains; most of the time, groups have been observed to solve problems more effectively than would be expected based on the solo performance of their average member, though less effectively, that would be expected based on the solo performance of their best member. By contrast, and as seen in Chapter 3, the predominant (though again not exclusive) finding in the idea-generation literature is one of net process loss—most of the time, face-to-face groups have been observed to generate fewer ideas than would be expected based on the solo performance of their average members. The synergy framework calls attention to such differences in group performance across task types. Steiner's (1966, 1972) model does not.

Even within a single task domain, the synergy framework calls attention to examples of exceptional performance by groups that are particularly worthy of further consideration and follow-up research. In some cases these involve strong synergistic gains in domains where weak synergy is the norm. This can be seen in the problem-solving literature, where Laughlin's empirical work on the letters-to-numbers task stands out (see Chapter 4, pp. 146–156), as does the conceptual work embodied in Larson's ValSeek model (see Chapter 9, pp. 331–343). Certain findings from the collective judgment literature considered in Chapter 5 also fit this description (e.g., Henry, 1993; Credé & Sniezek, 2003; Reagan-Cirincione, 1994). In other cases, the exceptional group performance involves only weak synergistic gains, but occurs in contexts where a net process loss is the norm. The clearest examples here come from the idea generation literature reviewed in Chapter 3 and concern electronic brainstorming (e.g., Dennis & Williams, 2005) and brainwriting (Coskun, 2005b; Paulus & Yang, 2000).

The value in highlighting such examples of exceptional group performance is that it gives direction to future research. Showing that collective action by groups can sometimes produce net process gains (synergy)— especially in domains where a lesser quality of performance is the norm— is apt to focus additional inquiry on what has gone right and what forms of interaction should be encouraged (e.g., because they lead to error correction in problem solving). By contrast, showing that collective action typically yields a net process loss should focus future inquiry on what has gone wrong and what forms of interaction should be avoided (e.g., because they lead to production blocking in idea generation). In short, how past research results are framed affects not only our thinking about the performance of small groups in the present, but also the research questions that we are likely to ask about their performance in the future.

Nearly all group performance is likely the result of both facilitative and inhibitory elements of group process. This seems most obviously true in the case of weak synergy, where group performance, by definition, lies between the average-member and best-member performance standards. Here, it is fairly evident that, although performance has benefited from the interaction among group members, there is still room for improvement. But it should be true as well when either strong synergistic gains or net process losses are observed. In all but the most extreme cases, some combination of facilitative and inhibitory factors is likely at play. The point here is simply that the synergy framework, relative to others that have gone before it, provides a more balanced platform for inquiring into both performance gains and losses and so the facilitative and inhibitory group processes that underlie them.

Challenges in Using the Synergy Framework

The principle challenge in using the synergy framework is properly operationalizing the standards associated with weak and strong synergy. As seen throughout the book, different types of tasks sometimes call for rather different operationalizations of these standards. Perhaps the starkest example is the weak synergy criterion when groups perform a conjunctive task. Whereas for most other task types this criterion is operationalized in terms of the solo performance of the average group member, on conjunctive tasks it is operationalized in terms of the solo performance of the group's weakest or least capable member. This shift is necessary in order to take account of the unique constraints on group performance that exist when working on conjunctive tasks (see Chapter 2, pp. 66–68, and Chapter 8, pp. 289–291).

The reverse can also occur; the same operation is sometimes employed to instantiate different synergy criteria in different task contexts. An example is the way the pooled performance of nominal groups is used when the task involves brainstorming (Chapter 3) versus collective-recall (Chapter 7). A nominal group's pooled performance is determined in essentially the same way in both cases—by counting the total number of unique ideas generated, or the total number of stimulus items recalled, regardless of how many nominal group members independently generated or recalled them. However, the resultant scores are interpreted very differently. In the case of brainstorming, the nominal group's pooled performance serves as the minimum criterion for establishing weak synergy in interactive groups (see Chapter 3, pp. 76–79). By contrast, for collective recall tasks, the nominal group's pooled performance serves as the minimum criterion for establishing strong synergy in interactive groups (see Chapter 7, pp. 228–230). This difference in interpretation is required by the different constraints that obtain when performing brainstorming versus collective recall tasks.

Finally, problems sometimes arise that make the synergy framework as a whole difficult or impossible to apply. In certain cases, these have to do with practical constraints on gathering the individual-level data necessary to create one or both of the synergy criteria. Such constraints are most commonly encountered when studying naturally occurring groups (e.g., the research on surgical teams discussed in connection with group learning curves in Chapter 7, pp. 220–223). But problems can turn up even when such individual-level data are readily available. For example, those data may occasionally be arrayed in ways that make it logically impossible to distinguish between weak and strong synergy. This occurs in collective estimation tasks, for instance, when the average of the group members' individual judgments is more accurate than the independent judgment of their best member (see Chapter 5, pp. 163–164).

Thus, although the synergy framework provides a useful metric for assessing and comparing group performance that can be applied much of the time, it cannot be applied in a blind or haphazard manner, and in some cases it cannot be applied fully or even at all. Still, careful thought and consideration of basic principles, along with the use of appropriate research designs, can help to make the synergy framework workable in a great many group performance contexts. On balance, then, it seems a beneficial, if imperfect, tool for both organizing empirical findings and for thinking about group performance more generally.

The Reality of Groups

Finally, there is also a meta-theoretical benefit to the synergy framework. By helping to see more clearly that certain group performances are emergent phenomena that cannot be explained by a simple combination of member contributions, the synergy framework speaks to a century-old debate about the psychological reality of groups.

On one side of this debate are those who deny the reality of groups, arguing that groups do not have properties that are independent of the individuals who make them up. One of the earliest and most ardent advocates of this point of view was Floyd Allport. In the introduction to his textbook on social psychology, Allport (1924a) famously wrote that "There is no psychology of groups which is not essentially and entirely a psychology of individuals" (p. 4; see also Allport, 1924b). Along similar lines, Krech and Crutchfield (1948) remarked nearly a quarter century later that "The study of groups as a whole can reveal nothing new beyond what is given by a synthesis of all the data pertaining to each of the group members" (p. 366). And just a half-dozen years after that, in an authoritative chapter in the *Handbook of Social Psychology*, Allport's younger brother, Gordon, declared that "[w]ith few exceptions, social psychologists regard their discipline as an attempt to understand and explain how the thought, feeling, and behavior of individuals are influenced by the actual, imagined, or implied presence of other human beings" (Allport, 1954, p. 5). This latter statement is important not only because it denies groups any meaningful standing in the discipline beyond that of a context variable, but also because it has became *the* definition of social psychology—as any survey of contemporary introductory social psychology textbooks will attest. It is all too apparent that today, perhaps even more than in the past, the dominant view is a distinctly individual-centric social psychology (cf. Greenwood, 2000, 2004).

And yet, as Gordon Allport (1954) conceded, there have been exceptions—and more than just a few. Standing on the other side of the debate about the psychological reality of groups, contemporaries of both Allports can be found who argued passionately that groups indeed are real, noting that they have emergent, irreducible properties, and that as such they merit close attention by a genuinely social social psychology (e.g., Cattell, 1948; Horowitz & Perlmutter, 1953; Le Bon, 1903; Lewin, 1947; McDougall, 1920; Warriner, 1956). Present-day writers have likewise argued for the reality of groups by calling attention to their irreducible "supervening qualities" (e.g., Sandelands & St. Clair, 1993). Taking a rather different tack, others have propose that the reality of groups itself be treated as a variable, with different collectives exhibiting different degrees of "groupness" depending on the extent to which they possess certain essential qualities (e.g., Arrow, McGrath, & Berdahl, 2000; Meneses, Ortega, Navarro, & de Quijaro, 2008).[1] Still others offer statistical approaches that, in effect, affirm the reality of groups by identifying unique variance in data obtained from individuals that is attributable to their group membership (e.g., Gonzalez & Griffin, 2002, 2003; Kenny, Mannetti, Pierro, Livi, & Kashy, 2002).

The synergy framework adds to this long-simmering dispute by delineating more clearly what is emergent and irreducible, and does so with respect to group products (i.e., performance) rather than properties. The reason why it is sometimes difficult to argue for the reality of groups when focused on group properties is that those properties must often be inferred from exactly the same data used to infer the properties of individuals. For example, at an experiential level, the same visual data that enables us to see individuals must be relied upon as well to provide evidence of their groupness (e.g., their proximity and similarity). This is true empirically as well. A cohesive group is one that displays a particular pattern (a group-level concept) of attraction (an individual-level concept) of members to the group. But how can one assess the group-level pattern except by measuring the individual-level attraction? A similar problem obtains when trying to assess a group's personality (what Cattell, 1948, called "group syntality"). The statistical challenge is to parse members' personality scores into independent individual and group components (cf. Gonzalez & Griffin, 2002). To see two separate things, individuals and groups, within exactly the same set of data is not impossible. It does, however, pose substantial statistical, conceptual, and experiential challenges.

The reality of groups seems more convincingly demonstrated by examining products instead of properties. Individual and group products are more easily distinguished because they can be estimated from wholly different observations. Individual products can be estimated directly from the efforts of people who work alone. These then become the standard of comparison for evaluating the products of people who work collectively. If the latter exceed the former in quality or quantity, they signal not only the superiority of the group, but its very existence and worthiness as an independent object of study. We know groups are real because they often do generate products that cannot readily be explained by a "synthesis of all the data pertaining to each of the group members" when studied individually. This is certainly the case for those products that signal a strong synergistic performance gain in groups. But it is true as well even for those that reflect a weak synergistic gain. Neither can be predicted a priori simply by studying the performance of the group members when working alone. Rather, in order to understand these performance gains, it is necessary to consider the group as an interacting whole.

☐ Future Directions in the Search for Synergy

Throughout the book I have called attention not only to examples of synergistic performance gains in groups, but also to avenues of inquiry that seem worth pursuing in order to better understand those gains. In this final section I consider three broad domains where research has lagged, and where additional efforts are apt to prove beneficial.

More Task-Focused Research

As argued in Chapter 2, in order to understand fully the performance of small groups, it seems essential to comprehend the requirements of the tasks that those groups are asked to perform. This includes knowing in detail all of the demands imposed by the tasks themselves and by the rules (both implicit and explicit) under which they must be performed.

Group process and productivity—and the prospect of synergistic performance gains—all become meaningful only in terms of such requirements. The varied pattern of results reported throughout this book makes it clear that, depending on the specific task being performed, collaborative work arrangements can be either more or less beneficial than working alone. Indeed, performance can sometimes vary widely even across tasks within the same broad category. One of the keys to solving the puzzle presented by this checkered pattern of results is to better understand the underlying nature of the tasks being performed. If task demands specify what is required of a group in order to perform well, then a comprehensive mapping of the similarities and differences among tasks with respect to such demands should be invaluable for helping to explain the variability in group performance across tasks.

What is needed in order to produce such a mapping is a detailed empirical analysis of group tasks, not simply a logical or intuitive analysis. Broad, conceptually-derived task category schemes, such as those offered by McGrath (1984) and Steiner (1966, 1972) (see Chapter 2, pp. 55–68), are helpful, but clearly have their limitations. Substantial differences exist even among tasks within the categories defined by such schemes, and some of those differences are apt to be crucially important for understanding group performance. Researchers have often paid too little attention to such differences. This would appear to be part of the reason why the search for synergy in groups has progressed so far in rather hit-or-miss fashion, and why no general theory of synergy (by whatever label) has yet emerged. It is reasonable to expect that this same slow progress will continue in the future until we evolve a deeper, more systematic appreciation of the similarities and differences among the tasks that groups are asked to perform, both in the laboratory and in field settings.

Regarding the latter, it is interesting to note that industrial psychologists have developed a variety of sophisticated approaches to job analysis in work organizations, some of which focus on the specific tasks being performed (Brannick, Levine, Morgeson, 2007; Harvey, 1991). But with few exceptions (e.g., Blicksenderfer, Cannon-Bower, Salas, & Baker, 2000), most of these approaches deal with tasks performed by individuals, not groups. Despite the fact that tasks performed by groups have become increasingly common in everyday work settings, relatively little effort has been devoted to understanding them—especially with regard to the interaction demands they place on group members.

The situation is only slightly better in laboratory research. Here, numerous examples can be found in which isolated characteristics of various group tasks have been manipulated as independent variables and their impact on group performance observed. Unfortunately, a great many of these are one-shot studies involving ad hoc tasks chosen with only limited regard for the full range of demands they place on individuals and groups or for how they may (or may not) be related to other superficially similar tasks.[2] As a result, it is difficult to abstract from this work broadly applicable principles concerning group tasks, their underlying dimensionality, and how those dimensions might be related to group performance.

To be sure, there are instances in which specific tasks have been studied more programmatically, and where some limited progress has been made in evolving principles and theories pertinent to them. The large body of work on brainstorming in groups (Chapter 3) is an example, as is the work by Laughlin and his colleagues on collective induction (Laughlin, 1999; Laughlin & Hollingshead, 1995; see Chapter 4, pp. 137–146). The more recent work by Kerr, Hertel, and others on the Köhler motivation gain effect (Weber & Hertel, 2007; see Chapter 8, pp. 284–291) might be included here as well. Further, instances can be found in which a specific variable has been manipulated across a wide range of tasks. Research that varies whether group members interact face-to-face or via computer is an example. This variable has been manipulated in conjunction with idea generation tasks (Chapter 3), problem-solving tasks (Chapter 4), and decision-making tasks (Chapter 6), among others. But even here it is rare to find any one study addressing more than a single type of task (for a recent exception, see Alge, Wiethoff, & Klein, 2003). Instead, we are forced to rely nearly exclusively on between-study comparisons in order to draw inferences about meaningful similarities and differences among group tasks (e.g., Laughlin & Ellis, 1986). As a result, very little progress has been made toward developing anything like a comprehensive, empirically-grounded "theory of group tasks" to match the conceptual models offered a generation ago.

The field of small group research, and of small group performance in particular, would benefit in two ways if greater attention were paid to the nature of, and interrelationship among, group tasks. First, a better understanding of the underlying dimensional structure of group tasks would be very helpful in guiding future research. It would enable us to see more clearly the interconnections among those things that we already do know about small group performance (i.e., how group performance on one task is related to performance on certain other tasks). Equally, it would bring into sharper focus those task domains about which more needs to be learned. It would in essence provide a territorial map and so a means of identifying those regions that are in need of further exploration.

Second, a deeper appreciation of group tasks would also be helpful for building better theories of group performance. In particular, developing a more complete understanding of tasks should make it easier to incorporate task attributes directly into our theories of small group performance, as opposed to creating separate theories for tasks with different attributes. To clarify what I mean by this, it is useful to consider an example.

Incorporating Task Attributes in Theories of Group Performance: An Example

There are a number of theories about leadership in groups that take explicit account of task characteristics. One is Fiedler's Contingency Model of Leadership Effectiveness (1967, 1978a; Fiedler & Chemers, 1974; Fiedler & Garcia, 1987). The Contingency Model defines leader effectiveness in terms of the accomplishments of the group being led; a leader is considered to be effective to the extent that his or her group performs well. Consequently, the Contingency Model can be seen as a theory of group performance as well as a theory of leadership. A central tenet of the model is that leader effectiveness, and so group performance, depends on the match between the leader's style and the situation that he or she is in. Importantly, no one style of leadership is presumed to be effective across all situations. Rather, different situations call for different leadership styles. Of primary interest for the present discussion is the situational portion of this model.

Fiedler (1967, 1978a) points out that situations vary in the extent to which they make it easy or difficult for the leader to influence group members. He argues that three aspects of the situation are especially important in this regard. One has to do with the quality of the interpersonal relationship between the leader and his or her group members, and is captured by the variable "leader-member relations." To the extent that the leader has a positive, high quality relationship with the members of his or her group, it should be easier for the leader to gain member cooperation—members will do what the leader asks because they like the leader and want to maintain their good relationship with him or her. A second factor concerns the organizational context within which the group is embedded, and is captured by the variable "position power." To the extent the leader's position gives him or her legitimate authority to reward and punish group members, it should be easier for the leader to exert influence—members will do what the leader asks in order to gain rewards and avoid punishment.

Finally, the third situational factor considered by Fiedler (1967, 1978a), and the one of greatest concern here, has to do with the group's task. It is captured by the variable "task structure," which Fiedler defines as the extent to which (a) the requirements of the task are clearly stated and well understood by group members, (b) there is one best way to perform the task, (c) there is a single correct solution, and (d) the correctness of that solution is easily demonstrated. Thus, for example, tasks are more structured when they are accompanied by construction plans, operating manuals, checklists, a picture, drawing, or model of what the final product should look like, or some other type of specification for how the work is to be accomplished. In essence, these all supply procedural directives that can be used to justify the leader's task-relevant requests and demands.

Thus, they make it easier for the leader to secure member compliance—members will do what the leader asks because it is correct.

Fiedler (1967) argued on rational grounds that the structure of the group's task is twice as important as position power, but only half as important as leader-member relations, in determining how easy it is over-all for a leader to influence the members of his or her group. This relationship can be summarized as follows:

$$SF = (4 \times LMR) + (2 \times TS) + PP,$$

where SF is situational favorableness,[3] or the extent to which the situation makes it easy for the leader to influence group members, LMR is leader-member relations, TS is task structure, and PP is position power. Subsequent empirical research found support for the validity of the 4:2:1 weighting scheme (Beach & Beach, 1978; Fiedler, 1978b; Nebeker, 1975). It also reaffirms a point made in Chapter 2, that task characteristics can have a surprisingly powerful effect on behavior in groups, and as such warrant at least as much attention in our theories as do interpersonal (e.g., leader-member relations) and context (e.g., position power) variables.

The Contingency Model predicts that situations differing in favorableness are best handled by leaders with different styles, where leadership style is conceived as a stable individual difference variable. A fuller description of these predictions, and of the body of evidence supporting them, is beyond the scope of this book (but see Fiedler, 1967, 1978a; Fiedler & Chemers, 1974; Fiedler & Garcia, 1987; see also Peters, Hartke, & Pohlmann, 1985; Strube & Garcia, 1981). My purpose here is simply to point out that task structure is one aspect of situational favorableness and to call attention to the fact that Fiedler's conceptualization of task structure derives directly from Marvin Shaw's (1963) earlier empirical work on the multidimensional nature of group tasks. Recall that Shaw's research was described in detail in Chapter 2 (see pp. 42–47). Note that all four of the defining features of task structure listed two paragraphs above are among the 10 task attributes assessed by Shaw (see Figure 2.2). Further, three of them were found by Shaw to be highly intercorrelated, all loading on his solution multiplicity dimension. Thus, to the extent that Shaw's findings are generalizable, they suggest that Fiedler's task structure variable is less factorially complex than it might appear, comprising just two underlying dimensions, not four, and even then reflecting one of those dimensions more strongly than the other. What Fiedler calls task structure consists primarily of what Shaw referred to as solution multiplicity, with a bit of task difficulty (specifically, goal clarity) tossed in. Fiedler's task structure variable would also appear to have much in common with Laughlin's (1980; 1999; Laughlin & Ellis, 1986) intellective–judgmental task continuum.

The Contingency Model is not the only leadership theory to consider the moderating influence of task structure (cf. House, 1971, 1996; Kerr & Jermier, 1978; Vroom & Jago, 2007). It is, however, one of the best examples of a theory that builds on prior task-focused research. This has benefited the model in several respects. First, it links this portion of the model to a wider nomological network of concepts—in this case, to the underlying multidimensional ordering of group tasks identified by Shaw (1963)—thus making it easier to understand what the term "task structure" does and does not imply (e.g., it does not refer in any way to the cooperative requirements of the task, which is another of Shaw's task dimensions). Second, building on Shaw's prior work has also benefited the model by providing a ready way to operationalize task structure. Indeed, for a number of years Fiedler measured task structure with a four-item instrument containing the exact measures used by Shaw (Fiedler, 1964). Only later was that instrument modified so that it could be used more reliably by untrained raters (Fiedler & Chemers, 1984).

Finally, adopting a dimensional perspective on group tasks gives Fiedler's (1967, 1978a) Contingency Model considerable flexibility and breadth of application, both cross-sectionally and longitudinally. The model predicts that changing the nature of the group's task can impact the favorableness of the situation, which in turn may imply the need for a different style of leadership. Furthermore, Fiedler argues that simply having experience with a task can make it more structured. That is, with increasing experience the requirements of the task become clearer and better understood, the correctness of various problem solutions becomes easier to demonstrate, and the task as a whole generally becomes more routine. This, too, can change the favorableness of the situational to the point where a different style of leadership may be called for. Although there is empirical evidence to support these ideas (e.g., Fiedler, 1978b, 1992, 1994; Fiedler & Garcia, 1987), it can be debated whether experience affects task structure per se or whether it might be better conceptualized as a separate determinant of situational favorableness.[4] It is not important to resolve this debate here. Rather, it is sufficient simply to note that the debate would not even be possible had task structure not been incorporated as a variable in the Contingency Model to begin with.

More Interaction-Focused Research

Synergy is a gain in performance that is attributable to group interaction. Surprisingly, we know less than we should about group interaction and about how it actually leads to synergistic performance gains. This is because detailed analysis of behavior in groups has fallen out of fashion among researchers concerned with group performance effectiveness. Only rarely is direct, behavioral process data obtained from groups as they perform their tasks. Instead, the modal approach is to manipulate one or more independent variables, then evaluate performance, without bothering to record (or even observe) the interaction among group members as they work. To be sure, researchers do routinely measure members' *perceptions* of the group and its interaction (e.g., regarding cooperation, information exchange, interpersonal conflict, etc.). Such variables are often tested as potential mediators of the effects(s) of the independent variable(s), though they are nearly always assessed at the end of the experimental session, after the group has completed its task. Apart from the logical difficulties associated with inferring mediation from variables measured after the fact, the major shortcoming of this approach is that it tells us very little about the specific behaviors that prompted participants' end-of-session reports. This, in turn, makes it nearly impossible to link the group's performance to particular interaction processes. Thus, while contemporary research makes it plain *that* interaction often does benefit group performance (i.e., by comparison to the performance of individuals working alone), it typically provides few clues about *how* interaction actually generates that benefit.

Interestingly, it has not always been this way. In the early years of small group research, it was common practice for investigators to make careful observations of group interaction and to relate these in some way to performance. A good example is Marjorie Shaw's (1932) study of group problem-solving. I described her study in some detail in Chapters 1 and 4. Recall that Shaw had students from a graduate course in social psychology work either individually or in four-person groups on a series of problem-solving tasks. She found that on a majority of those tasks the students performed better when working in groups than when working alone. As part of that study, Shaw had a trained note-taker observed each group and record (among other things) how often members made and (separately) rejected suggestions. She found that five times as many incorrect as correct suggestions were rejected, and that three times as many suggestions were rejected by another group member as by the member who made the suggestion in the first place. On the basis of these observations, Shaw concluded that "one point of group supremacy is the rejection of incorrect ideas that escape the notice of the individual when working alone" (p. 502).

In subsequent decades, more sophisticated approaches to coding group interaction were developed, reaching a high-water mark with the widely cited work of Bales (1950, Bales & Cohen, 1979; Bales & Strodtbeck, 1951). But starting with the introduction by Lorge and Solomon (1955) of their Model A (see Chapter 4, pp. 124–126), and continuing with the development of Social Decision Scheme (SDS) Theory by Davis (1973) and others (see Chapter 4, pp. 126–137), research on group problem solving and decision making began to move in a different direction. Rather than focusing on group interaction directly, investigators began to model the statistical relationship between members' pre-interaction solution preferences, on the one hand, and the solution eventually chosen by the group, on the other, under the assumption that much of the interaction that takes place in problem-solving and decision-making groups is devoted to resolving disagreements about which solution alternative is best. By modeling the relationship between member preferences and the solution actually chosen by the group, it was hoped that inferences might be drawn about the underlying interaction processes that enabled the group to reach consensus on a single collective response.

Consider, for example, the Truth Wins SDS model. Truth Wins is often the model that best describes the relationship between member preferences and the solution actually chosen by the group when working on simple algebra problems (e.g., Laughlin & Ellis, 1986). As will be recalled from Chapter 4, Truth Wins means that a group will tend to solve a problem correctly if at least one of its members can solve the problem working alone. Laughlin (1999; Laughlin & Hollingshead, 1995) suggests that Truth Wins reflects an underlying process of demonstration; members resolve their differences of opinion about which solution alternative is best by demonstrating to one another the correctness of the solutions they prefer.[5] This stands in contrast to, for example, a Majority Wins model, which predicts that a group will choose correctly only when a majority of its members initially prefer the correct alternative and is presumed to reflect an underlying process of voting. Thus, the inference to be drawn when the Truth Wins rather than Majority Wins model best fits the data is that the task in question evokes behavior associated with demonstration rather than voting.

This approach has been extremely helpful, in part because it offers a formal method for making specific, testable predictions about performance. At the same time, however, and as noted in Chapter 4, even when confirmed empirically, those predictions do not always uniquely identify the group processes that generated them. Importantly, the same pattern of results may be indicative of several different forms of group interaction.

This point is easily illustrated with the Truth Wins model. Even when Truth Wins closely fits the obtained data (e. g., when groups attempt to solve algebra problems), a question can be raised about the extent to which demonstration actually occurs as part of the group's interaction. Demonstration seems most likely when only a single member is able to derive the correct answer working alone. It may play a role as well when two members independently are able to work out the correct answer, yet constitute a minority within their group (i.e., in groups with five or more members). But here there is also another possibility. Members who cannot solve a problem themselves, but who nevertheless understand the task to be demonstrable (i.e., they recognize that there are well accepted rules and procedures that would lead to an unambiguously correct solution if only one knew how to apply them), may be willing to accept at face value—without demonstration—any solution advocated by at least two members who come to it independently. That is, it may sometimes be the *perceived* demonstrability of the task, not actual behavioral demonstration, that is at play. Extending this idea, when a majority of the members prefer the correct solution, especially a strong majority, it seems quite reasonable that demonstration might routinely be set aside in favor of voting. This is likely to occur to the extent that voting is easier and less time consuming than demonstration, and to the extent that group members subscribe to the dictum "consensus implies correctness." Finally, when there is no disagreement among members (i.e., they all agree a priori on the same solution), that solution seems most likely to be adopted by acclamation. Indeed, acclamation is likely an important part of the reason why correct solutions seldom emerge when every member prefers the same incorrect choice alternative. If, rather than deciding by acclamation, members instead tried to demonstrate to one another the correctness of their consensus (but erroneous) preference, they might come to recognize its insufficiency and so search for a better alternative.

Thus, even when a single social decision scheme model closely fits a given set of data, the nature of the underlying group process may vary considerably, depending on (among other things) the specific distribution of individual member preferences and capabilities within the group.[6]

Surprisingly, there have been relatively few attempts to supplement the social decision scheme approach with direct observations of group behavior in order to confirm the nature of the underlying group process(es). Laughlin's extensive programs of research with his rule induction and letters-to-numbers tasks perhaps come closest (see Chapter 4, pp. 137–156). These two tasks are specifically designed to reveal intermediate information-generating actions and problem-solving steps taken by individuals and groups as they work toward a final solution. For example, on each trial of the letters-to-numbers task, problem solvers must propose both an equation and a mapping of one letter to one number. It has been found that, compared to even the best of an equivalent number of individuals working alone, groups propose more complex equations (i.e., equations involving more letters), which enables them to identify the coding of more letters per trial and so determine the full coding of letters-to-numbers in fewer trials overall (Laughlin, Bonner, & Miner, 2002; Laughlin, Hatch, Silver, & Boh, 2006; Laughlin, Zander, Knievel, & Tan, 2003). Or, to put it in Shaw's (1932) terms, "one point of group supremacy" on the letters-to-numbers task is that they use more complex equations than individuals. Laughlin et al. (2006) suggest that this occurs because multiletter equations are *"demonstrably* preferable" to two-letter equations, meaning that any member who proposes such an equation should be able to demonstrate its greater potential information yield to others in the group, provided he or she has the time and motivation to do so. Yet Laughlin et al. offer no concrete behavioral evidence that demonstration actually takes place while groups perform the letters-to-numbers task. Thus, it could be that groups simply stumble onto more complex equations, without an a priori demonstration of their superiority (i.e., by chance they try something more complex, learn that it actually does work better, and so stick with it on subsequent trials). Using a more complex equation because someone in the group has shown that it will yield a larger quantity of helpful information, as opposed to using it without much forethought, then discovering its superiority after the fact, are two very different processes that are unlikely to be distinguished except by a careful analysis of the interaction among group members as they work on the problem.

I do not mean to suggest here that Laughlin et al. (2006) are necessarily incorrect in assuming that demonstration is an integral part of the process that underlies the superiority of group performance on the letters-to-numbers task. Rather, I am simply pointing out that what they have proposed is indeed an assumption and that it deserves verification through direct observation of group interaction.

More generally, research concerned with group performance needs to become more fully engaged in the business of observing group interaction directly if we expect to better understand the unfolding process by which synergistic performance gains (and losses) actually emerge. Although research that links interaction to accomplishment is relatively rare, when such linkages have been established in the past, they have been quite informative. Our understanding of idea generation in brainstorming groups, for example, has been enriched by research that examines in detail the sequence of ideas voiced by members (e.g., Brown, Tumeo, Larey, & Paulus, 1998; Nijstad & Stroebe, 2006). Likewise, our understanding of group decision-making effectiveness has profited from research that traces the orderly pattern of member contributions during discussion (e.g., Larson, 1997; Larson, Christensen, Franz, & Abbott, 1998; Winquist & Larson, 1998).

Another good example is the study of transactive memory in groups conducted by Rulke and Rau (2000). As described in Chapter 7 (see p. 250), this study examined the interaction among group members as they learned how to assemble an AM radio from a hobby kit. It was found that transactive memory—the informal assignment of responsibility for learning and retaining bits of task-relevant information—evolved by means of small encoding cycles. These cycles were typically initiated by either a question or statement indicating a lack of expertise, followed by a declaration of expertise by another group member (and sometimes an evaluation of that expertise by a third member), and ended with an attempt to coordinate who would do what in the group. The elements of these cycles constitute the key behaviors by which members learned one another's competencies vis-à-vis the radio assembly task and developed appropriate coordination strategies. Rulke and Rau observed that, the more frequently these cycles occurred during training, the more members subsequently specialized in different aspects of the overall radio assembly process, worked together in a smoothly coordinated fashion, and trusted one another's knowledge. As a result of all this, groups that were trained together performed the assembly task better—made fewer assembly errors—than groups that were trained apart.

As a final example, consider the work on group problem-solving by Chiu (2008a, 2008b; Chiu & Khoo, 2005). Using a statistical approach to discourse analysis, Chiu examined the discussions of 20 four-person groups as they attempted to solve a problem requiring the application of algebra. For each group, he coded the content of every speaking turn, then assessed the impact of various types of remarks made by members on the subsequent emergence of new ideas relevant to solving the problem. Chiu found that expressions of disagreement were more likely to spark new ideas than were expressions of agreement and that new ideas improved a group's problem-solving performance. The effect of disagreements on the generation of new ideas was particularly strong when the disagreement recognized a previous incorrect idea or contribution, but occurred even when no specific incorrect idea or contribution was recognized (e.g., "I don't understand how we get that [intermediate result]"). Disagreements, of course, would seem to be a central element of any error correction process in group interaction. Unfortunately, Chiu did not compare the problem-solving performance of groups to that of individuals working alone. Thus, his work does not speak in a direct way to the question of performance gains in groups. Nevertheless, his analysis of group interaction does seem to corroborate the conclusion drawn by Shaw (1932) more than three quarters of a century ago that "one point of group supremacy [on problem-solving tasks] is the rejection of incorrect ideas."

The statistical analysis of group interaction has in the past been hampered by the many difficulties inherent in complex, sequential data (e.g., nonindependence of observations). However, several new analytic techniques have recently been developed to deal with such difficulties (for nontechnical overviews, see Bonito, 2002; Chiu & Khoo, 2005). As illustrated by Chiu (2008a, 2008b), these new approaches enable researchers to go well beyond what can be deduced from simple tallies and summary statistics describing the overall content of group interaction. It is now possible to create a more sophisticated understanding of the patterned, contingent, interconnected nature of task-oriented behavior in groups. Employing such methods, and so more directly linking interaction to outcomes, should greatly improve our understanding of how synergistic performance gains are generated.

More Research on Temporal and Developmental Processes

Finally, in addition to more task- and interaction-focused research, there is also a need for more empirical work that examines the development of synergistic performance gains over time. It should be evident by now that a very large proportion of the experimental literature on small group performance focuses on ad hoc groups of undergraduate students who work together for no more than an hour or two. These groups have neither a history nor a future. They are created, exist for a moment, then vanish. In this respect, they more closely resemble exotic elements forged in high-energy physics experiments than task-performing groups found in the real world.

One difficulty with such transient conditions is that they may not always be conducive to the emergence of synergy in groups. Rather, depending on the task, synergy may sometimes take a considerable amount of time to develop. If the task is complex, for example, synergistic performance gains might not materialize until after members have first learned what their groupmates know and are skilled at, what behaviors they are likely to enact in various situations, and what responses might be needed to those behaviors. Such learning almost certainly underlies the dramatic performance gains observed over time in the surgical teams studied by Pisano, Bohmer, and Edmondson (2001) and described in Chapter 7 (see pp. 220–223). It is also part and parcel of transactive memory development in groups, another topic discussed in Chapter 7 (see pp. 241–254). Group learning increases as a function of the amount of time that members spend working together. If there is important information about the task, or about one's groupmates vis-à-vis the task, that must be learned before synergistic performance gains emerge, then the hoped for synergy will not be found if the group has existed for too short a time.

This, of course, is hardly a new idea. Among many others, those who coach team sports are keenly aware of it. No coach of a basketball, hockey, or soccer team—at any level of competition—would consider sending his or her team into a game without them first having spent a substantial amount of time practicing together. Practice sessions are invariably designed not only to improve players' performance as individuals, but also to improve their coordination as a team. But coordination in these sports seldom comes about overnight. Rather, it usually develops slowly and requires the commitment of much time and effort. The same is true for many other groups whose tasks call for tightly coordinated behavior by two or more members.

Even tasks that involve the coordination of seemingly simple behaviors may sometimes require a good deal of practice before synergistic performance gains begin to materialize. Consider, for instance, the cycling scenario used to introduce the concept of synergy in Chapter 1. As noted there, two cyclists can travel faster and further riding together, one behind the other, than either of them would be able to do riding alone. However, in order to realize this performance gain, it is necessary that the following rider stay very closely behind the leader—so close that his or her front wheel might occasionally overlap the leader's rear wheel. This is a relatively simple behavior that nevertheless is extremely dangerous for both riders. The reason is clear; if their wheels accidentally touch, there is a chance that one or both of them will take a painful fall to the ground. Because of this, the cyclist following pace may be unwilling to ride close enough to gain any measurable advantage from the small pocket of low pressure that lies immediately behind the leader. Rather, he or she may prefer to hang back slightly, at a distance that is safer, but that also provides little shelter from the wind. Not until the two cyclists begin to trust one another's riding abilities is it likely that either of them will be inclined to ride consistently close enough behind the other to draft effectively. The following rider in particular must learn to trust that the leader will not make sudden moves to the left or right (or, in a panic, hit the brakes!), and likewise that the leader will safely navigate them through traffic and around obstacles in their path. Trust of this sort is apt to increase the more they ride together, though it might grow faster in some circumstances than others. Thus, their third ride together will likely yield a larger synergistic performance gain than their first ride, and their first ride together might yield no gain at all.

The development of trust in the cycling scenario, and its likely impact on performance, is just one example of a temporal process that seems essential to understand if we are ever to have a complete picture of how synergistic performance gains emerge in groups. Although it would be naïve to suppose that synergy is an inevitable consequence of working collectively, and that if we just wait long enough it will eventually appear, it seems equally naïve to suppose that synergy will never materialize if it is not evident within the first few minutes of a group's life. Rather, there are apt to be many groups, performing many different types of tasks, for whom synergistic performance gains evolve only gradually. It is precisely this sort of situation that requires more research attention.

Thus, it seems important to study groups over time. To a degree, such investigations might be informed by existing theory and research that takes a dynamic perspective on groups and that emphasizes developmental changes that occur as group members gain experience with one another (e.g., Arrow, McGrath, & Berdahl, 2000; McGrath & Tschan, 2004). However, what is really needed is research that is specifically designed to identify and understand those particular changes in groups that either facilitate or inhibit the emergence of synergistic performance gains. Further, that research must be sensitive to the possibility—indeed, likelihood—that some of the relevant variables may be highly task specific. The growth of trust in the cycling scenario is an example. This variable is particular to that task. It refers to the confidence that each rider has in his or her partner's ability and behavior as they relate to drafting. Importantly, it does not refer to a more general interpersonal trust, camaraderie, group cohesiveness, or the like. Changes in these latter variables may or may not impact the performance of a cycling team (cf. Mullen & Copper, 1994; Salas, Rozell, Mullen, & Driskell, 1999), but, if they do, they almost certainly operate via other mechanisms (e.g., motivation). My point here is simply that we need to think carefully about how temporal processes are related to performance gains in groups. Whereas some may be task independent, and so broadly relevant, others are apt to be quite task specific. Task specificity does not make a variable any less important. Rather, it seems necessary to understand both task-specific and task-independent temporal processes if we are to make significant progress in the future in the search for synergy.

☐ Chapter Summary

In this final chapter, I have provided a summary evaluation of the synergy framework used throughout the book. That framework offers a reasonably balanced platform for inquiring into group performance gains as well as losses and into the facilitative and inhibitory interaction processes that underlie them. One advantage of the synergy framework is that it employs objective criteria for assessing gains and losses. As such, it allows us to see more clearly examples of exceptional group performance that are particularly worthy of further consideration and follow-up research. The synergy framework also provides a common metric for comparing group performance across otherwise incommensurate tasks. In this capacity, it helps call attention to performance differences that arise as a function of task type. Finally, the synergy framework speaks to the long-standing debate about the psychological reality of groups by showing that certain group performances are emergent phenomena that cannot be explained by any simple combination of member contributions. Thus, despite occasional difficulties associated with implementing the synergy framework, it seems a beneficial tool both for organizing empirical findings and for thinking about group performance more generally.

I also suggested in this chapter three broad directions for future research. One concerns the tasks that groups are asked to perform. To fully understand the performance of small groups, we need to better appreciate the underlying nature of their assigned tasks. A comprehensive mapping of the similarities and differences among tasks would be especially valuable for helping to explain the variability that is found in group performance across tasks and would make it easier to integrate task characteristics into our theories of group performance. A second direction for the future concerns the behavior of group members. Although synergistic performance gains are rooted in group interaction, we know less than we should about how interaction actually generates synergy. To learn more, we need to reacquaint ourselves with the detailed analysis of group behavior. This includes learning to apply new statistical tools to unpack the complex interdependence in group interaction and reveal the linkages between specific forms of interaction and performance. Finally, a third direction for further research is to examine the emergence of synergistic performance gains over time. This should be done with an eye toward identifying developmental changes in groups that either facilitate or inhibit synergy. The impact on performance of some of these changes may be task independent and so broadly relevant. But others are apt to be quite task specific. It seems necessary to understand both types if we are to fully comprehend synergistic performance gains in groups.

The future in the search for synergy seems brighter now than it once did. Evidence is slowly accumulating that groups are capable of more than just weak synergistic performance gains; they are capable as well of strong synergistic gains. There is good reason to expect that significant progress can be made not only in uncovering further examples of both, but also in understanding more precisely how such performance gains arise.

☐ Endnotes

1. The concept of "groupness" is akin to what Campbell (1958) originally referred to as "entitativity," which he defined as "the degree of having the nature of an entity, of having real existence." It is noteworthy that, within contemporary social psychology, research on entitativity is concerned not with the reality of groups per se, but with factors that determine when perceivers will and will not judge a set of persons to be a group (e.g., Hamilton & Hewstone, 2007; Yzerbyt, Judd, & Corneille, 2004). In other words, even here social psychologists have succeeded in turning scholarly attention away from groups, focusing instead on individuals—as perceivers of groups, in this case.

2. Tasks (like research participants) are too often chosen for their convenience. Laboratory researchers generally prefer simple tasks that require little experience, minimal training, and can be completed with just a few minutes of effort—all characteristics that are apt to work against the discovery of significant synergistic performance gains.

3. Situational favorableness was later renamed situational control (e.g., Fiedler & Chemers, 1984; Fiedler & Garcia, 1987).

4. Fiedler's (1978b, 1992, 1994) claim that experience can affect task structure calls to mind the discussion of task demonstrability in Chapter 2, where it was noted that certain of the conditions for establishing demonstrability pertain as much or more to the group performing the task as to the task itself.

5. This includes attempting—and failing—to demonstrate the correctness of an incorrect solution. By definition, an incorrect solution cannot be demonstrated to be correct. Yet attempting to do so should cause members to recognize their error and so lead them to abandon that solution for another alternative.

6. I am indebted to Nick Aramovich for his helpful discussions on this point.

REFERENCES

Abele, S., & Diehl, M. (2008). Finding teammates who are not prone to sucker and free-riding effects: The Protestant work ethic as a moderator of motivation losses in group performance. *Group Processes and Intergroup Relations, 11,* 39–54.

Aiello, J. R., & Douthitt, E. A. (2001). Social facilitation from Triplett to electronic performance monitoring. *Group Dynamics: Theory, Research, and Practice, 5,* 163–180.

Alge, B. J., Wiethoff, C., & Klein, H. J. (2003). When does the medium matter: Knowledge-building experiences and opportunities in decision-making teams. *Organizational Behavior and Human Decision Processes, 91,* 26–37.

Allen, N. J., & Hecht, T. D. (2004). The "romance of teams": Toward an understanding of its psychological underpinnings and implications. *Journal of Occupational and Organizational Psychology, 77,* 439–461.

Allport, F. H. (1920). The influence of the group upon association and thought. *Journal of Experimental Psychology, 3,* 159–182.

Allport, F. H. (1924a). *Social Psychology.* Boston: Houghton-Mifflin.

Allport, F. H. (1924b). The group fallacy in relation to social science. *Journal of Abnormal and Social Psychology, 19,* 60–73.

Allport, G. W. (1954). The historical background of modern social psychology. In G. Lindsey (Ed.), *Handbook of Social Psychology* (Vol. 1, pp. 3–56). Reading: MA, Addison-Wesley.

Anderson, J. R. (1983). Retrieval of information from long-term memory. *Science, 220,* 25–30.

Andersson, J. (2001). Net effect of memory collaboration: How is collaboration affected by factors such as friendship, gender and age? *Scandinavian Journal of Psychology, 42,* 367–375.

Andersson, J., & Rönnberg, J. (1995). Recall suffers from collaboration: Joint recall effects of friendship and task complexity. *Applied Cognitive Psychology, 9,* 199–211.

Andersson, J., & Rönnberg, J. (1996). Collaboration and memory: Effects of dyadic retrieval on different memory tasks. *Applied Cognitive Psychology, 10,* 171–181.

Andersson, J., & Rönnberg, J. (1997). Cued memory collaboration: Effects of friendship and type of retrieval cue. *European Journal of Cognitive Psychology, 9,* 273–287.

Ang, S., & O'Connor, M. (1991). The effect of group interaction strategies on performance in time series extrapolation. *International Journal of Forecasting, 7,* 347–372.

Argote, L., Devadas, R., & Melone, N. (1990). The base-rate fallacy: Contrasting processes and outcomes of groups and individual judgment. *Organizational Behavior and Human Decision Processes, 46,* 296–310.

Argote, L., Insko, C. A., Yovetich, N., & Romero, A. A. (1995). Group learning curves: The effects of turnover and task complexity on group performance. *Journal of Applied Social Psychology, 25,* 512–529.

Arrow, H., McGrath, J. E., & Berdahl, J. L. (2000). *Small groups as complex systems: Foundation, coordination, development, and adaptation.* Thousand Oaks, CA: Sage.

Arthur, W., Jr., Bell, S. T., Villado, A. J., & Doverspike, D. (2006). The use of person-organization fit in employment decision making: An assessment of its criterion-related validity. *Journal of Applied Psychology, 91,* 786–801.

Aslan, A., Bäuml, K-H., & Grundgeiger, T. (2007). The role of inhibitory processes in part-list cuing. *Journal of Experimental Psychology: Learning, Memory, and Cognition, 33,* 335–341.

Austin, J. R. (2003). Transactive memory in organizational groups. The effects of content, consensus, specialization, and accuracy on group performance. *Journal of Applied Psychology, 88,* 866–878.

Axtell, R. L. (2001). Zipf Distribution of U.S. Firm Sizes. *Science, 293,* 1818–1820.

Bailey, K. D. (1994). *Typologies and taxonomies: An introduction to classification techniques.* Thousand Oaks, CA: Sage.

Bales, R. F. (1950). *Interaction process analysis: A method for the study of small groups.* Cambridge, MA: Addison-Wesley.

Bales, R. F., & Cohen, S. P. (1979). *SYMLOG: A system for the multiple level observation of groups.* New York: Free Press.

Bales, R. F., & Strodtbeck, F. L. (1951). Phases in group problem-solving. *Journal of Abnormal and Social Psychology, 46,* 485–495.

Baltes, B. B., Dickson, M. W., Sherman, M. P., Bauer, C. C., & LaGanke, J. (2002). Computer-mediated communication and group decision making: A meta-analysis. *Organizational Behavior and Human Decision Processes, 87,* 156–179.

Barber, A. E., Wesson, M. J., Roberson, Q. M., & Taylor, M. S. (1999). A tale of two job markets: Organizational size and its effects on hiring practices and job search behavior. *Personnel Psychology, 52,* 841–867.

Barkowski, D., Lamm, H., & Schwinger, T. (1982). Brainstorming in group (dyadic) and individual conditions. [Einfallsproduktion von Individuen und Dyaden unter "Brainstorming"-Bedingungen] *Psychologische Beitrage, 24,* 39–46.

Baron, R. S., Hoppe, S. I., Kao, C. F., Brunsman, B., Linneweh, B., & Rogers, D. (1996). Social corroboration and opinion extremity. *Journal of Experimental Social Psychology, 32,* 537–560.

Barron, B. (2003). When smart groups fail. *The Journal of the Learning Sciences, 12,* 307–359.

Barton, W. A., Jr. (1926). The effect of group activity and individual effort in developing ability to solve problems in first year algebra. *Educational Administration and Supervision, 12,* 512–518.

Basadur, M., & Thompson, R. (1986). Usefulness of the ideation principle of extended effort in real world professional and managerial creative problem solving. *Journal of Creative Behavior, 20,* 23–34.

Basden, B. H., Basden, D. R., Bryner, S., & Thomas, R. L., III. (1997). A comparison of group and individual remembering: Does collaboration disrupt retrieval strategies? *Journal of Experimental Psychology: Learning, Memory, and Cognition, 23,* 1176–1189.

Basden, D. R., & Basden, B. H. (1995). Part-list cuing inhibition as retrieval strategy disruption. *Journal of Experimental Psychology: Learning, Memory, and Cognition, 21,* 1659–1672.

Baumann, M. R., & Bonner, B. L. (2004). The effects of variability and expectations on utilization of member expertise and group performance. *Organizational Behavior and Human Decision Processes, 93*, 89–101.

Beach, B. H., & Beach, L. R. (1978). A note on judgments of situational favorableness and probability of success. *Organizational Behavior and Human Performance, 22*, 69–74.

Beal, D. J., Cohen, R. R., Burke, M. J., & McLendon, C. L. (2003). Cohesion and performance in groups: A meta-analytic clarification of construct relations. *Journal of Applied Psychology, 88*, 989–1004.

Beat a mile a minute. (1899, July 1). *The New York Times*, p. 1.

Bezrukova, K., Thatcher, S. M. B., & Jehn, K. A. (2007). Group heterogeneity and faultlines: Comparing alignment and dispersion theories of group composition. In K. J. Behfar and L. L. Thompson (Eds.), *Conflict in organizational groups: New directions in theory and practice* (pp. 57–92). Evanston: IL: Northwestern University Press.

Blascovich, J., Mendes, W. B., Hunter, S. B., & Salomon, K. A. (1999). Social "facilitation" as challenge and threat. *Journal of Personality and Social Psychology, 77*, 68–77.

Blascovich, J., Mendes, W. B., Tomaka, J., Salomon, K., & Seery, M. (2003). The robust nature of the biopsychosocial model of challenge and threat: A reply to Wright and Kirby. *Personality and Social Psychology Review, 7*, 234–243.

Blascovich, J., & Tomaka, J. (1996). The biopsychosocial model of arousal regulation. *Advances in Experimental Social Psychology, 28*, 1–51.

Blicksenderfer, E., Cannon-Bower, J. A., Salas, E., & Baker, D. P. (2000). Analyzing knowledge requirements in team tasks. In J. M. Schraagn, S. F. Chipman, & V. L. Shalin (Eds.), *Cognitive task analysis* (pp. 431–447). Mahwah, NJ: Erlbaum.

Blitzkrieger (1939; September 25). *Time Magazine, 34*, 25–27.

Bond, C. F., Jr. (1982). Social facilitation: A self-presentational view. *Journal of Personality and Social Psychology, 42*, 1042–1050.

Bond, C. F., Jr., & Titus, L. J. (1983). Social facilitation: A meta-analysis of 241 studies. *Psychological Bulletin, 94*, 265–292.

Bond, C. F., Jr., & van Leeuwen, M. D. (1991). Can a part be greater than a whole? On the relationship between primary and meta-analytic evidence. *Basic and Applied Social Psychology, 12*, 33–40.

Bonito, J. A. (2002). The analysis of participation in small groups: Methodological and conceptual issues related to interdependence. *Small Group Research, 33*, 412–438.

Bonner, B. L. (2004). Expertise in group problem solving: Recognition, social combination, and performance. *Group Dynamics: Theory, Research, and Practice, 8*, 277–290.

Bonner, B. L., Baumann, M. R., Lehn, A. K., Pierce, D. M., & Wheeler, E. C. (2006). Modeling collective choice: Decision-making on complex intellective tasks. *European Journal of Social Psychology, 36*, 617–633.

Bonner, B. L., Gonzalez, C. M., & Sommer, D. (2004). Centrality and accuracy in group quantity estimations. *Group Dynamics: Theory, Research, and Practice, 8*, 155–165.

Bonner, B. L., Sillito, S. D., & Baumann, M. R. (2007). Collective estimation: Accuracy, expertise, and extroversion as sources of intra-group influence. *Organizational Behavior and Human Decision Processes, 103*, 121–133.

Brandon, D. P., & Hollingshead, A. B. (2004). Transactive memory systems in organizations: Matching tasks, expertise, and people. *Organization Science, 15,* 633–644.

Brannick, M. T., Levine, E. L., & Morgeson, F. P. (2007). *Job and work analysis: Methods, research, and applications for human resource management.* Thousand Oaks, CA: Sage.

Bransford, D. J., & Johnson, M. K. (1972). Contextual prerequisites for understanding: Some investigations of comprehension and recall. *Journal of Verbal Learning and Verbal Behavior, 11,* 717–726.

Bransford, D. J., & Johnson, M. K. (1973). Consideration of some problems of comprehension. In W. G. Chase (Ed.), *Visual information processing* (pp. 383–438). New York: Academic Press.

Brewer, M. B. (1979). In-group bias in the minimal intergroup situation: A cognitive-motivational analysis. *Psychological Bulletin, 86,* 307–324.

Brewer, M. B., & Gaertner, S. L. (2003). Toward reduction of prejudice: Intergroup contact and social categorization. In R. Brown & S. Gaertner (Eds.), *Blackwell handbook of social psychology: Intergroup processes* (pp. 451–472). Malden, MA: Blackwell.

Brodbeck, F. C., & Greitemeyer, T. (2000a). A dynamic model of group performance: Considering the group members' capacity to learn. *Group Processes and Intergroup Relations, 3,* 159–182.

Brodbeck, F. C., & Greitemeyer, T. (2000b). Effects of individual versus mixed individual and group experience in rule induction on group member learning and group performance. *Journal of Experimental Social Psychology, 36,* 621–648.

Brodbeck, F. C., Kerschreiter, R., Mojzisch, A., Frey, D., & Schulz-Hardt, S. (2002). The dissemination of critical, unshared information in decision-making groups: The effects of pre-discussion dissent. *European Journal of Social Psychology, 32,* 35–56.

Brodbeck, F. C., Kerschreiter, R., Mojzisch, A., & Schulz-Hardt, S. (2007). Group decision making under conditions of distributed knowledge: The information asymmetries model. *Academy of Management Journal, 32,* 459–479.

Brown, D. W., & Konrad, A. M. (2001). Granovetter was right—The importance of weak ties to a contemporary job search. *Group and Organization Management, 26,* 434–462.

Brown, V. R., & Paulus, P. B. (1996). A simple dynamic model of social factors in group brainstorming. *Small Group Research, 27,* 91–114.

Brown, V. R., Tumeo, M., Larey, T. S., & Paulus, P. B. (1998). Modeling cognitive interaction during brainstorming. *Small Group Research, 29,* 495–526.

Brownstein, A. L. (2003). Biased predecision processing. *Psychological Bulletin, 129,* 545–568.

Buehler, R., Messervey, D., & Griffin, D. (2005). Collaborative planning and prediction: Does group discussion affect optimistic biases in time estimation? *Organizational Behavior and Human Decision Processes, 97,* 47–63.

Buffardi, L. C., Fleishman, E. A., Morath, R. A., & McCarthy, P. M. (2000). Relationships between ability requirements and human errors in job tasks. *Journal of Applied Psychology, 85,* 551–564.

Bunderson, J. S. (2003). Recognizing and utilizing expertise in work groups: A status characteristics perspective. *Administrative Science Quarterly, 48,* 557–591.

Burnstein, E. (1982). Persuasion as argument processing. In H. Brandstatter, J. H. Davis, & G. Stocker-Kreichgauer (Eds.), *Group decision making* (pp. 103–124). London: Academic Press.

Burnstein, E., & Vinokur, A. (1973). Testing two classes of theories about group induced shifts in individual choice. *Journal of Experimental Social Psychology, 9*, 123–137.

Burnstein, E., & Vinokur, A. (1977). Persuasive argumentation and social comparison as determinants of attitude polarization. *Journal of Experimental Social Psychology, 13*, 315–352.

Burtt, H. E. (1920). Sex differences in the effect of discussion. *Journal of Experimental Psychology, 3*, 390–395.

Buunk, A. P., & Gibbons, F. X. (2007). Social comparison: The end of a theory and the emergence of a field. *Organizational Behavior and Human Decision Processes, 102*, 3–21.

Buyer, L. S. (1988). Creative problem solving: A comparison of performance under different instructions. *Journal of Creative Behavior, 22*, 55–61.

Byrne, D. (1971). *The attraction paradigm.* New York: Academic Press.

Cacioppo, J. T., & Petty, R. E. (1986). Social processes. In M. G. H. Coles, E. Donchin, & S. W. Porges (Eds.), *Psychophysiology: Systems, processes, and applications* (pp. 646–679). New York: Guilford.

Camacho, L. M., & Paulus, P. B. (1995). The role of social anxiousness in group brainstorming. *Journal of Personality and Social Psychology, 68*, 1071–1080.

Campbell, D. J. (1988). Task complexity: A review and analysis. *Academy of Management Review, 13*, 40–52.

Campbell, D. T. (1958). Common fate, similarity, and other indices of the status of aggregates of persons as social entities. *Behavioral Science, 3*, 14–25.

Campbell, D. T., & Stanley, J. C. (1966). *Experimental and quasi-experimental designs for research.* Chicago, IL: Rand-McNally.

Carron, A. V., Burke, S. M., & Prapavessis, H. (2004). Self-Presentation and Group Influence. *Journal of Applied Sport Psychology, 16*, 41–58.

Carver, C. S., & Scheier, M. F. (1981). *Attention and self-regulation: A control-theory approach to human behavior.* New York: Springer-Verlag.

Carver, C. S., & Scheier, M. F. (1998). *On the self-regulation of behavior.* Cambridge, UK: Cambridge University Press.

Casey, J. T., Gettys, C. F., Pliske, R. M., & Mehle, T. (1984). A partition of small group predecision performance into informational and social components. *Organizational Behavior and Human Performance, 34*, 112–139.

Cattell, R. B. (1948). Concepts and methods in the measurement of group syntality. *Psychological Review, 55*, 48–63.

Cattell, R. B. (1957). *Personality and motivation: Structure and measurement.* Yonkers, NY: World Books.

Caudle, R. M., & Williams, G. M. (1993). The misuse of analysis of variance to detect synergy in combination drug studies. *Pain, 55*, 313–317.

Chakin, S. (1987). The heuristic model of persuasion. In M. P. Zanna, J. M. Olson, & C. P. Herman (Eds.), *Social influence: The Ontario Symposium* (Vol. 5, pp. 3–39). Hillsdale, NJ: Erlbaum.

Chapman, D. S., Uggerslev, K. L., Carroll, S. A., Piasentin, K. A., & Jones, D. A. (2005). Applicant attraction to organizations and job choice: A meta-analytic review of the correlates of recruiting outcomes. *Journal of Applied Psychology, 90*, 928–944.

Chen, F. F., & Kenrick, D. T. (2002). Repulsion or attraction? Group membership and assumed attitude similarity. *Journal of Personality and Social Psychology*, *83*, 111–125.

Chernyshenko, O. S., Miner, A. G., Baumann, M. R., & Sniezek, J. A. (2003). The impact of information distribution, ownership, and discussion on group member judgment: The differential cue weighting model. *Organizational Behavior and Human Decision Processes*, *91*, 12–25.

Chiu, M. M. (2008a). Effects of argumentation on group micro-creativity: Statistical discourse analyses of algebra students' collaborative problem solving. *Contemporary Educational Psychology*, *33*, 382–402.

Chiu, M. M. (2008b). Flowing toward correct contributions during group problem solving: A statistical discourse analysis. *Journal of the Learning Sciences*, *17*, 415–463.

Chiu, M. M., & Khoo, L. (2005). A new method for analyzing sequential processes: Dynamic multilevel analysis. *Small Group Research*, *36*, 600–631.

Christensen, C., Larson, J. R., Jr., Abbott, A. S., Ardolino, A., Franz, T. M., & Pfeiffer, C. (2000). Decision making of clinical teams: communication patterns and diagnostic error. *Medical Decision Making*, *20*, 45–50.

Clark, N. K., Stephenson, G. M., & Kniveton, B. H. (1990). Social remembering: Quantitative aspects of individual and collaborative remembering by police officers and students. *British Journal of Psychology*, *81*, 73–94.

Clark, S. E., Abbe, A., & Larson, R. P. (2006). Collaboration in associative recognition memory: Using recalled information to defend "new" judgments. *Journal of Experimental Psychology: Learning, Memory, and Cognition*, *32*, 1266–1273.

Clark, S. E., Hori, A., Putnam, A., & Martin, T. P. (2000). Group collaboration in recognition memory. *Journal of Experimental Psychology: Learning, Memory, and Cognition*, *26*, 1578–1588.

Cohen, D., Whitmyre, J. W., & Funk, D. W. (1960). Effects of group cohesion and training upon creative thinking. *Journal of Applied Psychology*, *44*, 319–322.

Coleman, J. S. (1988). Social capital in the creation of human capital. *American Journal of Sociology*, *94* (Supplement), S95–S120.

Collaros, P. A., & Anderson, L. R. (1969). Effect of perceived expertness upon creativity of members of brainstorming groups. *Journal of Applied Psychology*, *53*, 159–163.

Collins, A. M., & Loftus, E. F. (1975). A spreading-activation theory of semantic processing. *Psychological Review*, *82*, 407–428.

Collins, B. E., & Guetzkow, H. (1964). *A social psychology of group processes for decision making*. New York: Wiley.

Coskun, H. (2005a). Cognitive stimulation with convergent and divergent thinking exercises in brainwriting: Incubation, sequence priming, and group context. *Small Group Research*, *35*, 466–498.

Coskun, H. (2005b). The effect of divergent thinking and group composition on idea generation in brainwriting. *Turk Psikoloji Dergisi*, *20*, 25–42.

Coskun, H., Paulus, P. B., Brown, V. R., & Sherwood, J. J. (2000). Cognitive stimulation and problem presentation in idea-generating groups. *Group Dynamics*, *4*, 307–329.

Cottrell, N. B. (1972). Social facilitation. In C. G. McClintock (Ed.), *Experimental Social Psychology* (pp. 185–236). New York: Holt.

Credé, M., & Sniezek, J. A. (2003). Group judgment processes and outcomes in video-conferencing versus face-to-face groups. *International Journal of Human-Computer Studies, 59,* 875–897.

Crott, H. W., Giesel, M., & Hoffmann, C. (1998). The process of inductive inference in groups: The use of positive and negative hypothesis and target testing in sequential rule-discovery tasks. *Journal of Personality and Social Psychology, 75,* 938–952.

Crown, D. F. (2007a). Effects of structurally competitive multilevel goals for an interdependent task. *Small Group Research, 38,* 265–288.

Crown, D. F. (2007b). The use of group and groupcentric individual goals for culturally heterogeneous and homogeneous task goals. *Small Group Research, 38,* 489–508.

Crown, D. F., & Rosse, J. G. (1995). Yours, mine, and ours: Facilitating group productivity through the integration of individual and group goals. *Organizational Behavior and Human Decision Processes, 64,* 138–150.

Crowne, D. P., & Marlowe, D. (1964). *The approval motive: Studies in evaluative dependence.* New York: Wiley.

Dalessio, A., & Imada, A. (1984). Relationships between interview selection decisions and perceptions of applicant similarity to an ideal employee and self: A field study. *Human Relations, 37,* 67–80.

Danesi, M. (2004). *The Liar Paradox and the Towers of Hanoi: The ten greatest math puzzles of all time.* Hoboken, NJ: Wiley.

Darley, J. (2003). Social comparison in ongoing groups. In M. A. Hogg & R. S. Tindale (Eds.), *Blackwell handbook of social psychology: Group processes* (pp. 334–351). Malden, MA: Blackwell.

Dasgupta, N., Banaji, M. R., & Abelson, R. P. (1999). Group entitativity and group perception: Associations between physical features and psychological judgment. *Journal of Personality and Social Psychology, 77,* 991–1003.

Dashiell, J. F. (1930). An experimental analysis of some group effects. *Journal of Abnormal and Social Psychology, 25,* 190–199.

Dashiell, J. F. (1935). Experimental studies of the influence of social situations on the behavior of individual human adults. In C. Murchison (Ed.), *A Handbook of Social Psychology.* (pp. 1097–1158). Worcester, MA: Clark University Press.

Davis, J. H. (1969). *Group performance.* Reading, MA: Addison-Wesley.

Davis, J. H. (1973). Group decisions and social interaction: A theory of social decision schemes. *Psychological Review, 80,* 97–125.

Davis, J. H. (1996). Group decision making and quantitative judgments: A consensus model. In E. Witte & J. H. Davis (Eds.), *Understanding group behavior: Consensual action by small groups* (Vol. 1., pp. 35–60). Hillsdale, NJ: Erlbaum.

Davis, J. H., & Restle, F. (1963). The analysis of problems and prediction of group problem solving. *Journal of Abnormal and Social Psychology, 66,* 103–116.

Davis, J. P., Eisenhardt, K. M., & Bingham, C. B. (2007). Developing theory through simulation methods. *Academy of Management Review, 32,* 480–499.

Day, E. A., Arthur, W., Jr., Bell, S. T., Edwards, B. D., Bennett, W., Jr., Mendoza, J. L., & Tubre, T. C. (2005). Ability-based pairing strategies in the team-based training of a complex skill: Does the intelligence of your training partner matter? *Intelligence, 33,* 39–65.

Day, E. A., Arthur, W., Jr., Miyashiro, B., Edwards, B. D., Tubre, T. C., & Tubre, A. H. (2004). Criterion-related validity of statistical operations of group general cognitive ability as a function of task type: Comparing the mean, maximum, and minimum. *Journal of Applied Social Psychology, 34,* 1521–1549.

De Dreu, C. K. W. (2007). Cooperative outcome interdependence, task reflexivity, and team effectiveness: A motivated information processing perspective. *Journal of Applied Psychology, 92,* 628–638.

De Dreu, C. K. W., Nijstad, B. A., & van Knippenberg, D. (2008). Motivated information processing in group judgment and decision making. *Personality and Social Psychology Review, 12,* 22–49.

De Dreu, C. K. W., & Weingart, L. R. (2003). Task vs. relationship conflict, team performance, and team member satisfaction: A meta-analysis. *Journal of Applied Psychology, 88,* 741–749.

de Marchi, S. (2005). *Computational and mathematical modeling in the social sciences.* New York: Cambridge University Press.

Delbecq, A. L., Van de Ven, A. H., & Gustafson, D. H. (1975). *Group techniques for program planning.* Glenview, IL: Scott, Foresman.

Demographia (2008). *Demographia World Urban Areas Population and Projections.* Belleville, IL: Author. Retrieved July 18, 2008, from http://www.demographia.com/db-worldua.pdf.

Dennis, A. R. (1996). Information exchange and use in small group decision making. *Small Group Research, 27,* 532–550.

Dennis, A. R., & Williams, M. L. (2003). Electronic Brainstorming: Theory, research, and future directions. In P. B. Paulus & B. A. Nijstad (Eds.), *Group creativity: Innovation through collaboration* (pp. 160–178). Oxford, UK: Oxford University Press.

Dennis, A. R., & Williams, M. L. (2005). A meta-analysis of group size effects in electronic brainstorming: More heads are better than one. *International Journal of e-Collaboration, 1,* 24–42.

DeShon, R. P., Kozlowski, S. W. J., Schmidt, A. M., Milner, K. R., & Wiechmann, D. (2004). A multiple-goal, multilevel model of feedback effects on the regulation of individual and team performance. *Journal of Applied Psychology, 89,* 1035–1056.

Deutsch, M. (1949). A theory of cooperation and competition. *Human Relations, 2,* 129–152.

Devine, D. J. (1999). Effects of cognitive ability, task knowledge, information sharing, and conflict on group decision-making effectiveness. *Small Group Research, 30,* 608–634.

Devine, D. J. (2002). A review and integration of classification systems relevant to teams in organizations. *Group Dynamics, 6,* 291–310.

Devine, D. J., Clayton, L. D., Dunford, B. B., Seying, R., & Pryce, J. (2001). Jury decision making: 45 years of empirical research on deliberating groups. *Psychology, Public Policy, and Law, 7,* 622–727.

Devine, D. J., & Philips, J. L. (2001). Do smarter teams do better? A meta-analysis of cognitive ability and team performance. *Small Group Research, 32,* 507–532.

Diehl, M., & Stroebe, W. (1987). Productivity loss in brainstorming groups: Toward the solution of a riddle. *Journal of Personality and Social Psychology, 53,* 497–509.

Diehl, M., & Stroebe, W. (1991). Productivity loss in idea-generating groups: Tracking down the blocking effect. *Journal of Personality and Social Psychology, 61*, 392–403.

Doise, W., Mugny, G., & Perret-Clermont, A.-N. (1975). Social interaction and the development of cognitive operations. *European Journal of Social Psychology, 5*, 367–383.

Dugosh, K. L., & Paulus, P. B. (2005). Cognitive and social comparison processes in brainstorming. *Journal of Experimental Social Psychology, 41*, 313–320.

Dugosh, K. L., Paulus, P. B., Roland, E. J., & Yang, H.-C. (2000). Cognitive stimulation in brainstorming. *Journal of Personality and Social Psychology, 79*, 722–735.

Dunnette, M. D., Campbell, J., & Jaastad, K. (1963). The effect of group participation on brainstorming effectiveness for two industrial samples. *Journal of Applied Psychology, 47*, 30–37.

Edmondson, A. C., Bohmer, R. M. J., & Pisano, G. P. (2001). Disrupted routines: Team learning and new technology implementation in hospitals. *Administrative Science Quarterly, 46*, 685–716.

Edmondson, A. C., Dillon, J. R., & Roloff, K. S. (2007). Three Perspectives on Team Learning. *Academy of Management Annals, 1*, 269–314.

Edmondson, A. C., Winslow, A. B., Bohmer, R. M. J., & Pisano, G. P. (2003). Learning how and learning what: Effects of tacit and codified knowledge on performance improvement following technology adoption. *Decision Sciences, 34*, 197–223.

Edwards, B. D., Day, E. A., Arthur, W., Jr., & Bell, S. T. (2006). Relationships among team ability composition, team mental models, and team performance. *Journal of Applied Psychology, 91*, 727–736.

Einhorn, H. J., Hogarth, R. M., & Klempner, E. (1977). Quality of group judgment. *Psychological Bulletin, 84*, 158–172.

Ellis, A. P. J., Hollenbeck, J. R., Ilgen, D. R., Porter, C. O. L. H., West, B. J., & Moon, H. (2003). Team learning: Collectively connecting the dots. *Journal of Applied Psychology, 88*, 821–835.

Epstein, J. M. (2007). *Generative social science: Studies in agent-based computational modeling.* Princeton, NJ: Princeton University Press.

Erez, M., & Somech, A. (1996). Is group productivity loss the rule or the exception? Effects of culture and group-based motivation. *Academy of Management Journal, 39*, 1513–1537.

Farnsworth, P. R. (1928). Concerning so-called group effects. *Journal of Genetic Psychology, 35*, 587–594.

Faure, C. (2004). Beyond brainstorming: Effects of different group procedures on selection of ideas and satisfaction with the process. *Journal of Creative Behavior, 38*, 13–34.

Festinger, L. (1950). Informal social communication. *Psychological Review, 57*, 271–282.

Festinger, L. (1954). A theory of social comparison processes. *Human Relations, 7*, 117–140.

Fiedler, F. E. (1964). A contingency model of leadership effectiveness. *Advances in Experimental Social Psychology, 1*, 149–190.

Fiedler, F. E. (1967). *A theory of leadership effectiveness.* New York, McGraw-Hill.

Fiedler, F. E. (1978a). The contingency model and the dynamics of the leadership process. *Advances in Experimental Social Psychology, 11*, 59–112.

Fiedler, F. E. (1978b). Recent developments in research on the contingency model. In L. Berkowitz (Ed.), *Group processes* (pp. 209–225). New York: Academic Press.

Fiedler, F. E. (1992). Time-based measures of leadership experience and organizational performance: A review of research and a preliminary model. *Leadership Quarterly, 3*, 5–23.

Fiedler, F. E. (1994). *Leadership experience and leadership performance.* Washington, DC: United States Army Research Institute for the Behavioral and Social Sciences.

Fiedler, F. E., & Chemers, M. M. (1974). *Leadership and effective management.* Glenview IL: Scott Foresman.

Fiedler, F. E., & Chemers, M. M. (1984). *Improving leadership effectiveness: The leader-match concept* (2nd ed.). New York: Wiley.

Fiedler, F. E., & Garcia, J. E. (1987). *New approaches to effective leadership: Cognitive resources and organizational performance.* New York: Wiley.

Fine, S. A., & Cronshaw, S. F. (1999). *Functional job analysis: A foundation for human resources management.* Mahwah, NJ: Erlbaum.

Finlay, F., Hitch, G. J., & Meudell, P. R. (2000). Mutual inhibition in collaborative recall: Evidence for a retrieval-based account. *Journal of Experimental Psychology: Learning, Memory, and Cognition, 26*, 1556–1567.

Fischer, G. W. (1981). When oracles fail: A comparison of four procedures for aggregating subjective probabilities. *Organizational Behavior and Human Performance, 28*, 96–110.

Fiske, D. W. (1949). Consistency of the factorial structure of personality ratings from different sources. *Journal of Abnormal and Social Psychology, 44*, 329–344.

Fleishman, E. A., & Quaintance, M. K. (1984). *Taxonomies of human performance.* Orlando, FL: Academic Press.

Fox, S. I. (1996). *Human physiology* (5th ed.). Dubuque, IA: Wm. C. Brown.

Franz, T. M., & Larson, J. R., Jr. (2002). The impact of experts on information sharing during group discussion. *Small Group Research 33*, 383–411.

Frings, D., Hopthrow, T., Abrams, D., Hulbert, L., & Gutierrez, R. (2008). Groupthink: The effects of alcohol and group process in vigilance errors. *Group Dynamics: Theory, Research and Practice, 12*, 179–190.

Furnham, A., & Yazdanpanahi, T. (1995). Personality differences and group versus individual brainstorming. *Personality and Individual Differences, 19*, 73–80.

Geen, R. G. (1981). Effects of being observed on persistence at an insoluble task. *British Journal of Social Psychology, 20*, 211–216.

Geen, R. G. (1989). Alternative conceptions of social facilitation. In P. B. Paulus (Ed.), *Psychology of group influence* (pp. 15–51). Hillsdale, NJ: Erlbaum.

Geen, R. G. (1991). Social motivation. *Annual Review of Psychology, 42*, 377–399.

George, J. M. (1990). Personality, affect, and behavior in groups. *Journal of Applied Psychology, 75*, 107–116.

Gigone, D., & Hastie, R. (1993). The common knowledge effect: Information sharing and group judgment. *Journal of Personality and Social Psychology, 65*, 959–974.

Gigone, D., & Hastie, R. (1996). The impact of information on group judgment: A model and computer simulation. In E. Witte and J. H. Davis (Eds.), *Understanding group behavior: Consensual action by small groups* (Vol. 1, pp. 221–251). Mahwah, NJ: Erlbaum.

Gigone, D., & Hastie, R. (1997a). The impact of information on small group choice. *Journal of Personality and Social Psychology, 72*, 132–140.

Gigone, D., & Hastie, R. (1997b). Proper analysis of the accuracy of group judgments. *Psychological Bulletin, 121*, 149–167.

Ginsborg, J., Chaffin, R., & Nicholson, G. (2006). Shared performance cues in singing and conducting: A content analysis of talk during practice. *Psychology of Music, 34*, 167–194.

Gockel, C., Kerr, N. L., Seok, D.-H., & Harris, D. (2008). Indispensability and group identification as sources of task motivation. *Journal of Experimental Social Psychology, 44*, 1316–1321.

Goldberg, L. R. (1993). The structure of phenotypic personality traits. *American Psychologist, 48*, 26–34.

Goldenberg, J., Mazursky, D., & Solomon, S. (1999). Toward identifying the inventive templates of new products: A channeled ideation approach. *Journal of Marketing Research, 36*, 200–210.

Gonzalez, R., & Griffin, D. (2002). Modeling the personality of dyads and groups. *Journal of Personality, 70*, 901–924.

Gonzalez, R., & Griffin, D. (2003). A statistical framework for modeling homogeneity and interdependence in groups. In G. J. O. Fletcher & M. S. Clark (Eds.), *Blackwell handbook of social psychology: Interpersonal processes* (pp. 505–534). Malden, MA: Blackwell.

Granovetter, M. S. (1973). The strength of weak ties. *American Journal of Sociology, 78*, 1360–1380.

Greenwood, J. D. (2000). Individualism and the social in early American social psychology. *Journal of the History of the Behavioral Sciences, 36*, 443–455.

Greenwood, J. D. (2004). *The disappearance of the social in American social psychology.* Cambridge, UK: Cambridge University Press

Greitemeyer, T., & Schulz-Hardt, S. (2003). Preference-consistent evaluation of information in the hidden profile paradigm: Beyond group-level explanations for the dominance of shared information in group decisions. *Journal of Personality and Social Psychology, 84*, 322–339.

Greitemeyer, T., Schulz-Hardt, S., Brodbeck, F. C., & Frey, D. (2006). Information sampling and group decision making: The effects of an advocacy decision procedure and task experience. *Journal of Experimental Psychology: Applied, 12*, 31–42.

Griffith, T. L., Fitchman, M., & Moreland, R. L. (1989). Social loafing and social facilitation: An empirical test of the cognitive-motivational model of performance. *Basic and Applied Psychology, 10*, 253–271.

Gryskiewicz, S. S. (1988). Trial by fire in an industrial setting: A practical evaluation of three creative problem-solving techniques. In K. Gronhaug & C. Kaufmann (Eds.), *Innovation: A cross-disciplinary perspective* (pp. 205–232). Oslo: Norwegian University Press.

Guerin, B. (1993). *Social facilitation.* Cambridge, UK: Cambridge University Press.

Guetzkow, H., & Simon, H. A. (1955). The impact of certain communication nets upon organization and performance in task-oriented groups. *Management Science. 1*, 233–250.

Gully, S. M., Devine, D. J., & Whitney, D. J. (1995). A meta-analysis of cohesion and performance: Effects of level of analysis and task interdependence. *Small Group Research, 1995, 26*, 497–520.

Hackman, J. R. (1968). Effects of task characteristics on group products. *Journal of Experimental Social Psychology, 4*, 162–187.

Hackman, J. R. (1969). Toward understanding the role of tasks in behavioral research. *Acta Psychologica, 31*, 97–128.

Hackman, J. R. (1987). The design of work teams. In J. W. Lorsch (Ed.), *Handbook of organizational behavior* (pp. 315–342). Englewood Cliffs, NJ: Prentice-Hall.

Hackman, J. R., & Morris, C. G. (1975). Group tasks, group interaction process, and group performance effectiveness: A review and proposed integration. *Advances in Experimental Social Psychology, 8*, 45–99.

Hackman, J. R., & Vidmar, N. (1970). Effects of size and task type on group performance and member reactions. *Sociometry, 33*, 37–54.

Halfhill, T., Sundstrom, E., Lahner, J., Calderone, W., & Nielsen, T. M. (2005). Group personality composition and group effectiveness: An integrative review of empirical research. *Small Group Research, 36*, 83–105.

Hamilton, D. L., & Hewstone, M. (2007). Conceptualising group perception: A 35-year evolution. In M. Hewstone, A W. Henk, J. B. F. De Wit, K. Van Den Bos, & M. S. Stroebe (Eds.), *The scope of social psychology: Theory and applications* (pp. 87–106). NY: Psychology Press.

Hardy, C. J., & Crace, R. K. (1991). The effects of task structure and teammate competence on social loafing. *Journal of Sport and Exercise Psychology, 13*, 372–381.

Harkins, S. G. (1987). Social loafing and social facilitation. *Journal of Experimental Social Psychology, 23*, 1–18.

Harkins, S. G. (2000). The potency of the potential for experimenter and self-evaluation in motivating vigilance performance. *Basic and Applied Social Psychology, 22*, 277–289.

Harkins, S. G. (2001a). The three-variable model: From Occam's razor to the black box. In S. G. Harkins (Ed.), *Multiple perspectives on the effects of evaluation on performance: Toward an integration* (pp. 207–259). Norwell, MA: Kluwer Academic.

Harkins, S. G. (2001b). Social influence effects on task performance: The ascendancy of social evaluation over self-evaluation. In J. P. Forgas and K. D. Williams (Eds.), *Social influence: Direct and indirect processes* (pp. 271–292). Philadelphia, PA: Psychology Press.

Harkins, S. G. (2006). Mere effort as the mediator of the evaluation-performance relationship. *Journal of Personality and Social Psychology, 91*, 436–455.

Harkins, S. G., & Jackson, J. M. (1985). The role of evaluation in eliminating social loafing. *Personality and Social Psychology Bulletin, 11*, 457–465.

Harkins, S. G., & Petty, R. E. (1982). Effects of task difficulty and task uniqueness on social loafing. *Journal of Personality and Social Psychology, 43*, 1214–1229.

Harkins, S. G., White, P. J., & Utman, C. H. (2000). The role of internal and external sources of evaluation in motivating task performance. *Personality and Social Psychology Bulletin, 26*, 100–117.

Harris, C. B., Paterson, H. M., & Kemp, R. I. (2008). Collaborative recall and collective memory: What happens when we remember together? *Memory, 16*, 213–230.

Harrison, D. A., & Klein, K. J. (2007). What's the difference? Diversity constructs as separation, variety, or disparity in organizations. *Academy of Management Review, 32*, 1199–1228.

Harrison, D. A., Price, K. H., & Bell, M. P. (1998). Beyond relational demography: Time and the effects of surface- and deep-level diversity on work group cohesion. *Academy of Management Journal, 41*, 96–107.

Harrison, D. A., Price, K. H., Gavin, J. H., & Florey, A. T. (2002). Time, teams, and task performance: Changing effects of surface- and deep-level diversity on group functioning. *Academy of Management Journal, 45*, 1029–1045.

Hart, C., & Van Vugt, M. (2006). From fault line to group fission: Understanding membership changes in small groups. *Personality and Social Psychology Bulletin, 32*, 392–404.

Hart, J. W, Bridgett, D. J., & Karau, S. J. (2001). Coworker ability and effort as determinants of individual effort on a collective task. *Group Dynamics: Theory, Research, and Practice, 5*, 181–190.

Harvey, R. J. (1991). Job analysis. In M. D. Dunnette & L. M. Hough (Eds.), *Handbook of industrial and organizational psychology* (2nd ed., Vol. 2, pp. 71–163). Palo Alto, CA: Consulting Psychology Press.

Hastie, R., & Stasser, G. (2000). Computer simulation methods in social psychology. In H. Reis & C. Judd (Eds.), *Handbook of research methods in social and personality psychology* (pp. 85–114). Cambridge, UK: Cambridge University Press.

Heath, C., & Jourden, F. J. (1997). Illusion, disillusion, and the buffering effect of groups. *Organizational Behavior and Human Decision Processes, 69*, 103–116.

Henchy, T., & Glass, D. C. (1968). Evaluation apprehension and the social facilitation of dominant and subordinate responses. *Journal of Personality and Social Psychology, 10*, 446–454.

Henningsen, D. D., & Henningsen, M. L. M. (2004). The effect of individual difference variables on information sharing in decision-making groups. *Human Communication Research, 30*, 540–555.

Henry, R. A. (1993). Group judgment accuracy: Reliability and validity of postdiscussion confidence judgments. *Organizational Behavior and Human Decision Processes, 56*, 11–27.

Hertel, G., Deter, C., & Konradt, U. (2003). Motivation gains in computer-supported groups. *Journal of Applied Social Psychology, 33*, 2080–2105.

Hertel, G., Kerr, N. L., & Messé, L. A. (1999). Revisiting the Köhler effect: Does diversity enhance motivation and performance in groups? *Psychologische Beitrage, 41*, 320–337.

Hertel, G., Kerr, N. L., & Messé, L. A. (2000). Motivation gains in performance groups: Paradigmatic and theoretical developments on the Köhler effect. *Journal of Personality and Social Psychology, 79*, 580–601.

Hertel, G., Konradt, U., & Orlikowski, B. (2004). Managing distance by interdependence: Goal setting, task interdependence, and team-based rewards in virtual teams. *European Journal of Work and Organizational Psychology, 13*, 1–28.

Hertel, G., Niemeyer, G., & Clauss, A. (2008). Social indispensability or social comparison: The why and when of motivation gains of inferior group members. *Journal of Applied Social Psychology, 38*, 1329–1363.

Hill, G. W. (1982). Group versus individual performance: Are N + 1 heads better than one? *Psychological Bulletin, 91*, 517–539.

Hinsz, V. B. (1990). Cognitive and consensus processes in group recognition memory performance. *Journal of Personality and Social Psychology, 59*, 705–718.

Hinsz, V. B. (1995). Group and individual decision making for task performance goals: Processes in the establishment of goals in groups. *Journal of Applied Social Psychology, 25,* 353–370.

Hinsz, V. B., & Nickell, G. S. (2004). Positive reactions to working in groups in a study of group and individual goal decision making. *Group Dynamics: Theory, Research, and Practice, 8,* 253–264.

Hinsz, V. B., Tindale, R. S., & Nagao, D. H. (2008). Accentuation of information processes and biases in group judgments integrating base-rate and case-specific information. *Journal of Experimental Social Psychology, 44,* 116–126.

Hoffman, B. J., & Woehr, D. J. (2006). A quantitative review of the relationship between person-organization fit and behavioral outcomes. *Journal of Vocational Behavior, 68,* 389–399.

Hoffmann, C., & Crott, H. W. (2004). Effects of amount of evidence and range of rule on the use of hypothesis and target tests by groups in rule-discovery tasks. *Thinking and Reasoning, 10,* 321–354.

Hogg, M. A. (2003). Social categorization, depersonalization, and group behavior. In M. A. Hogg & R. S. Tindale (Eds.), *Blackwell handbook of social psychology: Group processes* (pp. 58–85). Malden, MA: Blackwell.

Hollingshead, A. B. (1996). The rank-order effect in group decision making. *Organizational Behavior and Human Decision Processes, 68,* 181–193.

Hollingshead, A. B. (1998a). Communication, learning, and retrieval in transactive memory systems. *Journal of Experimental Social Psychology, 34,* 423–442.

Hollingshead, A. B. (1998b). Group and individual training: The impact of practice on performance. *Small Group Research, 29,* 254–280.

Hollingshead, A. B. (2000). Perceptions of expertise and transactive memory in work relationships. *Group Processes and Intergroup Relations, 3,* 257–267.

Hollingshead, A. B. (2001). Cognitive interdependence and convergent expectations in transactive memory. *Journal of Personality and Social Psychology, 81,* 1080–1089.

Hollingshead, A. B. (2004). Communication technologies, the Internet, and group research. In M. B. Brewer, & M. Hewstone (Eds.), *Applied Social Psychology* (pp. 301–317). Malden, MA: Blackwell.

Hollingshead, A. B., & Fraidin, S. N. (2003). Gender stereotypes and assumptions about expertise in transactive memory. *Journal of Experimental Social Psychology, 39,* 355–363.

Homan, A. C., Hollenbeck, J. R., Humphrey, S. E., van Knippenberg, D., Ilgen, D. R., & Van Kleef, G. A. (2008). Facing differences with an open mind: Openness to experience, salience of intragroup differences, and performance of diverse work groups. *Academy of Management Journal, 51,* 1204–1222.

Homan, A. C., van Knippenberg, D., Van Kleef, G. A., & De Dreu, C. K. W. (2007a). Bridging faultlines by valuing diversity: Diversity beliefs, information elaboration, and performance in diverse work groups. *Journal of Applied Psychology, 92,* 1189–1199.

Homan, A. C., van Knippenberg, D., Van Kleef, G. A., & De Dreu, C. K. W. (2007b). Interacting dimensions of diversity: Cross-categorization and the functioning of diverse work groups. *Group Dynamics: Theory, Research, and Practice, 11,* 79–94.

Hoppe, R. A. (1962). Memorizing by individuals and groups: A test of the pooling-of-ability model. *Journal of Abnormal and Social Psychology, 65,* 64–67.

Horowitz, M. W., & Perlmutter, H. V. (1953). The concept of the social group. *Journal of Social Psychology, 37*, 69–95.

House, R. J. (1971). A path-goal theory of leader effectiveness. *Administrative Science Quarterly, 16*, 321–339.

House, R. J. (1996). Path-goal theory of leadership: Lessons, legacy, and a reformulated theory. *Leadership Quarterly, 7*, 323–352.

Humphrey, S. E., Hollenbeck, J., R., Meyer, C. J., & Ilgen, D. R. (2007). Trait configurations in self-managed teams: A conceptual examination of the use of seeding for maximizing and minimizing trait variance in teams. *Journal of Applied Psychology, 92*, 885–892.

Husband, R. W. (1940). Cooperative versus solitary problem solution. *Journal of Social Psychology, 11*, 405–409.

Hutchins, E. (1990). The technology of team navigation. In J. Glaegher, R. E. Kraut, & C. Egido (Eds.), *Intellectual teamwork: Social and technological foundations of cooperative work* (pp. 191–220). Hillsdale, NJ: Erlbaum.

Ilgen, D. R., & Hulin, C. L. (2000). *Computational modeling of behavior in organizations: The third scientific discipline*. Washington, DC: American Psychological Association.

Ingham, A. G., Levinger, G., Graves, J., & Peckham, V. (1974). The Ringelmann effect: Studies of group size and group performance. *Journal of Experimental Social Psychology, 10*, 371–384.

Jackson, C. L., & LePine, J. A. (2003). Peer responses to a team's weakest link: A test and extension of LePine and Van Dyne's model. *Journal of Applied Psychology, 88*, 459–475.

Jehn, K. A., Northcraft, G. B., & Neale, M. A. (1999). Why differences make a difference: A field study of diversity, conflict, and performance in workgroups. *Administrative Science Quarterly, 44*, 741–763.

Jenness, A. (1932). The role of discussion in changing opinion regarding a matter of fact. *Journal of Abnormal and Social Psychology, 27*, 279–296.

Johansson, N. O., Andersson, J., & Rönnberg, J. (2005). Compensating strategies in collaborative remembering in very old couples. *Scandinavian Journal of Psychology, 46*, 349–359.

Jones, M. B. (1974). Regressing group on individual effectiveness. *Organizational Behavior and Human Performance, 11*, 426–451.

Jourden, F. J., & Heath, C. (1996). The evaluation gap in performance perceptions: Illusory perceptions of groups and individuals. *Journal of Applied Psychology, 81*, 369–379.

Kabanoff, B., & O'Brien, G. E. (1979). The effects of task type and cooperation upon group products and performance. *Organizational Behavior and Human Performance, 23*, 163–181.

Kanter, R. M. (1988). When a thousand flowers bloom: Structural, collective, and social conditions for innovation in organization. In B. M. Staw, & L. L. Cummings (Eds.), *Research in organizational behavior* (vol. 10, pp. 169–211). Greenwich, CT: JAI Press.

Kaplan, M. F., & Miller, L. E. (1978). Reducing the effects of juror bias. *Journal of Personality and Social Psychology, 36*, 1443–1455.

Kaplan, M. F., & Wilke, H. (2001). Cognitive and social motivation in group decision making. In J. P. Forgas, K. D. Williams, & L. Wheeler (Eds.), *The social mind: Cognitive and motivational aspects of interpersonal behavior* (pp. 406–428). New York: Cambridge University Press.

Karau, S. J., & Kelly, J. R. (1992). The effects of time scarcity and time abundance on group performance quality and interaction processes. *Journal of Experimental Social Psychology, 28*, 542–571.

Karau, S. J., & Williams, K. D. (1993). Social loafing: A meta-analytic review and theoretical integration. *Journal of Personality and Social Psychology, 65*, 681–706.

Karau, S. J., & Williams, K. D. (1997). The effects of group cohesiveness on social loafing and social compensation. *Group Dynamics: Theory, Research, and Practice, 1*, 156–168.

Katzung, B. G. (1998). *Basic and clinical pharmacology* (7th ed.). Stamford CT: Appleton and Lang.

Kearney, E., & Gebert, D. (2009). Managing diversity and enhancing team outcomes: The promise of transformational leadership. *Journal of Applied Psychology, 94*, 77–89.

Keidell, R. W. (1987). Team sports models as a generic organizational framework. *Human Relations, 40*, 591–612.

Keller, R. T. (2001). Cross-functional project groups in research and new product development: Diversity, communications, job stress, and outcomes. *Academy of Management Journal, 44*, 547–555.

Kelley, H. H., Holms, J. G., Kerr, N. L., Reis, H. T., Rusbult, C. E., & Van Lange, P. A. M. (2003). *An atlas of interpersonal situations.* Cambridge, UK: Cambridge University Press.

Kelley, H. H., & Thibaut, J. W. (1954). Experimental studies in group problem solving and process. In G. Lindzey (Ed.), *The handbook of social psychology: Volume II, Special fields and applications* (pp. 735–785). Reading, MA: Addison-Wesley.

Kelly, J. R., & Karau, S. J. (1993). Entrainment of creativity in small groups. *Small Group Research, 24*, 179–198.

Kelly, J. R., & Karau, S. J. (1999). Group decision making: The effects of initial preferences and time pressure. *Personality and Social Psychology Bulletin, 25*, 1343–1354.

Kenny, D. A., Mannetti, L., Pierro, A., Livi, S., & Kashy, D. A. (2002). The statistical analysis of data from small groups. *Journal of Personality and Social Psychology, 83*, 126–137.

Kent, R. N., & McGrath, J. E. (1969). Task and group characteristics as factors influencing group performance. *Journal of Experimental Social Psychology, 5*, 429–440.

Kerr, N. L. (1983). Motivation losses in small groups: A social dilemma analysis. *Journal of Personality and Social Psychology, 45*, 819–828.

Kerr, N. L., & Bruun, S. E. (1983). Dispensability of member effort and group motivation losses: Free-rider effects. *Journal of Personality and Social Psychology, 44*, 78–94.

Kerr, N. L., & MacCoun, R. J. (1985). The effects of jury size and polling method on the process and product of jury deliberation. *Journal of Personality and Social Psychology, 48*, 349–363.

Kerr, N. L., Messé, L. A., Park, E. S., & Sambolec, E. J. (2005). Identifiability, performance feedback and the Köhler effect. *Group Processes and Intergroup Relations, 8*, 375–390.

Kerr, N. L., Messé, L. A., Seok, D.-H, Sambolec, E. J., Lount, R. B., Jr., & Park, E. S. (2007). Psychological mechanisms underlying the Köhler motivation gain. *Personality and Social Psychology Bulletin, 33*, 828–841.

Kerr, N. L., Stasser, G., & Davis, J. H. (1979). Model testing, model fitting, and social decision schemes. *Organizational Behavior and Human Performance, 23,* 399–410.

Kerr, S., & Jermier, J. M. (1978). Substitutes for leadership: Their meaning and measurement. *Organizational Behavior and Human Performance, 22,* 375–403.

Kerwin, J., & Schaffer, D. R. (1994). Mock jurors versus juries: The role of deliberations in reactions to inadmissible testimony. *Personality and Social Psychology Bulletin, 20,* 153–162.

Klein, H. J., Wesson, M. J., Hollenbeck, J. R., & Alge, B. J. (1999). Goal commitment and the goal-setting process: Conceptual clarification and empirical synthesis. *Journal of Applied Psychology, 84,* 885–896.

Klimoski, R., & Jones, R. G. (1995). Staffing for effective group decision making: Key issues in matching people and teams. In R. Guzzo & E. Salas (Eds.), *Team effectiveness and decision making in organizations* (pp. 291–332). San Francisco: Jossey-Bass.

Köhler, O. (1926). Kraftleistungen bei einzel- und gruppenarbeit [Physical performance in individual and group situations]. *Industrielle Psychotechnik, 3,* 274–282.

Köhler, O. (1927). Über den gruppenwirkungsgrad der menschlichen körperarbeit und die bedingung optimaler Kollektivkraftreaktion [On group efficiency of physical labor and the conditions of optimal collective performance]. *Industrielle Psychotechnik, 4,* 209–226.

Kokubo, T. (1996). An effect of internal incentives to task performance on social loafing. *Japanese Journal of Experimental Social Psychology, 36,* 12–19.

Kooij-de Bode, H. M. J., van Knippenberg, D., & van Ginkel, W. P. (2008). Ethnic diversity and distributed information in group decision making: The importance of information elaboration. *Group Dynamics: Theory, Research, and Practice, 12,* 307–320.

Kozlowski, S. W. J., & Ilgen, D. R. (2006). Enhancing the effectiveness of work groups and teams. *Psychological Science in the Public Interest, 7,* 77–124.

Kravitz, D. A., & Martin, B. (1986). Ringelmann Rediscovered: The original article. *Journal of Personality and Social Psychology, 50,* 936–941.

Krech, D., & Crutchfield, R. S. (1948). *Theory and problems of social psychology.* NY: McGraw-Hill.

Kristof-Brown, A. L., Zimmerman, R. D., & Johnson, E. C. (2005). Consequences of individuals' fit at work: A meta-analysis of person-job, person-organization, person-group, and person-supervisor fit. *Personnel Psychology, 58,* 281–342.

Kugihara, N. (1999). Gender and social loafing in Japan. *Journal of Social Psychology, 139,* 516–526.

Kuhn, K. M., & Sniezek, J. A. (1996). Confidence and uncertainty in judgmental forecasting: Differential effects of scenario presentation. *Journal of Behavioral Decision Making, 4,* 231–247.

Lamm, H., & Trommsdorff, G. (1973). Group versus individual performance on a task requiring ideation proficiency (brainstorming): A review. *European Journal of Social Psychology, 3,* 362–388.

Larey, T. S., & Paulus, P. B. (1999). Group preference and convergent tendencies in small groups: A content analysis of group brainstorming performance. *Creativity Research Journal, 12,* 175–184.

Larson, J. R., Jr. (1977). Evidence for a self-serving bias in the attribution of causality. *Journal of Personality, 45,* 430–441.

Larson, J. R., Jr. (1997). Modeling the entry of shared and unshared information into group discussion: A review and BASIC language computer program. *Small Group Research, 28*, 454–479.

Larson, J. R., Jr. (2006). *Deep diversity and strong synergy: Modeling the impact of variability in members' problem-solving strategies on group problem-solving performance.* Paper presented at the first annual conference of the Interdisciplinary Network for Group Research (INGRoup), Pittsburgh, PA.

Larson, J. R., Jr. (2007a). Deep diversity and strong synergy: Modeling the impact of variability in members' problem-solving strategies on group problem-solving performance. *Small Group Research, 38*, 413–436.

Larson, J. R., Jr. (2007b). *A computational modeling approach to understanding the impact of diverse member problem-solving strategies on group problem-solving performance.* Invited paper presented at the annual meeting of the Society for Experimental Social Psychology: Small Groups Research Preconference. Chicago, IL.

Larson, J. R., Jr. (in press). Computer simulation methods for groups: From formula translation to agent-based modeling. In A. B. Hollingshead & M. S. Poole (Eds.), *Research methods for studying groups: A behind-the-scenes guide.* NY: Routledge.

Larson, J. R., Jr., & Christensen, C. (1993). Groups as problem-solving units: Toward a new meaning of social cognition. *British Journal of Social Psychology, 32*, 5–30.

Larson, J. R., Jr., Christensen, C., Abbott, A. S., & Franz, T. M. (1996). Diagnosing groups: Charting the flow of information in medical decision making teams. *Journal of Personality and Social Psychology, 71*, 315–330.

Larson, J. R., Jr., Christensen, C., Franz, T. M., & Abbott, A. S. (1998). Diagnosing groups: The pooling, management, and impact of shared and unshared case information in team-based medical decision making. *Journal of Personality and Social Psychology, 75*, 93–108.

Larson, J. R., Jr., Foster-Fishman, P. G., & Franz, T. M. (1998). Leadership style and the discussion of shared and unshared information in decision-making groups. *Personality and Social Psychology Bulletin, 24*, 482–495.

Larson, J. R., Jr., Foster-Fishman, P. G., & Keys, C. B. (1994). Information sharing in decision making groups. *Journal of Personality and Social Psychology, 67*, 446–461.

Larson, J. R., Jr., & Harmon, V. M. (2007). Recalling shared vs. unshared information mentioned during group discussion: Toward understanding differential repetition rates. *Group Processes and Intergroup Relations, 10*, 311–322.

Larson, J. R., Jr., & Reenan, A. M. (1979). The equivalence interval as a measure of uncertainty. *Organizational Behavior and Human Performance, 23*, 49–55.

Larson, J. R., Jr., Sargis, E. G., & Bauman, C. W. (2004). Shared knowledge and subgroup influence during decision-making discussions. *Journal of Behavioral Decision Making, 17*, 245–262.

Larson, J. R., Jr., & Schaumann, L. J. (1993). Group goals, group coordination, and group member motivation. *Human Performance, 6*, 49–69.

Latané, B. (1981). The psychology of social impact. *American Psychologist, 36*, 343–356.

Latané, B., Williams, K. D., & Harkins, S. G. (1979). Many hands make light the work: The causes and consequences of social loafing. *Journal of Personality and Social Psychology, 37*, 822–932.

Lau, D. C., & Murninghan, J. K. (1998). Demographic diversity and faultlines: The compositional dynamics of organizational groups. *Academy of Management Review, 23*, 325–340.

Lau, D. C., & Murninghan, J. K. (2005). Interactions within groups and subgroups. The effects of demographic faultlines. *Academy of Management Journal, 48*, 645–659.

Laughlin, P. R. (1980). Social combination processes of cooperative problem-solving groups on verbal intellective tasks. In M. Fishbein (Ed.), *Progress in social psychology* (pp. 127–155). Hillsdale, NJ: Erlbaum.

Laughlin, P. R. (1988). Collective induction: Group performance, social combination processes, and mutual majority and minority influence. *Journal of Personality and Social Psychology, 54*, 254–267.

Laughlin, P. R. (1992). Performance and influence in simultaneous collective and individual induction. *Organizational Behavior and Human Decision Processes, 51*, 447–470.

Laughlin, P. R. (1996). Group decision making and collective induction. In E. Witte & J. H. Davis (Eds.), *Understanding group behavior: Vol. 1. Consensual action by small groups* (pp. 61–80). Hillsdale, NJ: Erlbaum

Laughlin, P. R. (1999). Collective induction: Twelve postulates. *Organizational Behavior and Human Decision Processes, 80*, 50–69.

Laughlin, P. R., & Adamopoulos, J. (1980). Social combination processes and individual learning for six-person cooperative groups on an intellective task. *Journal of Personality and Social Psychology, 38*, 941–947.

Laughlin, P. R., & Bonner, B. L. (1999). Collective induction: Effects of multiple hypotheses and multiple evidence in two problem domains. *Journal of Personality and Social Psychology, 77*, 1163–1172.

Laughlin, P. R., Bonner, B. L., & Altermatt, T. W. (1998). Collective versus individual induction with single versus multiple hypotheses. *Journal of Personality and Social Psychology, 75*, 1481–1489.

Laughlin, P. R., Bonner, B. L., & Miner, A. G. (2002). Groups perform better than the best individuals on letters-to-numbers problems. *Organizational Behavior and Human Decision Processes, 88*, 605–620.

Laughlin, P. R., Carey, H. R., & Kerr, N. L. (2008). Group-to-individual problem-solving transfer. *Group Processes and Intergroup Relations, 11*, 319–330.

Laughlin, P. R., & Ellis, A. L. (1986). Demonstrability and social combination processes on mathematical intellective tasks. *Journal of Experimental Social Psychology, 22*, 177–189.

Laughlin, P. R., & Futoran, G. C. (1985). Collective induction: Social combination and sequential transition. *Journal of Personality and Social Psychology, 48*, 608–613.

Laughlin, P. R., Gonzalez, C. M., & Sommer, D. (2003). Quantity estimations by groups and individuals: Effects of known domain boundaries. *Group Dynamics: Theory, Research, and Practice, 7*, 55–63.

Laughlin, P. R., Hatch, E. C., Silver, J. S., & Boh, L. (2006). Groups perform better than the best individuals on letters-to-numbers problems: Effect of group size. *Journal of Personality and Social Psychology, 90*, 644–651.

Laughlin, P. R., & Hollingshead, A. B. (1995). A theory of collective induction. *Organizational Behavior and Human Decision Processes, 61*, 94–107.

Laughlin, P. R., Kerr, N. L., Davis, J. H., Halff, H. M., & Marciniak, K. A. (1975). Group size, member ability, and social decision schemes on an intellective task. *Journal of Personality and Social Psychology, 31*, 522–535.

Laughlin, P. R., Kerr, N. L., Munch, M. M., & Haggarty, C. A. (1976). Social decision schemes of the same four-person groups on two different intellective tasks. *Journal of Personality and Social Psychology, 33*, 80–88.

Laughlin, P. R., Magley, V. J., & Shupe, E. I. (1997). Positive and negative hypothesis testing by cooperative groups. *Organizational Behavior and Human Decision Processes, 69*, 265–275.

Laughlin, P. R., & McGlynn, R. P. (1986). Collective induction: Mutual group and individual influence by exchange of hypotheses and evidence. *Journal of Experimental Social Psychology, 22*, 567–589.

Laughlin, P. R., & Shippy, T. A. (1983). Collective induction. *Journal of Personality and Social Psychology, 45*, 94–100.

Laughlin, P. R., & Shupe, E. I. (1996). Intergroup collective induction. *Organizational Behavior and Human Decision Processes, 68*, 44–57.

Laughlin, P. R., VanderStoep, S. W., & Hollingshead, A. B. (1991). Collective versus individual induction: Recognition of truth, rejection of error, and collective information processing. *Journal of Personality and Social Psychology, 61*, 50–67.

Laughlin, P. R., Zander, M. L., Knievel, E. M., & Tan, T. K. (2003). Groups perform better than the best individuals on letters-to-numbers problems: Informative equations and effective reasoning. *Journal of Personality and Social Psychology, 85*, 684–694.

Lavery, T. A., Franz, T. M., Winquist, J. R., & Larson, J. R., Jr. (1999). The role of information exchange in predicting group accuracy on a multiple judgment task. *Basic and Applied Social Psychology, 21*, 281–289.

Lawrence, B. S. (1997). The black box of organizational demography. *Organizational Science, 8*, 1–22.

Lawrence, M., O'Connor, M., & Edmundson, B. (2000). A field study of sales forecasting accuracy and processes. *European Journal of Operational Research, 122*, 151–160.

Lazarsfeld, P., & Merton, R. K. (1954). Friendship as social process: A substantive and methodological analysis. In M. Berger, T. Abel, & C. Page (Eds.), *Freedom and control in modern society* (pp. 18–66). NY: Octagon Books.

Le Bon, G. (1903). *The crowd.* NY: Holt.

Leary, M. R., & Forsyth, D. R. (1987). Attributions of responsibility for collective endeavors. In C. Hendrick (Ed.), *Review of personality and social psychology* (vol. 8, pp. 167–188). Newbury Park, CA: Sage.

Leavitt, H. J. (1951). Some effects of certain communication patterns on group performance. *The Journal of Abnormal and Social Psychology, 46*, 38–50.

Leung, A. (2003). Different ties for different needs: Recruitment practices of entrepreneurial firms at different developmental phases. *Human Resource Management, 42*, 303–320.

Levine, J. M., & Moreland, R. L. (1990). Progress in small group research. *Annual Review of Psychology, 41*, 585–634.

Levine, J. M., & Moreland, R. L. (1998). Small groups. In D. T. Gilbert, S. T. Fiske, & G. Lindzey (Eds.), *The handbook of social psychology* (4th ed., vol. 2, pp. 415–469). New York: McGraw-Hill.

Lewin, K. (1947). Frontiers of group dynamics: Concepts, methods, and reality in social science; Social equilibria and social change. *Human Relations, 1,* 5–41.

Lewis, K. (2004). Knowledge and performance in knowledge-worker teams: A longitudinal study of transactive memory systems. *Management Science, 50,* 1519–1533.

Lewis, K., Belliveau, M., Herndon, B., & Keller, J. (2007). Group cognition, membership change, and performance: Investigating the benefits and determinants of collective knowledge. *Organizational Behavior and Human Decision Processes, 103,* 159–178.

Lewis, K., Lange, D., & Gillis, L. (2005). Transactive memory systems, learning, and learning transfer. *Organization Science, 16,* 581–598.

Li, J., & Hambrick, D. C. (2005). Factional groups: A new vantage on demographic faultlines, conflict, and disintegration in work teams. *Academy of Management Journal, 48,* 794–813.

Liang, D. W., Moreland, R. L., & Argote, L. (1995). Group versus individual training and group performance: The mediating factor of transactive memory. *Personality and Social Psychology Bulletin, 21,* 384–393.

Liden, R. C., Wayne, S. J., Jaworski, R., & Bennett, N. (2004). Social loafing: A field investigation. *Journal of Management, 30,* 285–304.

Littlepage, G. E., Hollingshead, A. B., Drake, L. R., & Littlepage, A. M. (2008). Transactive memory and performance in work groups: Specificity, communication, ability differences, and work allocation. *Group Dynamics: Theory, Research, and Practice, 12,* 223–241.

Littlepage, G. E., Robison, W., & Reddington, K. (1997). Effects of task experience and group experience on group performance, member ability, and recognition of expertise. *Organizational Behavior and Human Decision Processes, 69,* 133–147.

Locke, E. A., & Latham, G. P. (1990). *A theory of goal setting and task performance.* Englewood Cliffs, NJ: Prentice-Hall.

Locke, E. A., & Latham, G. P. (2002). Building a practically useful theory of goal setting and task motivation: A 35-year odyssey. *American Psychologist, 57,* 705–717.

Locke, E. A., & Latham, G. P. (2006). New directions in goal-setting theory. *Current Directions in Psychological Science, 15,* 265–268.

Locke, E. A., Latham, G. P., & Erez, M. (1988). The determinants of goal commitment. *Academy of Management Review, 13,* 23–39.

Locke, E. A., Tirnauer, D., Roberson, Q. M., Goldman, B., Latham, M. E., & Weldon, E. (2001). The importance of the individual in an age of groupism. In M. E. Turner (Ed.), *Groups at work: Theory and research* (pp. 501–528). Mahwah, NJ: Erlbaum.

London, K., & Nunez, N. (2000). The effect of jury deliberations on jurors' propensity to disregard inadmissible evidence. *Journal of Applied Psychology, 85,* 932–939.

Lorge, I., Fox, D., Davitz, J., & Brenner, M. (1958). A survey of studies contrasting the quality of group performance and individual performance. *Psychological Bulletin, 55,* 337–372.

Lorge, I., & Solomon, H. (1955). Two models of group behavior in the solution of Eureka-type problems. *Psychometrika, 20,* 139–148.

Lorge, I., & Solomon, H. (1959). Individual performance and group performance in problem solving related to group size and previous exposure to the problem. *Journal of Psychology, 48,* 107–114.

Lorge, I., & Solomon, H. (1960). Group and individual performance in problem solving related to previous exposure to problem, level of aspiration, and group size. *Behavioral Science, 5,* 28–38.

Lount, R. B., Jr., Kerr, N. L., Messé, L. A., Seok, D.-H., & Park, E. S. (2008). An examination of the stability and persistence of the Köhler motivation gain effect. *Group Dynamics: Theory, Research, and Practice, 12,* 279–289.

Lount, R. B., Jr., Park, E. S., Kerr, N. L., Messé, L. A., & Seok, D-H. (2008). Evaluation concerns and the Köhler effect. *Small Group Research, 39,* 795–812.

Lount, R. B., Jr. & Phillips, K. W. (2007). Working harder with the out-group: The impact of social category diversity on motivation gains. *Organizational Behavior and Human Decision Processes, 103,* 214–224.

MacCoun, R. J., & Kerr, N. L. (1988). Asymmetric influence in mock jury deliberation: Jurors' bias for leniency. *Journal of Personality and Social Psychology, 54,* 21–33.

Maier, N. R. F. (1967). Assets and liabilities in group problem solving: The need for an integrative function. *Psychological Review, 74,* 239–249.

Marieb, E. N. (2004). *Human anatomy and physiology* (6th ed.). New York: Benjamin Cummings.

Marquart, D. I. (1955). Group problem solving. *Journal of Social Psychology, 41,* 103–113.

Marsh, R. L., Landau, J. D., & Hicks, J. L. (1997). Contributions of inadequate source monitoring to unconscious plagiarism during idea generation. *Journal of Experimental Psychology: Learning, Memory, and Cognition, 23,* 886–897.

Marston, W. M. (1924). Studies in testimony. *Journal of Criminal Law and Criminology, 15,* 5–31.

Martins, L. L., Gilson, L. L., & Maynard, M. T. (2004). Virtual teams: What do we know and where do we go from here? *Journal of Management, 30,* 805–835.

Matsui, T., Kakuyama, T., & Onglatco, M. L. U. (1987). Effects of goals and feedback on performance in groups. *Journal of Applied Psychology, 72,* 407–415.

McCrae, R. R., & Costa, P. T., Jr. (1985). Updating Norman's "adequate taxonomy": Intelligence and personality dimensions in natural language and questionnaires. *Journal of Personality and Social Psychology, 49,* 710–721.

McCrae, R. R., & Costa, P. T., Jr. (2003). *Personality in adulthood: A Five-Factor Theory, perspective* (2nd ed.). New York: Guilford.

McDougall, W. (1920). *The group mind.* NY: G. P. Putnam's Sons.

McGlynn, R. P., McGurk, D., Effland, V. S., Johll, N. L., & Harding, D. J. (2004). Brainstorming and task performance in groups constrained by evidence. *Organizational Behavior and Human Decision Processes, 93,* 75–87.

McGrath, J. E. (1984). *Groups: Interaction and performance.* Englewood Cliffs, NJ: Prentice-Hall.

McGrath, J. E. (1997). Small group research, that once and future field: An interpretation of the past with an eye toward the future. *Group Dynamics: Theory Research, and Practice, 7,* 7–27.

McGrath, J. E., & Argote, L. (2003). Group process in organizational contexts. In M. A. Hogg, & R. S. Tindale (Eds.). *Blackwell handbook of social psychology: Group processes* (pp. 603–627). Malden, MA: Blackwell.

McGrath, J. E., & Tschan, F. (2004). Dynamics in groups and teams: Groups as complex action systems. In M. S. Poole & A. H. Van de Ven (Eds.), *Handbook of organizational change and innovation* (pp. 50–72). New York: Oxford University Press.

McLeod, P. L., Baron, R. S., Marti, M. W., & Yoon, K. (1997). The eyes have it: Minority influence in face-to-face and computer mediated group discussion. *Journal of Applied Psychology, 82,* 706–718.

McPherson, J. M., Smith-Lovin, L., & Cook, J. M. (2001). Birds of a feather: Homophily in social networks. *Annual Review of Sociology, 27,* 415–444.

Meadow, A., & Parnes, S. J. (1959). Evaluation of training in creative problem solving. *Journal of Applied Psychology, 43,* 189–194.

Meadow, A., Parnes, S. J., & Reese, H. (1959). Influence of brainstorming instructions and problem sequence on a creative problem solving test. *Journal of Applied Psychology, 43,* 413–416.

Mednick, S. A. (1962). The associative basis of the creative process. *Psychological Review, 69,* 220–232.

Mednick, S. A., & Mednick, M. T. (1967). *Examiner's manual: Remote associates test.* Boston: Houghton Mifflin.

Meneses, R., Ortega, R., Navarro, J., & de Quijaro, S. D. (2008). Criteria for assessing the level of group development (LGD) of work groups: Groupness, entitativity, and groupality as theoretical perspectives. *Small Group Research, 39,* 492–514.

Mesmer-Magnus, J. R., & DeChurch, L. A. (2009). Information sharing and team performance: A meta-analysis. *Journal of Applied Psychology, 94,* 535–546.

Messé, L. A., Hertel, G., Kerr, N. L., Lount, R. B., Jr., & Park, E. S. (2002). Knowledge of partner's ability as a moderator of group motivation gains: An exploration of the Köhler discrepancy effect. *Journal of Personality and Social Psychology, 82,* 935–946.

Meudell, P. R., Hitch, G. J., & Boyle, M. M. (1995). Collaboration in recall: Do pairs of people cross-cue each other to produce new memories? *Quarterly Journal of Experimental Psychology, 48A,* 141–152.

Meudell, P. R., Hitch, G. J., & Kirby, P. (1992). Are two heads better than one? Experimental investigations of the social facilitation of memory. *Applied Cognitive Psychology, 6,* 525–543.

Michaelsen, L. K., Knight, A. B., & Fink, L. D. (2004). *Team-based learning: A transformative use of small groups in college teaching.* Sterling, VA: Stylus.

Michaelsen, L. K., Watson, W. E., & Black, R. H. (1989). A realistic test of individual vs. group consensus decision making. *Journal of Applied Psychology, 74,* 834–839.

Michalko, M. (2006). *Thinkertoys: A handbook of creative-thinking techniques* (2nd ed.). Berkeley CA: Ten Speed Press.

Miner, F. C. (1984). Group versus individual decision making: An investigation of performance measures, decision strategies, and process losses/gains. *Organizational Behavior and Human Performance, 33,* 112–124.

Mitchell, T. R., & Silver, W. S. (1990). Individual and group goals when workers are interdependent: Effects on task strategies and performance. *Journal of Applied Psychology, 75,* 185–193.

Mojzisch, A., & Schulz-Hardt, S. (2006). Information sampling in group decision making: Sampling biases and their consequences. In K. Fiedler & P. Juslin (Eds.), *Information sampling and adaptive cognition* (pp. 299–326). Cambridge, UK: Cambridge University Press.

Molleman, E. (2005). Diversity in demographic characteristics, abilities, and personality traits: Do faultlines affect team functioning? *Group Decision and Negotiation, 14,* 173–193.

Moreland, R. L., Argote, L., & Krishnan, R. (1996). Socially shared cognition at work: Transactive memory and group performance. In J. L. Nye & A. M. Brower (Eds.), *What's social about social cognition? Research on socially shared cognition in small groups* (pp. 57–84). Thousand Oaks, CA: Sage.

Moreland, R. L., Argote, L., & Krishnan, R. (1998). Training people to work in groups. In R. S. Tindale, J. E., Edwards, L. Heath, E. J. Posavac, F. B. Bryant, E. Henderson-King, Y. Suarez-Balcazar, & J. Myers (Eds.), *Social psychological applications to social issues: Applications of theory and research on groups* (Vol. 4, pp. 37–60). New York: Plenum.

Moreland, R. L., Hogg, M. A., & Hains, S. C. (1994). Back to the future: Social psychological research on groups. *Journal of Experimental Social Psychology, 30,* 527–555.

Moreland, R. L., & Levine, J. M. (1982). Socialization in small groups: Temporal changes in individual-group relations. In L. Berkowitz (Ed.), *Advances in Experimental Social Psychology, 15,* 137–192.

Moreland, R. L., & Levine, J. M. (1992). The composition of small groups. *Advances in Group Process, 9,* 237–280.

Moreland, R. L., & Levine, J. M. (2003). Group composition: Explaining similarities and differences among group members. In M. A. Hogg & J. Cooper (Eds.), *Sage handbook of social psychology* (pp. 367–380). London: Sage.

Moreland, R. L., & Myaskovsky, L. (2000). Exploring the performance benefits of group training: Transactive memory or improved communication. *Organizational Behavior and Human Decision Processes, 82,* 117–133.

Morris, C. G. (1966). Task effects on group interaction. *Journal of Personality and Social Psychology, 5,* 545–554.

Mullen, B., & Copper, C. (1994). The relation between group cohesiveness and performance: An integration. *Psychological Bulletin, 115,* 210–227.

Mullen, B., Johnson, C., & Salas, E. (1991). Productivity loss in brainstorming groups: A meta-analytic integration. *Basic and Applied Social Psychology, 12,* 3–24.

Muller, D., & Butera, F. (2007). The focusing effect of self-evaluation threat in coaction and social comparison. *Journal of Personality and Social Psychology, 93,* 194–211.

Munkes, J., & Diehl, M. (2003). Matching or competition? Performance comparison processes in an idea generation task. *Group Processes and Intergroup Relations, 6,* 305–320.

Naquin, C. E., & Tynan, R. O. (2003). The team halo effect: Why teams are not blamed for their failures. *Journal of Applied Psychology, 88,* 332–340.

Nebeker, D. M. (1975). Situational favorability and environmental uncertainty: An integrative study. *Administrative Science Quarterly, 20,* 281–294.

Nickerson, R. S. (1984). Retrieval inhibition from part-set cuing: A persisting enigma in memory research. *Memory and Cognition, 12,* 531–552.

Nijstad, B. A., Diehl, M., & Stroebe, W. (2003). Cognitive stimulation and interference in idea-generating groups. In P. B. Paulus & B. A. Nijstad (Eds.), *Group creativity: Innovation through collaboration* (pp. 137–159). Oxford, UK: Oxford University Press.

Nijstad, B. A., & Stroebe, W. (2006). How the group affects the mind: A cognitive model of idea generation in groups. *Personality and Social Psychology Review, 10*, 186–213.

Nijstad, B. A., Stroebe, W., & Lodewijkx, H. F. M. (2002). Cognitive stimulation and interference in groups: Exposure effects in an idea generation task. *Journal of Experimental Social Psychology, 38*, 535–544.

Nijstad, B. A., Stroebe, W., & Lodewijkx, H. F. M. (2003). Production blocking and idea generation: Does blocking interfere with cognitive processes? *Journal of Experimental Social Psychology, 39*, 531–548.

Nijstad, B. A., Stroebe, W., & Lodewijkx, H. F. M. (2006). The illusion of group productivity: A reduction of failures explanation. *European Journal of Social Psychology, 36*, 31–48.

O'Donnell, A. M., Hmelo-Silver, C. E., & Erkens, G. (Eds.) (2006). *Collaborative learning, reasoning, and technology*. Mahwah, NJ: Erlbaum.

Okhuysen, G. A., & Eisenhardt, K. M. (2002). Integrating knowledge in groups: How formal interventions enable flexibility. *Organizational Science, 13*, 370–386.

Olivera, F., & Straus, S. G. (2004). Group-to-individual transfer of learning—Cognitive and social factors. *Small Group Research, 35*, 440–465.

Olson, M. (1965). *The logic of collective action: Public goods and the theory of groups.* Cambridge, MA: Harvard University Press.

Olsson, A.-C., Juslin, P., & Olsson, H. (2006). Individuals and dyads in a multiple-cue judgment task: Cognitive processes and performance. *Journal of Experimental Social Psychology, 42*, 40–56.

O'Reilly, C. A. III., Caldwell, D. F., & Barnett, W. P. (1989). Work Group demography, social integration, and turnover. *Administrative Science Quarterly, 34*, 21–37.

Osborn, A. F. (1953). *Applied imagination: Principles and procedures of creative thinking.* New York: Scribners.

Osborn, A. F. (1957). *Applied imagination: Principles and procedures of creative thinking* (revised edition). New York: Scribners.

Overstreet, H. A. (1925). *Influencing human behavior*. New York: Norton.

Pape, T., & Bölle, I. (1984). Einfallsproduktion von individuen und dyaden unter "brainstorming"-bedingungen [Brainstorming productivity of individuals and dyads]. *Psychologische Beiträge, 26*, 459–468.

Parks, C. D., & Cowlin, R. A. (1996). Acceptance of uncommon information into group discussion when that information is or is not demonstrable. *Organizational Behavior and Human Decision Processes, 66*, 307–316.

Parnes, S. J. (1961). Effects of extended effort in creative problem solving. *Journal of Educational Psychology, 52*, 117–122.

Parnes, S. J., & Meadow, A. (1959). Effects of "brainstorming" instructions on creative problem solving by trained and untrained subjects. *Journal of Educational Psychology, 50*, 171–176.

Paulus, P. B. (1983). Group influence on individual task performance. In P. B. Paulus (Ed.), *Basic group processes* (pp. 97–120). New York: Springer-Verlag.

Paulus, P. B., & Brown, V. R. (2003). Enhancing ideational creativity in groups: Lessons from research on brainstorming. In P. B. Paulus & B. A. Nijstad (Eds.), *Group creativity: Innovation through collaboration* (pp. 110–136). Oxford, UK: Oxford University Press.

Paulus, P. B., Dugosh, K. L., Dzindolet, M. T., Coskun, H., & Putman, V. L. (2002). Social and cognitive influences in group brainstorming. Predicting production gains and losses. *European Review of Social psychology, 12*, 299–325.

Paulus, P. B., & Dzindolet, M. T. (1993). Social influence processes in group brainstorming. *Journal of Personality and Social Psychology, 64*, 575–586.

Paulus, P. B., Dzindolet, M. T., Poletes, G., & Camacho, L. M. (1993). Perception of performance in group brainstorming: The illusion of group productivity. *Personality and Social Psychology Bulletin, 19*, 78–89.

Paulus, P. B., Larey, T. S., & Ortega, A. H. (1995). Performance and perceptions of brainstormers in an organizational setting. *Basic and Applied Social Psychology, 17*, 249–265.

Paulus, P. B., & Yang, H.-C. (2000). Idea generation in groups: A basis for creativity in organizations. *Organizational Behavior and Human Decision Processes, 82*, 76–87.

Pelled, L. H. (1996). Demographic diversity, conflict, and work group outcomes: An intervening process theory. *Organization Science, 7*, 615–631.

Pelled, L. H., Eisenhardt, K. M., & Xin, K. R. (1999). Exploring the black box: An analysis of work group diversity, conflict, and performance. *Administrative Science Quarterly, 44*, 1–28.

Perlmutter, H. V., & DeMontmollin, G. (1952). Group learning of nonsense syllables. *Journal of Abnormal and Social Psychology, 47*, 762–769.

Pessin, J. (1933). The comparative effects of social and mechanical stimulation on memorizing. *American Journal of Psychology, 45*, 263–270.

Pessin, J., & Husband, R. W. (1933). Effects of social stimulation on human maze learning. *Journal of Abnormal and Social Psychology, 28*, 148–154.

Peters, L. H., Hartke, D. D., & Pohlmann, J. T. (1985). Fiedler's contingency model of leadership: An application of the meta-analysis procedure of Schmidt and Hunter. *Psychological Bulletin, 97*, 274–285.

Peterson, N. G., Mumford, M. D., Borman, W. C., Jenneret, P. R., & Fleishman, E. A. (1999). *An occupational information system for the 21st century.* Washington, DC: American Psychological Association.

Phillips, K. W. (2003). The effects of categorically based expectations on minority influence: The importance of congruence. *Personality and Social Psychology Bulletin, 29*, 3–13.

Phillips, K. W., & Loyd, D. L. (2006). When surface and deep-level diversity collide: The effects on dissenting group members. *Organizational Behavior and Human Decision Processes, 99*, 143–160.

Phillips, K. W., Mannix, E. A., Neale, M. A., & Gruenfeld, D. H. (2004). Diverse groups and information sharing. The effects of congruent ties. *Journal of Experimental Social Psychology, 40*, 497–510.

Phillips, K. W., Northcraft, G. B., & Neale, M. A. (2006). Surface-level diversity and decision-making in groups: When does deep-level similarity help? *Group Processes and Intergroup Relations, 9*, 467–482.

Pisano, G. P., Bohmer, R. M. J., & Edmondson, A. C. (2001). Organizational differences in rates of learning: Evidence from the adoption of minimally invasive cardiac surgery. *Management Science, 47*, 752–768.

Plaks, J. E., & Higgins, E. T. (2000). Pragmatic use of stereotyping in teamwork: Social loafing and compensation as a function of inferred partner-situation fit. *Journal of Personality and Social Psychology, 79*, 962–974.

Platt, M. B. (1992). The effects of selection-rules on group composition and selection outcome. *Journal of Social Behavior and Personality, 7*, 59–77.

Plous, S. (1995). A comparison of strategies for reducing interval overconfidence in group judgments. *Journal of Applied Psychology, 80*, 443–454.

Postmes, T., Spears, R., & Cihangir, S. (2001). Quality of decision making and group norms. *Journal of Personality and Social Psychology, 80*, 918–930.

Pressman, I., & Singmaster, D. (1989). The jealous husbands and the missionaries and cannibals. *Mathematical Gazette, 73*, 73–81.

Price, K. H. (1985). Problem-solving strategies: A comparison by problem-solving phases. *Group & Organization Studies, 10*, 278–299.

Price, K. H., Harrison, D. A., & Gavin, J. H. (2006). Withholding inputs in team contexts: Member composition, interaction processes, evaluation structure, and social loafing. *Journal of Applied Psychology, 91*, 1375–1384.

Prietula, M., Carley, K., & Gasser, L. (1998). *Simulating organizations: Computational models of institutions and groups.* Cambridge, MA: MIT Press.

Raaijmakers, J. G. W., & Shiffrin, R. M. (1981). Search of associative memory. *Psychological Review, 88*, 93–134.

Rantilla, A. (2000). Collective task responsibility allocation: Revisiting the group-serving bias. *Small Group Research, 31*, 739–766.

Reagan-Cirincione, P. (1994). Improving the accuracy of group judgment: A process intervention combining group facilitation, social judgment analysis, and information technology. *Organizational Behavior and Human Decision Processes, 58*, 246–270.

Reagan-Cirincione, P., & Rohrbaugh, J. (1992). Task bias and the accuracy of judgment: Setting a baseline for expected group performance. *Journal of Behavioral Decision Making, 5*, 233–252.

Reagans, R., Argote, L., & Brooks, D. (2005). Individual experience and experience working together: Predicting learning rates from knowing who knows what and knowing how to work together. *Management Science, 51*, 869–881.

Reimer, T., Kuendig, S., Hoffrage, U., Park, E. S,, & Hinsz, V. B. (2007). Effects of the information environment on group discussions and decisions in the hidden-profile paradigm. *Journal Communication Monographs, 74*, 1–28.

Rico, R., Sanchez-Manzanares, M., Gil, F., & Gibson, C. (2008). Team implicit coordination processes: A team knowledge-based approach. *Academy of Management Review, 33*, 163–184.

Rietzschel, E. F., Nijstad, B. A., & Stroebe, W. (2006). Productivity is not enough: A comparison of interactive and nominal brainstorming groups on idea generation and selection. *Journal of Experimental Social Psychology, 42*, 244–251.

Rietzschel, E. F., Nijstad, B. A., & Stroebe, W. (2007). Relative accessibility of domain knowledge and creativity: The effects of knowledge activation on the quantity and originality of generated ideas. *Journal of Experimental Social Psychology, 43*, 933–946.

Ringelmann, M. (1913). Recherches sur les moteurs animés: Travail de l'homme. [Research on animate sources of power: The work of man]. *Annales de l'Institut National Agronomique, 2e série, 12*, 1–40.

Roby, T. B., & Lanzetta, J. T. (1958). Considerations in the analysis of group tasks. *Psychological Bulletin, 55*, 88–101.

Roenker, D. L., Thompson, C. P., & Brown, S. C. (1971). Comparison of measures for the estimation of clustering in free recall. *Psychological Bulletin, 76*, 45–48.

Rohrbaugh, J. (1979). Improving the quality of group judgement: Social judgment analysis and the Delphi technique. *Organizational Behavior and Human Performance, 24*, 73–92.

Rosenbaum, M. E. (1986). The repulsion hypothesis: On the nondevelopment of relationships. *Journal of Personality and Social Psychology, 51*, 1156–1166.

Rosenberg, S., Erlick, D. E., & Berkowitz, L. (1955). Some effects of varying combinations of group members on group performance measures and leadership behaviors. *Journal of Abnormal and Social Psychology, 51*, 195–203.

Ross, M., Spencer, S. J., Blatz, C. W., & Restorick, E. (2008). Collaboration reduces the frequency of false memories in older and younger adults. *Psychology and Aging, 23*, 85–92.

Ross, M., Spencer, S. J., Linardatos, L., Lam, K. C. H., & Perunovic, M. (2004). Going shopping and identifying landmarks: Does collaboration improve older people's memory? *Applied Cognitive Psychology, 18*, 683–696.

Rousseau, D. M. (1985). Issues of level in organizational research: Multilevel and cross-level perspectives. In L. L. Cummings & B. M. Staw (Eds.), *Research in organizational behavior* (vol. 7, pp. 1–37). Greenwich, CT: JAI Press.

Rowatt, W. C., Nesselroade, K. P., Beggan, J. K., & Allison, S. T. (1997). Perception of brainstorming in groups: The quality over quantity hypothesis. *Journal of Creative Behavior, 31*, 130–150.

Ruef, M. (2002). A structural event approach to the analysis of group composition. *Social Networks, 24*, 135–160.

Ruef, M., Aldrich, H. E., & Carter, N. M. (2003). The structure of founding teams: Homophily, strong ties, and isolation among U.S. entrepreneurs. *American Sociological Review, 68*, 195–222.

Rulke, D. L., & Rau, D. (2000). Investigating the encoding process of transactive memory development in group training. *Group & Organization Management, 25*, 373–396.

Ryack, B. (1965). A comparison of individual and group learning of nonsense syllables. *Journal of Personality and Social Psychology, 2*, 296–299.

Sacco, J. M., & Schmitt, N. (2005). A dynamic multilevel model of demographic diversity and misfit effects. *Journal of Applied Psychology, 90*, 203–231.

Sackett, P. R., & Larson, J. R., Jr. (1990). Research strategies and tactics in industrial and organizational psychology. In M. D. Dunnette & L. M. Hough (Eds.), *Handbook of industrial and organizational psychology* (2nd. ed., Vol. 1, pp. 419–489). Palo Alto, CA: Consulting Psychologists Press.

Salas, E., Rozell, D., Mullen, B., & Driskell, J. E. (1999). The effect of team building on performance. *Small Group Research, 30*, 309–330.

Sandelands, L., & St. Clair, L. (1993). Toward an empirical concept of group. *Journal for the Theory of Social Behavior, 23*, 423–458.

Sanna, L. J. (1992). Self-efficacy theory: Implications for social facilitation and social loafing. *Journal of Personality and Social Psychology, 62*, 774–786.

Sanna, L. J., & Shotland, R. L. (1990). Valence of anticipated evaluation and social facilitation. *Journal of Experimental Social Psychology, 26,* 82–92.

Sassenberg, K., Boos, M., & Klapproth, F. (2001). Wissen und problem-lösekompetenz: Der einfluß von expertise auf den Informationsaustausch in computervermittelter kommunikation [Knowledge and competence: The influence of expertise on information exchange in computer-mediated communication]. *Zeitschrift für Sozialpsychologie, 32,* 45–56.

Savadori, L., Van Swol, L. M., & Sniezek, J. A. (2001). Information sampling and confidence within groups and judge advisor systems. *Communication Research, 28,* 737–771.

Sawyer, J. E., Houlette, M. A., & Yeagley, E. L. (2006). Decision performance and diversity structure: Comparing faultlines in convergent, crosscut, and racially homogeneous groups. *Organizational Behavior and Human Decision Processes, 99,* 1–15.

Schegloff, E. A. (2000). Overlapping talk and the organization of turn-taking for conversation. *Language in Society, 29,* 1–63.

Schittekatte, M. (1996). Facilitating information exchange in small decision-making groups. *European Journal of Social Psychology, 26,* 537–556.

Schittekatte, M., & Van Hiel, A. (1996). Effects of partially shared information and awareness of unshared information on information sampling. *Small Group Research, 27,* 431–449.

Schneider, B. (1987). The people make the place. *Personnel Psychology, 40,* 437–452.

Schneider, B., Goldstein, H. W., & Smith, D. B. (1995). The ASA framework: An update. *Personnel Psychology, 48,* 747–773.

Schneider, B., & Smith, D. B. (2004). Personality and organizational culture. In B. Schneider and D. B. Smith (Eds.). *Personality and organizations* (pp. 347–370). Mahwah, NJ: Erlbaum.

Schneider, B., Smith, D. B., & Paul, M. C. (2001). P-E fit and the attraction-selection-attrition model of organizational functioning: Introduction and overview. In M. Erez, U. Kleinbeck, & H. Thierry (Eds.), *Work motivation in the context of a globalizing economy* (pp. 231–246). Mahwah, NJ: Erlbaum.

Scholten, L., van Knippenberg, D., Nijstad, B. A., & De Dreu, C. K. W. (2007). Motivated information processing and group decision-making: Effects of process accountability on information processing and decision quality. *Journal of Experimental Social Psychology, 43,* 539–552.

Schulz-Hardt, S., Brodbeck, F. C., Mojzisch, A., Kerschreiter, R., & Frey, D. (2006). Group decision making in hidden profile situations: Dissent as a facilitator for decision quality. *Journal of Personality and Social Psychology, 91,* 1080–1093.

Shaver, J. M. (2006). A paradox of synergy: Contagion and capacity effects in mergers and acquisitions. *Academy of Management Review, 31,* 962–976.

Shaw, Marjorie E. (1932). A comparison of individuals and small groups in the rational solution of complex problems. *American Journal of Psychology, 44,* 491–504.

Shaw, Marvin E. (1963). Scaling group tasks: A method for dimensional analysis. Office of Naval Research, Contract NR 170–266, Nonr-580(11), Technical Report No. 1. Abstracted in the *JSAS Catalog of Selected Documents in Psychology,* 1973, *3,* 8.

Shaw, Marvin E., & Ashton, N. (1976). Do assembly bonus effects occur on disjunctive tasks? A test of Steiner's theory. *Bulletin of the Psychonomic Society, 8,* 469–471.

Shepperd, J. A. (1993). Productivity loss in performance groups: A motivation analysis. *Psychological Bulletin, 113,* 67–81.

Shepperd, J. A. (2001). Social loafing and expectancy-value theory. In S. G. Harkins (Ed.), *Multiple perspectives on the effects of evaluation on performance: Toward an integration* (pp. 1–24). Boston, MA: Kluwer.

Shin, S. J., & Zhou, J. (2007). When is educational specialization heterogeneity related to creativity in research and development teams? Transformational leadership as a moderator. *Journal of Applied Psychology, 92,* 1709–1721.

Simon, H. A. (1992). What is an "explanation" of behavior? *Psychological Science, 3,* 150–161.

Simon, H. A. (1997). *Administrative behavior* (4th ed.). New York: The Free Press.

Simons, T., Pelled, L. H., & Smith, K. A. (1999). Making use of differences: Diversity, debate, and decision comprehensiveness in top management teams. *Academy of Management Journal, 42,* 662–674.

Simonton, D. K. (2003). Scientific creativity as constrained stochastic behavior: The integration of product, person, and process perspectives. *Psychological Bulletin, 129,* 475–494.

Slavin, R. E., Hurley, E. A., & Chamberlain, A. (2003). Cooperative learning and achievement: Theory and research. In W. M. Reynolds & G. E. Miller (Eds.), *Handbook of psychology: Educational psychology* (Vol. 7, 177–198). Hoboken, NJ: Wiley.

Smith, E. R., & Conrey, F. R. (2007). Agent-based modeling: A new approach for theory building in social psychology. *Personality and Social Psychology Review, 11,* 87–104.

Smith, K. G., Smith, K. A., Olian, J. D., Sims, H. P., Jr., O'Bannon, D. P., & Scully, J. A. (1994). Top management team demography and process: The role of social integration and communication. *Administrative Science Quarterly, 39,* 412–438.

Smith, S. M. (2003). The constraining effects of initial ideas. In P. B. Paulus & B. A. Nijstad (Eds.), *Group creativity: Innovation through collaboration* (pp. 15–31). Oxford, UK: Oxford University Press.

Smoke, W. H., & Zajonc, R. B. (1962). On the reliability of group judgments and decisions. In J. H. Criswell, H. Solomon, & P. Suppes (Eds.), *Mathematical models in small group processes* (pp. 322–333). Stanford, CA: Stanford University Press.

Sniezek, J. A. (1989). An examination of group process in judgmental forecasting. *International Journal of Forecasting, 5,* 171–178.

Sniezek, J. A. (1990). A comparison of techniques for judgmental forecasting by groups with common information. *Group & Organization Studies, 15,* 5–19.

Sniezek, J. A. (1992). Groups under uncertainty: An examination of confidence in group decision making. *Organizational Behavior and Human Decision Processes, 52,* 124–155.

Sniezek, J. A., & Henry, R. A. (1989). Accuracy and confidence in group judgment. *Organizational Behavior and Human Decision Processes, 43,* 1–28.

Sniezek, J. A., & Henry, R. A. (1990). Revision, weighting, and commitment in consensus group judgment. *Organizational Behavior and Human Decision Processes, 45,* 66–84

Sokal, R. R. (1974). Classification: Purposes, principles, progress, prospects. *Science, 185*, 1115–1123.

Sommers, S. R. (2006). On racial diversity and group decision making: Identifying multiple effects of racial composition on jury deliberations. *Journal of Personality and Social Psychology, 90*, 597–612.

Souter, N. (2007). *Creative business solutions: Breakthrough thinking: Brainstorming for inspiration and ideas.* New York, NY: Sterling Publishing.

South, E. B. (1927). Some psychological aspects of committee work. *Journal of Applied Psychology, 11*, 437–464.

Spence, K. W. (1956). *Behavior theory and conditioning.* New Haven, CT: Yale University Press.

Stanne, M. B., Johnson, D. W., & Johnson, R. T. (1999). Does competition enhance or inhibit motor performance: A meta-analysis. *Psychological Bulletin, 125*, 133–154.

Stasser, G. (1992). Pooling of unshared information during group discussion. In S. Worchel, W. Wood, & J. A. Simpson (Eds.), *Group process and productivity* (pp. 48–67). Newbury Park, CA: Sage.

Stasser, G. (1999a). A primer of social decision scheme theory: Models of group influence, competitive model-testing, and prospective modeling. *Organizational Behavior and Human Decision Processes, 80*, 3–20.

Stasser, G. (1999b). The uncertain role of unshared information in collective choice. In L. Thompson, J. Levine, & D. Messick (Eds.), *Shared knowledge in organizations* (pp. 49–69). Hillsdale, NJ: Erlbaum.

Stasser, G., & Dietz-Uhler, B. (2001). Collective choice, judgment and problem solving. In M. A. Hogg & R. S. Tindale (Eds.), *Blackwell handbook of social psychology: Group processes* (pp. 31–55). Oxford, UK: Blackwell.

Stasser, G., Kerr, N. L., & Bray, R. M. (1982). The social psychology of jury deliberations: Structure, process, and product. In N. L. Kerr, & R. M. Bray (Eds.), *The psychology of the courtroom* (pp. 221–256). New York: Academic Press.

Stasser, G., & Stewart, D. D. (1992). Discovery of hidden profiles by decision-making groups: Solving a problem versus making a judgment. *Journal of Personality and Social Psychology, 63*, 426–434.

Stasser, G., Stewart, D. D., & Wittenbaum, G. M. (1995). Expert roles and information exchange during discussion: The importance of knowing who knows what. *Journal of Experimental Social Psychology, 31*, 244–265.

Stasser, G. Taylor, L. A., Hanna, C. (1989). Information sampling in structured and unstructured discussions of three- and six-person groups. *Journal of Personality and Social Psychology, 57*, 67–78.

Stasser, G., & Titus, W. (1985). Pooling of unshared information in group decision making: Biased information sampling during discussion. *Journal of Personality and Social Psychology, 48*, 1467–1478.

Stasser, G., & Titus, W. (1987). Effects of information load and percentage of shared information on the dissemination of unshared information during group discussion. *Journal of Personality and Social Psychology, 53*, 81–93.

Stasser, G., & Titus, W. (2003). Hidden profiles: A brief history. *Psychological Inquiry, 14*, 304–313.

Stasser, G., Vaughan, S. I., & Stewart, D. D. (2000). Pooling unshared information: The benefits of knowing how access to information is distributed among members. *Organizational Behavior and Human Decision Processes, 82,* 102–116.

Stasson, M. F., & Bradshaw, S. D. (1995). Explanations of individual-group performance differences: What sort of "bonus" can be gained through group interaction? *Small Group Research, 26,* 296–308.

Stasson, M. F., Kameda, T., Parks, C. D., Zimmerman, S. K., & Davis, J. H. (1991). Effects of assigned group consensus requirement on group problem solving and group members' learning. *Social Psychology Quarterly, 54,* 25–35.

Steblay, N., Hosch, H. M., Culhane, S. E., & McWethy, A. (2006). The impact on juror verdicts of judicial instruction to disregard inadmissible evidence: A meta-analysis. *Law and Human Behavior, 30,* 469–492.

Steiner, I. D. (1966). Models for inferring relationships between group size and potential group productivity. *Behavioral Science, 11,* 273–283.

Steiner, I. D. (1972). *Group process and productivity.* New York: Academic Press.

Steiner, I. D. (1974). Whatever happened to the group in social psychology? *Journal of Experimental Social Psychology, 10,* 94–108.

Steiner, I. D. (1986). Paradigms and groups. *Advances in experimental social psychology, 19,* 251–289.

Steiner, I. D., & Rajaratnam, N. (1961). A model for the comparison of individual and group performance scores. *Behavioral Science, 6,* 142–147.

Stewart, D. D., & Stasser, G. (1995). Expert role assignment and information sampling during collective recall and decision making. *Journal of Personality and Social Psychology, 69,* 619–628.

Stewart, D. D., & Stasser, G. (1998). The sampling of critical, unshared information in decision-making groups: The role of an informed minority. *European Journal of Social Psychology, 28,* 95–113.

Stroebe, W., & Diehl, M. (1994). Why groups are less effective than their members: On productivity losses in idea-generating groups. In W. Stroebe & M. Hewstone (Eds.), *European Review of Social Psychology* (vol. 5, pp. 271–303). London: Wiley.

Stroebe, W., Diehl, M., & Abakoumkin, G. (1992). The illusion of group effectivity. *Personality and Social Psychology Bulletin, 18,* 643–650.

Stroebe, W., Diehl, M., & Abakoumkin, G. (1996). Social compensation and the Köhler effect: Toward a theoretical explanation of motivation gains in group productivity. In E. Witte, & J. H. Davis (Eds.), *Understanding group behavior: Vol. 2, small group processes and interpersonal relations* (pp. 37–65). Mahwah, NJ: Erlbaum.

Strube, M. J. (2005). What did Triplett really find? A contemporary analysis of the first experiment in social psychology. *American Journal of Psychology, 118,* 271–286.

Strube, M. J., & Garcia, J. E. (1981). A meta-analytical investigation of Fiedler's contingency model of leadership effectiveness. *Psychological Bulletin, 90,* 307–321.

Student (1908). The probable error of a mean. *Biometrika, 6,* 1–25.

Sundstrom, E. (1999). The challenges of supporting work team effectiveness. In E. Sundstrom (Ed.), *Supporting work team effectiveness: Best management practices for fostering high performance* (pp. 3–23). San Francisco, CA: Jossey-Bass.

Sweeney, J. (2005). *Innovation at the speed of laughter: 8 secrets to world class idea generation*. Minneapolis, MN: Aerialist Press.

Szymanski, K., & Harkins, S. G. (1987). Social loafing and self-evaluation with a social standard. *Journal of Personality and Social Psychology, 53*, 891–897.

Takahashi, M. (2007). Does collaborative remembering reduce false memories? *British Journal of Psychology, 98*, 1–13.

Tasa, K., Taggar, S., & Seijts, G. (2007). The development of collective efficacy in teams: A multilevel and longitudinal perspective. *Journal of Applied Psychology, 92*, 17–27.

Taylor, D. W. (1955). Problem solving by groups. *Acta Psychologica, 11*, 218–219.

Taylor, D. W., Berry, P. C., & Block, C. H. (1958). Does group participation when using brainstorming facilitate or inhibit creative thinking. *Administrative Science Quarterly, 3*, 23–47.

Thatcher, S. M. B., Jehn, K. A., & Zanutto, E. (2003). Cracks in diversity research: The effects of diversity faultlines on conflict and performance. *Group Decision and Negotiation, 12*, 217–241.

Thibaut, J. W., & Kelley, H. H. (1959). *The social psychology of groups*. New York: Wiley.

Thomas-Hunt, M. C., & Phillips, K. W. (2004). When what you know is not enough: Expertise and gender dynamics in task groups. *Personality and Social Psychology Bulletin, 30*, 1585–1598.

Thorndike, R. L. (1938). On what type of task will a group do well? *Journal of Abnormal and Social Psychology, 33*, 409–413.

Thorndike, R. L., & Hagen, E. P. (1977). *Measurement and evaluation in psychology and education*. New York: Wiley.

Thurstone, L. L., & Chave, E. J. (1929). *The measurement of attitudes*. Chicago: University of Chicago Press.

Timmerman, T. A. (2000). Racial diversity, age diversity, interdependence, and team performance. *Small Group Research, 31*, 592–606.

Timmons, W. M. (1942). Can the product superiority of discussors be attributed to averaging or majority influences? *Journal of Social Psychology, 15*, 23–32.

Tindale, R. S., & Larson, J. R., Jr. (1992). Assembly bonus effect or typical group performance? A comment on Michaelsen, Watson, & Black (1989). *Journal of Applied Psychology, 77*, 102–105.

Tindale, R. S., Davis, J. H., Vollrath, D. A., Nagao, D. H., & Hinsz, V. B. (1990). Asymmetrical social influence in freely interaction groups: A test of three models. *Journal of Personality and Social Psychology, 58*, 438–449.

Todd, A. R., Seok, D-H., Kerr, N. L., & Messé, L. A. (2006). Social compensation: Fact or social-comparison artifact? *Group Processes and Intergroup Relations, 9*, 431–442.

Torrance, E. P. (1970). Influence of dyadic interaction on creative functioning. *Psychological Reports, 26*, 391–394.

Travis, L. E. (1928). The influence of the group upon the stutterer's speed in free associations. *Journal of Abnormal and Social Psychology, 23*, 45–51.

Triplett, N. (1898). The dynamogenic factors in pacemaking and competition. *American Journal of Psychology, 9*, 507–533.

Trotman, K. T. (1985). The review process and the accuracy of auditor judgments. *Journal of Accounting Research, 23*, 740–752.

Tschan, F. (2002). Ideal cycles of communication (or cognitions) in triads, dyads, and individuals. *Small Group Research, 33*, 615–643.

Tschan, F., & von Cranach, M. (1996). Group task structure, processes, and outcomes. In M. C. West (Ed.), *Handbook of work group psychology* (pp. 95–121). Chichester, UK: Wiley.

Tsui, A. S., Egan, T. D., & O'Reilly, C. A., III. (1992). Being different: Relational demography and organizational attachment. *Administrative Science Quarterly, 37,* 549–579.

Turner, J. C., & Haslam, S. A. (2001). Social identity, organizations, and leadership. In M. E. Turner (Ed.), *Groups at work: Theory and research* (pp. 25–65). Mahwah, NJ: Erlbaum.

Turner, J. C., & Oakes, P. J. (1989). Self-categorization theory and social influence. In P. B. Paulus (Ed.), *Psychology of group influence* (2nd ed., pp. 233–275). Hillsdale, NJ: Erlbaum.

van Ginkel, W. P., & van Knippenberg, D. (2008). Group information elaboration and group decision making: The role of shared task representations. *Organizational Behavior and Human Decision Processes, 105,* 82–97.

van Ginkel, W. P., & van Knippenberg, D. (2009). Knowledge about the distribution of information and group decision making: When and why does it work? *Organizational Behavior and Human Decision Processes, 108,* 218–229.

Van Hiel, A., & Schittekatte, M. (1998). Information exchange in context: Effects of gender composition of group, accountability, and intergroup perception on group decision making. *Journal of Applied Social Psychology, 28,* 2049–2067.

van Knippenberg, D., De Dreu, C. K. W., & Homan, A. C. (2004). Work group diversity and group performance. An integrative model and research agenda. *Journal of Applied Psychology, 89,* 1008–1022.

Van Swol, L. M. (2007). Perceived importance of information: The effects of mentioning information, shared information bias, ownership bias, reiteration, and confirmation bias. *Group Processes Intergroup Relations, 10,* 239–256.

Van Swol, L. M. (2008). Performance and process in collective and individual memory: The role of social decision schemes and memory bias in collective memory. *Memory, 16,* 274–287.

Van Swol, L. M. (2009). Factors affecting decision makers' preference for unshared information. *Group dynamics: Theory, research, and practice, 13,* 31–45.

Van Swol, L. M., Savadori, L., & Sniezek, J. A. (2003). Factors that may affect the difficulty of uncovering hidden profiles. *Group Processes and Intergroup Relations, 6,* 285–304.

VanGundy, A. B. (1981). *Techniques for structured problem solving.* New York: Van Nostrand Reinhold.

Vincente, K. (1999). *Cognitive work analysis.* Mahwah, NJ: Erlbaum.

Vollrath, D. A., Sheppard, B. H., Hinsz, V. B., & Davis, J. H. (1989). Memory performance by decision-making groups and individuals. *Organizational Behavior and Human Decision Processes, 43,* 289–300.

von Cranach, M. (1996). Toward a theory of the acting group. In E. H. Witte & J. H. Davis (Eds.), *Understanding group behavior: Vol. 2. Small group process and interpersonal relations* (pp. 147–187). Mahwah, NJ: Erlbaum.

Vroom, V. H. (1964). *Work and motivation.* Oxford, UK: Wiley.

Vroom, V. H., & Jago, A. G. (2007). The role of the situation in leadership. *American Psychologist, 62,* 17–24.

Wageman, R. (1999). Task design, outcome interdependence, and individual differences: Their joint effects on effort in task-performing teams (Commentary on Huguet et al., 1999). *Group Dynamics: Theory, Research, and Practice, 3,* 132–137.

Wageman, R. (2001). The meaning of interdependence. In M. E. Turner (Ed.), *Groups at work: Theory and research.* (pp. 197–217). Mahwah, NJ: Erlbaum.

Wageman, R., & Gordon, F. M. (2005). As the twig is bent: How group values shape emergent task interdependence in groups. *Organization Science, 16,* 687–700.

Wallsten, T. S., & Diederich, A. (2001). Understanding pooled subjective probability estimates. *Mathematical Social Sciences, 41,* 1–18.

Wang, C. S., & Thompson, L. L. (2006). The negative and positive psychology of leadership and group research. *Advances in Group Process, 23,* 31–61.

Warmke, C., & Buchanan, L. (2003). *Idea revolution: Guidelines and prompts for brainstorming alone, in groups or with clients.* Cincinnati, OH: HOW Design Books.

Warriner, C. K. (1956). Groups are real: A reaffirmation. *American Sociological Review, 21,* 549–554.

Watson, G. B. (1928). Do groups think more efficiently than individuals? *Journal of Abnormal and Social Psychology, 23,* 328–336.

Watson, W. E., Kumar, K., & Michaelsen, L. K. (1993). Cultural diversity's impact on interaction process and performance: Comparing homogeneous and diverse task groups. *Academy of Management Journal, 36,* 590–602.

Webber, S. S., & Donahue, L. M. (2001). Impact of highly and less job-related diversity on work group cohesion and performance: a meta-analysis. *Journal of Management, 27,* 141–162.

Weber, B., & Hertel, G. (2007). Motivation gains of inferior group members: A meta-analytic review. *Journal of Personality and Social Psychology, 93,* 973–993.

Weber, R. A., & Camerer, C. F. (2003). Cultural conflict and merger failure: An experimental approach. *Management Science, 49,* 400–415.

Wegge, J., & Haslam, S. A. (2005). Improving work motivation and performance in brainstorming groups: The effects of three group goal-setting strategies. *European Journal of Work and Organizational Psychology, 14,* 400–430.

Wegge, J., Roth, C., Neubach, B., Schmidt, K.-H., & Kanfer, R. (2008). Age and gender diversity as determinants of performance and health in a public organization: The role of task complexity and group size. *Journal of Applied Psychology, 93,* 1301–1313.

Wegner, D. M. (1987). Transactive memory: A contemporary analysis of the group mind. In B. Mullen & G. R. Goethals (Eds.), *Theories of group behavior* (pp. 185–208). New York: Springer.

Wegner, D. M., Erber, R., & Raymond, P. (1991). Transactive memory in close relationships. *Journal of Personality and Social Psychology, 61,* 923–929.

Wegner, D. M., Giuliano, T., & Hertel, P. T. (1985). Cognitive interdependence in close relationships. In W. I. Ickes (Ed.), *Compatible and incompatible relationships* (pp. 253–276). New York: Springer.

Weldon, E., & Gargano, G. M. (1985). Cognitive effort in additive task groups: The effects of shared responsibility on the quality of multiattribute judgments. *Organizational Behavior and Human Decision Processes, 36,* 348–361.

Weldon, E., & Gargano, G. M. (1988). Cognitive loafing: The effects of accountability and shared responsibility on cognitive effort. *Personality and Social Psychology Bulletin, 14,* 159–171.

Weldon, E., & Mustari, E. L. (1988). Felt dispensability in groups of coactors: The effects of shared responsibility and explicit anonymity on cognitive effort. *Organizational Behavior and Human Decision Processes, 41*, 330–351.

Weldon, M. S., & Bellinger, K. D. (1997). Collective memory: Collaborative and individual processes in remembering. *Journal of Experimental Psychology: Learning, Memory, and Cognition, 23*, 1160–1175.

Weldon, M. S., Blair, C., & Huebsch, D. (2000). Group remembering: Does social loafing underlie collaborative inhibition? *Journal of Experimental Psychology: Learning, Memory, and Cognition, 26*, 1568–1577.

West, M. A. (2002). Sparkling fountains or stagnant ponds: An integrative model of creativity and innovation implementation in work groups. *Applied Psychology: An International Review, 51*, 355–387.

Weston, S. B., & English, H. B. (1926). The influence of the group on psychological test scores. *American Journal of Psychology, 37*, 600–601.

Whyte, G., & Sebenius, J. K. (1997). The effect of multiple anchors on anchoring in individual and group judgment. *Organizational Behavior and Human Decision Processes, 69*, 75–85.

Wicklund, R. A. (1989). The appropriation of ideas. In P. B. Paulus (Ed.), *Psychology of group influence* (2nd ed., pp. 393–423). Hillsdale, NJ: Erlbaum.

Wiggins, J. S., & Trapnell, P. D. (1997). Personality structure: The return of the big five. In R. Hogan, J. A. Johnson, & S. R. Briggs (Eds.), *Handbook of personality psychology* (pp. 737–765). San Diego, CA: Academic Press.

Wilder, D. A. (1984). Predictions of belief homogeneity and similarity following social categorization. *British Journal of Social Psychology, 23*, 323–333.

Williams, K. D., Harkins, S. G., & Karau, S. J. (2003). Social performance. In M. A. Hogg & J. Cooper (Eds.), *Sage handbook of social psychology* (pp. 327–346). Thousand Oaks, CA: Sage.

Williams, K. D., Harkins, S. G., & Latané, B. (1981). Identifiability as a deterrent to social loafing: Two cheering experiments. *Journal of Personality and Social Psychology, 40*, 303–311.

Williams, K. D., & Karau, S. J. (1991). Social loafing and social compensation: The effects of expectations of co-worker performance. *Journal of Personality and Social Psychology, 61*, 570–581.

Williams, K. D., Nida, S. A., Baca, L. D., & Latané, B. (1989). Social loafing and swimming: Effects of identifiability on individual and relay performance of intercollegiate swimmers. *Basic and Applied Social Psychology, 10*, 73–81.

Williams, K. Y., & O'Reilly, C. A., III. (1998). Demography and diversity in organizations: A review of 40 years of research. In B. M. Staw & L. L. Cummings (Eds.), *Research in organizational behavior* (Vol. 20, pp. 77–140). Greenwich, CT: JAI Press.

Williams, W. M., & Sternberg, R. J. (1988). Group intelligence: Why some groups are better than others. *Intelligence, 12*, 351–377.

Williamson, E. G. (1926). Allport's experiments in "social facilitation." *Psychological Monographs, 35* (3), 138–143.

Wilson, D. G. (2004). *Bicycling Science* (3rd ed.). Cambridge, MA: MIT Press.

Winquist, J. R., & Larson, J. R., Jr. (1998). Information pooling: When it impacts group decision making. *Journal of Personality and Social Psychology, 74*, 371–377.

Wittchen, M., Schlereth, D., & Hertel, G. (2007). Indispensability effects under temporal and spatial separation: Motivation gains in a sequential task during anonymous cooperation on the Internet. *International Journal of Internet Science, 2*, 12–27.

Witte, E. (1989). Köhler rediscovered: The anti-Ringelmann effect. *European Journal of Social Psychology, 19*, 147–154.

Wittenbaum, G. M., & Bowman, J. M. (2004). A social validation explanation for mutual enhancement. *Journal of Experimental Social Psychology, 40*, 169–184.

Wittenbaum, G. M., Hubbell, A. P., & Zuckerman, C. (1999). Mutual enhancement: Toward an understanding of the collective preference for shared information. *Journal of Personality and Social Psychology, 77*, 967–978.

Wittenbaum, G. M., & Park, J. M. (2001). The collective preference for shared information. *Current Directions in Psychological Science, 10*, 72–75.

Wittenbaum, G. M., Stasser, G., & Merry, C. J. (1996). Tacit coordination in anticipation of small group task completion. *Journal of Experimental Social Psychology, 32*, 129–152.

Wittenbaum, G. M., Vaughan, S. I., & Stasser, G. (1998). Coordination in task-performing groups. In R. S. Tindale et al. (Eds.), *Theory and research on small groups* (pp. 177–204). New York: Plenum Press.

Wood, J. V. (1989). Theory and research concerning social comparisons of personal attributes. *Psychological Bulletin, 106*, 231–248.

Wood, J. V. (2000). Examining social comparisons with the test selection measure: Opportunities for the researcher and the research participant. In J. Suls & L. Wheeler (Eds.), *Handbook of social comparison: Theory and research* (pp. 201–222). New York: Kluwer Academic.

Wood, R. E. (1986). Task complexity: Definition of the construct. *Organizational Behavior and Human Decision Processes, 37*, 60–82.

Wright, D. B., & Klumpp, A. (2004). Collaborative inhibition is due to the product, not the process, of recalling in groups. *Psychonomic Bulletin & Review, 11*, 1080–1083.

Yzerbyt, V., Judd, C. M., & Corneille, O. (Eds.) (2004). *The psychology of group perception: Perceived variability, entitativity, and essentialism*. New York: Psychology Press.

Zajonc, R. B. (1965). Social facilitation. *Science, 149*, 269–274.

Zajonc, R. B. (1980). Compresence. In P. B. Paulus (Ed.), *Psychology of group influence* (pp. 35–60). Hillsdale, NJ: Erlbaum.

Zakarian, A., & Kusiak, A. (1999). Forming teams: An analytical approach. *IIE Transactions, 31*, 85–97.

Zellmer-Bruhn, M. E., Maloney, M. M., Bhappu, A. D., & Salvador, R. (2008). When and how do differences matter. An exploration of perceived similarity in teams. *Organizational Behavior and Human Decision Processes, 107*, 41–59.

Zhang, Z.-X., Hempel, P. S., Han, Y.-L., & Tjosvold, D. (2007). Transactive memory system links work team characteristics and performance. *Journal of Applied Psychology, 92*, 1722–1730.

Ziegler, R., Diehl, M., & Zijlstra, G. (2000). Idea production in nominal and virtual groups: Does computer-mediated communication improve group brainstorming? *Group Processes and Intergroup Relations, 3*, 141–158.

AUTHOR INDEX

SUBJECT INDEX